# AIR FRYER

# COOKBOOK

## FOR BEGINNERS

# ~ 700 ~

**Easy to make, healthy and delicious
air fryer recipes, #2020 edition.**
Includes Alphabetic Glossary, Nutritional
Facts and Some Low Carb Recipes

**STELLA QUEEN**

# Table of Contents

AND MORE!!!

# Introduction

An Air Fryer is a magic revolutionized kitchen appliance that helps you fry with less or even no oil at all. This kind of product applies Rapid Air technology, which offers a new way on how to fry with less oil. This new invention cooks food through the circulation of superheated air and generates 80% low-fat food. Although the food is fried with less oil, you don't need to worry as the food processed by the Air Fryer still has the same taste as the food that is cooked using the deep-frying method.

This technology uses a superheated element, which radiates heat close to the food and an exhaust fan in its lid to circulate airflow. An Air Fryer ensures that the food processed is cooked completely. The exhaust fan located at the top of the cooking chamber helps the food to get the same heating temperature in every part in short time, resulting to a cooked food of best and healthy quality. Besides, cooking with an Air Fryer is also good for those that are busy and do not have enough time. For example, an Air Fryer only needs half a spoonful of oil and takes 10 minutes to serve a medium bowl of crispy French fries.

In addition to serving healthier food, an Air Fryer also provides some other benefits to you. Since an Air Fryer helps you fry using less oil or without oil at all for some kind of food, it automatically reduces the fat and cholesterol content in food. Surely, no one will refuse to enjoy fried food without worrying about the greasy and fat content. Having fried food with no guilt is really a form of indulging your tongue. Besides having low fat and cholesterol, by consuming oil sparingly, you save some amount of money, which can be used for other needs. An Air Fryer also can reheat your food. Sometimes, when you have fried leftover and you reheat it, it will usually serve reheated greasy food with some addition of unhealthy reuse oil. Surely, the saturated fat in the fried food gets worse because of this process. An Air Fryer helps you reheat your food without being afraid of extra oils that the food may absorb. Fried banana, fish and chips, nuggets, or even fried chicken can be reheated so that they become as warm and crispy as they were before by using an Air Fryer.

Some people may think that spending some amount of money to buy a fryer is wasteful. I dare to say that they are wrong because actually, an Air Fryer is not only used to fry. It is a sophisticated multi-function appliance since it also helps you to roast chicken, make steak, grill fish, and even bake a cake. With a built-in air filter, an Air Fryer filters the air and saves your kitchen from smoke and grease.

An air Fryer is really a simple innovative method of cooking. Grab it fast and welcome to a clean and healthy kitchen.

## 01. Scrambled Eggs

Preparation Time: 20 minutes
Servings: 2

**Ingredients:**

- 4 large eggs.
- ½ cup shredded sharp Cheddar cheese.
- 2 tbsp. unsalted butter; melted.

**Directions:**

1. Crack eggs into 2-cup round baking dish and whisk. Place dish into the air fryer basket.
2. Adjust the temperature to 400 Degrees F and set the timer for 10 minutes
3. After 5 minutes, stir the eggs and add the butter and cheese. Let cook 3 more minutes and stir again
4. Allow eggs to finish cooking an additional 2 minutes or remove if they are to your desired liking. Use a fork to fluff. Serve warm.

**Nutrition: Calories: 359; Protein: 19.5g; Fiber: 0.0g; Fat: 27.6g; Carbs: 1.1g**

## 02. Fennel Frittata

Preparation Time: 20 minutes
Servings: 6

**Ingredients:**

- 1 fennel bulb; shredded
- 6 eggs; whisked
- 2 tsp. cilantro; chopped.
- 1 tsp. sweet paprika
- Cooking spray
- A pinch of salt and black pepper

**Directions:**

1. Take a bowl and mix all the ingredients except the cooking spray and stir well.
2. Grease a baking pan with the cooking spray, pour the frittata mix and spread well
3. Put the pan in the Air Fryer and cook at 370°F for 15 minutes. Divide between plates and serve them for breakfast.

**Nutrition: Calories: 200; Fat: 12g; Fiber: 1g; Carbs: 5g; Protein: 8g**

## 03. Strawberries Oatmeal

Preparation Time: 20 minutes
Servings: 4

**Ingredients:**

- ½ cup coconut; shredded
- ¼ cup strawberries
- 2 cups coconut milk
- ¼ tsp. vanilla extract
- 2 tsp. stevia
- Cooking spray

**Directions:**

1. Grease the Air Fryer's pan with the cooking spray, add all the ingredients inside and toss
2. Cook at 365°F for 15 minutes, divide into bowls and serve for breakfast

**Nutrition: Calories: 142; Fat: 7g; Fiber: 2g; Carbs: 3g; Protein: 5g**

## 04. Asparagus Salad

Preparation Time: 15 minutes
Servings: 4

**Ingredients:**

- 1 cup baby arugula
- 1 bunch asparagus; trimmed
- 1 tbsp. balsamic vinegar
- 1 tbsp. cheddar cheese; grated

- A pinch of salt and black pepper
- Cooking spray

**Directions:**
1. Put the asparagus in your air fryer's basket, grease with cooking spray, season with salt and pepper and cook at 360°F for 10 minutes.
2. Take a bowl and mix the asparagus with the arugula and the vinegar, toss, divide between plates and serve hot with cheese sprinkled on top

**Nutrition: Calories: 200; Fat: 5g; Fiber: 1g; Carbs: 4g; Protein: 5g**

## 05. Lemony Raspberries Bowls

Preparation Time: 17 minutes
Servings: 2

**Ingredients:**
- 1 cup raspberries
- 2 tbsp. butter
- 2 tbsp. lemon juice
- 1 tsp. cinnamon powder

**Directions:**
1. In your air fryer, mix all the ingredients, toss, cover, cook at 350°F for 12 minutes, divide into bowls and serve for breakfast

**Nutrition: Calories: 208; Fat: 6g; Fiber: 9g; Carbs: 14g; Protein: 3g**

## 06. Spaghetti Squash Fritters

Preparation Time: 23 minutes
Servings: 4

**Ingredients:**
- 2 cups cooked spaghetti squash
- 2 stalks green onion, sliced
- 1 large egg.
- ¼ cup blanched finely ground almond flour.
- 2 tbsp. unsalted butter; softened.

- ½ tsp. garlic powder.
- 1 tsp. dried parsley.

**Directions:**
2. Remove excess moisture from the squash using a cheesecloth or kitchen towel.
3. Mix all ingredients in a large bowl. Form into four patties
4. Cut a piece of parchment to fit your air fryer basket. Place each patty on the parchment and place into the air fryer basket
5. Adjust the temperature to 400 Degrees F and set the timer for 8 minutes. Flip the patties halfway through the cooking time. Serve warm.

**Nutrition: Calories: 131; Protein: 3.8g; Fiber: 2.0g; Fat: 10.1g; Carbs: 7.1g**

## 07. Mushrooms and Cheese Spread

Preparation Time: 25 minutes
Servings: 4

**Ingredients:**
- ¼ cup mozzarella; shredded
- ½ cup coconut cream
- 1 cup white mushrooms
- A pinch of salt and black pepper
- Cooking spray

**Directions:**
1. Put the mushrooms in your air fryer's basket, grease with cooking spray and cook at 370°F for 20 minutes.
2. Transfer to a blender, add the remaining ingredients, pulse well, divide into bowls and serve as a spread

**Nutrition: Calories: 202; Fat: 12g; Fiber: 2g; Carbs: 5g; Protein: 7g**

## 08. Tuna and Spring Onions Salad

Preparation Time: 20 minutes
Servings: 4

**Ingredients:**

- 14 oz. canned tuna, drained and flaked
- 2 spring onions; chopped.
- 1 cup arugula
- 1 tbsp. olive oil
- A pinch of salt and black pepper

**Directions:**

1. In a bowl, all the ingredients except the oil and the arugula and whisk.
2. Preheat the Air Fryer over 360°F, add the oil and grease it. Pour the tuna mix, stir well and cook for 15 minutes
3. In a salad bowl, combine the arugula with the tuna mix, toss and serve.

**Nutrition: Calories: 212; Fat: 8g; Fiber: 3g; Carbs: 5g; Protein: 8g**

## 09. Cinnamon Pudding

Preparation Time: 16 minutes
Servings: 2

**Ingredients:**

- 4 eggs; whisked
- 4 tbsp. erythritol
- 2 tbsp. heavy cream
- ½ tsp. cinnamon powder
- ¼ tsp. allspice, ground
- Cooking spray

**Directions:**

1. Take a bowl and mix all the ingredients except the cooking spray, whisk well and pour into a ramekin greased with cooking spray
2. Add the basket to your Air Fryer, put the ramekin inside and cook at 400°F for 12 minutes. Divide into bowls and serve for breakfast.

**Nutrition: Calories: 201; Fat: 11g; Fiber: 2g; Carbs: 4g; Protein: 6g**

## 10. Tomatoes and Swiss Chard Bake

Preparation Time: 20 minutes
Servings: 4

**Ingredients:**

- 4 eggs; whisked
- 3 oz. Swiss chard; chopped.
- 1 cup tomatoes; cubed
- 1 tsp. olive oil
- Salt and black pepper to taste.

**Directions:**

1. Take a bowl and mix the eggs with the rest of the ingredients except the oil and whisk well.
2. Grease a pan that fits the fryer with the oil, pour the swish chard mix and cook at 359°F for 15 minutes.
3. Divide between plates and serve for breakfast

**Nutrition: Calories: 202; Fat: 14g; Fiber: 3g; Carbs: 5g; Protein: 12g**

## 11. Egg, Bacon and Cheese Roll Ups

Preparation Time: 30 minutes
Servings: 4

**Ingredients:**

- 12 slices sugar-free bacon.
- ½ medium green bell pepper; seeded and chopped
- 6 large eggs.
- ¼ cup chopped onion
- 1 cup shredded sharp Cheddar cheese.
- ½ cup mild salsa, for dipping
- 2 tbsp. unsalted butter.

**Directions:**

1. In a medium skillet over medium heat, melt butter. Add onion and pepper to the skillet and sauté until fragrant and onions are translucent, about 3 minutes
2. Whisk eggs in a small bowl and pour into skillet. Scramble eggs with onions and peppers until fluffy and fully cooked, about 5 minutes. Remove from heat and

set aside

3. On work surface, place three slices of bacon side by side, overlapping about ¼-inch. Place ¼ cup scrambled eggs in a heap on the side closest to you and sprinkle ¼ cup cheese on top of the eggs.

4. Tightly roll the bacon around the eggs and secure the seam with a toothpick if necessary. Place each roll into the air fryer basket

5. Adjust the temperature to 350 Degrees F and set the timer for 15 minutes. Rotate the rolls halfway through the cooking time. Bacon will be brown and crispy when completely cooked. Serve immediately with salsa for dipping.

**Nutrition: Calories: 460; Protein: 28.2g; Fiber: 0.8g; Fat: 31.7g; Carbs: 6.1g**

## 12. Crispy Ham Egg Cups

Preparation Time: 17 minutes
Servings: 2

**Ingredients:**

- 4 large eggs.
- 4: 1-oz.slices deli ham
- ½ cup shredded medium Cheddar cheese.
- ¼ cup diced green bell pepper.
- 2 tbsp. diced red bell pepper.
- 2 tbsp. diced white onion.
- 2 tbsp. full-fat sour cream.

**Directions:**

1. Place one slice of ham on the bottom of four baking cups.
2. Take a large bowl, whisk eggs with sour cream. Stir in green pepper, red pepper and onion
3. Pour the egg mixture into ham-lined baking cups. Top with Cheddar. Place cups into the air fryer basket. Adjust the temperature to 320 Degrees F and set the timer for 12 minutes or until the tops are browned. Serve warm.

**Nutrition: Calories: 382; Protein: 29.4g; Fiber:**

1.4g; Fat: 23.6g; Carbs: 6.0g

## 13. Olives and Kale

Preparation Time: 25 minutes
Servings: 4

**Ingredients:**

- 4 eggs; whisked
- 1 cup kale; chopped.
- ½ cup black olives, pitted and sliced
- 2 tbsp. cheddar; grated
- Cooking spray
- A pinch of salt and black pepper

**Directions:**

1. Take a bowl and mix the eggs with the rest of the ingredients except the cooking spray and whisk well.
2. Now, take a pan that fits in your air fryer and grease it with the cooking spray, pour the olives mixture inside, spread
3. Put the pan into the machine and cook at 360°F for 20 minutes. Serve for breakfast hot.

**Nutrition: Calories: 220; Fat: 13g; Fiber: 4g; Carbs: 6g; Protein: 12g**

## 14. Stuffed Poblanos

Preparation Time: 30 minutes
Servings: 4

**Ingredients:**

- ½ lb. spicy ground pork breakfast sausage
- 4 large poblano peppers
- 4 large eggs.
- ½ cup full-fat sour cream.
- 4 oz. full-fat cream cheese; softened.
- ¼ cup canned diced tomatoes and green chiles, drained
- 8 tbsp. shredded pepper jack cheese

**Directions:**

1. In a medium skillet over medium heat,

crumble and brown the ground sausage until no pink remains. Remove sausage and drain the fat from the pan. Crack eggs into the pan, scramble and cook until no longer runny

2. Place cooked sausage in a large bowl and fold in cream cheese. Mix in diced tomatoes and chiles. Gently fold in eggs

3. Cut a 4"–5" slit in the top of each poblano, removing the seeds and white membrane with a small knife. Separate the filling into fourand spoon carefully into each pepper. Top each with 2 tbsp. pepper jack cheese

4. Place each pepper into the air fryer basket. Adjust the temperature to 350 Degrees F and set the timer for 15 minutes.

5. Peppers will be soft and cheese will be browned when ready. Serve immediately with sour cream on top.

**Nutrition: Calories: 489; Protein: 22.8g; Fiber: 3.8g; Fat: 35.6g; Carbs: 12.6g**

## 15. Raspberries Oatmeal

Preparation Time: 20 minutes
Servings: 4

**Ingredients:**

- 1 ½ cups coconut; shredded
- ½ cups raspberries
- 2 cups almond milk
- ¼ tsp. nutmeg, ground
- 2 tsp. stevia
- ½ tsp. cinnamon powder
- Cooking spray

**Directions:**

1. Grease the air fryer's pan with cooking spray, mix all the ingredients inside, cover and cook at 360°F for 15 minutes. Divide into bowls and serve

**Nutrition: Calories: 172; Fat: 5g; Fiber: 2g; Carbs: 4g; Protein: 6g**

## 16. Bell Pepper Eggs

Preparation Time: 25 minutes
Servings: 4

**Ingredients:**

- 4 medium green bell peppers
- ¼ medium onion; peeled and chopped
- 3 oz. cooked ham; chopped
- 8 large eggs.
- 1 cup mild Cheddar cheese

**Directions:**

2. Cut the tops off each bell pepper. Remove the seeds and the white membranes with a small knife. Place ham and onion into each pepper

3. Crack 2 eggs into each pepper. Top with ¼ cup cheese per pepper. Place into the air fryer basket

4. Adjust the temperature to 390 Degrees F and set the timer for 15 minutes. When fully cooked, peppers will be tender and eggs will be firm. Serve immediately.

**Nutrition: Calories: 314; Protein: 24.9g; Fiber: 1.7g; Fat: 18.6g; Carbs: 6.3g**

## 17. Avocado Cauliflower Toast

Preparation Time: 23 minutes
Servings: 2

**Ingredients:**

- 1: 12-oz.steamer bag cauliflower
- ½ cup shredded mozzarella cheese
- 1 large egg.
- 1 ripe medium avocado
- ½ tsp. garlic powder.
- ¼ tsp. ground black pepper

**Directions:**

1. Cook cauliflower according to package instructions. Remove from bag and place into cheesecloth or clean towel to remove excess moisture.

2. Place cauliflower into a large bowl and

mix in egg and mozzarella. Cut a piece of parchment to fit your air fryer basket

3. Separate the cauliflower mixture into two and place it on the parchment in two mounds. Press out the cauliflower mounds into a ¼-inch-thick rectangle. Place the parchment into the air fryer basket.
4. Adjust the temperature to 400 Degrees F and set the timer for 8 minutes
5. Flip the cauliflower halfway through the cooking time
6. When the timer beeps, remove the parchment and allow the cauliflower to cool 5 minutes.
7. Cut open the avocado and remove the pit. Scoop out the inside, place it in a medium bowl and mash it with garlic powder and pepper. Spread onto the cauliflower.

**Nutrition: Calories: 278; Protein: 14.1g; Fiber: 8.2g; Fat: 15.6g; Carbs: 15.9g**

## 18. Blackberries Bowls

Preparation Time: 20 minutes
Servings: 4

### Ingredients:

- 1 ½ cups coconut milk
- ½ cup coconut; shredded
- ½ cup blackberries
- 2 tsp. stevia

### Directions:

1. In your air fryer's pan, mix all the ingredients, stir, cover and cook at 360°F for 15 minutes.
2. Divide into bowls and serve

**Nutrition: Calories: 171; Fat: 4g; Fiber: 2g; Carbs: 3g; Protein: 5g**

## 19. Air Fryer Breakfast Frittata

Preparation Time: 15 minutes
Cooking Time: 20 minutes
Servings: 2

### Ingredients:

- ¼ pound breakfast sausage, fully cooked and crumbled
- 4 eggs, lightly beaten
- ½ cup Monterey Jack cheese, shredded
- 2 tablespoons red bell pepper, diced
- 1 green onion, chopped
- 1 pinch cayenne pepper

### Directions:

1. Preheat the Air fryer to 365 o F and grease a nonstick 6x2-inch cake pan.
2. Whisk together eggs with sausage, green onion, bell pepper, cheese and cayenne in a bowl.
3. Transfer the egg mixture in the prepared cake pan and place in the Air fryer.
4. Cook for about 20 minutes and serve warm.

### Nutrition:

Calories: 464, Fat: 33.7g, Carbohydrates: 10.4g, Sugar: 7g, Protein: 30.4g, Sodium: 704mg

## 20. Breakfast Pockets

Preparation Time: 15 minutes
Cooking Time: 30 minutes
Servings: 4

### Ingredients:

- 2 sheets: 17.25 ozalmond flour puff pastry, cut into 4 equal sized pieces
- 1 package: 6 oz.ground breakfast sausage, crumbled
- 2 eggs, lightly beaten
- 1 cup cheddar cheese, shredded
- 1 teaspoon kosher salt
- ½ teaspoon ground black pepper
- 2 tablespoons canola oil

### Directions:

1. Preheat the Air fryer to 375 o F and grease the Air fryer basket.
2. Arrange the sausages in the basket and roast for about 15 minutes.

3. Place the eggs into the basket and cook for about 5 minutes.

4. Season with salt and black pepper and divide the egg sausages mixture over the 4 puff pastry rectangles.

5. Top with shredded cheddar cheese and drizzle with canola oil.

6. Place 1 egg pocket in the basket and cook for 6 minutes at 400 o F.

7. Remove from the Air fryer and repeat with the remaining pockets.

8. Serve warm and enjoy.

**Nutrition:**
Calories: 197, Fats: 15.4g, Carbs: 8.5g, Sugar: 1.1g, Proteins: 7.9g, Sodium: 203mg

## 21. Ham and Egg Toast Cups

Preparation Time: 5 minutes
Cooking Time: 5 minutes
Servings: 2

**Ingredients:**
- 2 eggs
- 2 slices of ham
- 2 tablespoons butter
- Cheddar cheese, for topping
- Salt, to taste
- Black pepper, to taste

**Directions:**
1. Preheat the Air fryer to 400 o F and grease both ramekins with melted butter.

2. Place each ham slice in the greased ramekins and crack each egg over ham slices.

3. Sprinkle with salt, black pepper and cheddar cheese and transfer into the Air fryer basket.

4. Cook for about 5 minutes and remove the ramekins from the basket.

5. Serve warm.

**Nutrition:**
Calories: 202, Fat: 13.7g, Carbs: 7.4g, Sugar: 3.3g, Protein: 10.2g, Sodium: 203mg

## 22. Cauliflower Hash Brown

Preparation Time: 20 minutes
Cooking Time: 10 minutes
Servings: 4

**Ingredients:**
- 2 cups cauliflower, finely grated, soaked and drained
- 2 tablespoons xanthan gum
- Salt, to taste
- Pepper powder, to taste
- 2 teaspoons chili flakes
- 1 teaspoon garlic
- 1 teaspoon onion powder
- 2 teaspoons vegetable oil

**Directions:**
1. Preheat the Air fryer to 300 o F and grease an Air fryer basket with oil.

2. Heat vegetable oil in a nonstick pan and add cauliflower.

3. Sauté for about 4 minutes and dish out the cauliflower in a plate.

4. Mix the cauliflower with xanthum gum, salt, chili flakes, garlic and onion powder.

5. Mix well and refrigerate the hash for about 20 minutes.

6. Place the hash in the Air fryer basket and cook for about 10 minutes.

7. Flip the hash after cooking half way through and dish out to serve warm.

**Nutrition:**
Calories: 291, Fat: 2.8g, Carbs: 6.5g, Sugar: 4.5g, Protein: 6.6g, Sodium: 62mg

## 23. French toast Sticks

Preparation Time: 10 minutes
Cooking Time: 5 minutes
Servings: 4

**Ingredients:**
- 4 bread, sliced into sticks
- 2 tablespoons soft butter or margarine

- 2 eggs, gently beaten
- Salt, to taste
- 1 pinch cinnamon
- 1 pinch nutmeg
- 1 pinch ground cloves

**Directions:**
1. Preheat the Air fryer at 365 o F and grease an Air fryer pan with butter.
2. Whisk eggs with salt, cinnamon, nutmeg and ground cloves in a bowl.
3. Dip the bread sticks in the egg mixture and place in the pan.
4. Cook for about 5 minutes, flipping in between and remove from the Air fryer.
5. Dish out and serve warm.

**Nutrition:**
Calories: 186, Fat: 11.7g, Carbs: 6.8g, Sugar: 1.7g, Protein: 13.2g, Sodium: 498mg

## 24. Sausage Solo

Preparation Time: 5 minutes
Cooking Time: 22 minutes
Servings: 4

**Ingredients:**
- 6 eggs
- 4 cooked sausages, sliced
- 2 bread slices, cut into sticks
- ½ cup mozzarella cheese, grated
- ½ cup cream

**Directions:**
1. Preheat the Air fryer to 355 o F and grease 4 ramekins lightly.
2. Whisk together eggs and cream in a bowl and beat well.
3. Transfer the egg mixture into ramekins and arrange the bread sticks and sausage slices around the edges.
4. Top with mozzarella cheese evenly and place the ramekins in Air fryer basket.
5. Cook for about 22 minutes and dish out to serve warm.

**Nutrition:**
Calories: 180, Fat: 12.7g, Carbs: 3.9g, Sugar: 1.3g, Protein: 12.4g, Sodium: 251mg

## 25. Sausage Bacon Fandango

Preparation Time: 5 minutes
Cooking Time: 20 minutes
Servings: 4

**Ingredients:**
- 8 bacon slices
- 8 chicken sausages
- 4 eggs
- Salt and black pepper, to taste

**Directions:**
1. Preheat the Air fryer to 320 o F and grease 4 ramekins lightly.
2. Place bacon slices and sausages in the Air fryer basket.
3. Cook for about 10 minutes and crack 1 egg in each prepared ramekin.
4. Season with salt and black pepper and cook for about 10 more minutes.
5. Divide bacon slices and sausages in serving plates.
6. Place 1 egg in each plate and serve warm.

**Nutrition:**
Calories: 287, Fat: 21.5g, Carbs: 0.9g, Sugar: 0.3g, Protein: 21.4g, Sodium: 1007mg

## 26. Creamy Parsley Soufflé

Preparation Time: 5 minutes
Cooking Time: 10 minutes
Servings: 2

**Ingredients:**
- 2 eggs
- 1 tablespoon fresh parsley, chopped
- 1 fresh red chili pepper, chopped
- 2 tablespoons light cream
- Salt, to taste

**Directions:**

1. Preheat the Air fryer to 390 o F and grease 2 soufflé dishes.
2. Mix together all the ingredients in a bowl until well combined.
3. Transfer the mixture into prepared soufflé dishes and place in the Air fryer.
4. Cook for about 10 minutes and dish out to serve warm.

**Nutrition**:
Calories: 108, Fat: 9g, Carbs: 1.1g, Sugar: 0.5g, Protein: 6g, Sodium: 146mg

## 27. Sweet Potato Hash

Preparation Time: 10 minutes
Cooking Time: 15 minutes
Servings: 6

**Ingredients:**
- 2 large sweet potato, cut into small cubes
- 2 slices bacon, cut into small pieces
- 2 tablespoons olive oil
- 1 tablespoon smoked paprika
- 1 teaspoon sea salt
- 1 teaspoon ground black pepper
- 1 teaspoon dried dill weed

**Directions:**
1. Preheat the Air Fryer to 400 o F and grease an Air fryer pan.
2. Mix together sweet potato, bacon, olive oil, paprika, salt, black pepper and dill in a large bowl.
3. Transfer the mixture into the preheated air fryer pan and cook for about 15 minutes, stirring in between.
4. Dish out and serve warm.

**Nutrition:**
Calories: 191, Fat: 6g, Carbohydrates: 31.4g, Sugar: 6g, Protein: 3.7g, Sodium: 447mg

## 28. Toad-in-the-Hole Tarts

Preparation Time: 5 minutes
Cooking Time: 25 minutes

Servings: 4

**Ingredients:**
- 1 sheet frozen puff pastry, thawed and cut into 4 squares
- 4 tablespoons cheddar cheese, shredded
- 4 tablespoons cooked ham, diced
- 4 eggs
- 2 tablespoons fresh chives, chopped
- 1 tablespoon olive oil

**Directions:**
1. Preheat the Air fryer to 400 o F and grease an Air fryer basket.
2. Place 2 pastry squares in the air fryer basket and cook for about 8 minutes.
3. Remove Air fryer basket from the Air fryer and press each square gently with a metal tablespoon to form an indentation.
4. Place 1 tablespoon of ham and 1 tablespoon of cheddar cheese in each hole and top with 1 egg each.
5. Return Air fryer basket to Air fryer and cook for about 6 more minutes.
6. Remove tarts from the Air fryer basket and allow to cool.
7. Repeat with remaining pastry squares, cheese, ham, and eggs.
8. Dish out and garnish tarts with chives.

**Nutrition:**
Calories: 175, Fat: 13.7g, Carbohydrates: 4.1g, Sugar: 0.5g, Protein: 9.3g, Sodium: 233mg

## 29. Tex-Mex Hash Browns

Preparation Time: 15 minutes
Cooking Time: 30 minutes
Servings: 4

**Ingredients:**
- 1½ pounds potatoes, peeled, cut into 1-inch cubes and soaked
- 1 red bell pepper, seeded and cut into 1-inch pieces
- 1 small onion, cut into 1-inch pieces

- 1 jalapeno, seeded and cut into 1-inch rings
- 1 tablespoon olive oil
- ½ teaspoon taco seasoning mix
- ½ teaspoon ground cumin
- 1 pinch salt and ground black pepper, to taste

**Directions:**
1. Preheat the Air fryer to 330 o F and grease an Air fryer basket.
2. Coat the potatoes with olive oil and transfer into the Air fryer basket.
3. Cook for about 18 minutes and dish out in a bowl.
4. Mix together bell pepper, onion, and jalapeno in the bowl and season with taco seasoning mix, cumin, salt and black pepper.
5. Toss to coat well and combine with the potatoes.
6. Transfer the seasoned vegetables into the Air fryer basket and cook for about 12 minutes, stirring in between.
7. Dish out and serve immediately.

**Nutrition:**
Calories: 186, Fat: 4.3g, Carbohydrates: 33.7g, Sugar: 3g, Protein: 4g, Sodium: 79mg

## 30. Puffed Egg Tarts

Preparation Time: 10 minutes
Cooking Time: 42 minutes
Servings: 4

**Ingredients:**
- 1 sheet frozen puff pastry half, thawed and cut into 4 squares
- ¾ cup Monterey Jack cheese, shredded and divided
- 4 large eggs
- 1 tablespoon fresh parsley, minced
- 1 tablespoon olive oil

**Directions:**
1. Preheat the Air fryer to 390 o F

2. Place 2 pastry squares in the air fryer basket and cook for about 10 minutes.
3. Remove Air fryer basket from the Air fryer and press each square gently with a metal tablespoon to form an indentation.
4. Place 3 tablespoons of cheese in each hole and top with 1 egg each.
5. Return Air fryer basket to Air fryer and cook for about 11 minutes.
6. Remove tarts from the Air fryer basket and sprinkle with half the parsley.
7. Repeat with remaining pastry squares, cheese and eggs.
8. Dish out and serve warm.

**Nutrition:**
Calories: 246, Fat: 19.4g, Carbohydrates: 5.9g, Sugar: 0.6g, Protein: 12.4g, Sodium: 213mg

## 31. Air Fryer Bacon

Preparation Time: 1 minutes
Cooking Time: 9 minutes
Servings: 6

**Ingredients:**
- 6 bacon strips
- ½ tablespoon olive oil

**Directions:**
1. Preheat the Air fryer to 350 o F and grease an Air fryer basket with olive oil.
2. Cook for about 9 minutes and flip the bacon.
3. Cook for 3 more minutes until crispy and serve warm.

**Nutrition:**
Calories: 245, Fat: 17.1g, Carbohydrates: 10.2g, Sugar: 2.7g, Protein: 12.8g, Sodium: 580mg

## 32. Broccoli Cheese Quiche

Preparation Time: 10 minutes
Cooking Time: 40 minutes
Servings: 2

**Ingredients:**

- 1 large broccoli, chopped into florets
- 3 large carrots, peeled and diced
- 1 cup cheddar cheese, grated
- ¼ cup feta cheese
- 2 large eggs
- 1 teaspoon dried rosemary
- 1 teaspoon dried thyme
- Salt and black pepper, to taste

**Directions:**

1. Preheat the Air fryer to 360 o F and grease a quiche dish.
2. Place broccoli and carrots into a food steamer and cook for about 20 minutes until soft.
3. Whisk together eggs with milk, dried herbs, salt and black pepper in a bowl.
4. Place steamed vegetables at the bottom of the quiche pan and top with tomatoes and cheese.
5. Drizzle with the egg mixture and transfer the quiche dish in the Air fryer.
6. Cook for about 20 minutes and dish out to serve warm.

**Nutrition:**
Calories: 412, Fat: 28, Carbohydrates: 16.3g, Sugar: 7.5g, Protein: 25.3g, Sodium: 720mg

## 33. Bacon and Egg Bite Cups

Preparation Time: 15 minutes
Cooking Time: 15 minutes
Servings: 4

**Ingredients:**

- 6 large eggs
- ½ cup red peppers, chopped
- ¼ cup fresh spinach, chopped
- ¾ cup mozzarella cheese, shredded
- 3 slices bacon, cooked and crumbled
- 2 tablespoons heavy whipping cream
- Salt and black pepper, to taste

**Directions:**

1. Preheat the Air fryer to 300 o F and grease 4 silicone molds.
2. Whisk together eggs with cream, salt and black pepper in a large bowl until combined.
3. Stir in rest of the ingredients and transfer the mixture into silicone molds.
4. Place in the Air fryer and cook for about 15 minutes.
5. Dish out and serve warm.

**Nutrition:**
Calories: 233, Fats: 17.2g, Carbohydrates: 2.9g, Sugar: 1.6g, Proteins: 16.8g, Sodium: 472mg

## 34. Air Fryer Sausage

Preparation Time: 5 minutes
Cooking Time: 20 minutes
Servings: 5

**Ingredients:**

- 5 raw and uncooked sausage links
- 1 tablespoon olive oil

**Directions:**

1. Preheat the Air fryer to 360 o F and grease an Air fryer basket with olive oil.
2. Cook for about 15 minutes and flip the sausages.
3. Cook for 5 more minutes and serve warm.

**Nutrition:**
Calories: 131, Fat: 11.8g, Carbohydrates: 0g, Sugar: 0g, Protein: 6g, Sodium: 160mg

## 35. Bacon Grilled Cheese

Preparation Time: 5 minutes
Cooking Time: 7 minutes
Servings: 2

**Ingredients:**

- 4 slices of bread
- 1 tablespoon butter, softened
- 2 slices mild cheddar cheese

- 6 slices bacon, cooked
- 2 slices mozzarella cheese
- 1 tablespoon olive oil

**Directions:**
1. Preheat the Air fryer to 370 o F and grease an Air fryer basket with olive oil.
2. Spread butter onto one side of each bread slice and place in the Air Fryer basket.
3. Layer with cheddar cheese slice, followed by bacon, mozzarella cheese and close with the other bread slice.
4. Place in the Air fryer and cook for about 4 minutes.
5. Flip the sandwich and cook for 3 more minutes.
6. Remove from the Air fryer and serve.

**Nutrition:**
Calories: 518, Fat: 34.9g, Carbohydrates: 20g, Sugar: 0.6g, Protein: 29.9g, Sodium: 1475mg

## 36. Air Fryer Breakfast Casserole

Preparation Time: 10 minutes
Cooking Time: 25 minutes
Servings: 2

**Ingredients:**
- 3 red potatoes
- 3 eggs
- 2 turkey sausage patties
- ¼ cup cheddar cheese
- 1 tablespoon milk
- Olive oil cooking spray

**Directions:**
1. Preheat the Air fryer to 400 ° F and grease a baking dish with cooking spray.
2. Place the potatoes in the Air fryer basket and cook for about 10 minutes.
3. Whisk eggs with milk in a bowl.
4. Put the potatoes and sausage in the baking dish and pour egg mixture on top.
5. Sprinkle with cheddar cheese and arrange in the Air fryer.

6. Cook for about 15 minutes at 350 ° F and dish out to serve warm.

**Nutrition:**
Calories: 469, Fat: 16.3g, Carbohydrates: 51.9g, Sugar: 4.1g, Protein: 29.1g, Sodium: 623mg

## 37. Air Fryer Breakfast Bake

Preparation Time: 15 minutes
Cooking Time: 25 minutes
Servings: 2

**Ingredients:**
- 4 eggs
- 1 slice whole grain bread, torn into pieces
- 1½ cups baby spinach
- 1/3 cup cheddar cheese, shredded
- ½ cup bell pepper, diced
- ½ teaspoon kosher salt
- 1 teaspoon hot sauce

**Directions:**
1. Preheat the Air fryer to 250 o F and grease a 6-inch soufflé dish with nonstick cooking spray.
2. Whisk together eggs, salt and hot sauce in a bowl.
3. Dip the bread pieces, spinach, ¼ cup cheddar cheese and bell pepper in the whisked eggs.
4. Pour this mixture into prepared soufflé dish and sprinkle with remaining cheese.
5. Transfer into the Air fryer basket and cook for about 25 minutes.
6. Remove from the Air fryer basket and let it rest for 10 minutes before serving.

**Nutrition:**
Calories: 249, Fat: 15.7g, Carbohydrates: 10.3g, Sugar: 3.4g, Protein: 18.2g, Sodium: 979mg

## 38. Sausage Breakfast Casserole

Preparation Time: 10 minutes
Cooking Time: 20 minutes
Servings: 4

**Ingredients:**

- 1 pound hash browns
- 1 pound ground breakfast sausage
- 3 bell peppers, diced
- ¼ cup sweet onion, diced
- 4 eggs
- 1 tablespoon olive oil
- Salt and black pepper, to taste

**Directions:**

Preheat the Air fryer to 355 o F and grease the casserole dish with olive oil.

1. Place the hash browns on the bottom of the casserole dish and top with sausages, bell peppers and onions.
2. Transfer into the Air fryer and cook for about 10 minutes.
3. Crack eggs into the casserole dish and cook for 10 more minutes.
4. Season with salt and black pepper and serve warm.

**Nutrition:**

Calories: 472, Fat: 25g, Carbohydrates: 47.6g, Sugar: 6.8g, Protein: 15.6g, Sodium: 649mg

## 39. Egg Veggie Frittata

Preparation Time: 10 minutes
Cooking Time: 18 minutes
Servings: 2

**Ingredients:**

- 4 eggs
- ½ cup milk
- 2 green onions, chopped
- ¼ cup baby Bella mushrooms, chopped
- ¼ cup spinach, chopped
- ½ teaspoon salt
- ½ teaspoon black pepper
- Dash of hot sauce

**Directions:**

1. Preheat the Air fryer to 365 o F and grease 6x3 inch square pan with butter.

2. Whisk eggs with milk in a large bowl and stir in green onions, mushrooms and spinach.
3. Sprinkle with salt, black pepper and hot sauce and pour this mixture into the prepared pan.
4. Place in the Air fryer and cook for about 18 minutes.
5. Dish out in a platter and serve warm.

**Nutrition:**

Calories: 166, Fat: 10.1g, Carbohydrates: 5.8g, Sugar: 4g, Protein: 13.8g, Sodium: 748mg

## 40. Corn Pudding

Preparation Time: 1 hour 25 minutes
Servings: 6

**Ingredients:**

- 4 bacon slices; cooked and chopped.
- 3 eggs
- 3 cups bread; cubed
- 1/2 cup heavy cream
- 1½ cups whole milk
- 1 cup cheddar cheese; grated
- 2 cups corn
- 1/2 cup green bell pepper; chopped
- 1 yellow onion; chopped.
- 1/4 cup celery; chopped.
- 1 tsp. thyme; chopped.
- 2 tsp. garlic; grated
- 3 tbsp. parmesan cheese; grated
- 1 tbsp. olive oil
- Salt and black pepper

**Directions:**

1. Heat up the oil in a pan over medium heat. Add the corn, celery, onion, bell pepper, salt, pepper, garlic and thyme to the pan; stir, sauté for 15 minutes and transfer to a bowl
2. To the same bowl, add the bacon, milk, cream, eggs, salt, pepper, bread and the cheddar cheese. Stir well, then pour into a

casserole dish that fits your air fryer

3. Place the dish in the fryer and cook at 350°F for 30 minutes
4. Sprinkle the pudding with parmesan cheese and cook for 30 minutes more. Slice, divide between plates and serve.

## 41. Delicious Doughnuts

Preparation Time: 28 Minutes
Servings: 6

**Ingredients:**

- 1/2 cup sugar
- 2 ¼ cups white flour
- 1 tsp. cinnamon powder
- 2 egg yolks
- 1/3 cup caster sugar
- 4 tbsp. butter; soft
- 1 ½ tsp. baking powder
- 1/2 cup sour cream

**Directions:**

1. In a bowl; mix 2 tablespoon butter with simple sugar and egg yolks and whisk well
2. Add half of the sour cream and stir.
3. In another bowls; mix flour with baking powder, stir and also add to eggs mix
4. Stir well until you obtain a dough, transfer it to a floured working surface; roll it out and cut big circles with smaller ones in the middle.
5. Brush doughnuts with the rest of the butter; heat up your air fryer at 360 degrees F; place doughnuts inside and cook them for 8 minutes
6. In a bowl; mix cinnamon with caster sugar and stir. Arrange doughnuts on plates and dip them in cinnamon and sugar before serving.

## 42. Blackberries and Cornflakes

Preparation Time: 15 minutes
Servings: 4

**Ingredients:**

- 3 cups milk
- 1/4 cup blackberries
- 2 eggs; whisked
- 1 tbsp. sugar
- 1/4 tsp. nutmeg; ground
- 4 tbsp. cream cheese; whipped
- 1½ cups corn flakes

**Directions:**

1. In a bowl, mix all ingredients and stir well.
2. Heat up your air fryer at 350°F, add the corn flakes mixture, spread and cook for 10 minutes. Divide between plates, serve and enjoy

## 43. Fried Mushroom

Preparation Time: 25 minutes
Servings: 4

- **Ingredients:**
- 7 oz. spinach; torn
- 8 cherry tomatoes; halved
- 4 slices bacon; chopped.
- 4 eggs
- 8 white mushrooms; sliced
- 1 garlic clove; minced
- A drizzle of olive oil
- Salt and black pepper to taste

**Directions:**

1. In a pan greased with oil and that fits your air fryer, mix all ingredients except for the spinach; stir.
2. Put the pan in your air fryer and cook at 400°F for 15 minutes. Add the spinach, toss and cook for 5 minutes more. Divide between plates and serve

## 44. Smoked Bacon and Bread

Preparation Time: 40 minutes
Servings: 6

**Ingredients:**

- 1 lb. white bread; cubed
- 1 lb. smoked bacon; cooked and chopped.
- 1/2 lb. cheddar cheese; shredded
- 1/2 lb. Monterey jack cheese; shredded
- 30 oz. canned tomatoes; chopped.
- 1/4 cup avocado oil
- 1 red onion; chopped.
- 2 tbsp. chicken stock
- 2 tbsp. chives; chopped.
- 8 eggs; whisked
- Salt and black pepper to taste

**Directions:**

1. Add the oil to your air fryer and heat it up at 350°F
2. Add all other ingredients except the chives and cook for 30 minutes, shaking halfway. Divide between plates and serve with chives sprinkled on top

## 45. Pancakes

Preparation Time: 30 minutes
Servings: 4

**Ingredients:**

- 1¾ cups white flour
- 1 cup apple; peeled, cored and chopped.
- 1¼ cups milk
- 1 egg; whisked
- 2 tbsp. sugar
- 2 tsp. baking powder
- 1/4 tsp. vanilla extract
- 2 tsp. cinnamon powder
- Cooking spray

**Directions:**

1. In a bowl, mix all ingredients: except cooking sprayand stir until you obtain a smooth batter
2. Grease your air fryer's pan with the cooking spray and pour in 1/4 of the batter; spread it into the pan.
3. Cover and cook at 360°F for 5 minutes,

flipping it halfway
4. Repeat steps 2 and 3 with 1/4 of the batter 3 more times and then serve the pancakes right away.

## 46. Creamy Mushroom Pie

Preparation Time: 20 minutes
Servings: 4

**Ingredients:**

- 6 white mushrooms; chopped.
- 3 eggs
- 1 red onion; chopped.
- 9-inch pie dough
- 1/4 cup cheddar cheese; grated
- 1/2 cup heavy cream
- 2 tbsp. bacon; cooked and crumbled
- 1 tbsp. olive oil
- 1/2 tsp. thyme; dried
- Salt and black pepper to taste

**Directions:**

1. Roll the dough on a working surface, then press it on the bottom of a pie pan that fits your air fryer and grease with the oil
2. In a bowl, mix all other ingredients except the cheese, stir well and pour mixture into the pie pan
3. Sprinkle the cheese on top, put the pan in the air fryer and cook at 400°F for 10 minutes. Slice and serve.

## 47. Cheesy Hash Brown

Preparation Time: 30 minutes
Servings: 6

**Ingredients:**

- 1½ lbs. hash browns
- 6 bacon slices; chopped.
- 8 oz. cream cheese; softened
- 1 yellow onion; chopped.
- 6 eggs
- 6 spring onions; chopped.

- 1 cup cheddar cheese; shredded
- 1 cup almond milk
- A drizzle of olive oil
- Salt and black pepper to taste

**Directions:**
1. Heat up your air fryer with the oil at 350°F. In a bowl, mix all other ingredients except the spring onions and whisk well
2. Add this mixture to your air fryer, cover and cook for 20 minutes
3. Divide between plates, sprinkle the spring onions on top and serve.

## 48. Pear Oatmeal

Preparation Time: 17 minutes
Servings: 4

**Ingredients:**
- 1 cup milk
- 1/4 cups brown sugar
- 1/2 cup walnuts; chopped.
- 2 cups pear; peeled and chopped.
- 1 cup old fashioned oats
- 1/2 tsp. cinnamon powder
- 1 tbsp. butter; softened

**Directions:**
1. In a heat-proof bowl that fits your air fryer, mix all ingredients and stir well. Place in your fryer and cook at 360°F for 12 minutes. Divide into bowls and serve

## 49. Ham and Cheese Patties

Preparation Time: 20 minutes
Servings: 4

**Ingredients:**
- 8 ham slices; chopped.
- 4 handfuls mozzarella cheese; grated
- 1 puff pastry sheet
- 4 tsp. mustard

**Directions:**

1. Roll out puff pastry on a working surface and cut it in 12 squares. Divide cheese, ham and mustard on half of them, top with the other halves and seal the edges
2. Place all the patties in your air fryer's basket and cook at 370°F for 10 minutes. Divide the patties between plates and serve

## 50. Peppers and Lettuce Salad

Preparation Time: 15 minutes
Servings: 4

**Ingredients:**
- 2 oz. rocket leaves
- 4 red bell peppers
- 1 lettuce head; torn
- 2 tbsp. olive oil
- 1 tbsp. lime juice
- 3 tbsp. heavy cream
- Salt and black pepper to taste

**Directions:**
1. Place the bell peppers in your air fryer's basket and cook at 400°F for 10 minutes
2. Remove the peppers, peel, cut them into strips and put them in a bowl. Add all remaining ingredients, toss and serve

## 51. Cod Tortilla

Preparation Time: 27 minutes
Servings: 4

**Ingredients:**
- 4 cod fillets; skinless and boneless
- 4 tortillas
- 1 green bell pepper; chopped.
- 1 red onion; chopped.
- A drizzle of olive oil
- 1 cup corn
- 1/2 cup salsa
- 4 tbsp. parmesan cheese; grated
- A handful of baby spinach

**Directions:**

1. Put the fish fillets in your air fryer's basket, cook at 350°F for 6 minutes and transfer to a plate.
2. Heat up a pan with the oil over medium heat, add the bell peppers, onions and corn and stir
3. Sauté for 5 minutes and take off the heat. Arrange all the tortillas on a working surface and divide the cod, salsa, sautéed veggies, spinach and parmesan evenly between the 4 tortillas; then wrap / roll them
4. Place the tortillas in your air fryer's basket and cook at 350°F for 6 minutes. Divide between plates, serve.

## 52. Artichoke Omelet

Preparation Time: 20 minutes
Servings:

**Ingredients:**

- 3 artichoke hearts; canned, drained and chopped.
- 6 eggs; whisked
- 2 tbsp. avocado oil
- 1/2 tsp. oregano; dried
- Salt and black pepper to taste

**Directions:**

1. In a bowl, mix all ingredients except the oil; stir well. Add the oil to your air fryer's pan and heat it up at 320°F.
2. Add the egg mixture, cook for 15 minutes, divide between plates and serve

## 53. Carrot Oatmeal

Preparation Time: 20 minutes
Servings: 4

**Ingredients:**

- 1/2 cup steel cut oats
- 2 cups almond milk
- 1 cup carrots; shredded
- 2 tsp. sugar

- 1 tsp. cardamom; ground
- Cooking spray

**Directions:**

1. Spray your air fryer with cooking spray, add all ingredients, toss and cover. Cook at 365°F for 15 minutes. Divide into bowls and serve

## 54. Chicken Burrito

Preparation Time: 15 minutes
Servings: 2

**Ingredients:**

- 4 chicken breast slices; cooked and shredded
- 2 tortillas
- 1 avocado; peeled, pitted and sliced
- 1 green bell pepper; sliced
- 2 eggs; whisked
- 2 tbsp. mild salsa
- 2 tbsp. cheddar cheese; grated
- Salt and black pepper to taste

**Directions:**

2. In a bowl, whisk the eggs with the salt and pepper and pour them into a pan that fits your air fryer. Put the pan in the air fryer's basket, cook for 5 minutes at 400°F and transfer the mix to a plate
3. Place the tortillas on a working surface and between them divide the eggs, chicken, bell peppers, avocado and the cheese; roll the burritos
4. Line your air fryer with tin foil, add the burritos and cook them at 300°F for 3-4 minutes. Serve for breakfast-or lunch, or dinner!

## 55. Potato Frittata

Preparation Time: 25 minutes
Servings: 6

**Ingredients:**

- 1 lb. small potatoes; chopped.

- 1 oz. parmesan cheese; grated
- 1/2 cup heavy cream
- 2 red onions; chopped.
- 8 eggs; whisked
- 1 tbsp. olive oil
- Salt and black pepper to taste

**Directions:**
1. In a bowl, mix all ingredients except the potatoes and oil; stir well.
2. Heat up your air fryer's pan with the oil at 320°F. Add the potatoes, stir and cook for 5 minutes
3. Add the egg mixture, spread and cook for 15 minutes more. Divide the frittata between plates and serve

## 56. Herbed Omelet

Preparation Time: 20 minutes
Servings: 4

**Ingredients:**
- 6 eggs; whisked
- 2 tbsp. parmesan cheese; grated
- 4 tbsp. heavy cream
- 1 tbsp. parsley; chopped.
- 1 tbsp. tarragon; chopped.
- 2 tbsp. chives; chopped.
- Salt and black pepper to taste

**Directions:**
1. In a bowl, mix all ingredients except for the parmesan and whisk well. Pour this into a pan that fits your air fryer, place it in preheated fryer and cook at 350°F for 15 minutes
2. Divide the omelet between plates and serve with the parmesan sprinkled on top

## 57. Cheese Toast

Preparation Time: 13 minutes
Servings:2

**Ingredients:**

- 4 bread slices
- 4 cheddar cheese slices
- 4 tsp. butter; softened

**Directions:**
1. Spread the butter on each slice of bread. Place 2 cheese slices each on 2 bread slices, then top with the other 2 bread slices; cut each in half
2. Arrange the sandwiches in your air fryer's basket and cook at 370°F for 8 minutes. Serve hot and enjoy!

## 58. Carrots and Cauliflower Mix

Preparation Time: 30 minutes
Servings: 4

**Ingredients:**
- 1 cauliflower head; stems removed, florets separated and steamed
- 2 oz. milk
- 2 oz. cheddar cheese; grated
- 3 carrots; chopped and steamed
- 3 eggs
- 2 tsp. cilantro; chopped.
- Salt and black pepper to taste

**Directions:**
1. In a bowl, mix the eggs with the milk, parsley, salt and pepper; whisk. Put the cauliflower and the carrots in your air fryer, add the egg mixture and spread. Then sprinkle the cheese on top
2. Cook at 350°F for 20 minutes, divide between plates and serve

## 59. Vanilla Oatmeal

Preparation Time: 22 minutes
Servings: 4

**Ingredients:**
- 1 cup steel cut oats
- 1 cup milk
- 2½ cups water

- 2 tsp. vanilla extract
- 2 tbsp. brown sugar

**Directions:**

1. In a pan that fits your air fryer, mix all ingredients and stir well. Place the pan in your air fryer and cook at 360°F for 17 minutes. Divide into bowls and serve

## 60. Fish Tacos Breakfast

Preparation Time: 23 Minutes
Servings: 4

**Ingredients:**

- 4 big tortillas
- 1 yellow onion; chopped
- 1 cup corn
- 1 red bell pepper; chopped
- 1/2 cup salsa
- 4 white fish fillets; skinless and boneless
- A handful mixed romaine lettuce; spinach and radicchio
- 4 tbsp. parmesan; grated

**Directions:**

1. Put fish fillets in your air fryer and cook at 350°F, for 6 minutes
2. Meanwhile; heat up a pan over medium high heat, add bell pepper, onion and corn; stir and cook for 1 - 2 minutes
3. Arrange tortillas on a working surface, divide fish fillets, spread salsa over them; divide mixed veggies and mixed greens and spread parmesan on each at the end.
4. Roll your tacos; place them in preheated air fryer and cook at 350°F, for 6 minutes more. Divide fish tacos on plates and serve for breakfast

## 61. Tuna Sandwiches

Preparation Time: 14 minutes
Servings: 4

**Ingredients:**

- 16 oz. canned tuna; drained

- 6 bread slices
- 6 provolone cheese slices
- 2 spring onions; chopped.
- 1/4 cup mayonnaise
- 2 tbsp. mustard
- 1 tbsp. lime juice
- 3 tbsp. butter; melted

**Directions:**

1. In a bowl, mix the tuna, mayo, lime juice, mustard and spring onions; stir until combined.
2. Spread the bread slices with the butter, place them in preheated air fryer and bake them at 350°F for 5 minutes
3. Spread tuna mix on half of the bread slices and top with the cheese and the other bread slices
4. Place the sandwiches in your air fryer's basket and cook for 4 minutes more. Divide between plates and serve.

## 62. Tofu and Bell Peppers

Preparation Time: 15 minutes
Servings: 8

**Ingredients:**

- 3 oz. firm tofu; crumbled
- 1 green onion; chopped.
- 1 yellow bell pepper; cut into strips
- 1 orange bell pepper; cut into strips
- 1 green bell pepper; cut into strips
- 2 tbsp. parsley; chopped.
- Salt and black pepper to taste

**Directions:**

1. In a pan that fits your air fryer, place the bell pepper strips and mix
2. Then add all remaining ingredients, toss and place the pan in the air fryer. Cook at 400°F for 10 minutes. Divide between plates and serve

## 63. Broccoli Stew

Preparation Time: 20 minutes
Servings: 4

**Ingredients:**

- 1 broccoli head, florets separated
- ¼ cup celery; chopped.
- ¾ cup tomato sauce
- 3 spring onions; chopped.
- 3 tbsp. chicken stock
- Salt and black pepper to taste.

**Directions:**

1. In a pan that fits your air fryer, mix all the ingredients, toss, introduce the pan in your fryer and cook at 380°F for 15 minutes
2. Divide into bowls and serve for lunch.

**Nutrition: Calories: 183; Fat: 4g; Fiber: 2g; Carbs: 4g; Protein: 7g**

## 64. Eggplant Bake

Preparation Time: 25 minutes
Servings: 4

**Ingredients:**

- ½ lb. cherry tomatoes; cubed
- ½ cup cilantro; chopped.
- 4 garlic cloves; minced
- 2 eggplants; cubed
- 1 hot chili pepper; chopped.
- 4 spring onions; chopped.
- 2 tsp. olive oil
- Salt and black pepper to taste.

**Directions:**

1. Grease a baking pan that fits the air fryer with the oil and mix all the ingredients in the pan.

2. Put the pan in the preheated air fryer and cook at 380°F for 20 minutes, divide into bowls and serve

**Nutrition: Calories: 232; Fat: 12g; Fiber: 3g; Carbs: 5g; Protein: 10g**

## 65. Tomatoes and Cabbage Stew

Preparation Time: 25 minutes
Servings: 4

**Ingredients:**

- 14 oz. canned tomatoes; chopped.
- 1 green cabbage head; shredded
- 4 oz. chicken stock
- 2 tbsp. dill; chopped.
- 1 tbsp. sweet paprika
- Salt and black pepper to taste.

**Directions:**

1. In a pan that fits your air fryer, mix the cabbage with the tomatoes and all the other ingredients except the dill, toss, introduce the pan in the fryer and cook at 380°F for 20 minutes
2. Divide into bowls and serve with dill sprinkled on top.

**Nutrition: Calories: 200; Fat: 8g; Fiber: 3g; Carbs: 4g; Protein: 6g**

## 66. Bell Peppers Stew

Preparation Time: 20 minutes
Servings: 4

**Ingredients:**

- 2 yellow bell peppers; cut into wedges
- ½ cup tomato sauce
- 2 red bell peppers; cut into wedges
- 2 green bell peppers; cut into wedges
- 1 tbsp. chili powder

- ¼ tsp. sweet paprika
- 2 tsp. cumin, ground
- Salt and black pepper to taste.

**Directions:**

1. In a pan that fits your air fryer, mix all the ingredients, toss, introduce the pan in the machine and cook at 370°F for 15 minutes
2. Divide into bowls.

**Nutrition: Calories: 190; Fat: 4g; Fiber: 2g; Carbs: 4g; Protein: 7g**

## 67. Spinach and Shrimp

Preparation Time: 20 minutes
Servings: 4

**Ingredients:**

- 15 oz. shrimp; peeled and deveined
- ¼ cup veggie stock
- 2 tomatoes; cubed
- 4 spring onions; chopped.
- 2 cups baby spinach
- 1 tbsp. garlic; minced
- 2 tbsp. cilantro; chopped.
- 1 tbsp. lemon juice
- ½ tsp. cumin, ground
- Salt and black pepper to taste.

**Directions:**

1. In a pan that fits your air fryer, mix all the ingredients except the cilantro, toss, introduce in the air fryer and cook at 360°F for 15 minutes
2. Add the cilantro, stir, divide into bowls.

**Nutrition: Calories: 201; Fat: 8g; Fiber: 2g; Carbs: 4g; Protein: 8g**

## 68. Fennel and Tomato Stew

Preparation Time: 25 minutes
Servings: 4

**Ingredients:**

- 2 fennel bulbs; shredded
- ½ cup chicken stock
- 1 red bell pepper; chopped.
- 2 garlic cloves; minced
- 2 cups tomatoes; cubed
- 2 tbsp. tomato puree
- 1 tsp. rosemary; dried
- 1 tsp. sweet paprika
- Salt and black pepper to taste.

**Directions:**

1. In a pan that fits your air fryer, mix all the ingredients, toss, introduce in the fryer and cook at 380°F for 15 minutes
2. Divide the stew into bowls.

**Nutrition: Calories: 184; Fat: 7g; Fiber: 2g; Carbs: 3g; Protein: 8g**

## 69. Spinach and Olives

Preparation Time: 25 minutes
Servings: 4

**Ingredients:**

- ½ cup tomato puree
- 4 cups spinach; torn
- 2 cups black olives, pitted and halved
- 3 celery stalks; chopped.
- 1 red bell pepper; chopped.
- 2 tomatoes; chopped.
- Salt and black pepper to taste.

**Directions:**

1. In a pan that fits your air fryer, mix all the ingredients except the spinach, toss, introduce the pan in the air fryer and cook at 370°F for 15 minutes
2. Add the spinach, toss, cook for 5 - 6 minutes more, divide into bowls and serve.

**Nutrition: Calories: 193; Fat: 6g; Fiber: 2g; Carbs: 4g; Protein: 6g**

## 70. Courgettes Casserole

Preparation Time: 25 minutes

Servings: 4

**Ingredients:**

- 14 oz. cherry tomatoes; cubed
- 2 spring onions; chopped.
- 3 garlic cloves; minced
- 2 courgettes; sliced
- 2 celery sticks; sliced
- 1 yellow bell pepper; chopped.
- ½ cup mozzarella; shredded
- 1 tbsp. thyme; dried
- 1 tbsp. olive oil
- 1 tsp. smoked paprika

**Directions:**

1. In a baking dish that fits your air fryer, mix all the ingredients except the cheese and toss.
2. Sprinkle the cheese on top, introduce the dish in your air fryer and cook at 380°F for 20 minutes. Divide between plates and serve for lunch

**Nutrition: Calories: 254; Fat: 12g; Fiber: 2g; Carbs: 4g; Protein: 11g**

## 71. Chicken and Asparagus

Preparation Time: 25 minutes

Servings: 4

**Ingredients:**

- 4 chicken breasts, skinless; boneless and halved
- 1 bunch asparagus; trimmed and halved
- 1 tbsp. olive oil
- 1 tbsp. sweet paprika
- Salt and black pepper to taste.

**Directions:**

1. Take a bowl and mix all the ingredients, toss, put them in your Air Fryer's basket and cook at 390°F for 20 minutes
2. Divide between plates and serve.

**Nutrition: Calories: 230; Fat: 11g; Fiber: 3g; Carbs: 5g; Protein: 12g**

## 72. Basil Chicken Bites

Preparation Time: 30 minutes

Servings: 4

**Ingredients:**

- 1 ½ lb. chicken breasts, skinless; boneless and cubed
- ½ cup chicken stock
- ½ tsp. basil; dried
- 2 tsp. smoked paprika
- Salt and black pepper to taste.

**Directions:**

1. In a pan that fits the air fryer, combine all the ingredients, toss, introduce the pan in the fryer and cook at 390°F for 25 minutes
2. Divide between plates and serve for lunch with a side salad.

**Nutrition: Calories: 223; Fat: 12g; Fiber: 2g; Carbs: 5g; Protein: 13g**

## 73. Paprika Cod

Preparation Time: 17 minutes

Servings: 4

**Ingredients:**

- 1 lb. cod fillets, boneless, skinless and cubed
- 1 spring onion; chopped.
- 2 cups baby arugula
- 2 tbsp. fresh cilantro; minced
- ½ tsp. sweet paprika
- ½ tsp. oregano, ground
- A drizzle of olive oil
- Salt and black pepper to taste.

**Directions:**

1. Take a bowl and mix the cod with salt, pepper, paprika, oregano and the oil, toss, transfer the cubes to your air fryer's

basket and cook at 360°F for 12 minutes
2. In a salad bowl, mix the cod with the remaining ingredients, toss, divide between plates and serve.

**Nutrition: Calories: 240; Fat: 11g; Fiber: 3g; Carbs: 5g; Protein: 8g**

## 74. Turkey and Mushroom Stew

Preparation Time: 30 minutes
Servings: 4

**Ingredients:**

- ½ lb. brown mushrooms; sliced
- 1 turkey breast, skinless, boneless; cubed and browned
- ¼ cup tomato sauce
- 1 tbsp. parsley; chopped.
- Salt and black pepper to taste.

**Directions:**

1. In a pan that fits your air fryer, mix the turkey with the mushrooms, salt, pepper and tomato sauce, toss, introduce in the fryer and cook at 350°F for 25 minutes
2. Divide into bowls and serve for lunch with parsley sprinkled on top.

**Nutrition: Calories: 220; Fat: 12g; Fiber: 2g; Carbs: 5g; Protein: 12g**

## 75. Okra Casserole

Preparation Time: 25 minutes
Servings: 4

**Ingredients:**

- 2 red bell peppers; cubed
- 2 tomatoes; chopped.
- 3 garlic cloves; minced
- 3 cups okra
- ½ cup cheddar; shredded
- ¼ cup tomato puree
- 1 tbsp. cilantro; chopped.
- 1 tsp. olive oil

- 2 tsp. coriander, ground
- Salt and black pepper to taste.

**Directions:**

1. Grease a heat proof dish that fits your air fryer with the oil, add all the ingredients except the cilantro and the cheese and toss them really gently
2. Sprinkle the cheese and the cilantro on top, introduce the dish in the fryer and cook at 390°F for 20 minutes.
3. Divide between plates and serve for lunch.

**Nutrition: Calories: 221; Fat: 7g; Fiber: 2g; Carbs: 4g; Protein: 9g**

## 76. Tomato and Avocado

Preparation Time: 8 minutes
Servings: 4

**Ingredients:**

- ½ lb. cherry tomatoes; halved
- 2 avocados, pitted; peeled and cubed
- 1 ¼ cup lettuce; torn
- 1/3 cup coconut cream
- A pinch of salt and black pepper
- Cooking spray

**Directions:**

1. Grease the air fryer with cooking spray, combine the tomatoes with avocados, salt, pepper and the cream and cook at 350°F for 5 minutes shaking once
2. In a salad bowl, mix the lettuce with the tomatoes and avocado mix, toss and serve.

**Nutrition: Calories: 226; Fat: 12g; Fiber: 2g; Carbs: 4g; Protein: 8g**

## 77. Turkey and Broccoli Stew

Preparation Time: 30 minutes
Servings: 4

**Ingredients:**

- 1 broccoli head, florets separated
- 1 turkey breast, skinless; boneless and cubed
- 1 cup tomato sauce
- 1 tbsp. parsley; chopped.
- 1 tbsp. olive oil
- Salt and black pepper to taste.

**Directions:**

1. In a baking dish that fits your air fryer, mix the turkey with the rest of the ingredients except the parsley, toss, introduce the dish in the fryer, bake at 380°F for 25 minutes
2. Divide into bowls, sprinkle the parsley on top and serve.

**Nutrition: Calories: 250; Fat: 11g; Fiber: 2g; Carbs: 6g; Protein: 12g**

## 78. Zucchini Stew

Preparation Time: 17 minutes
Servings: 4

**Ingredients:**

- 8 zucchinis, roughly cubed
- ¼ cup tomato sauce
- 1 tbsp. olive oil
- ½ tsp. basil; chopped.
- ¼ tsp. rosemary; dried
- Salt and black pepper to taste.

**Directions:**

1. Grease a pan that fits your air fryer with the oil, add all the ingredients, toss, introduce the pan in the fryer and cook at 350°F for 12 minutes
2. Divide into bowls and serve.

**Nutrition: Calories: 200; Fat: 6g; Fiber: 2g; Carbs: 4g; Protein: 6g**

## 79. Pork Stew

Preparation Time: 35 minutes
Servings: 4

**Ingredients:**

- 2 lb. pork stew meat; cubed
- 1 eggplant; cubed
- ½ cup beef stock
- 2 zucchinis; cubed
- ½ tsp. smoked paprika
- Salt and black pepper to taste.
- A handful cilantro; chopped.

**Directions:**

1. In a pan that fits your air fryer, mix all the ingredients, toss, introduce in your air fryer and cook at 370°F for 30 minutes
2. Divide into bowls and serve right away.

**Nutrition: Calories: 245; Fat: 12g; Fiber: 2g; Carbs: 5g; Protein: 14g**

## 80. Chicken and Celery Stew

Preparation Time: 35 minutes
Servings: 6

**Ingredients:**

- 1 lb. chicken breasts, skinless; boneless and cubed
- 4 celery stalks; chopped.
- ½ cup coconut cream
- 2 red bell peppers; chopped.
- 2 tsp. garlic; minced
- 1 tbsp. butter, soft
- Salt and black pepper to taste.

**Directions:**

1. Grease a baking dish that fits your air fryer with the butter, add all the ingredients in the pan and toss them.
2. Introduce the dish in the fryer, cook at 360°F for 30 minutes, divide into bowls and serve

**Nutrition: Calories: 246; Fat: 12g; Fiber: 2g; Carbs: 6g; Protein: 12g**

## 81. Okra and Green Beans Stew

Preparation Time: 20 minutes
Servings: 4

**Ingredients:**

- 1 lb. green beans; halved
- 4 garlic cloves; minced
- 1 cup okra
- 3 tbsp. tomato sauce
- 1 tbsp. thyme; chopped.
- Salt and black pepper to taste.

**Directions:**

1. In a pan that fits your air fryer, mix all the ingredients, toss, introduce the pan in the air fryer and cook at 370°F for 15 minutes
2. Divide the stew into bowls and serve.

**Nutrition: Calories: 183; Fat: 5g; Fiber: 2g; Carbs: 4g; Protein: 8g**

## 82. Zucchini and Cauliflower Stew

Preparation Time: 25 minutes
Servings: 4

**Ingredients:**

- 1 cauliflower head, florets separated
- 1 ½ cups zucchinis; sliced
- 1 handful parsley leaves; chopped.
- ½ cup tomato puree
- 2 green onions; chopped.
- 1 tbsp. balsamic vinegar
- 1 tbsp. olive oil
- Salt and black pepper to taste.

**Directions:**

1. In a pan that fits your air fryer, mix the zucchinis with the rest of the ingredients except the parsley, toss, introduce the pan in the air fryer and cook at 380°F for 20 minutes
2. Divide into bowls and serve for lunch with parsley sprinkled on top.

**Nutrition: Calories: 193; Fat: 5g; Fiber: 2g; Carbs: 4g; Protein: 7g**

## 83. Eggplant and Leeks Stew

Preparation Time: 25 minutes
Servings: 4

**Ingredients:**

- 2 big eggplants, roughly cubed
- ½ bunch cilantro; chopped.
- 1 cup veggie stock
- 2 garlic cloves; minced
- 3 leeks; sliced
- 2 tbsp. olive oil
- 1 tbsp. hot sauce
- 1 tbsp. sweet paprika
- 1 tbsp. tomato puree
- Salt and black pepper to taste.

**Directions:**

1. In a pan that fits the air fryer, mix all the ingredients, toss, introduce in the fryer and cook at 380°F for 20 minutes
2. Divide the stew into bowls and serve for lunch.

**Nutrition: Calories: 183; Fat: 4g; Fiber: 2g; Carbs: 4g; Protein: 12g**

## 84. Fried Paprika Tofu

Preparation Time: 25 minutes
Servings:

**Ingredients:**

- 1 block extra firm tofu; pressed to remove excess water and cut into cubes
- 1/4 cup cornstarch
- 1 tablespoon smoked paprika
- salt and pepper to taste

**Directions:**

1. Line the Air Fryer basket with aluminum foil and brush with oil. Preheat the Air Fryer to 370 - degrees Fahrenheit.
2. Mix all ingredients in a bowl. Toss to combine. Place in the Air Fryer basket and cook for 12 minutes.

## 85. Amazing Mac and Cheese

Preparation Time: 15 minutes
Servings:

**Ingredients:**
- 1 cup cooked macaroni
- 1/2 cup warm milk
- 1 tablespoon parmesan cheese
- 1 cup grated cheddar cheese
- salt and pepper; to taste

**Directions:**
1. Preheat the Air Fryer to 350 - degrees Fahrenheit. Stir all of the ingredients; except Parmesan, in a baking dish.
2. Place the dish inside the Air Fryer and cook for 10 minutes. Top with the Parmesan cheese.

## 86. Delicious Pasta Salad

Preparation Time: 2 hours 25 minutes
Servings:

**Ingredients:**
- 4 tomatoes; medium and cut in eighths
- 3 eggplants; small
- 3 zucchinis; medium sized
- 2 bell peppers; any color
- 4 cups large pasta; uncooked in any shape
- 1 cup cherry tomatoes; sliced
- 1/2 cup Italian dressing; fat-free
- 8 tablespoon parmesan; grated
- 2 tablespoon extra virgin olive oil
- 2 teaspoon pink Himalayan salt
- 1 teaspoon basil; dried
- high quality cooking spray

**Directions:**
1. Wash eggplant; pat it dry and then slice off and discard the stem. Do not peel the eggplant. Slice it into 1/2-inch-thick rounds.
2. Toss the eggplant with 1 tablespoon of extra virgin olive oil, and put the rounds in the Air Fryer basket.
3. Cook eggplant for 40 minutes at 350 - degrees Fahrenheit. Once it is soft and has no raw taste remaining, set the eggplant aside.
4. Wash the zucchini; pat it dry and then slice off and discard the stem. Do not peel the zucchini. Slice the zucchini into 1/2 -inch rounds.
5. Toss together with extra virgin olive oil, and put it in the Air Fryer basket.
6. Cook zucchini for about 25 minutes at 350 - degrees Fahrenheit. Once it is soft with no raw taste remaining set the zucchini aside.
7. Wash the tomatoes and slice them into eighths. Arrange them in the Air Fryer basket and spray gently with high quality cooking spray. Roast the tomatoes for 30 minutes at 350 - degrees Fahrenheit. Once they have shrunk and are starting to brown, set them aside.
8. Cook the pasta according to the directions on the package, drain them through a colander, and run them under cold water. Set them aside so they will cool off.
9. Wash the bell peppers; cut them in half, take off the stem and remove the seeds. Rinse under water if you need to, and then pat them dry.
10. Wash the cherry tomatoes and cut them in half.
11. In a large bowl; combine bell peppers and cherry tomatoes. Then; add in the roasted vegetables, cooked pasta, pink Himalayan salt, dressing, chopped basil leaves, and grated parmesan. Mix thoroughly.
12. Set the salad in the fridge to chill and marinade. Serve the salad chilled or at room temperature.

## 87. Cheesy Prosciutto and Potato Salad

Preparation Time: 15 minutes
Servings:

**Ingredients:**

- 4 pounds potatoes; boiled and cubed
- 15 slices prosciutto; diced
- 15 ounces. sour cream
- 2 cups shredded cheddar cheese
- 2 tablespoon mayonnaise
- 1 teaspoon salt
- 1 teaspoon black pepper
- 1 teaspoon dried basil

**Directions:**

1. Preheat the Air Fryer to 350 - degrees Fahrenheit.
2. Combine potatoes, prosciutto, and cheddar in a baking dish. Place in the Air Fryer and cook for 7 minutes.
3. In another bowl; whisk together the sour cream, mayonnaise, salt, pepper, and basil.
4. Stir the dressing into the salad; making sure to coat the ingredients well.

## 88. Chicken Quesadillas

Preparation Time: 20 minutes
Servings:

**Ingredients:**

- 2 soft taco shells
- 1-pound chicken breasts; boneless
- 1 large green pepper; sliced
- 1 medium-sized onion; sliced
- 1/2 cup Cheddar cheese; shredded
- 1/2 cup salsa sauce
- 2 tablespoon olive oil
- Salt and pepper; to taste

**Directions:**

1. Preheat the Air Fryer to 370 - degrees Fahrenheit and sprinkle the basket with 1 tablespoon of olive oil.
2. Place 1 taco shell on the bottom of the fryer. Spread salsa sauce on the taco. Cut chicken breast into stripes and lay on taco shell.
3. Place onions and peppers on the top of the chicken.
4. Sprinkle with salt and pepper. Then; add shredded cheese and cover with second taco shell.
5. Sprinkle with 1 tablespoon of olive oil and put the rack over taco to hold it in place.
6. Cook for 4 – 6 minutes; until cooked and lightly brown. Cut and serve either hot or cold.

## 89. Mozzarella and Tomato Bruschetta

Preparation Time: 10 minutes
Servings:

**Ingredients:**

- 6 small french loaf slices
- 1/2 cup finely chopped tomatoes
- 3 ounces grated mozzarella cheese
- 1 tablespoon. fresh basil; chopped
- 1 tablespoon olive oil

**Directions:**

1. Preheat the Air Fryer to 350 - degrees Fahrenheit. Cook the bread for about 3 minutes.
2. Top with tomato, mozzarella, and prosciutto.
3. Drizzle the olive oil over this.
4. Place the bruschetta in the Air Fryer and cook for an additional minute. Serve and enjoy.

## 90. Cheesy Chicken Sausage Casserole

Preparation Time: 30 minutes
Servings:

**Ingredients:**

- 2 cloves minced garlic
- ten eggs
- 1 cup chopped broccoli
- 1/2 tablespoon salt
- 1 cup divided shredded cheddar
- 1/4 tablespoon pepper

- 3/4 cup whipping cream
- 1 [12-oz ] package of cooked chicken sausage

**Directions:**
1. Preheat the Air Fryer to 400 - degrees Fahrenheit. Whisk the eggs in a large bowl. Add the whipping cream, and cheese and mix well.
2. In another bowl add in the garlic, broccoli, salt, pepper and cooked sausage.
3. Arrange the chicken sausage mix onto a casserole dish. Add the cheese mixture on top. Add to the Air Fryer and bake for nearly 20 minutes.

## 91. Cashew and Chicken Manchurian

Preparation Time: 30 minutes
Servings:

**Ingredients:**
- 1 cup chicken boneless
- 1 spring onions [chopped]
- 1 onion [chopped]
- 3 green chili
- 6 cashew nuts
- 1 teaspoon ginger [chopped]
- 1/2 teaspoon garlic [chopped]
- One Egg
- 2 tablespoon flour
- 1 tablespoon cornstarch
- 1 teaspoon soy sauce
- 2 teaspoon chili paste
- 1 teaspoon pepper
- 1 pinch msg & sugar
- water as needed
- 1 tablespoon oil

**Directions:**
1. Coat chicken with egg, salt and pepper. Mix cornstarch and flour, coat chicken and cook at preheated to 360 - degrees Fahrenheit Air Fryer for 10 minutes.
2. Cook nuts with oil in a pan.

3. Add onions and cook until translucent. Add the remaining ingredients and cook sauce.
4. Add chicken and garnish with spring onions.

## 92. Cheese and Bacon Rolls

Preparation Time: 25 minutes
Servings:

**Ingredients:**
- 8 ounces. refrigerated crescent roll dough [usually 1 can]
- 6 ounces. very sharp cheddar cheese; grated
- 1-pound bacon; cooked and chopped

**Directions:**
1. Unroll the crescent dough and, using a sharp knife, cut it into 1-inch by 1 1/2 - inch pieces.
2. In a medium bowl; combine the cheese and bacon. Spread about 1/4 cup of this mixture on each piece of dough.
3. Briefly preheat your Air Fryer to 330 – degrees Fahrenheit.
4. Place the rolls in the Fryer; either on the Air Fry tray or in the food basket.
5. Bake until golden brown; 6 – 8 minutes, and enjoy!
6. Note: The timing of this recipe can vary from one Fryer to the next; so watch carefully for the browning of the rolls.

## 93. Healthy Kidney Beans Oatmeal

Preparation Time: 25 minutes
Servings: 2 – 4

**Ingredients:**
- 2 large bell peppers; halved lengthwise, deseeded
- 2 tablespoon cooked kidney beans
- 2 tablespoon cooked chick peas
- 2 cups oatmeal; cooked
- 1 teaspoon ground cumin

- 1/2 teaspoon paprika
- 1/2 teaspoon salt or to taste
- 1/4 teaspoon black pepper powder
- 1/4 cup yogurt

**Directions:**

1. Place the bell peppers with its cut side down in the Air Fryer. Air fry in a preheated Air Fryer at 355 - degrees Fahrenheit for 2 – 3 minutes.
2. Remove from the Air Fryer and keep it aside.
3. Mix together rest of the ingredients in a bowl.
4. When the bell peppers are cool enough to handle, divide and stuff this mixture into the bell peppers.
5. Place it back in the Air Fryer and air fry at 355 – degrees Fahrenheit for 4 minutes. Serve hot and enjoy!.

## 94. Chicken Fillet with Brie and Turkey

Preparation Time: 40 minutes
Servings:

**Ingredients:**

- 4 slices turkey [cured]
- 2 chicken fillets [large]
- 4 slices brie cheese
- 1 tablespoon chives [chopped]
- pepper and salt to taste

**Directions:**

1. Preheat Air Fryer to 360 - degrees Fahrenheit. Cut chicken fillets into 4 pieces and season with salt and pepper.
2. Add chives and brie to it.
3. Add the ingredients onto the plain piece of turkey.
4. Close and wrap Turkey. Hold closed with toothpick. Air fry for 15 minutes, then roast until brown.

## 95. Cheese and Macaroni Balls

Preparation Time: 25 minutes

Servings:

**Ingredients:**

- 2 cups leftover macaroni
- 1 cup cheddar cheese; shredded
- 3 large eggs
- 1 cup milk
- 1/2 cup flour
- 1 cup breadcrumbs
- 1/2 teaspoon salt
- 1/4 teaspoon black pepper

**Directions:**

1. In a large bowl combine leftover macaroni and shredded cheese. Set aside.
2. In another bowl place flour; and in other - breadcrumbs. In medium bowl whisk eggs and milk.
3. Using ice-cream scoop, make balls from mac'n cheese mixture and roll them first in a flour, then in eggs mixture and then in breadcrumbs.
4. Preheat the Air Fryer to 365 - degrees Fahrenheit and cook mac'n cheese balls for about 10 minutes, stirring occasionally until cook and crispy. Serve with ketchup or another sauce.

## 96. Pita Bread Cheese Pizza

Preparation Time: 15 minutes
Servings:

**Ingredients:**

- 1-piece Pita bread
- 1/2-pound Mozzarella cheese
- 1 tablespoon olive oil
- 2 tablespoon ketchup
- 1/3 cup sausage
- 1 teaspoon garlic powder

**Directions:**

1. Using a tablespoon spread ketchup over Pita bread.
2. Then; add sausage and cheese. Sprinkle with garlic powder and with 1 tablespoon

olive oil.

3. Preheat the Air Fryer to 340 - degrees Fahrenheit and carefully transfer your pizza to a fryer basket. Cook for 6 minutes and enjoy your quick & easy pizza.

## 97. Tasty Portabella Pizza

Preparation Time: 15 minutes
Servings:

**Ingredients:**

- 3 tablespoon olive oil
- 3 portabella mushroom caps; cleaned and scooped
- 3 tablespoon mozzarella; shredded
- 3 tablespoon tomato sauce
- 1 pinch salt
- 12 slices pepperoni
- 1 pinch dried Italian seasonings

**Directions:**

1. Preheat the Air Fryer to 330 - degrees Fahrenheit.
2. On both sides of the portabella; drizzle oil and then season the inside with Italian seasonings and salt. Spread tomato sauce evenly over the mushroom and top with cheese.
3. Place the portabella into the cooking basket of the Air Fryer. Place pepperoni slices on top of the portabella pizza after 1 minute of cooking. Cook for 3 to 5 minutes.

## 98. Amazing Hot Dogs

Preparation Time: 20 minutes
Servings: 4

**Ingredients:**

- 3 brazilian sausages; cut into 3 equal pieces
- 9 bacon fillets; raw
- black pepper to taste

- salt to taste

**Directions:**

1. Preheat the Air Fryer for 5 min on 355 - degrees Fahrenheit.
2. Wrap the bacon fillets around each piece of sausages then season them with some salt and pepper. Fry the wrapped sausages for 15 min then serve them and enjoy.
3. Tip: To make it tastier, sprinkle 1/2 teaspoon of Italian seasoning on the sausages pieces.

## 99. Roasted Potatoes with Garlic and Bacon

Preparation Time: 40 minutes
Servings:

**Ingredients:**

- 4 potatoes; peeled and cut into bite-size chunks
- 6 cloves garlic; unpeeled
- 4 strips bacon; chopped
- 1 tablespoon fresh rosemary; finely chopped

**Directions:**

1. In a large bowl; combine the potatoes, garlic, bacon, and rosemary and mix thoroughly. Transfer to a baking dish.
2. Briefly preheat your Air Fryer to 350 - degrees Fahrenheit. Cook the potatoes in the Fryer until golden brown; 25 – 30 minutes.

## 100. Homemade Mexican Pizza

Preparation Time: 15 minutes
Servings:

**Ingredients:**

- 3/4 cup of refried beans
- 1 cup salsa
- 12 frozen beef meatballs; pre-cooked
- 2 jalapeno peppers; sliced
- 6 whole-wheat pita bread

- 1 cup pepper Jack cheese; shredded
- 1 cup Colby cheese; shredded

## Directions:

1. Take a bowl and combine salsa, meatball, jalapeno pepper and beans. Preheat the Air Fryer for 4 minutes at 370 - degrees Fahrenheit.
2. Top the pita with the mixture and sprinkle pepper jack and Colby cheese on top. Bake in Air Fryer for 10 minutes. Serve and enjoy.

## 101. Mozzarella Patties

Preparation Time: 25 minutes
Servings:

## Ingredients:

- 1-pound Mozzarella cheese
- 20 slices pepperoni
- 4 large eggs
- 1 tablespoon Italian seasoning
- 1 cup all-purpose flour
- 2 cups breadcrumbs
- Salt and black pepper; to taste

## Directions:

1. Slice Mozzarella cheese into 1/4-inch slices and cut each slice in half.
2. Create cheese sandwiches with Mozzarella halves and pepperoni inside. Press to seal.
3. In three different bowls place beaten eggs, breadcrumbs with Italian seasoning, and flour. Dip each cheese sandwich into flour; then into eggs and then into breadcrumb mixture.
4. Preheat the Air Fryer to 390 - degrees Fahrenheit and cook cheese patties for about 6 – 8 minutes, turning once while cooking. Serve with dipping sauce and enjoy.

## 102. Roasted Heirloom Tomato with Feta

Preparation Time: 55 minutes
Servings:

## Ingredients:

*For the Tomato:*

- 2 heirloom tomatoes
- 1 8-oz block of feta cheese
- 1/2 cup red onions; sliced paper thin
- 1 tablespoon olive oil
- 1 pinch salt

*For the Basil Pesto:*

- 1/2 cup parsley; roughly chopped
- 1/2 cup basil; rough chopped
- 1/2 cup parmesan cheese; grated
- 3 tablespoon pine nuts; toasted
- 1 garlic clove
- 1/2 cup olive oil
- 1 pinch salt

## Directions:

1. Make the pesto. In a food processor; add parsley, basil, parmesan, garlic, toasted pine nuts and salt.
2. Turn on the food processor and slowly add the olive oil.
3. Once all of the olive oil is incorporated into the pesto, store and refrigerate until ready to use.
4. Preheat the Air Fryer to 390 - degrees Fahrenheit.
5. Slice the tomato and the feta into 1/2 - inch thick circular slices. Pat tomato dry with a paper towel.
6. Spread 1 tablespoon of the pesto on top of each tomato slice and top with the feta.
7. Toss the red onions with 1 tablespoon of olive oil and place on top of the feta.
8. Place the tomatoes/feta into the cooking basket and cook for 12 – 14 minutes or until the feta starts to soften and brown.
9. Finish with a pinch of salt and an additional spoonful of basil pesto.

## 103. Easy Pesto Gnocchi

Preparation Time: 30 minutes
Servings:

**Ingredients:**

- 1 package [16-ounce] shelf-stable gnocchi
- 1 medium-sized onion; chopped
- 3 garlic cloves; minced
- 1 jar [8 ounce] pesto
- 1/3 cup Parmesan cheese; grated
- 1 tablespoon extra-virgin olive oil
- salt and black pepper; to taste

**Directions:**

1. In the large mixing bowl combine onion, garlic, and gnocchi and sprinkle with the olive oil. Stir to combine.
2. Preheat the Air Fryer to 340 - degrees Fahrenheit. Cook for 15 – 20 minutes; stirring couple time while cooking, until gnocchi are lightly browned and crisp.
3. Stir in the pesto and Parmesan cheese.
4. Serve immediately.

## 104. Cheeseburger Sliders

Preparation Time: 20 minutes
Servings:

**Ingredients:**

- 1-pound ground beef
- 6 slices cheddar cheese
- 6 dinner rolls
- salt to taste
- black pepper

**Directions:**

1. Preheat the Air Fryer to 390 – degrees Fahrenheit. Form the ground beef into 6 2.5-ounce patties and season with salt and pepper.
2. Add the burgers to the cooking basket and cook for 10 minutes. Remove from the Air Fryer and place the cheese on top of the burgers and return to the Air Fryer to cook for one more minute.

## 105. Delicious Meatloaf with Black Peppercorns

Preparation Time: 55 minutes
Servings:

**Ingredients:**

- 4 Pounds beef [minced]
- 1 onion [large; diced]
- 3 tablespoon tomato ketchup
- 1 teaspoon Worcester sauce
- 1 tablespoon oregano
- 1 tablespoon basil
- 1 tablespoon parsley
- 1 tablespoon mixed herbs
- salt according to taste
- pepper to taste
- 3 tablespoon breadcrumbs

**Directions:**

1. Put beef mince in a bowl and mix it with onion, herbs, ketchup and Worcester sauce. Stir well.
2. Add breadcrumbs to the mixture.
3. Put the seasoned beef in a dish and put in Air Fryer. Cook for 25 minutes at 390 - degrees Fahrenheit.
4. Serve with rice or mashed potatoes.

## 106. Homemade Falafel Burger

Preparation Time: 35 minutes
Servings:

**Ingredients:**

- 14 ounces. can chickpeas
- 1 small red onion
- 1 small lemon
- 5 ounces. gluten free oats
- 2 tablespoon cheese
- 2 tablespoon feta cheese
- 3 tablespoon greek yoghurt
- 4 tablespoon soft cheese
- 1 tablespoon garlic puree
- 1 tablespoon coriander
- 1 tablespoon oregano

- 1 tablespoon parsley
- salt & pepper to taste

**Directions:**
1. Place in a food processor or blender all the seasonings, the garlic, the lemon rind, red onion and the drained chickpeas. Whiz until they are coarse but not smooth.
2. Mix them in bowl with 1/2 the soft cheese, the hard cheese and the feta.
3. Combine them into burger shapes.
4. Roll them in gluten free oats until you cannot see any of the chickpea mixture. Place them in the Air Fryer inside the Air Fryer baking pan and cook for 8 minutes at 360 - degrees Fahrenheit.
5. Make the burger sauce. In a mixing bowl add the rest of the soft cheese, the Greek Yoghurt and some extra salt and pepper.
6. Mix well until it is nice and fluffy. Add the juice of the lemon and mix one last time.
7. Place the falafel burger inside your homemade buns with garnish.
8. Load up with your burger sauce.

## 107. Simple Cheese Wraps

Preparation Time: 35 minutes
Servings:

**Ingredients:**
- 1/2-pound cheese [provolone; diced]
- 1 steak [frozen; sliced]
- 1 pack egg roll wrapper
- 1 onion; chopped
- 1 bell pepper [green; chopped]
- salt and pepper to taste

**Directions:**
1. Sauté onion and bell pepper for 5 minutes. Cook steak; then shred it.
2. Mix these with cheese. Fill the wrappers and roll them.
3. Air fry for 5 min at 350 - degrees Fahrenheit; then raise temp to 392 - degrees Fahrenheit and fry for 5 minutes.

## 108. The meal is ready to be served. Enjoy the taste.

Special Mac and Cheese
Preparation Time: 25 minutes
Servings:

**Ingredients:**
- 1 cup elbow macaroni
- 1/2 cup broccoli or cauliflower; chopped
- 1/2 cup milk; warmed
- 1 ½ cups cheddar cheese; grated
- salt and pepper to taste
- 1 tablespoon parmesan; grated

**Directions:**
1. Bring a medium pot of water to a boil and add the macaroni and vegetables.
2. Cook until just tender; 7 – 10 minutes, and drain.
3. Toss the still-hot macaroni and vegetables with the milk and cheddar and transfer to a baking dish. Season with salt and pepper.
4. Briefly preheat your Air Fryer to 350 - degrees Fahrenheit.
5. Sprinkle the macaroni with the parmesan and bake until bubbling; about 15 minutes.
6. Let cool slightly before serving.

## 109. Fried Veggies with Golden Polenta Bites

Preparation Time: 50 minutes
Servings: 6

**Ingredients:**
- 1 cup onions; chopped
- 2 cloves garlic; finely minced
- 1/2-pound zucchini; cut into bite-sized chunks
- 1/2-pound potatoes; peeled and cut into bite-sized chunks
- 1 tablespoon olive oil

- 1 teaspoon paprika
- 1/2 teaspoon salt
- 1/2 teaspoon freshly ground black pepper; or more to taste
- 1/2 teaspoon dried dill weed; or more to taste
- 14 ounces pre-cooked polenta tube; cut into slices
- 1/4 cup Cheddar cheese; shaved

**Directions:**

1. Add the vegetables to an Air Fryer cooking basket.
2. Sprinkle them with olive oil, paprika, salt, pepper, and dill.
3. Now; set the machine to cook at 400 - degrees Fahrenheit. Cook for 6 minutes.
4. After that; pause the machine, shake the basket and set the timer for 6 minutes more. Set aside.
5. Next; spritz the polenta slices with non-stick cooking oil. Spritz the cooking basket too.
6. Set your Air Fryer to cook at 400 - degrees Fahrenheit Air-fry for 20 to 25 minutes.
7. Turn the polenta slices over and cook for another 10 minutes.
8. Top each polenta slice with air-fried vegetables and shaved cheese.

## 110. Hot Buttery Dinner Rolls

Preparation Time: 3 hours 15 minutes
Servings: 6

**Ingredients:**
*For the Rolls:*

- 1 1/3 cups plain flour
- 1 ½ tablespoons white sugar
- 1 teaspoon of instant yeast
- A pinch of kosher salt
- 2 tablespoons melted butter
- One Egg yolk
- 1/3 cup milk
- A pinch of nutmeg

*For the Topping:*

- 2 tablespoons softened butter
- 2 tablespoons honey

**Directions:**

1. Mix the flour, sugar, instant yeast, and salt using a stand mixer. Whisk on low speed for 1 minute or until smooth.
2. Now; stir in the butter. Continue to mix for 1 more minute as it all combines.
3. Lay the dough onto a lightly floured surface and knead several times.
4. Transfer the dough to a large bowl, cover and place it in a warm room to rise until doubled in size.
5. Now; whisk the egg yolk with milk and nutmeg. Coat the balls with the egg mixture.
6. Shape into balls; loosely cover and allow the balls to rise until doubled, it takes about 1 hour.
7. Then; bake them in the preheated Air Fryer at 320 - degrees Fahrenheit for 14 to 15 minutes.
8. In the meantime; make the topping by simply mixing the very soft butter with honey. Afterward, spread the topping onto each warm roll.
9. Cover the leftovers and keep in your fridge.

# Sides

## 111. Parmesan Zucchini Rounds

Preparation Time: 25 minutes
Servings: 4

**Ingredients:**

- 4 zucchinis; sliced
- 1 ½ cups parmesan; grated
- ¼ cup parsley; chopped.
- 1 egg; whisked
- 1 egg white; whisked
- ½ tsp. garlic powder
- Cooking spray

**Directions:**

1. Take a bowl and mix the egg with egg whites, parmesan, parsley and garlic powder and whisk.
2. Dredge each zucchini slice in this mix, place them all in your air fryer's basket, grease them with cooking spray and cook at 370°F for 20 minutes
3. Divide between plates and serve as a side dish.

**Nutrition: Calories: 183; Fat: 6g; Fiber: 2g; Carbs: 3g; Protein: 8g**

## 112. Green Bean Casserole

Preparation Time: 25 minutes
Servings: 4

**Ingredients:**

- 1 lb. fresh green beans, edges trimmed
- ½ oz. pork rinds, finely ground
- 1 oz. full-fat cream cheese
- ½ cup heavy whipping cream.
- ¼ cup diced yellow onion
- ½ cup chopped white mushrooms
- ½ cup chicken broth
- 4 tbsp. unsalted butter.
- ¼ tsp. xanthan gum

**Directions:**

1. In a medium skillet over medium heat, melt the butter. Sauté the onion and mushrooms until they become soft and fragrant, about 3–5 minutes.
2. Add the heavy whipping cream, cream cheese and broth to the pan. Whisk until smooth. Bring to a boil and then reduce to a simmer. Sprinkle the xanthan gum into the pan and remove from heat
3. Chop the green beans into 2-inch pieces and place into a 4-cup round baking dish. Pour the sauce mixture over them and stir until coated. Top the dish with ground pork rinds. Place into the air fryer basket
4. Adjust the temperature to 320 Degrees F and set the timer for 15 minutes. Top will be golden and green beans fork tender when fully cooked. Serve warm.

**Nutrition: Calories: 267; Protein: 3.6g; Fiber: 3.2g; Fat: 23.4g; Carbs: 9.7g**

## 113. Zucchini Spaghetti

Preparation Time: 20 minutes
Servings: 4

**Ingredients:**

- 1 lb. zucchinis, cut with a spiralizer
- 1 cup parmesan; grated
- ¼ cup parsley; chopped.
- ¼ cup olive oil
- 6 garlic cloves; minced
- ½ tsp. red pepper flakes
- Salt and black pepper to taste.

**Directions:**

1. In a pan that fits your air fryer, mix all

the ingredients, toss, introduce in the fryer and cook at 370°F for 15 minutes

2. Divide between plates and serve as a side dish.

**Nutrition: Calories: 200; Fat: 6g; Fiber: 3g; Carbs: 4g; Protein: 5g**

## 114. Cabbage and Radishes Mix

Preparation Time: 20 minutes
Servings: 4

**Ingredients:**

- 6 cups green cabbage; shredded
- ½ cup celery leaves; chopped.
- ¼ cup green onions; chopped.
- 6 radishes; sliced
- 3 tbsp. olive oil
- 2 tbsp. balsamic vinegar
- ½ tsp. hot paprika
- 1 tsp. lemon juice

**Directions:**

1. In your air fryer's pan, combine all the ingredients and toss well.
2. Introduce the pan in the fryer and cook at 380°F for 15 minutes. Divide between plates and serve as a side dish

**Nutrition: Calories: 130; Fat: 4g; Fiber: 3g; Carbs: 4g; Protein: 7g**

## 115. Jicama Fries

Preparation Time: 30 minutes
Servings: 4

**Ingredients:**

- 1 small jicama; peeled.
- ¼ tsp. onion powder.
- ¾tsp. chili powder
- ¼ tsp. ground black pepper
- ¼ tsp. garlic powder.

**Directions:**

1. Cut jicama into matchstick-sized pieces.

2. Place pieces into a small bowl and sprinkle with remaining ingredients. Place the fries into the air fryer basket

3. Adjust the temperature to 350 Degrees F and set the timer for 20 minutes. Toss the basket two or three times during cooking. Serve warm.

**Nutrition: Calories: 37; Protein: 0.8g; Fiber: 4.7g; Fat: 0.1g; Carbs: 8.7g**

## 116. Kale Chips

Preparation Time: 10 minutes
Servings: 4

**Ingredients:**

- 4 cups stemmed kale
- ½ tsp. salt
- 2 tsp. avocado oil

**Directions:**

1. Take a large bowl, toss kale in avocado oil and sprinkle with salt. Place into the air fryer basket.
2. Adjust the temperature to 400 Degrees F and set the timer for 5 minutes. Kale will be crispy when done. Serve immediately.

**Nutrition: Calories: 25; Protein: 0.5g; Fiber: 0.4g; Fat: 2.2g; Carbs: 1.1g**

## 117. Coriander Artichokes

Preparation Time: 20 minutes
Servings: 4

**Ingredients:**

- 12 oz. artichoke hearts
- 1 tbsp. lemon juice
- 1 tsp. coriander, ground
- ½ tsp. cumin seeds
- ½ tsp. olive oil
- Salt and black pepper to taste.

**Directions:**

1. In a pan that fits your air fryer, mix all the ingredients, toss, introduce the pan in

the fryer and cook at 370°F for 15 minutes

2. Divide the mix between plates and serve as a side dish.

**Nutrition: Calories: 200; Fat: 7g; Fiber: 2g; Carbs: 5g; Protein: 8g**

## 118. Spinach and Artichokes Sauté

Preparation Time: 20 minutes
Servings: 4

**Ingredients:**

- 10 oz. artichoke hearts; halved
- 2 cups baby spinach
- 3 garlic cloves
- ¼ cup veggie stock
- 2 tsp. lime juice
- Salt and black pepper to taste.

**Directions:**

1. In a pan that fits your air fryer, mix all the ingredients, toss, introduce in the fryer and cook at 370°F for 15 minutes
2. Divide between plates and serve as a side dish.

**Nutrition: Calories: 209; Fat: 6g; Fiber: 2g; Carbs: 4g; Protein: 8g**

## 119. Green Beans

Preparation Time: 25 minutes
Servings: 4

**Ingredients:**

- 6 cups green beans; trimmed
- 1 tbsp. hot paprika
- 2 tbsp. olive oil
- A pinch of salt and black pepper

**Directions:**

1. Take a bowl and mix the green beans with the other ingredients, toss, put them in the air fryer's basket and cook at 370°F for 20 minutes

2. Divide between plates and serve as a side dish.

**Nutrition: Calories: 120; Fat: 5g; Fiber: 1g; Carbs: 4g; Protein: 2g**

## 120. Balsamic Cabbage

Preparation Time: 25 minutes
Servings: 4

**Ingredients:**

- 6 cups red cabbage; shredded
- 4 garlic cloves; minced
- 1 tbsp. olive oil
- 1 tbsp. balsamic vinegar
- Salt and black pepper to taste.

**Directions:**

1. In a pan that fits the air fryer, combine all the ingredients, toss, introduce the pan in the air fryer and cook at 380°F for 15 minutes
2. Divide between plates and serve as a side dish.

**Nutrition: Calories: 151; Fat: 2g; Fiber: 3g; Carbs: 5g; Protein: 5g**

## 121. Herbed Radish Sauté

Preparation Time: 20 minutes
Servings: 4

**Ingredients:**

- 2 bunches red radishes; halved
- 2 tbsp. parsley; chopped.
- 2 tbsp. balsamic vinegar
- 1 tbsp. olive oil
- Salt and black pepper to taste.

**Directions:**

1. Take a bowl and mix the radishes with the remaining ingredients except the parsley, toss and put them in your air fryer's basket.
2. Cook at 400°F for 15 minutes, divide between plates, sprinkle the parsley on

top and serve as a side dish

**Nutrition: Calories: 180; Fat: 4g; Fiber: 2g; Carbs: 3g; Protein: 5g**

## 122. Roasted Tomatoes

Preparation Time: 20 minutes
Servings: 4

**Ingredients:**

- 4 tomatoes; halved
- ½ cup parmesan; grated
- 1 tbsp. basil; chopped.
- ½ tsp. onion powder
- ½ tsp. oregano; dried
- ½ tsp. smoked paprika
- ½ tsp. garlic powder
- Cooking spray

**Directions:**

1. Take a bowl and mix all the ingredients except the cooking spray and the parmesan.
2. Arrange the tomatoes in your air fryer's pan, sprinkle the parmesan on top and grease with cooking spray
3. Cook at 370°F for 15 minutes, divide between plates and serve.

**Nutrition: Calories: 200; Fat: 7g; Fiber: 2g; Carbs: 4g; Protein: 6g**

## 123. Kale and Walnuts

Preparation Time: 20 minutes
Servings: 4

**Ingredients:**

- 3 garlic cloves
- 10 cups kale; roughly chopped.
- 1/3 cup parmesan; grated
- ½ cup almond milk
- ¼ cup walnuts; chopped.
- 1 tbsp. butter; melted
- ¼ tsp. nutmeg, ground

- Salt and black pepper to taste.

**Directions:**

1. In a pan that fits the air fryer, combine all the ingredients, toss, introduce the pan in the machine and cook at 360°F for 15 minutes
2. Divide between plates and serve.

**Nutrition: Calories: 160; Fat: 7g; Fiber: 2g; Carbs: 4g; Protein: 5g**

## 124. Bok Choy and Butter Sauce

Preparation Time: 20 minutes
Servings: 4

**Ingredients:**

- 2 bok choy heads; trimmed and cut into strips
- 1 tbsp. butter; melted
- 2 tbsp. chicken stock
- 1 tsp. lemon juice
- 1 tbsp. olive oil
- A pinch of salt and black pepper

**Directions:**

1. In a pan that fits your air fryer, mix all the ingredients, toss, introduce the pan in the air fryer and cook at 380°F for 15 minutes.
2. Divide between plates and serve as a side dish

**Nutrition: Calories: 141; Fat: 3g; Fiber: 2g; Carbs: 4g; Protein: 3g**

## 125. Turmeric Mushroom

Preparation Time: 20 minutes
Servings: 4

**Ingredients:**

- 1 lb. brown mushrooms
- 4 garlic cloves; minced
- ¼ tsp. cinnamon powder
- 1 tsp. olive oil

- ½ tsp. turmeric powder
- Salt and black pepper to taste.

**Directions:**

1. In a bowl, combine all the ingredients and toss.
2. Put the mushrooms in your air fryer's basket and cook at 370°F for 15 minutes
3. Divide the mix between plates and serve as a side dish.

**Nutrition: Calories: 208; Fat: 7g; Fiber: 3g; Carbs: 5g; Protein: 7g**

## 126. Creamy Fennel

Preparation Time: 17 minutes
Servings: 4

**Ingredients:**

- 2 big fennel bulbs; sliced
- ½ cup coconut cream
- 2 tbsp. butter; melted
- Salt and black pepper to taste.

**Directions:**

1. In a pan that fits the air fryer, combine all the ingredients, toss, introduce in the machine and cook at 370°F for 12 minutes
2. Divide between plates and serve as a side dish.

**Nutrition: Calories: 151; Fat: 3g; Fiber: 2g; Carbs: 4g; Protein: 6g**

## 127. Air Fried Green Tomatoes

Preparation Time: 17 minutes
Servings: 4

**Ingredients:**

- 2 medium green tomatoes
- ⅓ cup grated Parmesan cheese.
- ¼ cup blanched finely ground almond flour.
- 1 large egg.

**Directions:**

1. Slice tomatoes into ½-inch-thick slices. Take a medium bowl, whisk the egg. Take a large bowl, mix the almond flour and Parmesan.
2. Dip each tomato slice into the egg, then dredge in the almond flour mixture. Place the slices into the air fryer basket
3. Adjust the temperature to 400 Degrees F and set the timer for 7 minutes. Flip the slices halfway through the cooking time. Serve immediately

**Nutrition: Calories: 106; Protein: 6.2g; Fiber: 1.4g; Fat: 6.7g; Carbs: 5.9g**

## 128. Sausage Mushroom Caps

Preparation Time: 18 minutes
Servings: 2

**Ingredients:**

- ½ lb. Italian sausage
- 6 large Portobello mushroom caps
- ¼ cup grated Parmesan cheese.
- ¼ cup chopped onion
- 2 tbsp. blanched finely ground almond flour
- 1 tsp. minced fresh garlic

**Directions:**

1. Use a spoon to hollow out each mushroom cap, reserving scrapings.
2. In a medium skillet over medium heat, brown the sausage about 10 minutes or until fully cooked and no pink remains. Drain and then add reserved mushroom scrapings, onion, almond flour, Parmesan and garlic.
3. Gently fold ingredients together and continue cooking an additional minute, then remove from heat
4. Evenly spoon the mixture into mushroom caps and place the caps into a 6-inch round pan. Place pan into the air fryer basket
5. Adjust the temperature to 375 Degrees F and set the timer for 8 minutes. When

finished cooking, the tops will be browned and bubbling. Serve warm.

**Nutrition: Calories: 404; Protein: 24.3g; Fiber: 4.5g; Fat: 25.8g; Carbs: 18.2g**

## 129. Cheesy Garlic Biscuits

Preparation Time: 17 minutes
Servings: 4

**Ingredients:**

- 1 large egg.
- 1 scallion, sliced
- ¼ cup unsalted butter; melted and divided
- ½ cup shredded sharp Cheddar cheese.
- ⅓ cup coconut flour
- ½ tsp. baking powder.
- ½ tsp. garlic powder.

**Directions:**

1. Take a large bowl, mix coconut flour, baking powder and garlic powder.
2. Stir in egg, half of the melted butter, Cheddar cheese and scallions. Pour the mixture into a 6-inch round baking pan. Place into the air fryer basket
3. Adjust the temperature to 320 Degrees F and set the timer for 12 minutes
4. To serve, remove from pan and allow to fully cool. Slice into four pieces and pour remaining melted butter over each.

**Nutrition: Calories: 218; Protein: 7.2g; Fiber: 3.4g; Fat: 16.9g; Carbs: 6.8g**

## 130. Roasted Garlic

Preparation Time: 25 minutes
Servings: 12 cloves

**Ingredients:**

- 1 medium head garlic
- 2 tsp. avocado oil

**Directions:**

1. Remove any hanging excess peel from the garlic but leave the cloves covered. Cut off ¼ of the head of garlic, exposing the tips of the cloves
2. Drizzle with avocado oil. Place the garlic head into a small sheet of aluminum foil, completely enclosing it. Place it into the air fryer basket. Adjust the temperature to 400 Degrees F and set the timer for 20 minutes. If your garlic head is a bit smaller, check it after 15 minutes
3. When done, garlic should be golden brown and very soft
4. To serve, cloves should pop out and easily be spread or sliced. Store in an airtight container in the refrigerator up to 5 days.
5. You may also freeze individual cloves on a baking sheet, then store together in a freezer-safe storage bag once frozen.

**Nutrition: Calories: 11; Protein: 0.2g; Fiber: 0.1g; Fat: 0.7g; Carbs: 1.0g**

## 131. Cilantro Roasted Cauliflower

Preparation Time: 17 minutes
Servings: 4

**Ingredients:**

- 2 cups chopped cauliflower florets
- 1 medium lime
- 2 tbsp. chopped cilantro
- 2 tbsp. coconut oil; melted
- ½ tsp. garlic powder.
- 2 tsp. chili powder

**Directions:**

1. Take a large bowl, toss cauliflower with coconut oil. Sprinkle with chili powder and garlic powder. Place seasoned cauliflower into the air fryer basket
2. Adjust the temperature to 350 Degrees F and set the timer for 7 minutes
3. Cauliflower will be tender and begin to turn golden at the edges. Place into serving bowl. Cut the lime into quarters and squeeze juice over cauliflower. Garnish with cilantro.

**Nutrition: Calories: 73; Protein: 1.1g; Fiber: 1.1g; Fat: 6.5g; Carbs: 3.3g**

## 132. Parmesan Zucchini Chips

Preparation Time: 20 minutes
Servings: 4

**Ingredients:**

- 1 oz. pork rinds.
- ½ cup grated Parmesan cheese.
- 2 medium zucchini
- 1 large egg.

**Directions:**

1. Slice zucchini in ¼-inch-thick slices. Place between two layers of paper towels or a clean kitchen towel for 30 minutes to remove excess moisture
2. Place pork rinds into food processor and pulse until finely ground. Pour into medium bowl and mix with Parmesan
3. Beat egg in a small bowl.
4. Dip zucchini slices in egg and then in pork rind mixture, coating as completely as possible. Carefully place each slice into the air fryer basket in a single layer, working in batches as necessary.
5. Adjust temperature to 320 Degrees F and set the timer for 10 minutes. Flip chips halfway through the cooking time. Serve warm.

**Nutrition: Calories: 121; Protein: 9.9g; Fiber: 0.6g; Fat: 6.7g; Carbs: 3.8g**

## 133. Easy Home Fries

Preparation Time: 20 minutes
Servings: 4

**Ingredients:**

- ½ medium white onion; peeled and diced
- 1 medium green bell pepper; seeded and diced
- 1 medium jicama; peeled.
- 1 tbsp. coconut oil; melted

- ½ tsp. pink Himalayan salt
- ¼ tsp. ground black pepper

**Directions:**

1. Cut jicama into 1-inch cubes. Place into a large bowl and toss with coconut oil until coated. Sprinkle with pepper and salt. Place into the air fryer basket with peppers and onion.
2. Adjust the temperature to 400 Degrees F and set the timer for 10 minutes. Shake two or three times during cooking. Jicama will be tender and dark around edges. Serve immediately.

**Nutrition: Calories: 97; Protein: 1.5g; Fiber: 8.0g; Fat: 3.3g; Carbs: 15.8g**

## 134. Healthy Garlic Stuffed Mushrooms

Preparation Time: 25 minutes
Servings:

**Ingredients:**

- 6 mushrooms [small]
- 1 ounce. onion [peeled; diced]
- 1 tablespoon breadcrumbs
- 1 tablespoon oil [olive]
- 1 teaspoon garlic [pureed]
- 1 teaspoon parsley
- salt to taste
- pepper to taste

**Directions:**

1. Mix breadcrumbs, oil, onion, parsley, salt, pepper and garlic in a medium sized bowl. Remove middle stalks from mushrooms and fill them with crumb mixture.
2. Cook in Air Fryer for 10 minutes at 350 - degrees Fahrenheit. Serve with mayo dip and enjoy the right combination.

## 135. Zucchini and Peppers with Saucy Sweet Potatoes

Preparation Time: 20 minutes

Servings: 4

**Ingredients:**

- 2 large-sized sweet potatoes; peeled and quartered
- 1 medium-sized zucchini; sliced
- 1 Serrano pepper; deveined and thinly sliced
- 1 bell pepper; deveined and thinly sliced
- 1 – 2 carrots; cut into matchsticks
- 1/4 cup olive oil
- 1 ½ tablespoon maple syrup
- 1/2 teaspoon porcini powder
- 1/4 teaspoon mustard powder
- 1/2 teaspoon fennel seeds
- 1 tablespoon garlic powder
- 1/2 teaspoon fine sea salt
- 1/4 teaspoon ground black pepper
- Tomato ketchup; to serve

**Directions:**

1. Place the sweet potatoes, zucchini, peppers, and the carrot into the Air Fryer cooking basket.
2. Drizzle with olive oil and toss to coat, cook in the preheated machine at 350 - degrees Fahrenheit for 15 minutes.
3. While the vegetables are cooking; prepare the sauce by thoroughly whisking the other ingredients, without the tomato ketchup.
4. Lightly grease a baking dish that fits into your machine.
5. Transfer cooked vegetables to the prepared baking dish; add the sauce and toss to coat well.
6. Turn the machine to 390 - degrees Fahrenheit and cook the vegetables for 5 more minutes.
7. Serve warm with tomato ketchup on the side.

## 136. Amazing Cheese Lings

Preparation Time: 25 minutes

Servings:

**Ingredients:**

- 1 cup flour [all-purpose]
- 3 small cubes cheese [grated]
- 1/4 teaspoon chili powder
- 1 teaspoon butter
- salt to taste
- 1 teaspoon baking powder

**Directions:**

1. Make dough with all the ingredients mentioned above and add small amount water if needed.
2. Roll and cut the pieces into round shape.
3. Preheat Air Fryer to 360 - degrees Fahrenheit and air fry for 5 minutes. Stir halfway and periodically.

## 137. Special Potatoes Side Dish

Preparation Time: 30 minutes
Servings:

**Ingredients:**

- 2 potatoes [medium]
- 1 teaspoon butter
- 3 tablespoon sour cream
- 1 teaspoon chives 1 teaspoon
- 1 ½ tablespoon cheese [grated]
- salt according to taste
- pepper according to taste

**Directions:**

1. Stab potatoes with fork and put in Air Fryer having boiled water so they are cooked from the inside to the outside properly.
2. Cook for 15 minutes at 350 - degrees Fahrenheit.
3. In the meantime, mix sour cream, cheese and chives in a bowl. Cut open potatoes and spread butter and add toppings to them. Serve with raw salad.

## 138. Delicious Potatoes with

## Mediterranean Dipping Sauce

Preparation Time: 55 minutes
Servings: 4

**Ingredients:**

- 2 pounds Russet potatoes; peeled and cubed
- 1 ½ tablespoons melted butter
- 1 teaspoon sea salt flakes
- 1 sprig rosemary; leaves only, crushed
- 2 sprigs thyme; leaves only, crushed
- 1/2 teaspoon freshly cracked black peppercorns
- For Mediterranean Dipping Sauce:
- 1/2 cup mascarpone cheese
- 1/3 cup yogurt
- 1 tablespoon fresh dill; chopped
- 1 tablespoon olive oil

**Directions:**

1. First; set your Air Fryer to cook at 350 - degrees Fahrenheit.
2. Now; add the potato cubes to the bowl with cold water and soak them approximately for 35 minutes.
3. After that; dry the potato cubes using a paper towel.
4. In a mixing dish; thoroughly whisk the melted butter with sea salt flakes, rosemary, thyme, and freshly cracked peppercorns.
5. Rub the potato cubes with this butter/spice mix.
6. Air-fry the potato cubes in the cooking basket for 18 to 20 minutes or until cooked through, make sure to shake the potatoes to cook them evenly.
7. Meanwhile; make the Mediterranean dipping sauce by mixing the remaining ingredients.
8. Serve warm potatoes with Mediterranean sauce for dipping and enjoy

## 139. Roasted Potatoes, Asparagus and

## Cheese

Preparation Time: 55 minutes
Servings:

**Ingredients:**

- 4 potatoes [medium]
- 1 asparagus bunch
- 1/3 cup cheese [cottage]
- 1/3 cup crème fraiche [low fat]
- 1 tablespoon mustard [wholegrain]

**Directions:**

1. Add oil and preheat Air Fryer to 390 - degrees Fahrenheit.
2. Cook potatoes in it for 20 minutes.
3. Boil asparagus in salted water for about 3 minutes.
4. Spoon out potatoes and make mash them with rest of ingredients mentioned above.
5. Refill the skins and season with salt and pepper. Serve with rice and enjoy!

## 140. Amazing Peppery Vegetable Omelet with Cheese

Preparation Time: 15 minutes
Servings: 2

**Ingredients:**

- 3 tablespoons plain milk
- four eggs; whisked
- 1 teaspoon melted butter
- Kosher salt and freshly ground black pepper; to taste
- 1 red bell pepper; deveined and chopped
- 1 green bell pepper; deveined and chopped
- 1 white onion; finely chopped
- 1/2 cup baby spinach leaves; roughly chopped
- 1/2 cup Halloumi cheese; shaved

**Directions:**

1. Start with spreading the canola cooking spray onto the Air Fryer baking pan.
2. Add all of the above ingredients to the baking pan, give them a good stir. Then; set your machine to cook at 350 degrees F; cook your omelet for 13 minutes.
3. Serve warm and enjoy!

## 141. Scrambled Eggs with Tomato and Spinach

Preparation Time: 15 minutes
Servings: 2

**Ingredients:**
- 2 tablespoons olive oil; melted
- four eggs; whisked
- 5 ounces fresh spinach; chopped
- 1 medium-sized tomato; chopped
- 1 teaspoon fresh lemon juice
- 1/2 teaspoon coarse salt
- 1/2 teaspoon ground black pepper
- 1/2 cup of fresh basil; roughly chopped

**Directions:**
1. Add the olive oil to an Air Fryer baking pan.
2. Make sure to tilt the pan to spread the oil evenly.
3. Simply combine the remaining ingredients; except for the basil leaves, whisk well until everything is well incorporated.
4. Cook in the preheated Air Fryer for 8 to 12 minutes at 280 - degrees Fahrenheit.
5. Garnish with fresh basil leaves.
6. Serve warm with a dollop of sour cream if desired.

## 142. Kernel and Sweet Corn Fritters

Preparation Time: 20 minutes
Servings: 4

**Ingredients:**
- 1 medium-sized carrot; grated

- 1 yellow onion; finely chopped
- 4 ounces canned sweet corn kernels; drained
- 1 teaspoon sea salt flakes
- 1 heaping tablespoon fresh cilantro; chopped
- 1 medium-sized egg; whisked
- 2 tablespoons plain milk
- 1 cup of Parmesan cheese; grated
- 1/4 cup of self-rising flour
- 1/3 teaspoon baking powder
- 1/3 teaspoon brown sugar

**Directions:**
1. Press down the grated carrot in the colander to remove excess liquid.
2. Then; spread the grated carrot between several sheets of kitchen towels and pat it dry.
3. Then; mix the carrots with the remaining ingredients in the order listed above.
4. Roll 1 tablespoon of the mixture into a ball; gently flatten it using the back of a spoon or your hand.
5. Now; repeat with the remaining ingredients.
6. Spitz the balls with a nonstick cooking oil. Cook in a single layer at 350 degrees for 8 to 11 minutes or until they're firm to touch in the center.
7. Serve warm and enjoy.

## 143. Amazing Onion Rings

Preparation Time: 30 minutes
Servings: 8

**Ingredients:**
- 2 medium-sized yellow onions; cut into rings
- 2 cups white flour
- 1/2 teaspoon baking soda
- 1 teaspoon baking powder
- 1 ½ teaspoons sea salt flakes
- 2 medium-sized eggs

- 1 ½ cups plain milk
- 1 ¼ cups seasoned breadcrumbs
- 1/2 teaspoon green peppercorns; freshly cracked
- 1/2 teaspoon dried dill weed
- 1/4 teaspoon paprika

**Directions:**

1. Begin by preheating your Air Fryer to 356 - degrees Fahrenheit.
2. Place the onion rings into the bowl with icy cold water and let them stay 15 to 20 minutes.
3. Drain the onion rings and dry them using a kitchen towel.
4. In a shallow bowl; mix the sifted flour together with baking soda, baking powder and sea salt flakes.
5. Then; coat each onion ring with the flour mixture.
6. In another shallow bowl; beat the eggs with milk, add the mixture to the remaining flour mixture and whisk well. Dredge the coated onion rings into this batter.
7. In a third bowl; mix the seasoned breadcrumbs, green peppercorns, dill, and paprika. Roll the onion rings over the breadcrumb mix, covering well. Air-fry them in the cooking basket for 8 to 11 minutes or until thoroughly cooked to golden.

## 144. Rosemary Cornbread

Preparation Time: 1 hr.
Servings: 6

**Ingredients:**

- 1 cup cornmeal
- 1 ½ cups of flour
- 1/2 teaspoon baking soda
- 1/2 teaspoon baking powder
- 1/4 teaspoon kosher salt
- 1 teaspoon dried rosemary
- 1/4 teaspoon garlic powder

- 2 tablespoons caster sugar
- two eggs
- 1/4 cup melted butter
- 1 cup buttermilk
- 1/2 cup corn kernels

**Directions:**

1. In a bowl; mix all dry Ingredients until well combined. In another bowl, combine all liquid Ingredients
2. Add the liquid mix to the dry mix. Fold in the corn kernels and stir to combine well.
3. Press the batter into the round loaf pan that is lightly greased with a non-stick cooking spray. Air-fry for 1 hour at 380 - degrees Fahrenheit.

## 145. Delicious Broccoli Bites with Hot Sauce

Preparation Time: 20 minutes
Servings: 6

**Ingredients:**

*For the Broccoli Bites:*

- 1 medium-sized head broccoli; broken into florets
- 1/2 teaspoon lemon zest; freshly grated
- 1/3 teaspoon fine sea salt
- 1/2 teaspoon hot paprika
- 1 teaspoon shallot powder
- 1 teaspoon porcini powder
- 1/2 teaspoon granulated garlic
- 1/3 teaspoon celery seeds
- 1 ½ tablespoons olive oil

*For the Hot Sauce:*

- 1/2 cup tomato sauce
- 3 tablespoons brown sugar
- 1 tablespoon balsamic vinegar
- 1/2 teaspoon ground allspice

**Directions:**

1. Toss all the ingredients for the broccoli

bites in a mixing bowl; covering the broccoli florets on all sides.

2. Cook them in the preheated Air Fryer at 360 degrees for 13 to 15 minutes.

3. In the meantime; mix all ingredients for the hot sauce.

4. Pause your Air Fryer; mix the broccoli with the prepared sauce and cook for further 3 minutes.

## 146. Roasted Potatoes & Yoghurt

Preparation Time: 55 minutes
Servings:

**Ingredients:**

- Pounds potatoes [waxy]
- 1 tablespoon paprika [spicy]
- salt to taste
- black pepper [freshly ground] to taste
- 1 tablespoon olive oil
- ounces. yoghurt [Greek]

**Directions:**

1. Preheat Air Fryer at 350 – degrees Fahrenheit.

2. Peel and cut potatoes in small pieces of about 3 cm cubes, soak the pieces in cold water for 30 minutes.

3. After 30 minutes' drain and pat dry the potato pieces.

4. In a medium size bowl add 1 tablespoon. of oil, paprika and sprinkle pepper and stir well. Coat the cubes with the mixture.

5. Put in fryer and air fry for about 20 minutes. Serve them with dip or pari-pari sauce. Enjoy the delicious combination.

## 147. Easy Veggie Rolls

Preparation Time: 30 minutes
Servings:

**Ingredients:**

- 2 potatoes [mashed]
- 1/4 cup peas
- 1/4 cup carrots [mashed]
- 1 cabbage [small; sliced]
- 1/4 beans
- 2 tablespoon sweet corn
- 1 onion [small; chopped]
- 1 teaspoon capsicum
- 1 teaspoon coriander
- 2 tablespoon butter
- ginger garlic to taste
- 1/2 teaspoon masala powder
- 1/2 teaspoon chili powder
- 1/2 cup breadcrumbs
- 1 packet roll sheets
- 1/2 cup cornstarch slurry

**Directions:**

1. Boil all the vegetables in half cup of water on a low heat and let them dry.

2. Spread the roll sheet and place the filling onto it then make the fillings into rolls and coat the rolls with slurry and breadcrumbs.

3. Preheat Air Fryer to 390 - degrees Fahrenheit and cook it for 10 minutes. Serve with boiled rice and have a treat.

## 148. Special Grilled Cheese

Preparation Time: 25 minutes
Servings:

**Ingredients:**

- 4 slices of brioche or white bread
- 1/2 cup sharp cheddar cheese
- 1/4 cup butter; melted

**Directions:**

1. Preheat the Air Fryer to 360 - degrees Fahrenheit. Place cheese and butter in separate bowls. Brush the butter on each side of the 4 slices of bread.

2. Place the cheese on 2 of the 4 pieces of bread. Put the grilled cheese together and add to the cooking basket.

3. Cook for 5 – 7 minutes or until golden

brown and the cheese has melted.

## 149. Different Potatoes Gratin

Preparation Time: 55 minutes
Servings:

**Ingredients:**

- 1/2 cup milk
- 7 medium russet potatoes; peeled
- 1 teaspoon black pepper
- 1/2 cup cream
- 1/2 cup semi-mature cheese; grated
- 1/2 teaspoon nutmeg

**Directions:**

1. Preheat the Air Fryer to 390 – degrees Fahrenheit.
2. Slice the potatoes wafer-thin. In a bowl; mix the milk and cream and season to taste with salt, pepper, and nutmeg.
3. Coat the potato slices with this mixture. Transfer the potato slices to an 8-inch heat-resistant baking dish. Pour the rest of the cream mixture on top of the potatoes.
4. In the cooking basket of the Air Fryer; place the baking dish and set the timer to 25 minutes.
5. Remove cooking basket and distribute the cheese evenly over the potatoes. Set the timer for 10 minutes and bake the gratin until it is nicely browned.

## 150. Yummy Potatoes Gratin

Preparation Time: 55 minutes
Servings:

**Ingredients:**

- 7 medium russet potatoes; peeled
- 1/2 cup milk
- 1/2 cup cream
- 1 teaspoon black pepper
- 1/2 teaspoon nutmeg
- 1/2 cup Gruyère or semi-mature cheese;

grated

**Directions:**

1. Preheat the Air Fryer to 390 - degrees Fahrenheit.
2. Slice the potatoes wafer-thin. In a bowl; mix the milk and cream and season to taste with salt, pepper and nutmeg.
3. Coat the potato slices with the milk mixture.
4. Transfer the potato slices to 8-inch heat resistant baking dish and pour the rest of the cream mixture from the bowl on top of the potatoes.
5. Place the baking dish in the cooking basket into the Air Fryer.
6. Set the timer and cook for 25 minutes. Remove cooking basket and distribute the cheese evenly over the potatoes.
7. Set the timer for 10 minutes and bake the gratin until it is nicely browned.
8. Tips: Instead of milk you can substitute two eggs

## 151. Roasted Vegetables Dish

Preparation Time: 30 minutes
Servings:

**Ingredients:**

- 1 1/3 cup parsnips [1 small]
- 1 1/3 cup celery [3 – 4 stalks]
- 2 red onions
- 1 1/3 cup butternut squash [1 small]
- 1 tablespoon fresh thyme needles
- 1 tablespoon olive oil
- pepper and salt to taste

**Directions:**

1. Preheat the Air Fryer to 390 - degrees Fahrenheit.
2. Peel the parsnips and onions. Cut the parsnips and celery into 2 Cm cubes and the onions into wedges.
3. Halve the butternut squash; remove the seeds and cut into cubes. [There's no need to peel it.]

4. Mix the cut vegetables with the thyme and olive oil. Season to taste.
5. Place the vegetables into the basket and slide the basket into the Air Fryer.
6. Set the timer for 20 minutes and roast the vegetables until the timer rings and the vegetables are nicely brown and done.
7. Stir the vegetables once while roasting.

## 152. Easy Sweet Potato Curry Fries

Preparation Time: 55 minutes
Servings:

**Ingredients:**
- Pounds sweet potatoes
- 1 teaspoon curry powder
- 2 tablespoon olive oil
- salt to taste

**Directions:**
1. Preheat Air Fryer to 390 - degrees Fahrenheit.
2. Wash and cut sweet potatoes into fine long fries. Add oil in the pan and bake the fried for 25 minutes.
3. Now season them with curry and salt. Serve with ketchup and enjoy.

## 153. Awesome Tartar Sauce Chips

Preparation Time: 55 minutes
Servings:

**Ingredients:**
- 2 potatoes [large]
- 1 teaspoon rosemary
- 2 cloves garlic [crushed]
- 1 tablespoon oil [olive]

*Sauce:*
- 1 shallot [chopped]
- 3 tablespoon capers [drained; chopped]
- 1 squeeze lemon juice
- 2 tablespoon jalapenos [drained; chopped]

- 3 tablespoon parsley [fresh; chopped]
- 1 cup mayonnaise
- salt and pepper to taste

**Directions:**
1. Cut potatoes into wedges and soak in salted water for about 20 minutes.
2. Preheat Air Fryer to 350 - degrees Fahrenheit.
3. Mix all the ingredients and coat it over the potatoes. Cook the coated potatoes for about 25 minutes.
4. Make a sauce and serve with it. Enjoy the delicious taste.

## 154. Rosemary Potato Chips

Preparation Time: 1 hour 15 minutes
Servings:

**Ingredients:**
- 4 medium russet potatoes
- 1 tablespoon olive oil
- 2 teaspoon rosemary; chopped
- 2 pinches salt

**Directions:**
1. Scrub the potatoes under running water to clean.
2. Cut the potatoes lengthwise and peel them into thin chips directly into a mixing bowl full of water.
3. Soak the potatoes for 30 minutes; changing the water several times. Drain thoroughly and pat completely dry with a paper towel.
4. Preheat the Air Fryer to 330 - degrees Fahrenheit. In a mixing bowl; toss the potatoes with olive oil. Place them into the cooking basket and cook for 30 minutes or until golden brown, shaking frequently to ensure the chips are cooked evenly.
5. When finished and still warm, toss in a large bowl with rosemary and salt.

## 155. Tasty Turkey Wrapped Prawns

Preparation Time: 30 minutes
Servings:

**Ingredients:**

- 1 Pound. Turkey [sliced]
- 1 Pound. Prawns [tiger]

**Directions:**

1. Preheat Air Fryer to 390 - degrees Fahrenheit.
2. Wrap prawns with Turkey and secure with toothpick. Refrigerate for 20 minutes.
3. Cook for 10 minutes in batches. Serve with tartar sauce and enjoy the yummy taste.

## 156. Yummy Cheesy Rice Balls

Preparation Time: 40 minutes
Servings:

**Ingredients:**

- 1 cup rice [boiled]
- 1 cup paneer
- 1 tablespoon corn flour
- 1 green chili; chopped
- 1 cup cheese mozzarella; cubed
- 2 tablespoon carrot; chopped
- 2 tablespoon sweet corn
- 1 tablespoon corn flour slurry
- salt to taste
- garlic powder [optional] to taste
- 1/2 breadcrumbs
- 1 teaspoon oregano

**Directions:**

1. Preheat Air Fryer to 390 - degrees Fahrenheit.
2. Mix all the above-mentioned ingredients and form into small ball shape.
3. Roll the mixture in slurry and breadcrumbs. Cook for 15 minutes.

## 157. Delicious French Fries

Preparation Time: 25 minutes
Servings:

**Ingredients:**

- 6 medium russet potatoes; peeled
- 2 tablespoon olive oil

**Directions:**

1. Peel the potatoes and cut them into 1/4 inch by 3-inch strips.
2. Soak the potatoes in water for at least 30 minutes; then drain thoroughly and pat dry with a paper towel.
3. Preheat the Air Fryer to 360 - degrees Fahrenheit.
4. Place the potatoes in a large bowl and mix in oil, coating the potatoes lightly. Add the potatoes to the cooking basket and cook for 30 minutes or until golden brown and crisp. Shake 2 – 3 times during cooking.
5. Tip: Thicker cut potatoes will take longer to cook; while thinner cut potatoes will cook faster.

## 158. Roasted Brussels Sprouts

Preparation Time: 30 minutes
Servings:

**Ingredients:**

- 2 cups Brussels sprouts
- 1/4 cup pine nuts [toasted]
- 1 orange [juice and zest]
- 1/4 raisins [drained]
- 1 tablespoon oil [olive]

**Directions:**

1. Preheat Air Fryer to 390 – degrees Fahrenheit.
2. Boil sprouts for about 4 minutes and then put them in cold water and drain the sprouts properly.
3. Meanwhile; soak raisins in orange juice for 15 minutes. Now roast the cooled sprouts with oil for 15 minutes. Serve with nuts, raisins and zest.

## 159. Cheese and Spinach Balls

Preparation Time: 35 minutes
Servings:

**Ingredients:**
- 1 cup corn flour
- 1 cup bread crumbs
- 1 cup spinach [boiled]
- 2 onion [chopped]
- 1 tablespoon red chili flakes
- 1/2 cup mozzarella [grated]
- 1 teaspoon garlic [grated]
- 1 tablespoon salt
- 2 tablespoon olive oil

**Directions:**
1. Mix all ingredients and form the mixture into small balls. Brush the pan with oil.
2. Air fry at 390 - degrees Fahrenheit for 15 minutes. Serve them with tartar sauce.

## 160. Special Walnut Stilton Circles

Preparation Time: 45 minutes
Servings:

**Ingredients:**
- 1/4 cup flour [plain]
- 1/4 cup walnuts
- 1/4 cup butter
- 1/4 cup stilton

**Directions:**
1. Make dough with the all the ingredients mentioned above by mixing them well till a thick texture appears. Cut dough into log shapes, approx. 3cm.
2. Wrap it in aluminum foil and let it freeze for about 30 minutes. Now cut the dough into circles.
3. Line Air Fryer with baking sheet and preheat to 350 - degrees Fahrenheit. Cook 20 minutes. And it is ready! Serve while its hot.

# Seafood

## 161. Lemon Garlic Shrimps

Preparation Time: 15 minutes
Cooking Time: 8 minutes
Servings: 2

**Ingredients:**

- ¾ pound medium shrimp, peeled and deveined
- 1½ tablespoons fresh lemon juice
- 1 tablespoon olive oil
- 1 teaspoon lemon pepper
- ¼ teaspoon paprika
- ¼ teaspoon garlic powder

**Directions:**

1. Preheat the Air fryer to 400 o F and grease an Air fryer basket.
2. Mix lemon juice, olive oil, lemon pepper, paprika and garlic powder in a large bowl.
3. Stir in the shrimp and toss until well combined.
4. Arrange shrimp into the Air fryer basket in a single layer and cook for about 8 minutes.
5. Dish out the shrimp in serving plates and serve warm.

**Nutrition:**
Calories: 260, Fat: 12.4g, Carbohydrates: 0.3g, Sugar: 0.1g, Protein: 35.6g, Sodium: 619mg

## 162. Creamy Tuna Cakes

Preparation Time: 15 minutes
Cooking Time: 15 minutes
Servings: 4

**Ingredients:**

- 2: 6-ouncescans tuna, drained
- 1½ tablespoon almond flour
- 1½ tablespoons mayonnaise

- 1 tablespoon fresh lemon juice
- 1 teaspoon dried dill
- 1 teaspoon garlic powder
- ½ teaspoon onion powder
- Pinch of salt and ground black pepper

**Directions:**

1. Preheat the Air fryer to 400 o F and grease an Air fryer basket.
2. Mix the tuna, mayonnaise, almond flour, lemon juice, dill, and spices in a large bowl.
3. Make 4 equal-sized patties from the mixture and arrange in the Air fryer basket.
4. Cook for about 10 minutes and flip the sides.
5. Cook for 5 more minutes and dish out the tuna cakes in serving plates to serve warm.

**Nutrition:**
Calories: 200, Fat: 10.1g, Carbohydrates: 2.9g, Sugar: 0.8g, Protein: 23.4g, Sodium: 122mg

## 163. Cheesy Shrimp

Preparation Time: 20 minutes
Cooking Time: 20 minutes
Servings: 4

**Ingredients:**

- 2/3 cup Parmesan cheese, grated
- 2 pounds shrimp, peeled and deveined
- 4 garlic cloves, minced
- 2 tablespoons olive oil
- 1 teaspoon dried basil
- ½ teaspoon dried oregano
- 1 teaspoon onion powder
- ½ teaspoon red pepper flakes, crushed
- Ground black pepper, as required

- 2 tablespoons fresh lemon juice

**Directions:**

1. Preheat the Air fryer to 350 o F and grease an Air fryer basket.
2. Mix Parmesan cheese, garlic, olive oil, herbs, and spices in a large bowl.
3. Arrange half of the shrimp into the Air fryer basket in a single layer and cook for about 10 minutes.
4. Dish out the shrimps onto serving plates and drizzle with lemon juice to serve hot.

**Nutrition:**
Calories: 386, Fat: 14.2g, Carbohydrates: 5.3g, Sugar: 0.4g, Protein: 57.3g, Sodium: 670mg

## 164. Creamy Breaded Shrimp

Preparation Time: 15 minutes
Cooking Time: 20 minutes
Servings: 3

**Ingredients:**

- ¼ cup all-purpose flour
- 1 cup panko breadcrumbs
- 1 pound shrimp, peeled and deveined
- ½ cup mayonnaise
- ¼ cup sweet chili sauce
- 1 tablespoon Sriracha sauce

**Directions:**

1. Preheat the Air fryer to 400 o F and grease an Air fryer basket.
2. Place flour in a shallow bowl and mix the mayonnaise, chili sauce, and Sriracha sauce in another bowl.
3. Place the breadcrumbs in a third bowl.
4. Coat each shrimp with the flour, dip into mayonnaise mixture and finally, dredge in the breadcrumbs.
5. Arrange half of the coated shrimps into the Air fryer basket and cook for about 10 minutes.
6. Dish out the coated shrimps onto serving plates and repeat with the remaining mixture.

**Nutrition:**
Calories: 540, Fat: 18.2g, Carbohydrates: 33.1g, Sugar: 10.6g, Protein: 36.8g, Sodium: 813mg

## 165. Breaded Shrimp with Lemon

Preparation Time: 15 minutes
Cooking Time: 14 minutes
Servings: 3

**Ingredients:**

- ½ cup plain flour
- 2 egg whites
- 1 cup breadcrumbs
- 1 pound large shrimp, peeled and deveined
- Salt and ground black pepper, as required
- ¼ teaspoon lemon zest
- ¼ teaspoon cayenne pepper
- ¼ teaspoon red pepper flakes, crushed
- 2 tablespoons vegetable oil

**Directions:**

1. Preheat the Air fryer to 400 o F and grease an Air fryer basket.
2. Mix flour, salt, and black pepper in a shallow bowl.
3. Whisk the egg whites in a second bowl and mix the breadcrumbs, lime zest and spices in a third bowl.
4. Coat each shrimp with the flour, dip into egg whites and finally, dredge in the breadcrumbs.
5. Drizzle the shrimp evenly with olive oil and arrange half of the coated shrimps into the Air fryer basket.
6. Cook for about 7 minutes and dish out the coated shrimps onto serving plates.
7. Repeat with the remaining mixture and serve hot.

**Nutrition:**
Calories: 432, Fat: 11.3g, Carbohydrates: 44.8g, Sugar: 2.5g, Protein: 37.7g, Sodium: 526mg

## 166. Coconut Crusted Shrimp

Preparation Time: 15 minutes
Cooking Time: 40 minutes
Servings: 3

**Ingredients:**

- 8 ounces coconut milk
- ½ cup sweetened coconut, shredded
- ½ cup panko breadcrumbs
- 1 pound large shrimp, peeled and deveined
- Salt and black pepper, to taste

**Directions:**

1. Preheat the Air fryer to 350 o F and grease an Air fryer basket.
2. Place the coconut milk in a shallow bowl.
3. Mix coconut, breadcrumbs, salt, and black pepper in another bowl.
4. Dip each shrimp into coconut milk and finally, dredge in the coconut mixture.
5. Arrange half of the shrimps into the Air fryer basket and cook for about 20 minutes.
6. Dish out the shrimps onto serving plates and repeat with the remaining mixture to serve.

**Nutrition:**
Calories: 408, Fats: 23.7g, Carbohydrates: 11.7g, Sugar: 3.4g, Proteins: 31g, Sodium: 253mg

## 167. Shrimp Scampi

Preparation Time: 15 minutes
Cooking Time: 7 minutes
Servings: 6

**Ingredients:**

- 4 tablespoons salted butter
- 1 pound shrimp, peeled and deveined
- 2 tablespoons fresh basil, chopped
- 1 tablespoon fresh chives, chopped
- 1 tablespoon fresh lemon juice
- 1 tablespoon garlic, minced
- 2 teaspoons red pepper flakes, crushed
- 2 tablespoons dry white wine

**Directions:**

1. Preheat the Air fryer to 325 o F and grease an Air fryer pan.
2. Heat butter, lemon juice, garlic, and red pepper flakes in a pan and return the pan to Air fryer basket.
3. Cook for about 2 minutes and stir in shrimp, basil, chives and wine.
4. Cook for about 5 minutes and dish out the mixture onto serving plates.
5. Serve hot.

**Nutrition:**
Calories: 250, Fat: 13.7g, Carbohydrates: 3.3g, Sugar: 0.3g, Protein: 26.3g, Sodium: 360mg

## 168. Rice Flour Coated Shrimp

Preparation Time: 20 minutes
Cooking Time: 20 minutes
Servings: 3

**Ingredients:**

- 3 tablespoons rice flour
- 1 pound shrimp, peeled and deveined
- 2 tablespoons olive oil
- 1 teaspoon powdered sugar
- Salt and black pepper, as required

**Directions:**

1. Preheat the Air fryer to 325 o F and grease an Air fryer basket.
2. Mix rice flour, olive oil, sugar, salt, and black pepper in a bowl.
3. Stir in the shrimp and transfer half of the shrimp to the Air fryer basket.
4. Cook for about 10 minutes, flipping once in between.
5. Dish out the mixture onto serving plates and repeat with the remaining mixture.

**Nutrition:**
Calories: 299, Fat: 12g, Carbohydrates: 11.1g, Sugar: 0.8g, Protein: 35g, Sodium: 419mg

## 169. Shrimp Kebabs

Preparation Time: 15 minutes
Cooking Time: 10 minutes
Servings: 2

**Ingredients:**

- ¾ pound shrimp, peeled and deveined
- 1 tablespoon fresh cilantro, chopped
- Wooden skewers, presoaked
- 2 tablespoons fresh lemon juice
- 1 teaspoon garlic, minced
- ½ teaspoon paprika
- ½ teaspoon ground cumin
- Salt and ground black pepper, as required

**Directions:**

1. Preheat the Air fryer to 350 o F and grease an Air fryer basket.
2. Mix lemon juice, garlic, and spices in a bowl.
3. Stir in the shrimp and mix to coat well.
4. Thread the shrimp onto presoaked wooden skewers and transfer to the Air fryer basket.
5. Cook for about 10 minutes, flipping once in between.
6. Dish out the mixture onto serving plates and serve garnished with fresh cilantro.

**Nutrition:**
Calories: 212, Fat: 3.2g, Carbohydrates: 3.9g, Sugar: 0.4g, Protein: 39.1g, Sodium: 497mg

## 170. Garlic Parmesan Shrimp

Preparation Time: 20 minutes
Cooking Time: 10 minutes
Servings: 2

**Ingredients:**

- 1 pound shrimp, deveined and peeled
- ½ cup parmesan cheese, grated
- ¼ cup cilantro, diced
- 1 tablespoon olive oil
- 1 teaspoon salt
- 1 teaspoon fresh cracked pepper

- 1 tablespoon lemon juice
- 6 garlic cloves, diced

**Directions:**

1. Preheat the Air fryer to 350 o F and grease an Air fryer basket.
2. Drizzle shrimp with olive oil and lemon juice and season with garlic, salt and cracked pepper.
3. Cover the bowl with plastic wrap and refrigerate for about 3 hours.
4. Stir in the parmesan cheese and cilantro to the bowl and transfer to the Air fryer basket.
5. Cook for about 10 minutes and serve immediately.

**Nutrition:**
Calories: 602, Fat: 23.9g, Carbohydrates: 46.5g, Sugar: 2.9g, Protein: 11.3g, Sodium: 886mg

## 171. Prawn Burgers

Preparation Time: 20 minutes
Cooking Time: 6 minutes
Servings: 2

**Ingredients:**

- ½ cup prawns, peeled, deveined and finely chopped
- ½ cup breadcrumbs
- 2-3 tablespoons onion, finely chopped
- 3 cups fresh baby greens
- ½ teaspoon ginger, minced
- ½ teaspoon garlic, minced
- ½ teaspoon red chili powder
- ½ teaspoon ground cumin
- ¼ teaspoon ground turmeric
- Salt and ground black pepper, as required

**Directions:**

1. Preheat the Air fryer to 390 o F and grease an Air fryer basket.
2. Mix the prawns, breadcrumbs, onion, ginger, garlic, and spices in a bowl.
3. Make small-sized patties from the mixture

4. Cook for about 6 minutes and dish out in a platter.
5. Serve immediately warm alongside the baby greens.

**Nutrition:**
Calories: 240, Fat: 2.7g, Carbohydrates: 37.4g, Sugar: 4g, Protein: 18g, Sodium: 371mg

## 172. Buttered Scallops

Preparation Time: 15 minutes
Cooking Time: 4 minutes
Servings: 2

**Ingredients:**

- ¾ pound sea scallops, cleaned and patted very dry
- 1 tablespoon butter, melted
- ½ tablespoon fresh thyme, minced
- Salt and black pepper, as required

**Directions:**

1. Preheat the Air fryer to 390 o F and grease an Air fryer basket.
2. Mix scallops, butter, thyme, salt, and black pepper in a bowl.
3. Arrange scallops in the Air fryer basket and cook for about 4 minutes.
4. Dish out the scallops in a platter and serve hot.

**Nutrition:**
Calories: 202, Fat: 7.1g, Carbohydrates: 4.4g, Sugar: 0g, Protein: 28.7g, Sodium: 393mg

## 173. Scallops with Capers Sauce

Preparation Time: 15 minutes
Cooking Time: 6 minutes
Servings: 2

**Ingredients:**

- 10: 1-ouncesea scallops, cleaned and patted very dry
- 2 tablespoons fresh parsley, finely chopped
- 2 teaspoons capers, finely chopped
- Salt and ground black pepper, as required
- ¼ cup extra-virgin olive oil
- 1 teaspoon fresh lemon zest, finely grated
- ½ teaspoon garlic, finely chopped

**Directions:**

1. Preheat the Air fryer to 390 o F and grease an Air fryer basket.
2. Season the scallops evenly with salt and black pepper.
3. Arrange the scallops in the Air fryer basket and cook for about 6 minutes.
4. Mix parsley, capers, olive oil, lemon zest and garlic in a bowl.
5. Dish out the scallops in a platter and top with capers sauce.

**Nutrition:**
Calories: 344, Fat: 26.3g, Carbohydrates: 4.2g, Sugar: 0.1g, Protein: 24g, Sodium: 393mg

## 174. Crispy Scallops

Preparation Time: 15 minutes
- Cooking Time: 6 minutes
- Servings: 4

**Ingredients:**

- 18 sea scallops, cleaned and patted very dry
- 1/8 cup all-purpose flour
- 1 tablespoon 2% milk
- ½ egg
- ¼ cup cornflakes, crushed
- ½ teaspoon paprika
- Salt and black pepper, as required

**Directions:**

1. Preheat the Air fryer to 400 o F and grease an Air fryer basket.
2. Mix flour, paprika, salt, and black pepper in a bowl.
3. Whisk egg with milk in another bowl and place the cornflakes in a third bowl.

4. Coat each scallop with the flour mixture, dip into the egg mixture and finally, dredge in the cornflakes.
5. Arrange scallops in the Air fryer basket and cook for about 6 minutes.
6. Dish out the scallops in a platter and serve hot.

**Nutrition:**
Calories: 150, Fat: 1.7g, Carbohydrates: 8g, Sugar: 0.4g, Protein: 24g, Sodium: 278mg

## 175. Scallops with Spinach

Preparation Time: 20 minutes
Cooking Time: 10 minutes
Servings: 2

**Ingredients:**

- 1: 12-ouncespackage frozen spinach, thawed and drained
- 8 jumbo sea scallops
- Olive oil cooking spray
- 1 tablespoon fresh basil, chopped
- Salt and ground black pepper, as required
- ¾ cup heavy whipping cream
- 1 tablespoon tomato paste
- 1 teaspoon garlic, minced

**Directions:**

1. Preheat the Air fryer to 350 o F and grease an Air fryer pan.
2. Season the scallops evenly with salt and black pepper.
3. Mix cream, tomato paste, garlic, basil, salt, and black pepper in a bowl.
4. Place spinach at the bottom of the Air fryer pan, followed by seasoned scallops and top with the cream mixture.
5. Transfer into the Air fryer and cook for about 10 minutes.
6. Dish out in a platter and serve hot.

**Nutrition:**
Calories: 203, Fat: 18.3g, Carbohydrates: 12.3g, Sugar: 1.7g, Protein: 26.4g, Sodium: 101mg

## 176. Bacon Wrapped Scallops

Preparation Time: 15 minutes
Cooking Time: 12 minutes
Servings: 4

**Ingredients:**

- 5 center-cut bacon slices, cut each in 4 pieces
- 20 sea scallops, cleaned and patted very dry
- Olive oil cooking spray
- 1 teaspoon lemon pepper seasoning
- ½ teaspoon paprika
- Salt and ground black pepper, to taste

**Directions:**

1. Preheat the Air fryer to 400 o F and grease an Air fryer basket.
2. Wrap each scallop with a piece of bacon and secure each with a toothpick.
3. Season the scallops evenly with lemon pepper seasoning and paprika.
4. Arrange half of the scallops into the Air fryer basket and spray with cooking spray.
5. Season with salt and black pepper and cook for about 6 minutes.
6. Repeat with the remaining half and serve warm.

**Nutrition:**
Calories: 330, Fat: 16.3g, Carbohydrates: 4.5g, Sugar: 0g, Protein: 38.7g, Sodium: 1118mg

## 177. Glazed Calamari

Preparation Time: 20 minutes
Cooking Time: 13 minutes
Servings: 3

**Ingredients:**

- ½ pound calamari tubes, cut into ¼ inch rings
- 1 cup club soda
- 1 cup flour
- ½ tablespoon red pepper flakes, crushed

- Salt and black pepper, to taste

*For Sauce*

- ½ cup honey
- 2 tablespoons Sriracha sauce
- ¼ teaspoon red pepper flakes, crushed

**Directions:**

1. Preheat the Air fryer to 375 o F and grease an Air fryer basket.
2. Soak the calamari in the club soda in a bowl and keep aside for about 10 minutes.
3. Mix flour, red pepper flakes, salt, and black pepper in another bowl.
4. Drain the club soda from calamari and coat the calamari rings evenly with flour mixture.
5. Arrange calamari rings into the Air fryer basket and cook for about 11 minutes.
6. Meanwhile, mix the honey, Sriracha sauce and red pepper flakes in a bowl.
7. Coat the calamari rings with the honey sauce and cook for 2 more minutes.
8. Dish out the calamari rings onto serving plates and serve hot.

**Nutrition:**
Calories: 307, Fats: 1.4g, Carbohydrates: 62.1g, Sugar: 35g, Proteins: 12g, Sodium: 131mg

## 178. Buttered Crab Shells

Preparation Time: 20 minutes
Cooking Time: 10 minutes
Servings: 4

**Ingredients:**

- 4 soft crab shells, cleaned
- 1 cup buttermilk
- 3 eggs
- 2 cups panko breadcrumb
- 2 tablespoons butter, melted
- 2 teaspoons seafood seasoningo
- 1½ teaspoons lemon zest, grated

**Directions:**

1. Preheat the Air fryer to 375 o F and grease an Air fryer basket.
2. Place the buttermilk in a shallow bowl and whisk the eggs in a second bowl.
3. Mix the breadcrumbs, seafood seasoning, and lemon zest in a third bowl.
4. Soak the crab shells into the buttermilk for about 10 minutes, then dip in the eggs.
5. Dredge in the breadcrumb mixture and arrange the crab shells into the Air fryer basket.
6. Cook for about 10 minutes and dish out in a platter.
7. Drizzle melted butter over the crab shells and immediately serve.

**Nutrition:**
Calories: 521, Fat: 16.8g, Carbohydrates: 11.5g, Sugar: 3.3g, Protein: 47.8g, Sodium: 1100mg
(Note: Seafood Seasoning - Mix the salt, celery seed, dry mustard powder, red pepper, black pepper, bay leaves, paprika, cloves, allspice, ginger, cardamom, and cinnamon together in a bowl until thoroughly combined. Or, you can buy at your local store or on Amazon.

## 179. Crab Cakes

Preparation Time: 20 minutes
Cooking Time: 20 minutes
Servings: 4

**Ingredients:**

- 1 pound lump crab meat
- 1/3 cup panko breadcrumbs
- ¼ cup scallion, finely chopped
- 2 large eggs
- 2 tablespoons mayonnaise
- 1 teaspoon Dijon mustard
- 1 teaspoon Worcestershire sauce
- 1½ teaspoons Old Bay seasoning
- Ground black pepper, as required

**Directions:**

1. Preheat the Air fryer to 375 o F and

grease an Air fryer basket.

2. Mix all the ingredients in a large bowl and cover to refrigerate for about 1 hour.
3. Make 8 equal-sized patties from the mixture and transfer 4 patties into the Air fryer.
4. Cook for about 10 minutes, flipping once in between and repeat with the remaining patties.
5. Dish out and serve warm.

**Nutrition:**
Calories: 183, Fat: 14.8g, Carbohydrates: 5.9g, Sugar: 1.1g, Protein: 20.1g, Sodium: 996mg

## 180. Wasabi Crab Cakes

Preparation Time: 20 minutes
Cooking Time: 24 minutes
Servings: 6

**Ingredients:**
- 3 scallions, finely chopped
- 1 celery rib, finely chopped
- 1/3 cup plus ½ cup dry breadcrumbs, divided
- 2 large egg whites
- 1½ cups lump crab meat, drained
- 3 tablespoons mayonnaise
- 1 medium sweet red pepper, finely chopped
- ¼ teaspoon prepared wasabi
- Salt, to taste

**Directions:**
1. Preheat the Air fryer to 375 o F and grease an Air fryer basket.
2. Mix scallions, red pepper, celery, 1/3 cup of breadcrumbs, egg whites, mayonnaise, wasabi, and salt in a large bowl.
3. Fold in the crab meat gently and mix well.
4. Place the remaining breadcrumbs in another bowl.
5. Make ¾-inch thick patties from the mixture and arrange half of the patties into the Air fryer.

6. Cook for about 12 minutes, flipping once halfway through and repeat with the remaining patties.
7. Dish out and serve warm.

**Nutrition:**
Calories: 112, Fat: 4g, Carbohydrates: 15.5g, Sugar: 2.7g, Protein: 4.9g, Sodium: 253mg

## 181. Lemony Tuna

Preparation Time: 15 minutes
Cooking Time: 12 minutes
Servings: 8

**Ingredients:**
- 4 tablespoons fresh parsley, chopped
- 4: 6-ouncecans water packed plain tuna
- 1 cup breadcrumbs
- 2 eggs
- 4 teaspoons Dijon mustard
- 2 tablespoons fresh lime juice
- 6 tablespoons canola oil
- Dash of hot sauce
- Salt and black pepper, to taste

**Directions:**
1. Preheat the Air fryer to 360 o F and grease an Air fryer basket.
2. Mix tuna fish, breadcrumbs, mustard, parsley, hot sauce, canola oil, eggs, salt and lime juice in a large bowl.
3. Make equal-sized patties from the mixture and refrigerate for about 3 hours.
4. Transfer the patties into the Air fryer basket and cook for about 12 minutes.
5. Dish out and serve warm.

**Nutrition:**
Calories: 388, Fat: 21.8g, Carbohydrates: 31.7g, Sugar: 1.2g, Protein: 14.2g, Sodium: 680mg

## 182. Haddock with Cheese Sauce

Preparation Time: 15 minutes
Cooking Time: 8 minutes

Servings: 4

**Ingredients:**

- 4: 6-ouncehaddock fillets
- 6 tablespoons fresh basil, chopped
- 4 tablespoons pine nuts
- 2 tablespoons Parmesan cheese, grated
- 2 tablespoons olive oil
- Salt and black pepper, to taste

**Directions:**

1. Preheat the Air fryer to 360 o F and grease an Air fryer basket.
2. Season the haddock fillets with salt and black pepper and coat evenly with olive oil.
3. Transfer the haddock fillets in the Air fryer basket and cook for about 8 minutes.
4. Meanwhile, put rest of the ingredients in a food processor and pulse until smooth to make cheese sauce.
5. Dish out the haddock fillets in the bowl and top with cheese sauce to serve.

**Nutrition:**
Calories: 354, Fat: 17.5g, Carbohydrates: 1.7g, Sugar: 0.3g, Protein: 47g, Sodium: 278mg

## 183. Crumbed Cod

Preparation Time: 15 minutes
Cooking Time: 7 minutes
Servings: 4

**Ingredients:**

- 1 cup flour
- 4: 4-ounceskinless codfish fillets, cut into rectangular pieces
- 6 eggs
- 2 green chilies, finely chopped
- 6 scallions, finely chopped
- 4 garlic cloves, minced
- Salt and black pepper, to taste
- 2 teaspoons soy sauce

**Directions:**

1. Preheat the Air fryer to 375 o F and grease an Air fryer basket.
2. Place the flour in a shallow dish and mix remaining ingredients except cod in another shallow dish.
3. Coat each cod fillet into the flour and then dip in the egg mixture.
4. Arrange the cod fillets in the Air fryer basket and cook for about 7 minutes.
5. Dish out and serve warm.

**Nutrition:**
Calories: 462, Fat: 16.9g, Carbohydrates: 51.3g, Sugar: 3.3g, Protein: 24.4g, Sodium: 646mg

## 184. Lemony and Spicy Coconut Crusted Salmon

Preparation Time: 10 minutes
Cooking Time: 6 minutes
Servings: 4

**Ingredients:**

- 1 pound salmon
- ½ cup flour
- 2 egg whites
- ½ cup breadcrumbs
- ½ cup unsweetened coconut, shredded
- ¼ teaspoon lemon zest
- Salt and freshly ground black pepper, to taste
- ¼ teaspoon cayenne pepper
- ¼ teaspoon red pepper flakes, crushed
- Vegetable oil, as required

**Directions:**

1. Preheat the Air fryer to 400 o F and grease an Air fryer basket.
2. Mix the flour, salt and black pepper in a shallow dish.
3. Whisk the egg whites in a second shallow dish.
4. Mix the breadcrumbs, coconut, lime zest, salt and cayenne pepper in a third shallow dish.

5. Coat salmon in the flour, then dip in the egg whites and then into the breadcrumb mixture evenly.

6. Place the salmon in the Air fryer basket and drizzle with vegetable oil.

7. Cook for about 6 minutes and dish out to serve warm.

**Nutrition:**
Calories: 558, Fat: 22.2g, Carbohydrates: 18.6g, Sugar: 8.7g, Protein: 43g, Sodium: 3456mg

## 185. Rice in Crab Shell

Preparation Time: 20 minutes
Cooking Time: 8 minutes
Servings: 2

**Ingredients:**
- 1 bowl cooked rice
- 4 tablespoons crab meat
- 2 tablespoons butter
- 2 tablespoons Parmesan cheese, shredded
- 2 crab shells
- Paprika, to taste

**Directions:**
1. Preheat the Air fryer to 390 o F and grease an Air fryer basket.
2. Mix rice, crab meat, butter and paprika in a bowl.
3. Fill crab shell with rice mixture and top with Parmesan cheese.
4. Arrange the crab shell in the Air fryer basket and cook for about 8 minutes.
5. Sprinkle with more paprika and serve hot.

**Nutrition:**
Calories: 285, Fat: 33g, Carbohydrates: 0g, Sugar: 0g, Protein: 33g, Sodium: 153mg

## 186. Fish Sticks

Preparation Time: 25 minutes
Servings: 4

**Ingredients:**

- 1 lb. cod fillet; cut into 3/4-inch strips
- 1 oz. pork rinds, finely ground
- 1 large egg.
- ¼ cup blanched finely ground almond flour.
- 1 tbsp. coconut oil
- ½ tsp. Old Bay seasoning

**Directions:**
1. Place ground pork rinds, almond flour, Old Bay seasoning and coconut oil into a large bowl and mix together. Take a medium bowl, whisk egg
2. Dip each fish stick into the egg and then gently press into the flour mixture, coating as fully and evenly as possible. Place fish sticks into the air fryer basket
3. Adjust the temperature to 400 Degrees F and set the timer for 10 minutes or until golden. Serve immediately.

**Nutrition: Calories: 205; Protein: 24.4g; Fiber: 0.8g; Fat: 10.7g; Carbs: 1.6g**

## 187. Swordfish Steaks and Tomatoes

Preparation Time: 15 minutes
Servings: 2

**Ingredients:**

- 30 oz. canned tomatoes; chopped.
- 2 1-inch thick swordfish steaks
- 2 tbsp. capers, drained
- 1 tbsp. red vinegar
- 2 tbsp. oregano; chopped.
- A pinch of salt and black pepper

**Directions:**
1. In a pan that fits the air fryer, combine all the ingredients, toss, put the pan in the fryer and cook at 390°F for 10 minutes, flipping the fish halfway
2. Divide the mix between plates and serve

**Nutrition: Calories: 280; Fat: 12g; Fiber: 4g; Carbs: 6g; Protein: 11g**

## 188. Lime Trout and Shallots

Preparation Time: 17 minutes
Servings: 4

**Ingredients:**

- 4 trout fillets; boneless
- 3 garlic cloves; minced
- 6 shallots; chopped.
- ½ cup butter; melted
- ½ cup olive oil
- Juice of 1 lime
- A pinch of salt and black pepper

**Directions:**

1. In a pan that fits the air fryer, combine the fish with the shallots and the rest of the ingredients, toss gently
2. Put the pan in the machine and cook at 390°F for 12 minutes, flipping the fish halfway.
3. Divide between plates and serve with a side salad.

**Nutrition: Calories: 270; Fat: 12g; Fiber: 4g; Carbs: 6g; Protein: 12g**

## 189. Trout and Zucchinis

Preparation Time: 20 minutes
Servings: 4

**Ingredients:**

- 3 zucchinis, cut in medium chunks
- 4 trout fillets; boneless
- ¼ cup tomato sauce
- 1 garlic clove; minced
- ½ cup cilantro; chopped.
- 1 tbsp. lemon juice
- 2 tbsp. olive oil
- Salt and black pepper to taste.

**Directions:**

1. In a pan that fits your air fryer, mix the fish with the other ingredients, toss, introduce in the fryer and cook at 380°F

for 15 minutes. Divide everything between plates and serve right away

**Nutrition: Calories: 220; Fat: 12g; Fiber: 4g; Carbs: 6g; Protein: 9g**

## 190. Butter Trout

Preparation Time: 22 minutes
Servings: 4

**Ingredients:**

- 4 trout fillets; boneless
- Juice of 1 lime
- 1 tbsp. parsley; chopped.
- 1 tbsp. chives; chopped.
- 4 tbsp. butter; melted
- Salt and black pepper to taste.

**Directions:**

1. Mix the fish fillets with the melted butter, salt and pepper, rub gently, put the fish in your air fryer's basket and cook at 390°F for 6 minutes on each side.
2. Divide between plates and serve with lime juice drizzled on top and with parsley and chives sprinkled at the end.

**Nutrition: Calories: 221; Fat: 11g; Fiber: 4g; Carbs: 6g; Protein: 9g**

## 191. Roasted Red Snapper

Preparation Time: 20 minutes
Servings: 4

**Ingredients:**

- 4 red snapper fillets; boneless
- 2 garlic cloves; minced
- 1 tbsp. hot chili paste
- 2 tbsp. olive oil
- 2 tbsp. coconut aminos
- 2 tbsp. lime juice
- A pinch of salt and black pepper

**Directions:**

1. Take a bowl and mix all the ingredients

except the fish and whisk well

2. Rub the fish with this mix, place it in your air fryer's basket and cook at 380°F for 15 minutes

3. Serve with a side salad.

**Nutrition: Calories: 220; Fat: 13g; Fiber: 4g; Carbs: 6g; Protein: 11g**

## 192. Pesto Almond Salmon

Preparation Time: 17 minutes
Servings: 2

**Ingredients:**

- 2: 1 ½-inch-thicksalmon fillets: about 4 oz. each
- ¼ cup sliced almonds, roughly chopped
- ¼ cup pesto
- 2 tbsp. unsalted butter; melted.

**Directions:**

1. In a small bowl, mix pesto and almonds. Set aside. Place fillets into a 6-inch round baking dish

2. Brush each fillet with butter and place half of the pesto mixture on the top of each fillet. Place dish into the air fryer basket. Adjust the temperature to 390 Degrees F and set the timer for 12 minutes

3. Salmon will easily flake when fully cooked and reach an internal temperature of at least 145 Degrees F. Serve warm.

**Nutrition: Calories: 433; Protein: 23.3g; Fiber: 2.4g; Fat: 34.0g; Carbs: 6.1g**

## 193. Shrimp Scampi

Preparation Time: 18 minutes
Servings: 4

**Ingredients:**

- 1 lb. medium peeled and deveined shrimp
- ½ medium lemon.
- ¼ cup heavy whipping cream.
- 1 tbsp. chopped fresh parsley

- 4 tbsp. salted butter
- ¼ tsp. xanthan gum
- ¼ tsp. red pepper flakes
- 1 tsp. minced roasted garlic

**Directions:**

1. In a medium saucepan over medium heat, melt butter. Zest the lemon, then squeeze juice into the pan. Add garlic

2. Pour in the cream, xanthan gum and red pepper flakes. Whisk until the mixture begins to thicken, about 2–3 minutes

3. Place shrimp into a 4-cup round baking dish. Pour the cream sauce over the shrimp and cover with foil. Place the dish into the air fryer basket.

4. Adjust the temperature to 400 Degrees F and set the timer for 8 minutes. Stir twice during cooking. When done, garnish with parsley and serve warm.

**Nutrition: Calories: 240; Protein: 16.7g; Fiber: 0.4g; Fat: 17.0g; Carbs: 2.4g**

## 194. Fish and Salsa

Preparation Time: 20 minutes
Servings: 4

**Ingredients:**

- 4 sea bass fillets; boneless
- 3 garlic cloves; minced
- 3 tomatoes; roughly chopped.
- 2 spring onions; chopped.
- ¼ cup chicken stock
- 1 tbsp. balsamic vinegar
- 1 tbsp. olive oil
- A pinch of salt and black pepper

**Directions:**

1. In a blender, combine all the ingredients except the fish and pulse well.

2. Put the mix in a pan that fits the air fryer, add the fish, toss gently, introduce the pan in the fryer and cook at 380°F for 15 minutes. Divide between plates and serve.

**Nutrition: Calories: 261; Fat: 11g; Fiber: 4g; Carbs: 7g; Protein: 11g**

## 195. Salmon Jerky

Preparation Time: 4 hours 5 minutes
Servings: 4

**Ingredients:**

- 1 lb. salmon, skin and bones removed
- ¼ cup soy sauce
- ½ tsp. ground ginger
- ¼ tsp. red pepper flakes
- ½ tsp. liquid smoke
- ¼ tsp. ground black pepper
- Juice of ½ medium lime

**Directions:**

1. Slice salmon into ¼-inch-thick slices, 4-inch long
2. Place strips into a large storage bag or a covered bowl and add remaining ingredients. Allow to marinate for 2 hours in the refrigerator
3. Place each strip into the air fryer basket in a single layer. Adjust the temperature to 140 Degrees F and set the timer for 4 hours. Cool then store in a sealed container until ready to eat.

**Nutrition: Calories: 108; Protein: 15.1g; Fiber: 0.2g; Fat: 4.1g; Carbs: 1.0g**

## 196. Lemony Flounder Fillets

Preparation Time: 17 minutes
Servings: 2

**Ingredients:**

- 2 flounder fillets; boneless
- 2 garlic cloves; minced
- 2 tbsp. olive oil
- 2 tbsp. lemon juice
- 2 tsp. coconut aminos
- ½ tsp. stevia
- A pinch of salt and black pepper

**Directions:**

1. In a pan that fits your air fryer, mix all the ingredients, toss, introduce in the fryer and cook at 390°F for 12 minutes. Divide into bowls and serve.

**Nutrition: Calories: 251; Fat: 13g; Fiber: 3g; Carbs: 5g; Protein: 10g**

## 197. Garlic Lemon Shrimp

Preparation Time: 11 minutes
Servings: 2

**Ingredients:**

- 8 oz. medium shelled and deveined shrimp
- 1 medium lemon.
- 2 tbsp. unsalted butter; melted.
- ½ tsp. minced garlic
- ½ tsp. Old Bay seasoning

**Directions:**

1. Zest lemon and then cut in half. Place shrimp in a large bowl and squeeze juice from ½ lemon on top of them.
2. Add lemon zest to bowl along with remaining ingredients. Toss shrimp until fully coated
3. Pour bowl contents into 6-inch round baking dish. Place into the air fryer basket.
4. Adjust the temperature to 400 Degrees F and set the timer for 6 minutes. Shrimp will be bright pink when fully cooked. Serve warm with pan sauce.

**Nutrition: Calories: 190; Protein: 16.4g; Fiber: 0.4g; Fat: 11.8g; Carbs: 2.9g**

## 198. Delicious Shrimp recipe

Preparation Time: 17 minutes
Servings: 4

**Ingredients:**

- 1 lb. medium shelled and deveined shrimp
- ¼ cup full-fat mayonnaise
- 2 tbsp. sriracha

- 2 tbsp. salted butter; melted.
- ¼ tsp. powdered erythritol
- ¼ tsp. garlic powder.
- ⅛ tsp. ground black pepper
- ½ tsp. Old Bay seasoning

**Directions:**

1. Take a large bowl, toss shrimp in butter, Old Bay seasoning and garlic powder. Place shrimp into the air fryer basket
2. Adjust the temperature to 400 Degrees F and set the timer for 7 minutes.
3. Flip the shrimp halfway through the cooking time. Shrimp will be bright pink when fully cooked
4. In another large bowl, mix sriracha, powdered erythritol, mayonnaise and pepper.
5. Toss shrimp in the spicy mixture and serve immediately.

**Nutrition: Calories: 143; Protein: 16.4g; Fiber: 0.0g; Fat: 6.4g; Mg; Carbs: 3.0g**

## 199. Air Fried Tuna Salad Bites

Preparation Time: 17 minutes
Servings: 12 bites

**Ingredients:**

- 1: 10-oz.can tuna, drained
- ½ cup blanched finely ground almond flour, divided.
- ¼ cup full-fat mayonnaise
- 1 stalk celery; chopped
- 1 medium avocado; peeled, pitted and mashed
- 2 tsp. coconut oil

**Directions:**

1. Take a large bowl, mix tuna, mayonnaise, celery and mashed avocado. Form the mixture into balls.
2. Roll balls in almond flour and spritz with coconut oil. Place balls into the air fryer basket.
3. Adjust the temperature to 400 Degrees F

and set the timer for 7 minutes.

4. Gently turn tuna bites after 5 minutes. Serve warm.

**Nutrition: Calories: 323; Protein: 17.3g; Fiber: 4.0g; Fat: 25.4g; Carbs: 6.3g**

## 200. Cod Fillets

Preparation Time: 20 minutes
Servings: 4

**Ingredients:**

- 4 cod fillets; boneless
- 1 fennel; sliced
- 2 garlic cloves; minced
- 1 red bell pepper; chopped.
- 2 tbsp. olive oil
- 1 tbsp. thyme; chopped.
- ½ tsp. black peppercorns
- 2 tsp. Italian seasoning
- A pinch of salt and black pepper

**Directions:**

1. Take a bowl and mix the fennel with bell pepper and the other ingredients except the fish fillets and toss.
2. Put this into a pan that fits the air fryer, add the fish on top
3. Introduce the pan in your air fryer and cook at 380°F for 15 minutes. Divide between plates and serve.

**Nutrition: Calories: 241; Fat: 12g; Fiber: 4g; Carbs: 7g; Protein: 11g**

## 201. Tarragon and Parmesan Trout

Preparation Time: 20 minutes
Servings: 4

**Ingredients:**

- 4 trout fillets; boneless
- ¾ cup parmesan; grated
- 2 garlic cloves; minced
- ½ cup chicken stock

- ¼ cup tarragon; chopped.
- 2 tbsp. olive oil
- Salt and black pepper to taste.

**Directions:**

1. In a pan that fits your air fryer, mix all the ingredients except the fish and the parmesan and whisk. Add the fish and grease it well with this mix
2. Sprinkle the parmesan on top, put the pan in the air fryer and cook at 380°F for 15 minutes
3. Divide everything between plates and serve.

**Nutrition: Calories: 271; Fat: 12g; Fiber: 4g; Carbs: 6g; Protein: 11g**

## 202. Crab Dip

Preparation Time: 18 minutes
Servings: 4

**Ingredients:**

- 8 oz. full-fat cream cheese; softened.
- 2: 6-oz.cans lump crabmeat
- ¼ cup chopped pickled jalapeños.
- ¼ cup full-fat sour cream.
- ¼ cup sliced green onion
- ½ cup shredded Cheddar cheese
- ¼ cup full-fat mayonnaise
- 1 tbsp. lemon juice
- ½ tsp. hot sauce

**Directions:**

1. Place all ingredients into a 4-cup round baking dish and stir until fully combined. Place dish into the air fryer basket
2. Adjust the temperature to 400 Degrees F and set the timer for 8 minutes. Dip will be bubbling and hot when done. Serve warm.

**Nutrition: Calories: 441; Protein: 17.8g; Fiber: 0.6g; Fat: 33.8g; Carbs: 8.2g**

## 203. Crab Cakes

Preparation Time: 20 minutes
Servings: 4

**Ingredients:**

- ½ medium green bell pepper; seeded and chopped
- ¼ cup chopped green onion
- 1 large egg.
- 2: 6-oz.cans lump crabmeat
- ¼ cup blanched finely ground almond flour.
- ½ tbsp. lemon juice
- 2 tbsp. full-fat mayonnaise
- ½ tsp. Old Bay seasoning
- ½ tsp. Dijon mustard

**Directions:**

1. Take a large bowl, combine all ingredients. Form into four balls and flatten into patties. Place patties into the air fryer basket
2. Adjust the temperature to 350 Degrees F and set the timer for 10 minutes.
3. Flip patties halfway through the cooking time. Serve warm.

**Nutrition: Calories: 151; Protein: 13.4g; Fiber: 0.9g; Fat: 10.0g; Carbs: 2.3g**

## 204. Buttery Shrimp

Preparation Time: 11 minutes
Servings: 2

**Ingredients:**

- 8 oz. medium shelled and deveined shrimp
- 2 tbsp. salted butter; melted.
- ¼ tsp. onion powder.
- ½ tsp. garlic powder.
- ½ tsp. Old Bay seasoning
- 1 tsp. paprika

**Directions:**

1. Toss all ingredients together in a large bowl. Place shrimp into the air fryer

basket.

2. Adjust the temperature to 400 Degrees F and set the timer for 6 minutes. Turn the shrimp halfway through the cooking time to ensure even cooking. Serve immediately.

**Nutrition: Calories: 192; Protein: 16.6g; Fiber: 0.5g; Fat: 11.9g; Carbs: 2.5g**

## 205. Lime Baked Salmon

Preparation Time: 22 minutes
Servings: 2

**Ingredients:**

- 2: 3-oz.salmon fillets, skin removed
- ¼ cup sliced pickled jalapeños
- ½ medium lime, juiced
- 2 tbsp. chopped cilantro
- 1 tbsp. salted butter; melted.
- ½ tsp. finely minced garlic
- 1 tsp. chili powder

**Directions:**

1. Place salmon fillets into a 6-inch round baking pan. Brush each with butter and sprinkle with chili powder and garlic
2. Place jalapeño slices on top and around salmon. Pour half of the lime juice over the salmon and cover with foil. Place pan into the air fryer basket. Adjust the temperature to 370 Degrees F and set the timer for 12 minutes
3. When fully cooked, salmon should flake easily with a fork and reach an internal temperature of at least 145 Degrees F.
4. To serve, spritz with remaining lime juice and garnish with cilantro.

**Nutrition: Calories: 167; Protein: 15.8g; Fiber: 0.7g; Fat: 9.9g; Carbs: 1.6g**

## 206. Black Sea Bass with Rosemary Vinaigrette

Preparation Time: 17 minutes

Servings: 4

**Ingredients:**

- 4 black sea bass fillets; boneless and skin scored
- 3 garlic cloves; minced
- 2 tbsp. olive oil
- 1 tbsp. rosemary; chopped.
- 3 tbsp. black olives, pitted and chopped.
- A pinch of salt and black pepper
- Juice of 1 lime

**Directions:**

1. Take a bowl and mix the oil with the olives and the rest of the ingredients except the fish and whisk well.
2. Place the fish in a pan that fits the air fryer, spread the rosemary vinaigrette all over.
3. Put the pan in the machine and cook at 380°F for 12 minutes, flipping the fish halfway. Divide between plates and serve

**Nutrition: Calories: 220; Fat: 12g; Fiber: 4g; Carbs: 6g; Protein: 10g**

## 207. Tuna Zoodle Casserole

Preparation Time: 30 minutes
Servings: 4

**Ingredients:**

- 1 oz. pork rinds, finely ground
- 2 medium zucchini, spiralized
- 2: 5-oz.cans albacore tuna
- ¼ cup diced white onion
- ¼ cup chopped white mushrooms
- 2 stalks celery, finely chopped
- ½ cup heavy cream
- ½ cup vegetable broth
- 2 tbsp. full-fat mayonnaise
- 2 tbsp. salted butter
- ½ tsp. red pepper flakes
- ¼ tsp. xanthan gum

**Directions:**

1. In a large saucepan over medium heat, melt butter. Add onion, mushrooms and celery and sauté until fragrant, about 3–5 minutes.

2. Pour in heavy cream, vegetable broth, mayonnaise and xanthan gum. Reduce heat and continue cooking an additional 3 minutes, until the mixture begins to thicken

3. Add red pepper flakes, zucchini and tuna. Turn off heat and stir until zucchini noodles are coated

4. Pour into 4-cup round baking dish. Top with ground pork rinds and cover the top of the dish with foil. Place into the air fryer basket. Adjust the temperature to 370 Degrees F and set the timer for 15 minutes.

5. When 3 minutes remain, remove the foil to brown the top of the casserole. Serve warm.

**Nutrition: Calories: 339; Protein: 19.7g; Fiber: 1.8g; Fat: 25.1g; Carbs: 6.1g**

## 208. Spicy Avocado Cod

Preparation Time: 20 minutes

- Servings: 2

**Ingredients:**

- 1 medium avocado; peeled, pitted and sliced
- ¼ cup chopped pickled jalapeños.
- 2: 3-oz.cod fillets
- ½ medium lime
- 1 cup shredded cabbage
- ¼ cup full-fat sour cream.
- 2 tbsp. full-fat mayonnaise
- ½ tsp. paprika
- ¼ tsp. garlic powder.
- 1 tsp. chili powder
- 1 tsp. cumin

**Directions:**

1. Take a large bowl, place cabbage, sour cream, mayonnaise and jalapeños. Mix until fully coated. Let sit for 20 minutes in the refrigerator

2. Sprinkle cod fillets with chili powder, cumin, paprika and garlic powder. Place each fillet into the air fryer basket. Adjust the temperature to 370 Degrees F and set the timer for 10 minutes.

3. Flip the fillets halfway through the cooking time. When fully cooked, fish should have an internal temperature of at least 145 Degrees F

4. To serve, divide slaw mixture into two serving bowls, break cod fillets into pieces and spread over the bowls and top with avocado. Squeeze lime juice over each bowl. Serve immediately.

**Nutrition: Calories: 342; Protein: 16.1g; Fiber: 6.4g; Fat: 25.2g; Carbs: 11.7g**

## 209. Air-Fried Crab Sticks

Servings: 2-3

**Ingredients:**

- Crab sticks: 1 package
- Cooking oil spray: as needed

**Directions:**

1. Take each of the sticks out of the package and unroll until flat. Tear the sheets into thirds.

2. Arrange them on a plate and lightly spritz using cooking spray. Set the timer for 10 minutes.

3. Note: If you shred the crab meat; you can cut the time in half, but they will also easily fall through the holes in the basket.

## 210. Breaded Cod Sticks

Servings: 5

**Ingredients:**

- Milk: 3 tbsp.
- Large eggs: 2

- Breadcrumbs: 2 cups
- Salt: .25 tsp.
- Black pepper: .5 tsp.
- Almond flour: 1 cup
- Cod: 1 lb.

**Directions:**
1. Set the Air Fryer at 350° Fahrenheit.
2. Prepare three bowls; 1 with the milk and eggs; 1 with the pepper, salt, and breadcrumbs; and another with almond flour.
3. Dip the sticks in the flour, egg mixture, and lastly - the breadcrumbs.
4. Arrange in the basket and set the timer for 12 minutes – shaking halfway through the cooking process.
5. Serve with your favorite sauce.

## 211. Breaded Fried Shrimp

Servings: 4

**Ingredients:**
- Raw shrimp: 1 lb.
- Egg white: 3 tbsp. or 1 egg
- All-purpose flour: .5 cup
- Panko breadcrumbs: .75 cup
- Paprika: 1 tsp.
- Pepper & salt: as desired
- McCormick's Grill Mates Montreal Chicken Seasoning
- Cooking oil spray: as needed

*Ingredients - The Sauce:*
- Sriracha: 2 tbsp.
- Plain non-fat Greek yogurt: .33 cup
- Sweet chili sauce: .25 cup

**Directions:**
1. Peel and devein the shrimp.
2. Set the temperature of the Air Fryer to 400° Fahrenheit.
3. Add the seasonings to the shrimp.
4. Use three bowls for the breadcrumbs, egg whites, and flour.

5. Dip the shrimp into the flour, the egg, and the breadcrumbs.
6. Lightly spritz the shrimp with the cooking spray and add to the fryer basket for four minutes.
7. Flip the shrimp and continue cooking for another four minutes.
8. Combine all of the fixings for the sauce and toss with the shrimp before serving.

## 212. Cajun Salmon

Servings: 1-2

**Ingredients:**
- Salmon fillet – ¾-inch thick: 1)
- Juice of ¼ lemon
- For Breading: Cajun seasoning for coating
- Optional: Sprinkle of sugar

**Directions:**
1. Warm the Air Fryer to 356° Fahrenheit : approx. 5 min.).
2. Rinse and pat the salmon dry. Thoroughly coat the fish with the coating mix.
3. Arrange the fillet in the fryer basket and set the timer for seven minutes with the skin side facing upward.
4. Serve with a drizzle of lemon.

## 213. Cajun Shrimp

Servings: 4-6

**Ingredients:**
- Olive oil: 1 tbsp.
- Old Bay seasoning: .5 tsp.
- Tiger shrimp: 1.25 lb. or 16-20
- Smoked paprika: .25 tsp.
- Cayenne pepper: .25 tsp.
- Salt: 1 pinch

**Directions:**
1. Heat the Air Fryer to reach 390° Fahrenheit.
2. Coat the shrimp using the oil and spices.

3. Place the shrimp in the fryer basket and set the timer for five minutes.
4. Serve with your favorite side dish.

## 214. Coconut Shrimp

Servings: 3

**Ingredients:**

- Coconut – unsweetened & dried: 1 cup
- Gluten-free breadcrumbs: 1 cup
- Shrimp: 12 large
- Gluten-free flour: 1 cup
- Egg white: 1 cup
- Cornstarch: 1 tbsp.

**Directions:**

1. Set the Air Fryer to 350º Fahrenheit.
2. Select a shallow platter and combine coconut and the breadcrumbs.
3. In another bowl, mix the flour and cornstarch. Break the egg into a small bowl.
4. Coat the shrimp with the egg white, flour, and lastly the breadcrumbs.
5. Place in the fryer basket and fry for 10 minutes.
6. Serve with your favorite sides or as a quick snack.

## 215. Creamy Salmon

Servings: 2

**Ingredients:**

- Salmon: .75 lb. - 6 pieces
- Salt: 1 pinch
- Olive oil: 1 tbsp.
- Chopped dill: 1 tbsp.
- Sour cream: 3 tbsp.
- Plain yogurt: 1.75 oz.

**Directions:**

1. Program the temperature setting on the Air Fryer to 285º Fahrenheit.
2. Pour oil into the fryer basket. Shake the

salt over the salmon and add it to the fryer basket. Air fry for 10 minutes.
3. Whisk the yogurt, dill, and salt.
4. Serve the salmon with the sauce and your favorite sides.

## 216. Crispy Halibut

Servings: 4

**Ingredients:**

- Halibut fillets: 4
- Fresh chives: .25 cup
- Fresh parsley: .5 cup
- Fresh dill: .25 cup
- Black pepper & sea salt: to your liking
- Pork rinds: .75 cup
- Extra-virgin olive oil: 1 tbsp.
- Finely grated lemon zest: 1 tbsp.

**Directions:**

1. Warm the Air Fryer to reach 390º Fahrenheit.
2. Chop the chives, dill, and parsley. Combine all of the dry fixings – parsley, pork rinds, chives, dill, lemon zest, black pepper, sea salt, and olive oil.
3. Rinse the halibut well and let them drain well on paper towels.
4. Prepare a baking tin to fit in the cooker. Spoon the rinds over the fish and press in.
5. Add the prepared fillets in the fryer for 30 minutes.

## 217. Dill Salmon

Servings: 4

**Ingredients:**

- Salmon: 4 - 6-oz. pieces or 1.5 lb.
- Salt: 1 pinch
- Olive oil: 2 tsp.

*Ingredients - The Sauce:*

- Sour cream: .5 cup
- Non-fat Greek yogurt: .5 cup

- Dill: 2 finely chopped tbsp.
- Salt: 1 pinch

**Directions:**

1. Preheat the Air Fryer prior to baking time: 270° Fahrenheit).
2. Chop the salmon into the four portions. Drizzle with about half of the oil: 1 tsp.). Flavor with a pinch of salt and add to the basket for about 20-23 minutes.
3. Lastly, blend the yogurt, salt, sour cream, and dill in a mixing container. Pour the sauce over the cooked salmon with a pinch of chopped dill.

## 218. E-Z Catfish

Servings: 3

**Ingredients:**

- Olive oil: 1 tbsp.
- Seasoned fish fry: .25 cup
- Catfish fillets: 4

**Directions:**

1. Prepare the fryer to 400° Fahrenheit.
2. First, rinse the fish, and pat dry with a paper towel.
3. Dump the seasoning into a large zip-type baggie. Add the fish and shake to cover each fillet. Spray with a spritz of cooking oil spray. Add to the basket.
4. Set the timer for ten minutes. Flip, and reset the timer for ten more minutes. Flip once more and cook for two to three minutes.
5. Once it reaches the desired crispiness, transfer to a plate to serve.

## 219. Fish & Chips

Servings: 4

**Ingredients:**

- Catfish fillets or similar fish: 2
- Wholemeal bread for breadcrumbs: 3 slices

- Medium beaten egg: 1
- Bag tortilla chips: 0.88 oz. or approximately/25g
- Juice and rind of 1 lemon
- Pepper and salt
- Parsley: 1 tbsp.

**Directions:**

1. Warm the fryer before baking time to reach 356° Fahrenheit.
2. Zest and juice the lemon.
3. Slice the fillets into four pieces ready for cooking. Season each one with the lemon juice and set aside for a few minutes.
4. Use a food processor to mix the tortillas, parsley, pepper, breadcrumbs, and lemon zest.
5. Whisk the egg and egg wash the fish. Run it through the crumb mixture. Place them onto the baking tray and cook until crispy.
6. Preparation time is ten minutes with a total cooking time of fifteen minutes; so, wait patiently to enjoy.

## 220. Fish Nuggets

Servings: 4

**Ingredients:**

- Cod fillet: 1 lb.
- Eggs: 3
- Olive oil: 4 tbsp.
- Almond flour: 1 cup
- Gluten-free breadcrumbs: 1 cup
- Salt: 1 tsp.

**Directions:**

1. Set the temperature of the Air Fryer at 390° Fahrenheit.
2. Cut the cod into nuggets.
3. Prepare three dishes. Beat the eggs in one. Combine the salt, oil, and breadcrumbs in another. The last one will be almond flour.
4. Cover each of the nuggets using the flour, a dip in the eggs, and the breadcrumbs.

5. Arrange the prepared nuggets in the basket and set the timer for 20 minutes. Serve.

## 221. Fish Tacos

Servings: 6

**Ingredients:**

- Tempura batter: 1 cupmade from:
- Flour: 1 cup
- Cornstarch: 1 tbsp.
- Salt & pepper: 1 pinch each
- Cold seltzer water: .5 cup
- Salsa: .5 cup
- Coleslaw: 1 cup
- White pepper: 1 tsp.
- Chopped cilantro: 2 tbsp.
- Guacamole: .5 cup
- Lemon wedges: 1

**Directions:**

1. Prep the tempura batter using the salt, pepper. cornstarch, and flour.
2. Slice the cod into two-ounce pieces: 6 piecesand sprinkle using the salt and pepper.
3. Use the batterto coat the cod. Dredge them in the panko.
4. Use the French fry setting and set the timer for ten minutes. Turn after five minutes.
5. Top each portion with coleslaw, salsa, guacamole, cilantro, or lemon juice.

## 222. Ginger Cod Steaks

Servings: 2

**Ingredients:**

- Large cod steaks: 2 slices
- Turmeric powder: .25 tsp.
- Ginger powder: .5 tsp.
- Garlic powder: .5 tsp.
- Salt & pepper: 1 pinch

- Plum sauce: 1 tbsp.
- Ginger slices: as desired
- Kentucky Kernel Seasoned Flour: +Corn flour: 1 part of each

**Directions:**

1. Dry off the steaks and marinate using the pepper, salt, ginger powder, and turmeric powder for a few minutes.
2. Lightly coat the steaks with the corn flour/Kentucky mix.
3. Set the temperature in the fryer to 356° Fahrenheit for 15 minutes and increase to 400° Fahrenheit for 5 minutes.: Time may vary depending on the size of the cod.
4. Prepare the sauce in a wok. Brown the ginger slices and remove from the heat. Stir in the plum sauce adding water to thin as needed.
5. Serve the steaks with a drizzle of the prepared sauce.

## 223. Grilled Shrimp

Servings: 4

**Ingredients:**

- Medium shrimp/prawns: 8
- Melted butter: 1 tbsp.
- Rosemary: 1 sprig
- Pepper and salt: as desired
- Minced garlic cloves: 3

**Directions:**

1. Combine all of the fixings in a mixing bowl. Toss well and arrange in the fryer basket.
2. Set the timer for 7 minutes: 356° Fahrenheitand serve.

## 224. Honey & Sriracha Tossed Calamari

Servings: 1-2

**Ingredients:**

- Calamari tubes - tentacles if you prefer: .5 lb.

- Club soda: 1 cup
- Four: 1 cup
- Salt - red pepper & black pepper: 2 dashes each
- Honey: .5 cup + 1-2 tbsp. Sriracha
- Red pepper flakes: 2 shakes

**Directions:**

1. Fully rinse the calamari and blot it dry using a bunch of paper towels. Slice into rings: .25-inch wide). Toss the rings into a bowl. Pour in the club soda and stir until all are submerged. Wait for about 10 minutes.
2. Sift the salt, flour, red & black pepper. Set aside for now.
3. Dredge the calamari into the flour mixture and set on a platter until ready to fry.
4. Spritz the basket of the Air Fryer with a small amount of cooking oil spray. Arrange the calamari in the basket, careful not to crowd it too much.
5. Set the temperature at 375° Fahrenheit and the timer for 11 minutes.
6. Shake the basket twice during the cooking process, loosening any rings that may stick.
7. Remove from the basket, toss with the sauce, and return to the fryer for two more minutes.
8. Serve with additional sauce as desired.
9. Make the sauce by combining honey, sriracha, and red pepper flakes in a small bowl, mix until fully combined.

## 225. Lemon Fish

Servings: 4

**Ingredients:**

- Water: .5 cup + 3 tbsp.
- Sugar: .25 cup
- Juice of 1 lemon
- Green chili sauce: 2 tsp.
- Salt: to your liking

- Egg white: 1
- Corn flour slurry: 4 tsp.
- Red chili sauce: 1 tsp.
- Lettuce: 2-3 leaves
- Catfish: 2 - cut into 4 pieces
- Oil: 2 tsp.

**Directions:**

1. Boil the water and sugar in a saucepan. Slice the lemon and place it in a dish.
2. Add the egg white, oil, chili sauce, salt, and flour in a bowl, mixing well. Add three tablespoons of water and whisk to make a smooth slurry batter.
3. Sprinkle flour onto a plate. Dip in the batter and then the flour.
4. Lightly grease the Air Fryer basket with a spritz of cooking oil spray and heat to reach 356° Fahrenheit.
5. Arrange the fillets in the basket and cook for 15 to 20 minutes until crispy.
6. Add salt to the pan and stir well. Add the corn flour slurry and mix it again. Blend in the red sauce juice, and lemon slices, mixing well and cooking until thickened.
7. Remove the fish from the basket, brush with a spritz of oil, and place back into the pan. Cook for about five additional minutes.
8. Tear the leaves apart to make a serving bed. Add the fish and pour the lemon sauce over the top of the fish. Serve.

## 226. Oregano Clams

Servings: 4

**Ingredients:**

- Shucked clams: 2 dozen
- Dried oregano: 1 tsp.
- Chopped parsley: .25 cup
- Grated parmesan cheese: .25 cup
- Unseasoned breadcrumbs: 1 cup
- Melted butter: 4 tbsp.
- Minced garlic cloves: 3

- For the Pan: Sea salt: 1 cup

**Directions:**

1. Warm up the Air Fryer a few minutes at 400° Fahrenheit.
2. Mince the garlic and combine with the breadcrumbs, oregano, parsley, parmesan cheese, and melted butter in a medium mixing bowl.
3. Using a heaping tablespoon of the crumb mixture, add it to the clams.
4. Fill the insert with salt, arrange the clams inside, and air fry for three minutes.
5. Garnish with fresh parsley and lemon wedges.

## 227. Salmon Croquettes

Servings: 4

**Ingredients:**

- Red salmon: 1 lb. can
- Breadcrumbs: 1 cup
- Vegetable oil: .33 cup
- Chopped parsley: half of 1 bunch
- Eggs: 2

**Directions:**

1. Set the Air Fryer at 392° Fahrenheit.
2. Drain and mash the salmon. Whisk and add the eggs and parsley.
3. In another dish, mix the breadcrumbs and oil.
4. Prepare 16 croquettes using the breadcrumb mixture.
5. Arrange in the preheated fryer basket for seven minutes.
6. Serve.

## 228. Salmon Patties

Servings: 6-8

**Ingredients:**

- Salmon fillet: 1 portion - approx. 7 oz.
- Russet potatoes: 3 large - approx. 14 oz.
- Frozen veggies: .33 cup
- Dill sprinkles: 2 pinches
- Salt and pepper: 1 dash each
- Egg: 1

**Ingredients - The Coating:**

- Breadcrumbs
- Olive oil spray

**Preparation Steps:**

1. Warm the Air Fryer to reach 356° Fahrenheit.
2. Peel and chop the potatoes into small bits. Boil for about ten minutes.
3. Mash and place in the refrigerator to cool.
4. Grill the salmon for five minutes. Flake it apart and set it aside for now.
5. Combine all of the fixings and shape into patties. Evenly coat with the breadcrumbs, and spray with a bit of olive oil spray.
6. Place in the fryer for 10-12 minutes.

## 229. Shrimp Scampi

Servings: 4
Ingredients:

- Butter: 4 tbsp.
- Minced garlic: 1 tbsp.
- Dried chives: 1 tsp.or Chopped chives: 1 tbsp.
- Red pepper flakes: 2 tsp.
- Dried: 1 tsp.or Minced basil leaves plus more for sprinkling: 1 tbsp.
- Lemon juice: 1 tbsp.
- Chicken stock or white wine: 2 tbsp.
- Defrosted shrimp: 1 lb. or about 21-25 count
- Also Needed: 6x3 metal pan & silicone mitts

**Directions:**

1. Set the Air Fryer at 330° Fahrenheit. Warm the pan at the same time.
2. Add the garlic, pepper flakes, and butter to the hot pan. Sauté for two minutes,

stirring once to infuse the garlic.

3. Open the Air Fryer, stirring gently.
4. Set the timer for 5 minutes, stirring once.
5. At this point, the butter should be melted.
6. Remove the pan with oven mitts. The shrimp will continue cooking, but let it sit on the countertop to cool.
7. Stir well and dust with a layer of freshly chopped basil leaves.

## 230. Teriyaki Glazed Halibut Steak

Servings: 3

**Ingredients:**
- Halibut steak: 1 lb.

*Ingredients - The Marinade:*
- Low-sodium soy sauce: .66 cup
- Mirin Japanese cooking wine: .5 cup
- Sugar: .25 cup
- Orange juice: .25 cup
- Lime juice: 2 tbsp.
- Ground ginger: .25 tsp.
- Crushed red pepper flakes: .25 tsp.
- Smashed garlic: 1 clove

**Directions:**
1. Warm the Air Fryer at 390° Fahrenheit.
2. Mix all of the marinade fixings in a saucepan, bringing it to a boil. Lower the heat setting to medium and cool.
3. Pour half of the marinade in a plastic bag with the halibut and zip it closed. Marinate in the refrigerator for about 30 minutes.
4. Air fry the halibut for 10-12 minutes. Brush using the remaining glaze over the steak.
5. Serve with a bed of rice. Add a little basil or mint or basil for extra flavoring.

## 231. Tomato & Basil Scallops

Servings: 2

**Ingredients:**

- Jumbo sea scallops: 8
- Frozen spinach: 12 oz.
- Vegetable oil to spray: as needed
- Tomato paste: 1 tbsp.
- Heavy whipping cream: .75 cup
- Chopped fresh basil: 1 tbsp.
- Minced garlic: 1 tsp.
- Black pepper & salt: .5 tsp. each
- Additional salt and pepper - to season scallops
- Also Needed: 7-inch heat-proof pan

**Directions:**
1. Thaw and drain the spinach.
2. Spray the pan. Scoop a layer of spinach in the pan.
3. Spray both sides of the scallops with vegetable oil. Dust with pepper and salt. Arrange the scallops in the pan on top of the spinach.
4. Combine the basil, garlic, cream, tomato paste, salt, and pepper. Pour the mixture over the spinach and scallops.
5. Set the Air Fryer at 350° Fahrenheit for 10 minutes until the scallops are cooked thoroughly. The sauce will also be bubbling.
6. Serve immediately.

## 232. Salmon Fillets and Pineapple Mix

Preparation Time: 15 minutes
Servings: 2

**Ingredients:**
- 20 oz. canned pineapple pieces
- 2 tsp. garlic powder
- 1 tbsp. balsamic vinegar
- 2 medium salmon fillets; boneless
- 1/2 tsp. ginger; grated
- A drizzle of olive oil
- Salt and black pepper to taste

**Directions:**
1. Grease a pan that fits your air fryer with

the oil and add the fish inside.

2. Add the remaining ingredients and place the pan in the air fryer.

3. Cook at 350°F for 10 minutes. Divide between plates and serve

## 233. Herbed Tuna

Preparation Time: 18 minutes
Servings: 4

**Ingredients:**

- 1/2 cup cilantro; chopped.
- 1/3 cup olive oil
- 1 jalapeno pepper; chopped.
- 2 tbsp. parsley; chopped.
- 2 tbsp. basil; chopped.
- 1 tsp. red pepper flakes
- 1 tsp. thyme; chopped.
- 4 sushi tuna steaks
- 3 garlic cloves; minced
- 1 small red onion; chopped.
- 3 tbsp. balsamic vinegar
- Salt and black pepper to taste

**Directions:**

1. Place all ingredients except the fish into a bowl and stir well.

2. Add the fish and toss, coating it well

3. Transfer everything to your air fryer and cook at 360°F for 4 minutes on each side. Divide the fish between plates and serve

## 234. Shrimp and Tomatoes

Preparation Time: 25 minutes
Servings: 4

**Ingredients:**

- 2 lbs. shrimp; peeled and deveined
- 1 lb. tomatoes; peeled and chopped
- 4 onions; chopped.
- 1 tsp. coriander; ground
- Juice of 1 lemon

- 1/4 cup veggie stock
- 4 tbsp. olive oil
- Salt and black pepper to taste

**Directions:**

1. In a pan that fits your air fryer, mix all the ingredients well

2. Place the pan in the fryer and cook at 360°F for 15 minutes. Divide into bowls and serve; enjoy!

## 235. Peas and Cod Fillets

Preparation Time: 20 Minutes
Servings: 4

**Ingredients:**

- 4 cod fillets; boneless
- 2 cups peas
- 1/2 tsp. oregano; dried
- 1/2 tsp. sweet paprika
- 2 tbsp. parsley; chopped
- 4 tbsp. wine
- 2 garlic cloves; minced
- Salt and pepper to the taste

**Directions:**

1. In your food processor mix garlic with parsley, salt, pepper, oregano, paprika and wine and blend well.

2. Rub fish with half of this mix, place in your air fryer and cook at 360°F, for 10 minutes

3. Meanwhile; put peas in a pot, add water to cover, add salt, bring to a boil over medium high heat, cook for 10 minutes; drain and divide among plates. Also divide fish on plates, spread the rest of the herb dressing all over and serve

## 236. Awesome Shrimp Mix

Preparation Time: 20 minutes
Servings: 4

**Ingredients:**

- 18 oz. shrimp; peeled and deveined
- 2 green chilies; minced
- 1 tbsp. olive oil
- 1 tsp. turmeric powder
- 2 onions; chopped.
- 4 oz. curd; beaten
- 1-inch ginger; chopped.
- 1/2 tbsp. mustard seeds
- Salt and black pepper to taste

**Directions:**
1. In a pan that fits your air fryer, place and mix all the ingredients.
2. Place the pan in the fryer and cook at 380°F for 10 minutes. Divide into bowls and serve

## 237. Pea Pods and Shrimp Mix

Preparation Time: 18 minutes
Servings: 4

**Ingredients:**
- 1 lb. shrimp; peeled and deveined
- 3/4 cup pineapple juice
- 2 tbsp. soy sauce
- 1/2 lb. pea pods
- 3 tbsp. sugar
- 3 tbsp. balsamic vinegar

**Directions:**
1. In a pan that fits your air fryer, mix all the ingredients.
2. Place the pan in the fryer and cook at 380°F for 8 minutes. Divide into bowls and serve

## 238. Halibut and Sun Dried Tomatoes

Preparation Time: 20 Minutes
Servings: 2

**Ingredients:**
- 2 medium halibut fillets
- 2 garlic cloves; minced

- 9 black olives; pitted and sliced
- 6 sun dried tomatoes; chopped
- 2 small red onions; sliced
- 1 fennel bulb; sliced
- 4 rosemary springs; chopped
- 1/2 tsp. red pepper flakes; crushed
- 2 tsp. olive oil
- Salt and black pepper to the taste

**Directions:**
1. Season fish with salt, pepper, rub with garlic and oil and put in a heat proof dish that fits your air fryer.
2. Add onion slices, sun dried tomatoes, fennel, olives, rosemary and sprinkle pepper flakes, transfer to your air fryer and cook at 380°F, for 10 minutes. Divide fish and veggies on plates and serve

## 239. Baked Cod

Preparation Time: 18 minutes
Servings: 4

**Ingredients:**
- 4 cod fillets; boneless
- 3/4 tsp. sweet paprika
- 1/2 tsp. oregano; dried
- 1/2 tsp. thyme; dried
- 1/2 tsp. basil; dried
- 2 tbsp. parsley; chopped.
- 2 tbsp. butter; melted
- A drizzle of olive oil
- Juice of 1 lemon
- Salt and black pepper to taste

**Directions:**
1. Add all ingredients to a bowl and toss gently.
2. Transfer the fish to your air fryer and cook at 380°F for 6 minutes on each side. Serve right away

## 240. Simple Lime Salmon

Preparation Time: 17 minutes
Servings: 5

**Ingredients:**

- 1/2 cup butter; melted
- 1/2 cup olive oil
- 2 salmon fillets; boneless
- 1 lime; sliced
- 6 green onions; chopped.
- 3 garlic cloves; minced
- 2 shallots; chopped.
- Juice of 1 lime
- Salt and black pepper to taste

**Directions:**

1. In a bowl, mix the salmon with the lime juice, butter, oil, garlic, shallots, salt, pepper and the green onions; rub well
2. Transfer the fish to your air fryer, top with the lime slices and cook at 380°F for 6 minutes on each side. Serve with a side salad.

## 241. Sea Bass Paella

Preparation Time: 35 minutes
Servings: 4

**Ingredients:**

- 1 lb. sea bass fillets; cubed
- 1 red bell pepper; deseeded and chopped.
- 6 scallops
- 8 shrimp; peeled and deveined
- 5 oz. wild rice
- 2 oz. peas
- 14 oz. dry white wine
- 3½ oz. chicken stock
- A drizzle of olive oil
- Salt and black pepper to taste

**Directions:**

1. In a heatproof dish that fits your air fryer, place all the ingredients and toss
2. Place the dish in your air fryer and cook at 380°F and cook for 25 minutes, stirring

halfway. Divide between plates and serve.

## 242. Spicy Cod

Preparation Time: 15 minutes
Servings: 4

**Ingredients:**

- 4 cod fillets; boneless
- 2 tbsp. assorted chili peppers
- 1 lemon; sliced
- Juice of 1 lemon
- Salt and black pepper to taste

**Directions:**

1. In your air fryer, mix the cod with the chili pepper, lemon juice, salt and pepper
2. Arrange the lemon slices on top and cook at 360°F for 10 minutes. Divide the fillets between plates and serve.

## 243. Cilantro Trout Fillets

Preparation Time: 18 minutes
Servings: 4

**Ingredients:**

- 4 trout fillets; boneless
- 4 garlic cloves; minced
- 1 cup black olives; pitted and chopped.
- 1 tbsp. olive oil
- 3 tbsp. cilantro; chopped.

**Directions:**

1. Add all of the ingredients to your air fryer and mix well
2. Cook at 360°F for 6 minutes on each side. Divide everything between plates and serve.

## 244. Snapper Fillets

Preparation Time: 20 minutes
Servings: 4

**Ingredients:**

- 4 medium snapper fillets; boneless

- 8 garlic cloves; minced
- 1/3 cup olive oil
- 1 tbsp. lemon zest
- 1½ tbsp. green olives; pitted and sliced
- Juice of 2 limes
- Salt and black pepper to taste

**Directions:**
1. Add all the ingredients except the fish to a baking dish that fits your air fryer; mix well.
2. Add the fish and toss gently, then place in the fryer
3. Cook at 360°F for 15 minutes. Divide everything between plates and serve

## 245. Salmon and Jasmine Rice

Preparation Time: 35 minutes
Servings: 2

**Ingredients:**
- 2 wild salmon fillets; boneless
- 1/2 cup jasmine rice
- 1 tbsp. butter; melted
- 1/4 tsp. saffron
- 1 cup chicken stock
- Salt and black pepper to taste

**Directions:**
1. Add all ingredients except the fish to a pan that fits your air fryer; toss well
2. Place the pain in the air fryer and cook at 360°F for 15 minutes
3. Add the fish, cover and cook at 360°F for 12 minutes more. Divide everything between plates and serve right away.

## 246. Mussels and Shrimp

Preparation Time: 25 minutes
Servings: 4

**Ingredients:**
- 1½ lbs. large shrimp; peeled and deveined
- 20 oz. canned tomatoes; chopped.

- 1/2 cup parsley; chopped.
- 1/2 tsp. marjoram; dried
- 1 tbsp. basil; dried
- 8 oz. clam juice
- 12 mussels
- 2 tbsp. butter; melted
- 2 yellow onions; chopped.
- 3 garlic cloves; minced
- Salt and black pepper to taste

**Directions:**
1. Place all the ingredients in a pan that fits your air fryer; toss well
2. Put the pan into the fryer and cook at 380°F for 15 minutes. Divide into bowls and serve right away.

## 247. Fried Salmon

Preparation Time: 22 minutes
Servings: 4

**Ingredients:**
- 4 salmon fillets; boneless
- 1 white onion; chopped.
- 3 tbsp. olive oil
- 3 tomatoes; sliced
- 4 thyme sprigs; chopped.
- 4 cilantro sprigs; chopped.
- 1 lemon; sliced
- Salt and black pepper to taste

**Directions:**
1. In your air fryer, mix the salmon with the oil, onions, tomatoes, thyme, cilantro, salt and pepper
2. Top with the lemon slices and cook at 360°F for 12 minutes. Divide everything between plates and serve.

## 248. Trout Bites

Preparation Time: 18 minutes
Servings: 4

**Ingredients:**

- 1 lb. trout fillets; boneless and cut into cubes
- 1 sweet onion; chopped.
- 2 celery stalks; sliced
- 1 garlic clove; crushed
- 1 shallot; sliced
- 1/3 cup sake
- 1/3 cup mirin
- 1/4 cup miso
- 1-inch ginger piece; chopped
- 1 tsp. mustard
- 1 tsp. sugar
- 1 tbsp. rice vinegar

**Directions:**

1. Add all ingredients to a pan that fits your air fryer and toss
2. Place the pan in the fryer and cook at 370°F for 12 minutes. Divide into bowls and serve.

## 249. Shrimp and Spaghetti

Preparation Time: 20 minutes
Servings: 4

**Ingredients:**

- 1 lb. shrimp; cooked, peeled and deveined
- 10 oz. canned tomatoes; chopped.
- 1 cup parmesan cheese; grated
- 2 tbsp. olive oil
- 1/4 tsp. oregano; dried
- 12 oz. spaghetti; cooked
- 1 garlic clove; minced
- 1 tbsp. parsley; finely chopped.

**Directions:**

1. In a pan that fits your air fryer, add the shrimp with the oil, garlic, tomatoes, oregano and parsley; toss well.
2. Place the pan in the fryer and cook at 380°F for 10 minutes
3. Add the spaghetti and the parmesan; toss

well. Divide between plates, serve and enjoy!

## 250. Hawaiian Salmon Recipe

Preparation Time: 20 Minutes
Servings: 2

**Ingredients:**

- 20-ounce canned pineapple pieces and juice
- 2 medium salmon fillets; boneless
- 1/2 tsp. ginger; grated
- 2 tsp. garlic powder
- 1 tsp. onion powder
- 1 tbsp. balsamic vinegar
- Salt and black pepper to the taste

**Directions:**

1. Season salmon with garlic powder, onion powder, salt and black pepper, rub well, transfer to a heat proof dish that fits your air fryer, add ginger and pineapple chunks and toss them really gently
2. Drizzle the vinegar all over, put in your air fryer and cook at 350°F, for 10 minutes. Divide everything on plates and serve

## 251. Easy Trout

Preparation Time: 25 minutes
Servings: 4

**Ingredients:**

- 4 whole trout
- 3 oz. breadcrumbs
- 1 tbsp. chives; chopped.
- 1 tbsp. olive oil
- 1 egg; whisked
- 1 tbsp. butter
- Juice of 1 lemon
- Salt and black pepper to taste

**Directions:**

1. In a bowl, combine the breadcrumbs,

lemon juice, salt, pepper, egg and chives; stir very well.

2. Coat the trout with the breadcrumb mix
3. Heat up your air fryer with the oil and the butter at 370°F; add the trout and cook for 10 minutes on each side. Divide between plates and serve with a side salad

## 252. Clams and Potatoes

Preparation Time: 20 minutes
Servings: 4

**Ingredients:**

- 1 lb. baby red potatoes; scrubbed
- 10 oz. beer
- 15 small clams; shucked
- 2 tbsp. cilantro; chopped.
- 2 chorizo links; sliced
- 1 yellow onion; chopped.
- 1 tsp. olive oil

**Directions:**

1. In a pan that fits your air fryer, add all of the ingredients and toss
2. Place the pan in the fryer and cook at 390°F for 15 minutes. Divide into bowls and serve.

## 253. Mussels Bowls

Preparation Time: 18 minutes
Servings: 4

**Ingredients:**

- 2 lbs. mussels; scrubbed
- 8 oz. spicy sausage; chopped.
- 1 yellow onion; chopped.
- 1 tbsp. olive oil
- 12 oz. black beer
- 1 tbsp. paprika

**Directions:**

1. Combine all the ingredients in a pan that fits your air fryer
2. Place the pan in the air fryer and cook at

400°F for 12 minutes. Divide the mussels into bowls, serve and enjoy!

## 254. Shrimp and Corn

Preparation Time: 20 minutes
Servings: 4

**Ingredients:**

- 1½ lbs. shrimp; peeled and deveined
- 2 cups corn
- 1/4 cup chicken stock
- 2 sweet onions; cut into wedges
- 1 tbsp. old bay seasoning
- 1 tsp. red pepper flakes; crushed
- 8 garlic cloves; crushed
- A drizzle of olive oil
- Salt and black pepper to taste

**Directions:**

1. Grease a pan that fits your air fryer with the oil.
2. Add all other ingredients to the oiled pan and toss well

Place the pan in the fryer and cook at 390°F for 10 minutes. Divide everything into bowls and serve

## 255. Salmon Thyme and Parsley

Preparation Time: 25 Minutes
Servings: 4

**Ingredients:**

- 4 salmon fillets; boneless
- 4 thyme springs
- 4 parsley springs
- 3 tbsp. extra virgin olive oil
- 1 yellow onion; chopped
- 3 tomatoes; sliced
- Juice from 1 lemon
- Salt and black pepper to the taste

**Directions:**

1. Drizzle 1 tablespoon oil in a pan that fits

your air fryer; add a layer of tomatoes, salt and pepper, drizzle 1 more tablespoon oil, add fish, season them with salt and pepper, drizzle the rest of the oil, add thyme and parsley springs, onions, lemon

3.

juice, salt and pepper, place in your air fryer's basket

2.  Cook at 360°F, for 12 minutes shaking once. Divide everything on plates and serve right away

## 256. Sweet Chicken Kabobs

Preparation Time: 20 minutes
Cooking Time: 14 minutes
Servings: 3

**Ingredients:**

- 4 scallions, chopped
- 2 teaspoons sesame seeds, toasted
- 1 pound chicken tenders
- Wooden skewers, pres oaked
- 1 tablespoon fresh ginger, finely grated
- 4 garlic cloves, minced
- ½ cup pineapple juice
- ½ cup soy sauce
- ¼ cup sesame oil
- A pinch of black pepper

**Directions:**

1. Preheat the Air fryer to 390 o F and grease an Air fryer pan.
2. Mix scallion, ginger, garlic, pineapple juice, soy sauce, oil, sesame seeds, and black pepper in a large baking dish.
3. Thread chicken tenders onto pre-soaked wooden skewers.
4. Coat the skewers generously with marinade and refrigerate for about 2 hours.
5. Transfer half of the skewers in the Air fryer pan and cook for about 7 minutes.
6. Repeat with the remaining mixture and dish out to serve warm.

**Nutrition:**
Calories: 392, Fat: 23g, Carbohydrates: 9.9g, Sugar: 4.1g, Protein: 35.8g, Sodium: 1800mg

## 257. Chicken with Apple

Preparation Time: 10 minutes
Cooking Time: 20 minutes

Servings: 8

**Ingredients:**

- 1 shallot, thinly sliced
- 1 teaspoon fresh thyme, minced
- 2: 4-ouncesboneless, skinless chicken thighs, sliced into chunks
- 1 large apple, cored and cubed
- 1 tablespoon fresh ginger, finely grated
- ½ cup apple cider
- 2 tablespoons maple syrup
- Salt and black pepper, as required

**Directions:**

1. Preheat the Air fryer to 390 o F and grease an Air fryer basket.
2. Mix the shallot, ginger, thyme, apple cider, maple syrup, salt, and black pepper in a bowl.
3. Coat the chicken generously with the marinade and refrigerate to marinate for about 8 hours.
4. Arrange the chicken pieces and cubed apples into the Air Fryer basket and cook for about 20 minutes, flipping once halfway.
5. Dish out the chicken mixture into a serving bowl to serve.

**Nutrition:**
Calories: 299, Fat: 26.2g, Carbohydrates: 39.9g, Sugar: 30.4g, Protein: 26.2g, Sodium: 125mg

## 258. Jerk Chicken, Pineapple and Veggie Kabobs

Preparation Time: 20 minutes
Cooking Time: 18 minutes
Servings: 8

**Ingredients:**

- 8: 4-ouncesboneless, skinless chicken thigh fillets, trimmed and cut into cubes

- 2 large zucchinis, sliced
- 8 ounces white mushrooms, stems removed
- 1: 20-ouncescan pineapple chunks, drained
- Wooden skewers, presoaked
- 1 tablespoon jerk seasoning
- Salt and black pepper, to taste
- 1 tablespoon jerk sauce

**Directions:**

1. Preheat the Air fryer to 370 o F and grease an Air fryer pan.
2. Mix the chicken cubes and jerk seasoning in a bowl.
3. Season the zucchini slices and mushrooms evenly with salt and black pepper.
4. Thread chicken, zucchinis, mushrooms and pineapple chunks onto presoaked wooden skewers.
5. Transfer half of the skewers in the Air fryer pan and cook for about 9 minutes.
6. Repeat with the remaining mixture and dish out to serve hot.

**Nutrition:**
Calories: 274, Fat: 8.7g, Carbohydrates: 14.1g, Sugar: 9.9g, Protein: 35.1g, Sodium: 150mg

## 259. Curried Chicken

Preparation Time: 15 minutes
Cooking Time: 18 minutes
Servings: 3

**Ingredients:**

- 1 pound boneless chicken, cubed
- ½ tablespoon cornstarch
- 1 egg
- 1 medium yellow onion, thinly sliced
- ½ cup evaporated milk
- 1 tablespoon light soy sauce
- 2 tablespoons olive oil
- 3 teaspoons garlic, minced

- 1 teaspoon fresh ginger, grated
- 5 curry leaves
- 1 teaspoon curry powder
- 1 tablespoon chili sauce
- 1 teaspoon sugar
- Salt and black pepper, as required

**Directions:**

1. Preheat the Air fryer to 390 o F and grease an Air fryer basket.
2. Mix the chicken cubes, soy sauce, cornstarch and egg in a bowl and keep aside for about 1 hour.
3. Arrange the chicken cubes into the Air Fryer basket and cook for about 10 minutes.
4. Heat olive oil in a medium skillet and add onion, green chili, garlic, ginger, and curry leaves.
5. Sauté for about 4 minutes and stir in the chicken cubes, curry powder, chili sauce, sugar, salt, and black pepper.
6. Mix well and add the evaporated milk.
7. Cook for about 4 minutes and dish out the chicken mixture into a serving bowl to serve.

**Nutrition:**
Calories: 363, Fat: 19g, Carbohydrates: 10g, Sugar: 0.8g, Protein: 37.1g, Sodium: 789mg

## 260. lazed Turkey Breast

Preparation Time: 15 minutes
Cooking Time: 55 minutes
Servings: 8

**Ingredients:**

- 1: 5-poundsboneless turkey breast
- 1 tablespoon butter, softened
- 1 teaspoon dried thyme, crushed
- ½ teaspoon dried sage, crushed
- ½ teaspoon smoked paprika
- Salt and ground black pepper, as required
- 2 teaspoons olive oil

- ¼ cup maple syrup
- 2 tablespoons Dijon mustard

**Directions:**
1. Preheat the Air fryer to 350 o F and grease an Air fryer basket.
2. Mix the herbs, paprika, salt, and black pepper in a bowl.
3. Drizzle the turkey breast with oil and season with the herb mixture.
4. Arrange the turkey breast into the Air Fryer basket and cook for about 50 minutes, flipping twice in between.
5. Meanwhile, mix the maple syrup, mustard, and butter in a bowl.
6. Coat the turkey evenly with maple glaze and cook for about 5 minutes.
7. Dish out the turkey breast onto a cutting board and cut into desired size slices to serve.

**Nutrition:**
Calories: 302, Fat: 3.3g, Carbohydrates: 5.6g, Sugar: 4.7g, Protein: 56.2g, Sodium: 170mg

## 261. Chicken with Carrots

Preparation Time: 15 minutes
Cooking Time: 25 minutes
Servings: 2

- **Ingredients:**
- 1 carrot, peeled and thinly sliced
- 2 tablespoons butter
- 2: 4-ounceschicken breast halves
- 1 tablespoon fresh rosemary, chopped
- Salt and black pepper, as required
- 2 tablespoons fresh lemon juice

**Directions:**
1. Preheat the Air fryer to 375 o F and grease an Air fryer basket.
2. Place 2 square-shaped parchment papers onto a smooth surface and arrange carrot slices evenly in the center of each parchment paper.
3. Drizzle ½ tablespoon of butter over

carrot slices and season with salt and black pepper.
4. Layer with chicken breasts and top with rosemary, lemon juice and remaining butter.
5. Fold the parchment paper on all sides and transfer into the Air fryer.
6. Cook for about 25 minutes and dish out in a serving platter to serve.

**Nutrition:**
Calories: 339, Fats: 20.3g, Carbohydrates: 4.4g, Sugar: 1.8g, Proteins: 33.4g, Sodium: 2822mg

## 262. Citrus Turkey Legs

Preparation Time: 15 minutes
Cooking Time: 30 minutes
Servings: 2

**Ingredients:**
- 1 tablespoon fresh rosemary, minced
- 2 turkey legs
- 2 garlic cloves, minced
- 1 teaspoon fresh lime zest, finely grated
- 2 tablespoons olive oil
- 1 tablespoon fresh lime juice
- Salt and black pepper, as required

**Directions:**
1. Preheat the Air fryer to 350 o F and grease an Air fryer basket.
2. Mix the garlic, rosemary, lime zest, oil, lime juice, salt, and black pepper in a bowl.
3. Coat the turkey legs with marinade and refrigerate to marinate for about 8 hours.
4. Arrange the turkey legs into the Air Fryer basket and cook for about 30 minutes, flipping once in between.
5. Dish out the turkey legs into serving plates.

**Nutrition:**
Calories: 458, Fat: 29.5g, Carbohydrates: 2.3g, Sugar: 0.1g, Protein: 44.6g, Sodium: 247mg

## 263. Chicken with Veggies and Rice

Preparation Time: 15 minutes
Cooking Time: 20 minutes
Servings: 3

**Ingredients:**

- 3 cups cold boiled white rice
- 1 cup cooked chicken, diced
- ½ cup frozen carrots
- ½ cup frozen peas
- ½ cup onion, chopped
- 6 tablespoons soy sauce
- 1 tablespoon vegetable oil

**Directions:**

1. Preheat the Air fryer to 360 o F and grease a 7" nonstick pan.
2. Mix the rice, soy sauce, and vegetable oil in a bowl.
3. Stir in the remaining ingredients and mix until well combined.
4. Transfer the rice mixture into the pan and place in the Air fryer.
5. Cook for about 20 minutes and dish out to serve immediately.

**Nutrition:**
Calories: 405, Fat: 6.4g, Carbohydrates: 63g, Sugar: 3.5g, Protein: 21.7g, Sodium: 1500mg

## 264. Delicious Chicken Burgers

Preparation Time: 20 minutes
Cooking Time: 30 minutes
Servings: 4

**Ingredients:**

- 4 boneless, skinless chicken breasts
- 1¾ ounces plain flour
- 2 eggs
- 4 hamburger buns, split and toasted
- 4 mozzarella cheese slices
- 1 teaspoon mustard powder
- ½ teaspoon paprika
- 1 teaspoon Worcestershire sauce
- ¼ teaspoon dried parsley
- ¼ teaspoon dried tarragon
- ¼ teaspoon dried oregano
- 1 teaspoon dried garlic
- 1 teaspoon chicken seasoning
- ½ teaspoon cayenne pepper
- Salt and black pepper, as required

**Directions:**

1. Preheat the Air fryer to 355 o F and grease an Air fryer basket.
2. Put the chicken breasts, mustard, paprika, Worcestershire sauce, salt, and black pepper in a food processor and pulse until minced.
3. Make 4 equal-sized patties from the mixture.
4. Place the flour in a shallow bowl and whisk the egg in a second bowl.
5. Combine dried herbs and spices in a third bowl.
6. Coat each chicken patty with flour, dip into whisked egg and then coat with breadcrumb mixture.
7. Arrange the chicken patties into the Air fryer basket in a single layer and cook for about 30 minutes, flipping once in between.
8. Place half bun in a plate, layer with lettuce leaf, patty and cheese slice.
9. Cover with bun top and dish out to serve warm.

**Nutrition:**
Calories: 562, Fat: 20.3g, Carbohydrates: 33g, Sugar: 3.3g, Protein: 58.7g, Sodium: 560mg

## 265. Simple Turkey Breast

Preparation Time: 20 minutes
Cooking Time: 40 minutes
Servings: 10

**Ingredients:**

- 1: 8-poundsbone-in turkey breast

- Salt and black pepper, as required
- 2 tablespoons olive oil

**Directions:**
1. Preheat the Air fryer to 360 o F and grease an Air fryer basket.
2. Season the turkey breast with salt and black pepper and drizzle with oil.
3. Arrange the turkey breast into the Air Fryer basket, skin side down and cook for about 20 minutes.
4. Flip the side and cook for another 20 minutes.
5. Dish out in a platter and cut into desired size slices to serve.

**Nutrition:**
Calories: 719, Fat: 35.9g, Carbohydrates: 0g, Sugar: 0g, Protein: 97.2g, Sodium: 386mg

## 266. Buttermilk Brined Turkey Breast

Preparation Time: 15 minutes
Cooking Time: 20 minutes
Servings: 8

**Ingredients:**
- ¾ cup brine from a can of olives
- 3½ pounds boneless, skinless turkey breast
- 2 fresh thyme sprigs
- 1 fresh rosemary sprig
- ½ cup buttermilk

**Directions:**
1. Preheat the Air fryer to 350 o F and grease an Air fryer basket.
2. Mix olive brine and buttermilk in a bowl until well combined.
3. Place the turkey breast, buttermilk mixture and herb sprigs in a resealable plastic bag.
4. Seal the bag and refrigerate for about 12 hours.
5. Remove the turkey breast from bag and arrange the turkey breast into the Air fryer basket.

6. Cook for about 20 minutes, flipping once in between.
7. Dish out the turkey breast onto a cutting board and cut into desired size slices to serve.

**Nutrition:**
Calories: 215, Fat: 3.5g, Carbohydrates: 9.4g, Sugar: 7.7g, Protein: 34.4g, Sodium: 2000mg

## 267. Delightful Turkey Wings

Preparation Time: 10 minutes
Cooking Time: 26 minutes
Servings: 4

**Ingredients:**
- 2 pounds turkey wings
- 4 tablespoons chicken rub
- 3 tablespoons olive oil

**Directions:**
1. Preheat the Air fryer to 380 o F and grease an Air fryer basket.
2. Mix the turkey wings, chicken rub, and olive oil in a bowl until well combined.
3. Arrange the turkey wings into the Air fryer basket and cook for about 26 minutes, flipping once in between.
4. Dish out the turkey wings in a platter and serve hot.

**Nutrition:**
Calories: 204, Fat: 15.5g, Carbohydrates: 3g, Sugar: 0g, Protein: 12g, Sodium: 465mg

## 268. Duck Rolls

Preparation Time: 20 minutes
Cooking Time: 40 minutes
Servings: 3

**Ingredients:**
- 1 pound duck breast fillet, each cut into 2 pieces
- 3 tablespoons fresh parsley, finely chopped
- 1 small red onion, finely chopped

- 1 garlic clove, crushed
- 1½ teaspoons ground cumin
- 1 teaspoon ground cinnamon
- ½ teaspoon red chili powder
- Salt, to taste
- 2 tablespoons olive oil

**Directions:**

1. Preheat the Air fryer to 355 o F and grease an Air fryer basket.
2. Mix the garlic, parsley, onion, spices, and 1 tablespoon of olive oil in a bowl.
3. Make a slit in each duck piece horizontally and coat with onion mixture.
4. Roll each duck piece tightly and transfer into the Air fryer basket.
5. Cook for about 40 minutes and cut into desired size slices to serve.

**Nutrition:**
Calories: 239, Fats: 8.2g, Carbohydrates: 3.2g, Sugar: 0.9g, Proteins: 37.5g, Sodium: 46mg

## 269. Turkey Meatloaf

Preparation Time: 20 minutes
Cooking Time: 20 minutes
Servings: 4

**Ingredients:**

- 1 pound ground turkey
- 1 cup kale leaves, trimmed and finely chopped
- 1 cup onion, chopped
- ½ cup fresh breadcrumbs
- 1 cup Monterey Jack cheese, grated
- 2 garlic cloves, minced
- ¼ cup salsa verde
- 1 teaspoon red chili powder
- ½ teaspoon ground cumin
- ½ teaspoon dried oregano, crushed
- Salt and ground black pepper, as required

**Directions:**

1. Preheat the Air fryer to 400 o F and

grease an Air fryer basket.

2. Mix all the ingredients in a bowl and divide the turkey mixture into 4 equal-sized portions.
3. Shape each into a mini loaf and arrange the loaves into the Air fryer basket.
4. Cook for about 20 minutes and dish out to serve warm.

**Nutrition:**
Calories: 435, Fat: 23.1g, Carbohydrates: 18.1g, Sugar: 3.6g, Protein: 42.2g, Sodium: 641mg

## 270. Buttered Duck Breasts

Preparation Time: 15 minutes
Cooking Time: 22 minutes
Servings: 4

**Ingredients:**

- 2: 12-ouncesduck breasts
- 3 tablespoons unsalted butter, melted
- Salt and ground black pepper, as required
- ½ teaspoon dried thyme, crushed
- ¼ teaspoon star anise powder

**Directions:**

1. Preheat the Air fryer to 390 o F and grease an Air fryer basket.
2. Season the duck breasts generously with salt and black pepper.
3. Arrange the duck breasts into the prepared Air fryer basket and cook for about 10 minutes.
4. Dish out the duck breasts and drizzle with melted butter.
5. Season with thyme and star anise powder and place the duck breasts again into the Air fryer basket.
6. Cook for about 12 more minutes and dish out to serve warm.

**Nutrition:**
Calories: 296, Fat: 15.5g, Carbohydrates: 0.1g, Sugar: 0g, Protein: 37.5g, Sodium: 100mg

## 271. Beer Coated Duck Breast

Preparation Time: 15 minutes
Cooking Time: 20 minutes
Servings: 2

**Ingredients:**

- 1 tablespoon fresh thyme, chopped
- 1 cup beer
- 1: 10½-ouncesduck breast
- 6 cherry tomatoes
- 1 tablespoon olive oil
- 1 teaspoon mustard
- Salt and ground black pepper, as required
- 1 tablespoon balsamic vinegar

**Directions:**

1. Preheat the Air fryer to 390 o F and grease an Air fryer basket.
2. Mix the olive oil, mustard, thyme, beer, salt, and black pepper in a bowl.
3. Coat the duck breasts generously with marinade and refrigerate, covered for about 4 hours.
4. Cover the duck breasts and arrange into the Air fryer basket.
5. Cook for about 15 minutes and remove the foil from breast.
6. Set the Air fryer to 355 o F and place the duck breast and tomatoes into the Air Fryer basket.
7. Cook for about 5 minutes and dish out the duck breasts and cherry tomatoes.
8. Drizzle with vinegar and serve immediately.

**Nutrition:**

Calories: 332, Fat: 13.7g, Carbohydrates: 9.2g, Sugar: 2.5g, Protein: 34.6g, Sodium: 88mg

## 272. Duck Breast with Figs

Preparation Time: 20 minutes
Cooking Time: 45 minutes
Servings: 2

**Ingredients:**

- 1 pound boneless duck breast

---

- 6 fresh figs, halved
- 1 tablespoon fresh thyme, chopped
- 2 cups fresh pomegranate juice
- 2 tablespoons lemon juice
- 3 tablespoons brown sugar
- 1 teaspoon olive oil
- Salt and black pepper, as required

**Directions:**

1. Preheat the Air fryer to 400 o F and grease an Air fryer basket.
2. Put the pomegranate juice, lemon juice, and brown sugar in a medium saucepan over medium heat.
3. Bring to a boil and simmer on low heat for about 25 minutes.
4. Season the duck breasts generously with salt and black pepper.
5. Arrange the duck breasts into the Air fryer basket, skin side up and cook for about 14 minutes, flipping once in between.
6. Dish out the duck breasts onto a cutting board for about 10 minutes.
7. Meanwhile, put the figs, olive oil, salt, and black pepper in a bowl until well mixed.
8. Set the Air fryer to 400 o F and arrange the figs into the Air fryer basket.
9. Cook for about 5 more minutes and dish out in a platter.
10. Put the duck breast with the roasted figs and drizzle with warm pomegranate juice mixture.
11. Garnish with fresh thyme and serve warm.

**Nutrition:**

Calories: 699, Fat: 12.1g, Carbohydrates: 90g, Sugar: 74g, Protein: 519g, Sodium: 110mg

## 273. Herbed Duck Legs

Preparation Time: 10 minutes
Cooking Time: 30 minutes
Servings: 2

**Ingredients:**

- ½ tablespoon fresh thyme, chopped
- ½ tablespoon fresh parsley, chopped
- 2 duck legs
- 1 garlic clove, minced
- 1 teaspoon five spice powder
- Salt and black pepper, as required

**Directions:**

1. Preheat the Air fryer to 340 o F and grease an Air fryer basket.
2. Mix the garlic, herbs, five spice powder, salt, and black pepper in a bowl.
3. Rub the duck legs with garlic mixture generously and arrange into the Air fryer basket.
4. Cook for about 25 minutes and set the Air fryer to 390 o F.
5. Cook for 5 more minutes and dish out to serve hot.

**Nutrition:**

Calories: 138, Fat: 4.5g, Carbohydrates: 1g, Sugar: 0g, Protein: 25g, Sodium: 82mg

## 274. Chicken Wings with Prawn Paste

Preparation Time: 20 minutes
Cooking Time: 8 minutes
Servings: 6

**Ingredients:**

- Corn flour, as required
- 2 pounds mid-joint chicken wings
- 2 tablespoons prawn paste
- 4 tablespoons olive oil
- 1½ teaspoons sugar
- 2 teaspoons sesame oil
- 1 teaspoon Shaoxing wine
- 2 teaspoons fresh ginger juice

**Directions:**

1. Preheat the Air fryer to 360 o F and grease an Air fryer basket.
2. Mix all the ingredients in a bowl except wings and corn flour.

3. Rub the chicken wings generously with marinade and refrigerate overnight.
4. Coat the chicken wings evenly with corn flour and keep aside.
5. Set the Air fryer to 390 o F and arrange the chicken wings in the Air fryer basket.
6. Cook for about 8 minutes and dish out to serve hot.

**Nutrition:**

Calories: 416, Fat: 31.5g, Carbohydrates: 11.2g, Sugar: 1.6g, Protein: 24.4g, Sodium: 661mg

## 275. Spicy Green Crusted Chicken

Preparation Time: 10 minutes
Cooking Time: 40 minutes
Servings: 6

**Ingredients:**

- 6 eggs, beaten
- 6 teaspoons parsley
- 4 teaspoons thyme
- 1 pound chicken pieces
- 6 teaspoons oregano
- Salt and freshly ground black pepper, to taste
- 4 teaspoons paprika

**Directions:**

1. Preheat the Air fryer to 360 o F and grease an Air fryer basket.
2. Whisk eggs in a bowl and mix all the ingredients in another bowl except chicken pieces.
3. Dip the chicken in eggs and then coat generously with the dry mixture.
4. Arrange half of the chicken pieces in the Air fryer basket and cook for about 20 minutes.
5. Repeat with the remaining mixture and dish out to serve hot.

**Nutrition:**

Calories: 218, Fat: 10.4g, Carbohydrates: 2.6g, Sugar: 0.6g, Protein: 27.9g, Sodium: 128mg

## 276. Creamy Chicken Tenders

Preparation Time: 15 minutes
Cooking Time: 20 minutes
Servings: 8

### Ingredients:

- 2 pounds chicken tenders
- 1 cup feta cheese
- 4 tablespoons olive oil
- 1 cup cream
- Salt and black pepper, to taste

### Directions:

1. Preheat the Air fryer to 340 o F and grease an Air fryer basket.
2. Season the chicken tenders with salt and black pepper.
3. Arrange the chicken tenderloins in the Air fryer basket and drizzle with olive oil.\
4. Cook for about 15 minutes and set the Air fryer to 390 o F.
5. Cook for about 5 more minutes and dish out to serve warm.
6. Repeat with the remaining mixture and dish out to serve hot.

### Nutrition:

Calories: 344, Fat: 21.1g, Carbohydrates: 1.7g, Sugar: 1.4g, Protein: 35.7g, Sodium: 317mg

## 277. Chicken Breasts with Chimichurri

Preparation Time: 15 minutes
Cooking Time: 35 minutes
Servings: 1

### Ingredients:

- 1 chicken breast, bone-in, skin-on
- Chimichurri
- ½ bunch fresh cilantro
- 1/4 bunch fresh parsley
- ½ shallot, peeled, cut in quarters
- ½ tablespoon paprika ground
- ½ tablespoon chili powder
- ½ tablespoon fennel ground

- ½ teaspoon black pepper, ground
- ½ teaspoon onion powder
- 1 teaspoon salt
- ½ teaspoon garlic powder
- ½ teaspoon cumin ground
- ½ tablespoon canola oil
- Chimichurri
- 2 tablespoons olive oil
- 4 garlic cloves, peeled
- Zest and juice of 1 lemon
- 1 teaspoon kosher salt

### Directions:

1. Preheat the Air fryer to 300 o F and grease an Air fryer basket.
2. Combine all the spices in a suitable bowl and season the chicken with it.
3. Sprinkle with canola oil and arrange the chicken in the Air fryer basket.
4. Cook for about 35 minutes and dish out in a platter.
5. Put all the ingredients in the blender and blend until smooth.
6. Serve the chicken with chimichurri sauce.

### Nutrition:

Calories: 140, Fats: 7.9g, Carbohydrates: 1.8g, Sugar: 7.1g, Proteins: 7.2g, Sodium: 581mg

## 278. Fried Chicken Thighs

Preparation Time: 10 minutes
Cooking Time: 25 minutes
Servings: 4

### Ingredients:

- ½ cup almond flour
- 1 egg beaten
- 4 small chicken thighs
- 1½ tablespoons Old Bay Cajun Seasoning
- 1 teaspoon seasoning salt

### Directions:

1. Preheat the Air fryer to 400 o F for 3 minutes and grease an Air fryer basket.

2. Whisk the egg in a shallow bowl and place the old bay, flour and salt in another bowl.
3. Dip the chicken in the egg and coat with the flour mixture.
4. Arrange the chicken thighs in the Air fryer basket and cook for about 25 minutes.
5. Dish out in a platter and serve warm.

**Nutrition:**
Calories: 180, Fat: 20g, Carbohydrates: 3g, Sugar: 1.2g, Protein: 21g, Sodium: 686mg

## 279. Sweet Sriracha Turkey Legs

Preparation Time: 10 minutes
Cooking Time: 35 minutes
Servings: 2

**Ingredients:**
- 1-pound turkey legs
- 1 tablespoon butter
- 1 tablespoon cilantro
- 1 tablespoon chives
- 1 tablespoon scallions
- 4 tablespoons sriracha sauce
- 1½ tablespoons soy sauce
- ½ lime, juiced

**Directions:**
1. Preheat the Air fryer on Roasting mode to 360 o F for 3 minutes and grease an Air fryer basket.
2. Arrange the turkey legs in the Air fryer basket and cook for about 30 minutes, flipping several times in between.
3. Mix butter, scallions, sriracha sauce, soy sauce and lime juice in the saucepan and cook for about for 3 minutes until the sauce thickens.
4. Drizzle this sauce over the turkey legs and garnish with cilantro and chives to serve.

**Nutrition:**
Calories: 361, Fat: 16.3g, Carbohydrates: 9.3g, Sugar: 18.2g, Protein: 33.3g, Sodium: 515mg

## 280. Gyro Seasoned Chicken

Preparation Time: 10 minutes
Cooking Time: 30 minutes
Servings: 4

**Ingredients:**
- 2 pounds chicken thighs
- 1 tablespoon avocado oil
- 2 tablespoons primal palate super gyro seasoning
- 2 tablespoons primal palate new bae seasoning
- 1 tablespoon Himalayan pink salt

**Directions:**
1. Preheat the Air fryer to 350 o F and grease an Air fryer basket.
2. Rub the chicken with avocado oil and half of the spices.
3. Arrange the chicken thighs in the Air fryer basket and cook for about 25 minutes, flipping once in between.
4. Sprinkle the remaining seasoning and cook for 5 more minutes.
5. Dish out and serve warm.

**Nutrition:**
Calories: 545, Fat: 36.4g, Carbohydrates: 0.7g, Sugar: 0g, Protein: 42.5g, Sodium: 272mg

## 281. Special Salsa Chicken Steak

Preparation Time: 10 minutes
Cooking Time: 30 minutes
Servings: 6

**Ingredients:**
- 2 pounds chicken steak
- ½ cup shredded Monterey Jack cheese
- 1 cup tomato sauce
- ½ teaspoon garlic powder
- 2 cups salsa
- ½ teaspoon hot pepper sauce
- Salt and black pepper, to taste

**Directions:**

1. Preheat the Air fryer to 450 o F and grease an Air fryer basket.
2. Season the chicken steak with garlic powder, salt and black pepper and marinate for about 8 hours.
3. Mix salsa, tomato sauce and hot pepper sauce in a bowl.
4. Arrange the steak pieces in the Air fryer basket and drizzle with the salsa mixture.
5. Cook for about 30 minutes and dish out to serve hot.

**Nutrition:**
Calories: 345, Fat: 14.3g, Carbohydrates: 7.6g, Sugar: 4.3g, Protein: 45.1g, Sodium: 828mg

## 282. Chicken with Veggies and Rice

Preparation Time: 35 minutes
Servings: 3

**Ingredients:**

- 3 cups cold boiled white rice
- 1 cup cooked chicken, diced
- 1/2 cup frozen carrots
- 1/2 cup frozen peas
- 1/2 cup onion; chopped
- 1 tbsp. vegetable oil
- 6 tbsp. soy sauce

**Directions:**

1. In a large bowl, add the rice, soy sauce and oil and mix thoroughly.
2. Add the remaining Ingredients and mix until well combined. Transfer the rice mixture into a 7" nonstick pan.
3. Arrange the pan into an Air Fryer basket. Set the temperature of Air Fryer to 360°F. Air Fry for about 20 minutes.
4. Remove the pan from Air Fryer and transfer the rice mixture onto serving plates. Serve immediately.

## 283. Turkey Wings Orange Sauce

Preparation Time: 45 minutes

Servings: 4

**Ingredients:**

- 2 turkey wings
- 1½ cups cranberries
- 1 cup orange juice
- 2 tbsp. butter; melted
- 1 yellow onion; sliced
- 1 bunch thyme; roughly chopped.
- Salt and black pepper to taste

**Directions:**

1. Place the butter in a pan that fits your air fryer and heat up over medium-high heat.
2. Add the cranberries, salt, pepper, onions and orange juice; whisk and cook for 3 minutes
3. Add the turkey wings, toss and cook for 3-4 minutes more
4. Transfer the pan to your air fryer and cook at 380°F for 25 minutes
5. Add the thyme, toss and divide everything between plates. Serve and enjoy!

## 284. Chicken and Yogurt

Preparation Time: 1 hour 15 minutes
Servings: 4

**Ingredients:**

- 17 oz. chicken meat; boneless and cubed
- 14 oz. yogurt
- 3½ oz. cherry tomatoes; halved
- 1 red bell pepper; deseeded and cubed
- 1 yellow bell pepper; deseeded and cubed
- 2 tbsp. coriander powder
- 2 tsp. olive oil
- 1 tsp. turmeric powder
- 3 mint leaves; torn
- 1 green bell pepper; deseeded and cubed
- 1 tbsp. ginger; grated
- 2 tbsp. red chili powder
- 2 tbsp. cumin powder
- Salt and black pepper to taste

**Directions:**

1. In a bowl, mix all of the ingredients, toss well and place in the fridge for 1 hour
2. Transfer the whole mix to a pan that fits your air fryer and cook at 400°F for 15 minutes, shaking the pan halfway. Divide everything between plates and serve

## 285. Chicken and Peppercorns

Preparation Time: 25 minutes
Servings: 4

**Ingredients:**

- 8 chicken thighs; boneless
- 1 tsp. black peppercorns
- 4 garlic cloves; minced
- 1/2 cup soy sauce
- 1/2 cup balsamic vinegar
- Salt and black pepper to taste

**Directions:**

1. In a pan that fits your air fryer; mix the chicken with all the other ingredients and toss
2. Place the pan in the fryer and cook at 380°F for 20 minutes. Divide everything between plates and serve.

## 286. Duck and Sauce

Preparation Time: 30 minutes
Servings: 4

**Ingredients:**

- 2 duck breasts; skin scored
- 8 oz. white wine
- 1 tbsp. garlic; minced
- 2 tbsp. heavy cream
- 1 tbsp. sugar
- 2 tbsp. cranberries
- 1 tbsp. olive oil
- Salt and black pepper to taste

**Directions:**

1. Season the duck breasts with salt and

pepper and put them in preheated air fryer

2. Cook at 350°F for 10 minutes on each side and divide between plates
3. Heat up a pan with the oil over medium heat and add the cranberries, sugar, wine, garlic and the cream; whisk well. Cook for 3-4 minutes, drizzle over the duck and serve.

## 287. Barbeque Chicken Wings

Preparation Time: 40 minutes
Servings: 4

**Ingredients:**

- 1/2 cup BBQ sauce
- 2 lbs. chicken wings; cut into drumettes and flats

**Directions:**

1. Set the temperature of Air Fryer to 380°F. Grease an Air Fryer basket. Arrange chicken wings into the prepared Air Fryer basket in a single layer.
2. Air Fry for about 24 minutes, flipping once halfway through. Now, set the temperature of Air Fryer to 400°F.
3. Air Fry for about 6 minutes. Remove from Air Fryer and transfer the chicken wings into a bowl. Drizzle with the BBQ sauce and toss to coat well. Serve immediately.

## 288. Turkey and Spring Onions

Preparation Time: 40 minutes
Servings: 2

**Ingredients:**

- 2 small turkey breasts; boneless and skinless
- 1 bunch spring onions; chopped.
- 2 red chilies; chopped.
- 1 tbsp. Chinese rice wine
- 1 tbsp. oyster sauce
- 1 cup chicken stock

- 1 tbsp. olive oil
- 1 tbsp. soy sauce

**Directions:**
1. Add the oil to a pan that fits your air fryer and place it over medium heat
2. Then add the chilies, spring onions, oyster sauce, soy sauce, stock and rice wine; whisk and simmer for 3-4 minutes
3. Add the turkey, toss and place the pan in the air fryer and cook at 380°F for 30 minutes. Divide everything between plates and serve.

## 289. Chicken and Squash

Preparation Time: 35 minutes
Servings: 4

**Ingredients:**
- 14 oz. coconut milk
- 6 cups squash; cubed
- 8 chicken drumsticks
- 1/2 cup cilantro; chopped.
- 2 tbsp. olive oil
- 2 tbsp. green curry paste
- 1/4 tsp. coriander; ground
- 1/2 cup basil; chopped.
- 2 red chilies; minced
- 3 garlic cloves; minced
- A pinch of cumin; ground
- Salt and black pepper to taste

**Directions:**
1. Heat up a pan that fits your air fryer with the oil over medium heat.
2. Add the garlic, chilies, curry paste, cumin, coriander, salt and pepper; stir and cook for 3-4 minutes.
3. Add the chicken pieces and the coconut milk and stir
4. Place the pan in the fryer and cook at 380°F for 15 minutes
5. Add the squash, cilantro and basil; toss and cook for 5-6 minutes more. Divide

into bowls and serve. Enjoy!

## 290. Soy Sauce Chicken

Preparation Time: 50 minutes
Servings: 6

**Ingredients:**
- 1 whole chicken; cut into pieces
- 1 tsp. sesame oil
- 2 tsp. soy sauce
- 1 chili pepper; minced
- 1 tbsp. ginger; grated
- Salt and black pepper to taste

**Directions:**
1. In a bowl, mix the chicken with all the other ingredients and rub well
2. Transfer the chicken pieces to your air fryer's basket
3. Cook at 400°F for 30 minutes and then at 380°F for 10 minutes more. Divide everything between plates and serve

## 291. Chicken and Veggies

Preparation Time: 35 minutes
Servings: 4

**Ingredients:**
- 4 chicken breasts; boneless and skinless
- 3 garlic cloves; minced
- 1 celery stalk; chopped.
- 1 red onion; chopped.
- 2 tbsp. olive oil
- 1 tsp. sage; dried
- 1 carrot; chopped.
- 1 cup chicken stock
- 1/2 tsp. rosemary; dried
- Salt and black pepper to taste

**Directions:**
1. In a pan that fits your air fryer, place all ingredients and toss well
2. Put the pan in the fryer and cook at 360°F

for 25 minutes. Divide everything between plates, serve and enjoy!

## 292. Rosemary Chicken Breasts

Preparation Time: 35 minutes
Servings: 4

**Ingredients:**

- 2 chicken breasts; skinless, boneless and halved
- 1 yellow onion; sliced
- 1 cup chicken stock
- 4 garlic cloves; chopped.
- 2 tbsp. cornstarch mixed with 2½ tbsp. water
- 2 tbsp. butter; melted
- 1 tbsp. soy sauce
- 1 tsp. rosemary; dried
- 1 tbsp. fresh rosemary; chopped.
- Salt and black pepper to taste

**Directions:**

1. Heat up the butter in a pan that fits your air fryer over medium heat.
2. Add the onions, garlic, dried and fresh rosemary, stock, soy sauce, salt and pepper; stir and simmer for 2-3 minutes
3. Add the cornstarch mixture, whisk, cook for 2 minutes more and take off the heat
4. Add the chicken, toss gently and place the pan in the fryer; cook at 370°F for 20 minutes. Divide between plates and serve hot.

## 293. Sesame Chicken

Preparation Time: 30 minutes
Servings: 4

**Ingredients:**

- 2 lbs. chicken breasts; skinless, boneless and cubed
- 1/2 cup soy sauce
- 1/2 cup honey
- 1 tbsp. olive oil

- 2 tsp. sesame oil
- 1/4 tsp. red pepper flakes
- 1/2 cup yellow onion; chopped.
- 2 garlic cloves; minced
- 1 tbsp. sesame seeds; toasted
- Salt and black pepper to taste

**Directions:**

1. Heat up the oil in a pan that fits your air fryer oil over medium heat.
2. Add the chicken, toss and brown for 3 minutes
3. Add the onions, garlic, salt and pepper; stir and cook for 2 minutes more.
4. Add the soy sauce, sesame oil, honey and pepper flakes; toss well
5. Place the pan in the fryer and cook at 380°F for 15 minutes
6. Top with the sesame seeds and toss. Divide between plates and serve.

## 294. Turkey with Fig Sauce

Preparation Time: 40 minutes
Servings: 4

**Ingredients:**

- 2 turkey breasts; halved
- 1 shallot; chopped.
- 1 cup chicken stock
- 1/2 cup red wine
- 1 tbsp. olive oil
- 3 tbsp. butter; melted
- 1 tbsp. white flour
- 1/2 tsp. garlic powder
- 1/4 tsp. sweet paprika
- 4 tbsp. figs; chopped.
- Salt and black pepper to taste

**Directions:**

1. Heat up a pan with the olive oil and 1½ tbsp. of the butter over medium-high heat.
2. Add the shallots, stir and cook for 2 minutes

3. Add the garlic powder, paprika, stock, salt, pepper, wine and the figs; stir and cook for 7-8 minutes.

4. Next add the flour, stir well and cook the sauce for 1-2 minutes more; take off heat

5. Season the turkey with salt and pepper and drizzle the remaining 1½ tbsp. of butter over them

6. Place the turkey in your air fryer's basket and cook at 380°F for 15 minutes, flipping them halfway. Divide between plates, drizzle the sauce all over and serve.

## 295. Duck Breast and Potatoes

Preparation Time: 40 minutes
Servings: 2

**Ingredients:**
- 1 duck breast; halved and scored
- 1 oz. red wine
- 2 tbsp. butter; melted
- 2 gold potatoes; cubed
- Salt and black pepper to taste

**Directions:**
1. Season the duck pieces with salt and pepper, put them in a pan and heat up over medium-high heat.
2. Cook for 4 minutes on each side, transfer to your air fryer's basket and cook at 360°F for 8 minutes
3. Put the butter in a pan and heat it up over medium heat; then add the potatoes, salt, pepper and the wine and cook for 8 minutes
4. Add the duck pieces, toss and cook everything for 3-4 minutes more. Divide all between plates and serve.

## 296. Cajun Chicken and Okra

Preparation Time: 40 minutes
Servings: 4

**Ingredients:**
- 1 lb. chicken thighs; halved

- 1/2 lb. okra
- 1 red bell pepper; chopped.
- 1 yellow onion; chopped.
- 1 cup chicken stock
- 1 tbsp. Cajun spice
- 4 garlic cloves; minced
- 1 tbsp. olive oil
- Salt and black pepper to taste

**Directions:**
1. Add the oil to a pan that fits your air fryer and heat up over medium heat.
2. Then add the chicken and brown for 2-3 minutes
3. Next, add all remaining ingredients, toss and cook for 3-4 minutes more
4. Place the pan into the air fryer and cook at 380°F for 22 minutes. Divide everything between plates and serve.

## 297. Chicken and Beer

Preparation Time: 40 minutes
Servings: 4

**Ingredients:**
- 15 oz. beer
- 1 yellow onion; minced
- 1 chili pepper; chopped.
- 2 tbsp. olive oil
- 4 chicken drumsticks
- 1 tbsp. balsamic vinegar
- Salt and black pepper to taste

**Directions:**
1. Put the oil in a pan that fits your air fryer and heat up over medium heat.
2. Add the onion and the chili pepper, stir and cook for 2 minutes
3. Add the vinegar, beer, salt and pepper; stir and cook for 3 more minutes
4. Add the chicken, toss and put the pan in the fryer and cook at 370°F for 20 minutes. Divide everything between plates and serve.

## 298. Turkey M-eatballs

Preparation Time: 25 minutes
Servings: 8

**Ingredients:**

- 1 lb. turkey meat; ground
- 1/4 cup parsley; chopped.
- 1/4 cup milk
- 1/2 cup panko breadcrumbs
- 1 tsp. fish sauce
- 1 tsp. oregano; dried
- 1 egg; whisked
- 1/4 cup parmesan cheese; grated
- 1 yellow onion; minced
- 4 garlic cloves; minced
- 2 tsp. soy sauce
- Cooking spray
- Salt and black pepper to taste

**Directions:**

1. In a bowl, mix together all of the ingredients: except the cooking spray), stir well and then shape into medium-sized meatballs
2. Place the meatballs in your air fryer's basket, grease them with cooking spray and cook at 380°F for 15 minutes. Serve the meatballs with a side salad

## 299. Chicken and Baby Carrots

Preparation Time: 35 minutes
Servings: 4

**Ingredients:**

- 6 chicken thighs
- 1/2 lb. baby carrots; halved
- 15 oz. canned tomatoes; chopped.
- 1 cup chicken stock
- 1 yellow onion; chopped.
- 1 tsp. olive oil
- 1/2 tsp. thyme; dried
- 1/2 cup white wine

- 2 tbsp. tomato paste
- Salt and black pepper to taste

**Directions:**

1. Put the oil into a pan that fits your air fryer and heat up over medium heat.
2. Add the chicken thighs and brown them for 1-2 minutes on each side
3. Add all the remaining ingredients, toss and cook for 4-5 minutes more
4. Place the pan in the air fryer and cook at 380°F for 22 minutes. Divide the chicken and carrots mix between plates and serve.

## 300. Balsamic Chicken

Preparation Time: 30 minutes
Servings: 4

**Ingredients:**

- 4 chicken breasts; skinless and boneless
- 1 yellow onion; minced
- 1/4 cup cheddar cheese; grated
- 1/4 tsp. garlic powder
- 1/4 cup balsamic vinegar
- 12 oz. canned tomatoes; chopped.
- Salt and black pepper to taste

**Directions:**

1. In a baking dish that fits your air fryer, mix the chicken with the onions, vinegar, tomatoes, salt, pepper and garlic powder
2. Sprinkle the cheese on top and place the pan in the air fryer; cook at 400°F for 20 minutes. Divide between plates and serve.

## 301. Chicken Curry

Preparation Time: 40 minutes
Servings: 4

**Ingredients:**

- 15 oz. chicken breast; skinless, boneless, cubed
- 6 potatoes; peeled and cubed
- 5 oz. heavy cream

- 1/2 bunch coriander; chopped
- 1 yellow onion; sliced
- 1 tbsp. olive oil
- 1 tsp. curry powder
- Salt and black pepper to taste

**Directions:**
1. Heat up the oil in a pan that fits your air fryer over medium heat.
2. Add the chicken, toss and brown for 2 minutes
3. Then add the onions, curry powder, salt and pepper; toss and cook for 3 minutes.
4. Next add the potatoes and the cream; toss well
5. Place the pan in the air fryer and cook at 370°F for 20 minutes
6. Add the coriander and stir. Divide the curry into bowls and serve.

## 302. Asian Atyle Chicken

Preparation Time: 40 minutes
Servings: 4

**Ingredients:**
- 1 lb. spinach; chopped.
- 1½ lbs. chicken drumsticks
- 15 oz. canned tomatoes; crushed
- 1/4 cup lemon juice
- 1/2 cup chicken stock
- 1/2 cup heavy cream
- 1/2 cup cilantro; chopped.
- 4 garlic cloves; minced
- 1 yellow onion; chopped.
- 2 tbsp. butter; melted
- 1 tbsp. ginger; grated
- 1½ tsp. coriander; ground
- 1½ tsp. paprika
- 1 tsp. turmeric powder
- Salt and black pepper to taste

**Directions:**
1. Place the butter in a pan that fits your air

fryer and heat over medium heat.
2. Add the onions and the garlic, stir and cook for 3 minutes
3. Add the ginger, paprika, coriander, turmeric, salt, pepper and the chicken; toss and cook for 4 minutes more.
4. Add the tomatoes and the stock and stir
5. Place the pan in the fryer and cook at 370°F for 15 minutes
6. Add the spinach, lemon juice, cilantro and the cream; stir and cook for 5-6 minutes more. Divide everything into bowls and serve.

## 303. Lemongrass Chicken

Preparation Time: 40 minutes
Servings: 4

**Ingredients:**
- 10 chicken drumsticks
- 1 cup coconut milk
- 1 bunch lemongrass; trimmed
- 1/4 cup parsley; chopped.
- 1 yellow onion; chopped.
- 2 tbsp. fish sauce
- 3 tbsp. soy sauce
- 1 tsp. butter; melted
- 1 tbsp. ginger; chopped.
- 4 garlic cloves; minced
- 1 tbsp. lemon juice
- Salt and black pepper to taste

**Directions:**
1. In a blender, combine the lemongrass, ginger, garlic, soy sauce, fish sauce and coconut milk; pulse well.
2. Put the butter in a pan that fits your air fryer and heat it up over medium heat; add the onions, stir and cook for 2-3 minutes
3. Add the chicken, salt, pepper and the lemongrass mix; toss well
4. Place the pan in the fryer and cook at 380°F for 25 minutes

5. Add the lemon juice and the parsley and toss. Divide everything between plates and serve.

## 304. Chicken and Chickpeas

Preparation Time: 35 minutes
Servings: 4

**Ingredients:**

- 2 lbs. chicken thighs; boneless
- 8 oz. canned chickpeas; drained
- 5 oz. bacon; cooked and crumbled
- 1 cup chicken stock
- 1 tsp. balsamic v*inegar
- 2 tbsp. olive oil
- 1 cup yellow onion; chopped.
- 2 carrots; chopped.
- 1 tbsp. parsley; chopped.
- Salt and black pepper to taste

**Directions:**

1. Heat up a pan that fits your air fryer with the oil over medium heat.
2. Add the onions, carrots, salt and pepper; stir and sauté for 3-4 minutes.
3. Add the chicken, stock, vinegar and chickpeas; then toss
4. Place the pan in the fryer and cook at 380°F for 20 minutes
5. Add the bacon and the parsley and toss again. Divide everything between plates and serve.

## 305. Pickle Fried Chicken

Cooking Time: 47 minutes
Servings: 4

**Ingredients:**

- 4 chicken legs; bone in, skin on, cut into drumsticks and thighs, about 3 ½ lbs.
- 2 eggs
- 1/2 cup almond flour
- Pickle juice from 24 oz. jar of kosher dill pickles
- 1 cup breadcrumbs
- 1 tsp. black pepper
- 1 tsp. sea salt
- 2 tbsp. olive oil
- 1/8 tsp. cayenne pepper
- 1/2 tsp. ground paprika

**Directions:**

1. Place chicken in a bowl and pour the pickle juice over it. Cover and transfer chicken to fridge to brine in pickle juice for 8 hours
2. Remove the chicken from the fridge. Place flour in a bowl and season it with salt and pepper. In another bowl, whisk egg and olive oil.
3. Place the breadcrumbs in a third bowl, along with paprika, salt, pepper and cayenne pepper. Preheat your air fryer to 370°F. Remove the chicken from the pickle brine and pat dry
4. Coat pieces of chicken with flour, then egg mixture and finally with breadcrumbs. Place the breaded chicken on a baking sheet and spray each piece with cooking spray. Air fry chicken in two batches.
5. Place two pieces thighs and two drumsticks into air fryer basket. Air fry for 10 minutes. Turn pieces of chicken over and cook for another 10 minutes
6. Remove chicken and set aside. Repeat with the second batch of chicken. Lower the temperature to 340°F.
7. Place the first batch of chicken on top of the second batch and air fry for an additional 7 minutes.

## 306. Spicy Buffalo Wings

Cooking Time: 26 minutes
Servings: 4

**Ingredients:**

- 2 lbs. chicken wings
- 1/2 cup hot & spicy sauce; divided
- 6 tbsp. melted butter; divided

- Salt to taste

**Directions:**

1. In a bowl, mix ¼ cup hot and spicy sauce and 3 tbsp. of melted butter. Cover chicken pieces with the mixture and marinate for 2 hours in the fridge
2. Preheat your air fryer to 400°F. Split the wings into 2 batches. Place the first batch into air fryer and cook for 12 minutes, shaking halfway through cook time
3. Repeat with the second batch. Place all the wings into air fryer for additional 2 minute cook time.
4. Finish preparing sauce by mixing the remaining 3 tbsp. of butter and ¼ cup of hot sauce. Dip cooked wings in sauce and enjoy!

## 307. Crunchy Chicken Strips

Cooking Time: 12 minutes
Servings: 8

**Ingredients:**

- 1 chicken breast; cut into strips
- 3/4 cup breadcrumbs
- 1/4 cup almond flour
- 1 egg; beaten
- 1 tsp. mix spice
- 1 tbsp. plain oats
- 1 tbsp. dried coconut
- Salt and pepper to taste

**Directions:**

1. In a bowl, mix oats, mix spice, coconut, pepper, salt and breadcrumbs. Add beaten egg to another bowl. Add the flour to a third dish
2. Take the flour and coat chicken strips with it, then dip in egg and roll in breadcrumb mixture. Place the coated chicken strips in air fryer basket and air fry at 350°F and cook for 4 minutes. Serve hot!

## 308. Teriyaki Chicken

(Cooking Time: 14 minutes
Servings: 2

**Ingredients:**

- 2 boneless; skinless chicken thighs
- 1 tsp. ginger; grated.
- 3 tbsp. teriyaki sauce
- 1 tbsp. cooking wine

**Directions:**

1. Mix all ingredients in a bowl. Place bowl in fridge for 30 minutes. Add marinated chicken to air fryer in a baking pan and cook at 350°F for 8 minutes
2. After 8 minutes, flip the chicken over and cook for an additional 6 minutes. Serve hot.

## 309. Crispy Honey Chicken Wings

(Cooking Time: 35 minutes
Servings: 8

**Ingredients:**

- 16 pieces chicken wings
- 1/4 cup clover honey
- 1/8 cup water; or as needed
- 3/4 cup potato starch
- 1/4 cup butter
- 4 tbsp. garlic; minced
- 1/2 tsp. kosher salt

**Directions:**

1. Rinse and dry the chicken wings. Place potato starch in a bowl and coat chicken wings. Add wings to the air fryer, then cook at 380°F for 25 minutes, shaking the basket every five minutes
2. Once done, cook again at 400°F for 5-10 minutes. All skin on all wings should be very dry and crisp.
3. Heat a small stainless-steel saucepan on low heat. Melt the butter, then add garlic. Sauté the for 5 minutes. Afterwards, add honey and salt
4. Simmer on low for about 20 minutes, stirring every few minutes so the sauce

does not burn. Add a few drops of water after 15 minutes to keep sauce from hardening.

5.  Remove chicken wings from air fryer and pour sauce over. Coat and serve.

## 310. Chicken Fried Rice

(Cooking Time: 20 minutes
Servings: 3

**Ingredients:**

- 1 cup chicken; cooked and diced
- 3 cups white rice; cooked
- 1 cup frozen peas and carrots
- 1/2 cup onion; diced
- 1 tbsp. vegetable oil
- 6 tbsp. soy sauce

**Directions:**

1.  Place white rice into the mixing bowl, adding the vegetable oil and the soy sauce. Mix thoroughly.
2.  Then, add the frozen peas and carrots, diced onions and diced chicken. Mix thoroughly once more
3.  Pour the rice mixture into the nonstick pan and place in air fryer. Cook at 360°F for 20 minutes. Once done, remove and serve.

## 311. Sweet Mustard Chicken

: Cooking Time: 12 minutes
Servings: 4

**Ingredients:**

- 12 oz. chicken breast; diced
- 1 cup cornstarch
- 6 oz. Sweet Mustard sauce
- 1/4 cup milk
- 1/2 tsp. white pepper

**Directions:**

1.  Add milk and chicken to a mixing bowl and set aside for 2 minutes. Drain the milk from chicken and toss chicken with

cornstarch

2.  Place the chicken in the air fryer at 350°F for 12 minutes. Place chicken in serving dish and sprinkle with white pepper along with a dish of sauce for dipping chicken pieces in.

## 312. Chicken Drumst-.0icks

(Cooking Time: 20 minutes
Servings: 4

**Ingredients:**

- 8 chicken drumsticks
- 1 large egg; lightly beaten.
- 1/3 cup oats
- 1/3 cup cauliflower
- 1 tsp. cayenne pepper
- 2 tbsp. thyme
- 2 tbsp. oregano
- 3 tbsp. coconut milk
- 2 tbsp. mustard powder
- Salt and pepper to taste

**Directions:**

1.  Preheat your oven to 350°F. Season chicken drumsticks with salt and pepper. Rub coconut milk all over chicken drumsticks
2.  Add cayenne pepper, mustard powder, oregano, oats, thyme, cauliflower, into food processor and mix until you have a consistency of breadcrumbs. In a small bowl, add beaten egg
3.  Dip the chicken into breadcrumb mixture then into egg and dip again into breadcrumbs. Place coated chicken drumsticks inside air fryer and cook for 20 minutes. Serve hot.

## 313. Popcorn Chicken

(Cooking Time: 10 minutes
Servings: 12

**Ingredients:**

- 1 chicken breast; boneless
- 1 cup breadcrumbs
- 1/4 cup almond flour
- 1 egg; beaten
- 2 tsp. mix spice
- Salt and pepper to taste

**Directions:**

1. Add the chicken to your food processor and process it until it is minced. In a bowl, add the beaten egg. In another bowl, add the flour
2. In a third shallow dish add the breadcrumbs, mix spice, pepper and salt and stir to combine. Make small chicken balls from minced chicken.
3. Roll chicken balls in flour, then dip into egg, then coat with breadcrumbs. Place coated chicken balls into air fryer and air fry at 350°F for 10 minutes. Serve hot!

## 314. Chicken Tenderloins

(Cooking Time: 12 minutes
Servings: 4

**Ingredients:**

- 8 chicken tenderloins
- 1 egg; beaten
- 1 cup breadcrumbs
- 2 tbsp. olive oil
- Salt and pepper to taste

**Directions:**

1. Preheat your air fryer to 350°F. Mix olive oil, breadcrumbs, pepper and salt in a bowl. Add the beaten egg in another dish
2. Dip chicken into egg then coat with breadcrumbs and place into air fryer basket and cook for 12 minutes.

## 315. Sweet and Spicy Chicken Wings

(Cooking Time: 16 minutes
Servings: 6

**Ingredients:**

- 6 chicken wings
- 2 garlic cloves; chopped.
- 1 tbsp. honey
- 2 tbsp. Worcestershire sauce
- 1 tsp. red chili flakes
- Salt and pepper to taste

**Directions:**

1. Mix in a bowl, garlic, red chili flakes, honey, Worcestershire sauce, salt and pepper. Toss chicken wings in mixture and place into fridge for an hour
2. Place the marinated chicken wings in the air fryer basket and spray them with cooking spray. Air fry chicken wings at 320°F for 8 minutes
3. After 8 minutes, turn the heat to 350°F for another 4 minutes. Serve hot!

## 316. Garlic Chicken Nuggets

(Cooking Time: 10 minutes
Servings: 4

**Ingredients:**

- 9 oz. chicken breast; thinly chopped
- 3/4 cup breadcrumbs
- 2 eggs; divided
- 1 tsp. tomato ketchup
- 1 tsp. parsley
- 1 tsp. garlic; minced.
- 1 tsp. paprika
- 1 tbsp. olive oil
- Salt and pepper to taste

**Directions:**

1. Mix breadcrumbs, salt, pepper, paprika and oil. Mix well to make a thick paste. Mix chopped chicken, ketchup, one egg, parsley in a bowl
2. Shape the chicken mixture into little nugget shapes and dip into other beaten egg. Coat the nuggets with breadcrumbs. Cook at 390°F for 10 minutes in air fryer.

## 317. Chicken Kebabs

(Cooking Time: 15 to 20 minutes
Servings: 5

**Ingredients:**

- 2 chicken breasts; diced
- 1 large yellow bell pepper; diced
- 1 large red bell pepper; diced
- 1 large green bell pepper; diced
- 3 button mushrooms; sliced
- Pepper; to taste
- 1/2 cup soy sauce
- 1/4 cup honey
- Sesame oil
- Sesame seeds
- Oil spray
- Salt; to taste

**Directions:**

1. Preheat the air fryer at 338°F. Season the chicken breast with pepper and salt. Mist some oil onto it, then add the soy sauce and honey
2. Mix thoroughly. Add some sesame oil and drizzle the chicken mixture with sesame seeds.
3. Take out the wooden skewers and arrange the ingredients in the following order: yellow bell pepper, chicken breast, red bell pepper, mushroom, chicken breast, green bell pepper, chicken breast, yellow bell pepper, red bell pepper
4. Do this until all the ingredients have been used up. Glaze with the remaining honey soy sauce mixture.
5. Add the kebabs to the basket and cook for 15-20 minutes. Drizzle with remaining sesame seeds and serve.

## 318. Chicken Burger Patties

(Cooking Time: 11 minutes
Servings: 1

**Ingredients:**

- 1-2 chicken patties.

**Directions:**

1. Preheat air fryer at 360 °F for 3 minutes. Place the frozen chicken patties into the basket and cook for 11 minutes. Serve as desired

## 319. Chicken Sandwich

(Cooking Time: 16 minutes
Servings: 2

**Ingredients:**

- 2 chicken breasts; boneless and skinless
- 2 eggs
- 4 hamburger buns; buttered or toasted
- 8 dill pickle chips
- 1/2 cup dill pickle juice
- 1/2 cup milk
- 1 cup all-purpose flour
- 2 tbsp. powdered sugar
- 1 tsp. paprika
- 1 tsp. sea salt
- 1/2 tsp. ground black pepper
- 1/2 tsp. garlic powder
- 1/4 tsp. ground celery seed
- 1 tbsp. extra-virgin olive oil

**Directions:**

1. Place chicken in a Ziploc bag and pound into ½ inch thickness. Then, depending on its size, cut chicken into 2-3 pieces
2. Return chicken to Ziploc bag and pour in pickle juice. Marinate for at least 30 minutes in the refrigerator.
3. In a bowl, beat the eggs together with the milk. Then, in another bowl, combine the flour with the sugar and spices.
4. Using tongs, coat the chicken with the egg mixture first, then with the flour mixture. Shake off the excess.
5. Spray the bottom of the air fryer with the olive oil and add the chicken. Spray the chicken with oil as well and cook at 340°F

for 6 minutes

6. Flip over the chicken and spray with oil again, then cook for another 6 minutes.

7. Raise the temperature to 400°F and cook for 2 minutes on each side. Then, serve on buttered and toasted buns along with the pickle chips.

## 320. Lemon Pepper Chicken

(Cooking Time: 15 minutes
Servings: 1

**Ingredients:**

- 2 lemons; rind and juice part
- 1 chicken breast
- A handful of black peppercorns
- 1 tbsp. chicken seasoning
- 1 tsp. garlic purée
- Salt and pepper; to taste

**Directions:**

1. Preheat the air fryer to 356°F. Place a large sheet of silver foil on a work top and place all the seasonings and the lemon rind inside

2. Lay out your chicken breasts onto a chopping board and trim off any fatty bits or bone. Season each side with salt and pepper

3. Rub the chicken seasoning into both sides. Afterwards, place chicken on the silver foil sheet and rub well.

4. Tightly seal the foil and flatten chicken further with a rolling pin. Then, place in the air fryer for 15 minutes until fully cooked in the middle. Serve.

## 321. Chicken Quesadillas

(Cooking Time: 8 minutes
Servings: 6

**Ingredients:**

- 2 soft taco shells
- Chicken fajita strips
- 1/2 cup onions; sliced

- 1/2 cup green peppers; sliced
- Vegetable oil
- Mexican cheese; shredded

**Directions:**

1. Preheat air fryer at 370°F for about 3 minutes. Spray pan lightly with vegetable oil. Place 1 soft taco shell on the pan, topping with shredded cheese

2. Lay out the fajita chicken strips in a single layer, then top with the onions and green peppers. Add more shredded cheese.

3. Place another soft taco shell on top and spray lightly with vegetable oil. Hold down with the fryer rack. Cook the quesadilla for 4 minutes, then flip over carefully with large spatula

4. Spray lightly with vegetable oil and return rack on top of shell to hold it in place. Cook for another 4 minutes. Once at your preferred level of crispiness, remove and cut into 4 slices or 6 slices. Serve

## 322. Rotisserie Chicken

(Cooking Time: 1 hour
Servings: 4

**Ingredients:**

- 1 to 2 tbsp. ghee or preferred oil
- 1 whole chicken; cleaned and blotted dry.
- 1 tbsp. seasoning salt

**Directions:**

1. Rub your chosen oil all over the chicken and season generously. Place it breast-side own on the air fryer and cook at 350°F for 30 minutes. Flip the chicken over and cook for another 30 minutes, or until it reaches 165°F. Let it rest for 10 minutes and serve

## 323. Coconut Chicken Tenders

(Cooking Time: 10 minutes
Servings: 5

**Ingredients:**

- 16 oz. chicken breast tenders
- 1/4 cup light coconut milk
- 1 egg
- 1/2 cup coconut flakes; sweetened
- 1/4 cup flour
- 1/2 cup panko breadcrumbs
- Oil spray
- 1/2 tsp. salt
- 1/2 tsp. ground ginger
- 1/2 tsp. onion powder
- 1/2 tsp. ground black pepper

**Directions:**

1. To prepare, rinse and pat the chicken tenders dry. Then, in 3 separate bowls, mix the following combinations: flour, salt, pepper, ground ginger and onion powder; egg and light coconut milk; and panko crumbs and coconut flakes
2. One by one, dip the chicken tenders into the flour mixture first, then the egg mixture, then the panko mixture. Make sure the chicken is well-covered with each before moving onto the next
3. Spray the bottom of your preheated basket with oil to prevent sticking. Lay chicken in single layer into the basket and spray the tops lightly with oil. Air fry at 360°F for 10 minutes, flipping once halfway through and spraying with oil once more. Serve once done

## 324. Bacon Wrapped Herb Chicken

(Cooking Time: 15 minutes
Servings: 6

**Ingredients:**

- 1 chicken breast; cut into 6 pieces
- 6 slices of bacon
- 1 tbsp. soft cheese
- 1/2 tsp. parsley; dried.
- 1/2 tsp. paprika
- 1/2 tsp. basil; dried.
- Salt and pepper to taste

**Directions:**

1. In a bowl, mix basil, parsley, salt, pepper and paprika. Place the bacon slices on a dish and spread them with soft cheese
2. Place the chicken pieces into basil mix and cover with seasoning. Place the chicken pieces on top of bacon slices. Roll up and secure with toothpick.
3. Place into air fryer and cook at 350°F and cook for 15 minutes

## 325. Chicken Pasta Salad

(Cooking Time: 27 minutes
Servings: 2

**Ingredients:**

- 3 chicken breasts
- 1 medium bag frozen vegetables of choice
- 1 cup rigatoni or pasta of choice; cooked
- Paprika
- Garlic and herb seasoning
- Italian dressing
- Black pepper
- Ground parsley
- Oil spray

**Directions:**

1. Wash the chicken breasts and season with paprika, garlic and herb seasoning and a tbsp. of the Italian dressing. Top a little with black pepper and ground parsley. Mist the air fryer with oil, then add the marinated chicken breasts. Spray oil over the chicken as well. Cook at 360°F for 15 minutes
2. Halfway through, flip the chicken breasts and season with pepper and parsley. Spray over with oil and allow to cook all the way
3. While the chicken is cooking, empty a bag of frozen vegetables into a bowl and season with the garlic and herb dressing and some Italian dressing. Mix well. Spray another air fryer and add in the

vegetables. Cook for 12 minutes at 380°F.

4. Dice the cooked chicken while waiting for the vegetables to cook. Season the cooked with some garlic and herb seasoning, along with some parsley and Italian dressing

5. Mix well, tasting to your preference. Add the diced chicken to the mix, mixing well. Once the vegetables have finished cooking, add to the chicken and pasta mixture and incorporate thoroughly. Serve

## 326. Flourless Chicken Cordon Bleu

(Cooking Time: 8 minutes
Servings: 2

**Ingredients:**

- 2 chicken breasts
- 1 slice cheddar cheese
- 1 slice ham
- 1 small egg; beaten
- 1 tbsp. oats
- 1 tbsp. thyme
- 1 tbsp. tarragon
- 1 tbsp. soft cheese
- 1 tsp. garlic purée
- 1 tsp. parsley
- Salt and pepper; to taste

**Directions:**

1. Preheat air fryer to 356°F. On a chopping board, chop the chicken breasts at a side angle to right near the corner. Sprinkle the chicken on all sides with salt, pepper and tarragon

2. In a mixing bowl, mix the soft cheese, garlic and parsley well. Place a layer of the cheese mixture in the middle of the breast along with ½ slice each of the cheddar cheese and ham. Once done, press the chicken down to seal

3. Place the egg and oats in different bowls. Add the thyme to the oats bowl and mix well. Roll the chicken in the oats first,

then in the egg, then back to the oats

4. Place chicken pieces on a baking sheet in your air fryer and cook for 30 minutes at 356°F. After 20 minutes, turn it over so both sides cook evenly. Serve.

## 327. Herby Chicken

(Cooking Time: 15 minutes
Servings: 2

**Ingredients:**

- 2 chicken breasts
- Mixed herb chicken seasoning
- 2 tbsp. soft cheese
- Salt and pepper; to taste

**Directions:**

1. Preheat air fryer at 356°F. Score the chicken by partly slicing into the breasts for the seasoning. Season with salt and pepper, then using your hands, cover the chicken in the soft cheese

2. Roll the chicken breasts in the mixed herbs and place in the air fryer on a reusable baking mat. Cook at 356°F for 15 minutes or until cooked in the middle. Serve.

## 328. Honey Chicken Wings

(Cooking Time: 30 minutes
Servings: 2

**Ingredients:**

- 1 lb. chicken wings; tips removed and wings separated.
- Cilantro; chives, or scallions for garnish
- For the sauce
- 1/4 cup honey
- 1 ½ tbsp. soy sauce
- 1 tbsp. butter
- 2 tbsp. sriracha sauce

- Juice of ½ a lime

**Directions:**

1. Preheat the air fryer to 360°F. Add the chicken wings to the air fryer basket and cook for 30 minutes, turning the chicken about every 7 minutes with tongs to make sure the wings are evenly browned

2. While the wings are cooking, add the sauce ingredients to a small sauce pan and bring to a boil for about 3 minutes. When the wings are cooked, toss them in a bowl with the sauce until fully coated. Sprinkle with the garnish and serve immediately.

## 329. Chicken Fajita Rollups

(Cooking Time: 12 minutes
Servings: 6

**Ingredients:**

- 3 chicken breasts
- 1/2 large red bell pepper; cut into strips
- 1/2 large green bell pepper; cut into strips
- 1/2 large yellow bell pepper; cut into strips
- 1/2 large red onion; sliced
- 2 tsp. paprika
6. .

- 1 tsp. garlic powder
- 1 tsp. cumin powder
- 1/2 tsp. cayenne pepper
- 1/2 tsp. Mexican oregano
- Cooking spray
- Salt and pepper; to taste

**Directions:**

1. Mix spices in a small bowl and set aside. Slice the chicken breasts lengthwise into 2 even slices.

2. Then, place each breast half between parchment paper and firmly pound it using a heavy object to an even thickness of ¼ of an inch

3. Liberally season both sides of the breast with the prepared spice rub

4. Afterwards, portion the vegetable strips evenly among the cuts and place each portion on one side of the chicken. Roll up the chicken tightly and secure with toothpicks. Sprinkle the remaining spice rub

5. Mist the air fryer basket with cooking spray and place the rollups in it. Spray the chicken with more cooking spray, then air fry for 12 minutes. Repeat until all the rollups are cooked, then serve

# Meat

## 330. Mustard Lamb Loin Chops

Preparation Time: 15 minutes
Cooking Time: 30 minutes
Servings: 4

**Ingredients:**

- 8: 4-ounceslamb loin chops
- 2 tablespoons Dijon mustard
- 1 tablespoon fresh lemon juice
- ½ teaspoon olive oil
- 1 teaspoon dried tarragon
- Salt and black pepper, to taste

**Directions:**

1. Preheat the Air fryer to 390 o F and grease an Air fryer basket.
2. Mix the mustard, lemon juice, oil, tarragon, salt, and black pepper in a large bowl.
3. Coat the chops generously with the mustard mixture and arrange in the Air fryer basket.
4. Cook for about 15 minutes, flipping once in between and dish out to serve hot.

**Nutrition:**
Calories: 433, Fat: 17.6g, Carbohydrates: 0.6g, Sugar: 0.2g, Protein: 64.1g, Sodium: 201mg

## 331. Herbed Lamb Chops

Preparation Time: 10 minutes
Cooking Time: 7 minutes
Servings: 2

**Ingredients:**

- 4: 4-ounceslamb chops
- 1 tablespoon fresh lemon juice
- 1 tablespoon olive oil
- 1 teaspoon dried rosemary
- 1 teaspoon dried thyme

- 1 teaspoon dried oregano
- ½ teaspoon ground cumin
- ½ teaspoon ground coriander
- Salt and black pepper, to taste

**Directions:**

1. Preheat the Air fryer to 390 o F and grease an Air fryer basket.
2. Mix the lemon juice, oil, herbs, and spices in a large bowl.
3. Coat the chops generously with the herb mixture and refrigerate to marinate for about 1 hour.
4. Arrange the chops in the Air fryer basket and cook for about 7 minutes, flipping once in between.
5. Dish out the lamb chops in a platter and serve hot.

**Nutrition:**
Calories: 491, Fat: 24g, Carbohydrates: 1.6g, Sugar: 0.2g, Protein: 64g, Sodium: 253mg

## 332. Za'atar Lamb Loin Chops

Preparation Time: 10 minutes
Cooking Time: 30 minutes
Servings: 4

**Ingredients:**

- 8: 3½-ouncesbone-in lamb loin chops, trimmed
- 3 garlic cloves, crushed
- 1 tablespoon fresh lemon juice
- 1 teaspoon olive oil
- 1 tablespoon Za'ataro
- Salt and black pepper, to taste

**Directions:**

1. Preheat the Air fryer to 400 o F and grease an Air fryer basket.
2. Mix the garlic, lemon juice, oil, Za'atar,

salt, and black pepper in a large bowl.

3. Coat the chops generously with the herb mixture and arrange the chops in the Air fryer basket.
4. Cook for about 15 minutes, flipping twice in between and dish out the lamb chops to serve hot.
5. Nutrition:
6. Calories: 433, Fat: 17.6g, Carbohydrates: 0.6g, Sugar: 0.2g, Protein: 64.1g, Sodium: 201mg
7. (Note: Za'atar - Za'atar is generally made with ground dried thyme, oregano, marjoram, or some combination thereof, mixed with toasted sesame seeds, and salt, though other spices such as sumac might also be added. Some commercial varieties also include roasted flour.

## 333. Pesto Coated Rack of Lamb

Preparation Time: 15 minutes
Cooking Time: 15 minutes
Servings: 4

**Ingredients:**

- ½ bunch fresh mint
- 1: 1½-poundsrack of lamb
- 1 garlic clove
- ¼ cup extra-virgin olive oil
- ½ tablespoon honey
- Salt and black pepper, to taste

**Directions:**

1. Preheat the Air fryer to 200 o F and grease an Air fryer basket.
2. Put the mint, garlic, oil, honey, salt, and black pepper in a blender and pulse until smooth to make pesto.
3. Coat the rack of lamb with this pesto on both sides and arrange in the Air fryer basket.
4. Cook for about 15 minutes and cut the rack into individual chops to serve.

**Nutrition:**
Calories: 406, Fat: 27.7g, Carbohydrates: 2.9g,

Sugar: 2.2g, Protein: 34.9g, Sodium: 161mg

## 334. Spiced Lamb Steaks

Preparation Time: 15 minutes
Cooking Time: 15 minutes
Servings: 3

**Ingredients:**

- ½ onion, roughly chopped
- 1½ pounds boneless lamb sirloin steaks
- 5 garlic cloves, peeled
- 1 tablespoon fresh ginger, peeled
- 1 teaspoon garam masala
- 1 teaspoon ground fennel
- ½ teaspoon ground cumin
- ½ teaspoon ground cinnamon
- ½ teaspoon cayenne pepper
- Salt and black pepper, to taste

**Directions:**

1. Preheat the Air fryer to 330 o F and grease an Air fryer basket.
2. Put the onion, garlic, ginger, and spices in a blender and pulse until smooth.
3. Coat the lamb steaks with this mixture on both sides and refrigerate to marinate for about 24 hours.
4. Arrange the lamb steaks in the Air fryer basket and cook for about 15 minutes, flipping once in between.
5. Dish out the steaks in a platter and serve warm.

**Nutrition:**
Calories: 252, Fat: 16.7g, Carbohydrates: 4.2g, Sugar: 0.7g, Protein: 21.7g, Sodium: 42mg

## 335. Leg of Lamb with Brussels Sprout

Preparation Time: 20 minutes
Cooking Time: 1 hour 30 minutes
Servings: 6

**Ingredients:**

- 2¼ pounds leg of lamb

- 1 tablespoon fresh rosemary, minced
- 1 tablespoon fresh lemon thyme
- 1½ pounds Brussels sprouts, trimmed
- 3 tablespoons olive oil, divided
- 1 garlic clove, minced
- Salt and ground black pepper, as required
- 2 tablespoons honey

**Directions:**
1. Preheat the Air fryer to 300 o F and grease an Air fryer basket.
2. Make slits in the leg of lamb with a sharp knife.
3. Mix 2 tablespoons of oil, herbs, garlic, salt, and black pepper in a bowl.
4. Coat the leg of lamb with oil mixture generously and arrange in the Air fryer basket.
5. Cook for about 75 minutes and set the Air fryer to 390 o F.
6. Coat the Brussels sprout evenly with the remaining oil and honey and arrange them in the Air fryer basket with leg of lamb.
7. Cook for about 15 minutes and dish out to serve warm.

**Nutrition:**
Calories: 449, Fats: 19.9g, Carbohydrates: 16.6g, Sugar: 8.2g, Proteins: 51.7g, Sodium: 185mg

## 336. Honey Mustard Cheesy Meatballs

Preparation Time: 15 minutes
Cooking Time: 15 minutes
Servings: 8

**Ingredients:**
- 2 onions, chopped
- 1 pound ground beef
- 4 tablespoons fresh basil, chopped
- 2 tablespoons cheddar cheese, grated
- 2 teaspoons garlic paste
- 2 teaspoons honey
- Salt and black pepper, to taste
- 2 teaspoons mustard

**Directions:**
1. Preheat the Air fryer to 385 o F and grease an Air fryer basket.
2. Mix all the ingredients in a bowl until well combined.
3. Shape the mixture into equal-sized balls gently and arrange the meatballs in the Air fryer basket.
4. Cook for about 15 minutes and dish out to serve warm.

**Nutrition:**
Calories: 134, Fat: 4.4g, Carbohydrates: 4.6g, Sugar: 2.7g, Protein: 18.2g, Sodium: 50mg

## 337. Spicy Lamb Kebabs

Preparation Time: 20 minutes
Cooking Time: 8 minutes
Servings: 6

**Ingredients:**
- 4 eggs, beaten
- 1 cup pistachios, chopped
- 1 pound ground lamb
- 4 tablespoons plain flour
- 4 tablespoons flat-leaf parsley, chopped
- 2 teaspoons chili flakes
- 4 garlic cloves, minced
- 2 tablespoons fresh lemon juice
- 2 teaspoons cumin seeds
- 1 teaspoon fennel seeds
- 2 teaspoons dried mint
- 2 teaspoons salt
- Olive oil
- 1 teaspoon coriander seeds
- 1 teaspoon freshly ground black pepper

**Directions:**
1. Preheat the Air fryer to 355 o F and grease an Air fryer basket.
2. Mix lamb, pistachios, eggs, lemon juice, chili flakes, flour, cumin seeds, fennel seeds, coriander seeds, mint, parsley, salt and black pepper in a large bowl.

3. Thread the lamb mixture onto metal skewers to form sausages and coat with olive oil.
4. Place the skewers in the Air fryer basket and cook for about 8 minutes.
5. Dish out in a platter and serve hot.

**Nutrition:**

Calories: 284, Fat: 15.8g, Carbohydrates: 8.4g, Sugar: 1.1g, Protein: 27.9g, Sodium: 932mg

## 338. Simple Beef Burgers

Preparation Time: 20 minutes
Cooking Time: 12 minutes
Servings: 6

**Ingredients:**

- 2 pounds ground beef
- 12 cheddar cheese slices
- 12 dinner rolls
- 6 tablespoons tomato ketchup
- Salt and black pepper, to taste

**Directions:**

1. Preheat the Air fryer to 390 o F and grease an Air fryer basket.
2. Mix the beef, salt and black pepper in a bowl.
3. Make small equal-sized patties from the beef mixture and arrange half of patties in the Air fryer basket.
4. Cook for about 12 minutes and top each patty with 1 cheese slice.
5. Arrange the patties between rolls and drizzle with ketchup.
6. Repeat with the remaining batch and dish out to serve hot.

**Nutrition:**

Calories: 537, Fat: 28.3g, Carbohydrates: 7.6g, Sugar: 4.2g, Protein: 60.6g, Sodium: 636mg

## 339. Lamb with Potatoes

Preparation Time: 20 minutes
Cooking Time: 15 minutes

Servings: 2

**Ingredients:**

- ½ pound lamb meat
- 2 small potatoes, peeled and halved
- ½ small onion, peeled and halved
- ¼ cup frozen sweet potato fries
- 1 garlic clove, crushed
- ½ tablespoon dried rosemary, crushed
- 1 teaspoon olive oil

Directions:

1. Preheat the Air fryer to 355 o F and arrange a divider in the Air fryer.
2. Rub the lamb evenly with garlic and rosemary and place on one side of Air fryer divider.
3. Cook for about 20 minutes and meanwhile, microwave the potatoes for about 4 minutes.
4. Dish out the potatoes in a large bowl and stir in the olive oil and onions.
5. Transfer into the Air fryer divider and change the side of lamb ramp.
6. Cook for about 15 minutes, flipping once in between and dish out in a bowl.

**Nutrition:**

Calories: 399, Fat: 18.5g, Carbohydrates: 32.3g, Sugar: 3.8g, Protein: 24.5g, Sodium: 104mg

## 340. Herbed Pork Burgers

Preparation Time: 15 minutes
Cooking Time: 45 minutes
Servings: 8

**Ingredients:**

- 2 small onions, chopped
- 21-ounce ground pork
- 2 teaspoons fresh basil, chopped
- 8 burger buns
- ½ cup cheddar cheese, grated
- 2 teaspoons mustard
- 2 teaspoons garlic puree

- 2 teaspoons tomato puree
- Salt and freshly ground black pepper, to taste
- 2 teaspoons dried mixed herbs, crushed

**Directions:**
1. Preheat the Air fryer to 395 o F and grease an Air fryer basket.
2. Mix all the ingredients in a bowl except cheese and buns.
3. Make 8 equal-sized patties from the pork mixture and arrange thee patties in the Air fryer basket.
4. Cook for about 45 minutes, flipping once in between and arrange the patties in buns with cheese to serve.

**Nutrition:**
Calories: 289, Fat: 6.5g, Carbohydrates: 29.2g, Sugar: 4.9g, Protein: 28.7g, Sodium: 384mg

## 341. Chinese Style Pork Meatballs

Preparation Time: 15 minutes
Cooking Time: 20 minutes
Servings: 3

**Ingredients:**
- 1 egg, beaten
- 6-ounce ground pork
- ¼ cup cornstarch
- 1 teaspoon oyster sauce
- ½ tablespoon light soy sauce
- ½ teaspoon sesame oil
- ¼ teaspoon five spice powder
- ½ tablespoon olive oil
- ¼ teaspoon brown sugar

**Directions:**
1. Preheat the Air fryer to 390 o F and grease an Air fryer basket.
2. Mix all the ingredients in a bowl except cornstarch and oil until well combined.
3. Shape the mixture into equal-sized balls and place the cornstarch in a shallow dish.
4. Roll the meatballs evenly into cornstarch

mixture and arrange in the Air fryer basket.
5. Cook for about 10 minutes and dish out to serve warm.

**Nutrition:**
Calories: 171, Fat: 6.6g, Carbohydrates: 10.8g, Sugar: 0.7g, Protein: 16.9g, Sodium: 254mg

## 342. Sausage Meatballs

Preparation Time: 15 minutes
Cooking Time: 15 minutes
Servings: 4

**Ingredients:**
- 3½-ounce sausage, casing removed
- ½ medium onion, minced finely
- 1 teaspoon fresh sage, chopped finely
- 3 tablespoons Italian breadcrumbs
- ½ teaspoon garlic, minced
- Salt and black pepper, to taste

**Directions:**
1. Preheat the Air fryer to 355 o F and grease an Air fryer basket.
2. Mix all the ingredients in a bowl until well combined.
3. Shape the mixture into equal-sized balls and arrange the balls in the Air fryer basket.
4. Cook for about 15 minutes and dish out to serve warm.

**Nutrition:**
Calories: 111, Fat: 7.3g, Carbohydrates: 5.2g, Sugar: 0.9g, Protein: 5.7g, Sodium: 224mg

## 343. Italian Beef Meatballs

Preparation Time: 10 minutes
Cooking Time: 15 minutes
Servings: 6

**Ingredients:**
- 2 large eggs
- 2 pounds ground beef

- ¼ cup fresh parsley, chopped
- 1¼ cups panko breadcrumbs
- ¼ cup Parmigiano Reggiano, grated
- 1 teaspoon dried oregano
- 1 small garlic clove, chopped
- Salt and black pepper, to taste
- 1 teaspoon vegetable oil

**Directions:**

1. Preheat the Air fryer to 350 o F and grease an Air fryer basket.
2. Mix beef with all other ingredients in a bowl until well combined.
3. Make equal-sized balls from the mixture and arrange the balls in the Air fryer basket.
4. Cook for about 13 minutes and dish out to serve warm.

**Nutrition:**
Calories: 398, Fat: 13.8g, Carbohydrates: 3.6g, Sugar: 1.3g, Protein: 51.8g, Sodium: 272mg

## 344. Beef and Veggie Spring Rolls

Preparation Time: 10 minutes
Cooking Time: 14 minutes
Servings: 8

**Ingredients:**

- 2-ounce Asian rice noodles, soaked in warm water, drained and cut into small lengths
- 7-ounce ground beef
- 1 small onion, chopped
- 1 cup fresh mixed vegetables
- 1 packet spring roll skins
- 2 tablespoons olive oil
- Salt and black pepper, to taste

**Directions:**

1. Preheat the Air fryer to 350 o F and grease an Air fryer basket.
2. Heat olive oil in a pan and add the onion and garlic.
3. Sauté for about 5 minutes and stir in the

beef.
4. Cook for about 5 minutes and add vegetables and soy sauce.
5. Cook for about 7 minutes and stir in the noodles.
6. Place the spring rolls skin onto a smooth surface and put the filling mixture diagonally in it.
7. Fold in both sides to seal properly and brush with oil.
8. Arrange the rolls in batches in the Air fryer basket and cook for about 14 minutes, tossing in between.
9. Cook for about 15 minutes, flipping once in between and dish out in a platter.

**Nutrition:**
Calories: 147, Fat: 5.4g, Carbohydrates: 15.9g, Sugar: 0.6g, Protein: 8.7g, Sodium: 302mg

## 345. Beef Pot Pie

Preparation Time: 10 minutes
Cooking Time: 1 hour 27 minutes
Servings: 3

**Ingredients:**

- 1 pound beef stewing steak, cubed
- 1 can ale mixed into 1 cup water
- 2 beef bouillon cubes
- 1 tablespoon plain flour
- 1 prepared short crust pastry
- 1 tablespoon olive oil
- 1 tablespoon tomato puree
- 2 tablespoons onion paste
- Salt and black pepper, to taste

**Directions:**

1. Preheat the Air fryer to 390 o F and grease 2 ramekins lightly.
2. Heat olive oil in a pan and add steak cubes.
3. Cook for about 5 minutes and stir in the onion paste and tomato puree.
4. Cook for about 6 minutes and add the ale mixture, bouillon cubes, salt and black

pepper.

5. Bring to a boil and reduce the heat to simmer for about 1 hour.

6. Mix flour and 3 tablespoons of warm water in a bowl and slowly add this mixture into the beef mixture.

7. Roll out the short crust pastry and line 2 ramekins with pastry.

8. Divide the beef mixture evenly in the ramekins and top with extra pastry.

9. Transfer into the Air fryer and cook for about 10 minutes.

10. Set the Air fryer to 335 o F and cook for about 6 more minutes.

11. Dish out and serve warm.

**Nutrition:**
Calories: 442, Fat: 14.2g, Carbohydrates: 19g, Sugar: 1.2g, Protein: 50.6g, Sodium: 583mg

## 346. Veggie Stuffed Beef Rolls

Preparation Time: 20 minutes
Cooking Time: 14 minutes
Servings: 6

**Ingredients:**
- 2 pounds beef flank steak, pounded to 1/8-inch thickness
- 6 Provolone cheese slices
- 3-ounce roasted red bell peppers
- ¾ cup fresh baby spinach
- 3 tablespoons prepared pesto
- Salt and black pepper, to taste

**Directions:**
1. Preheat the Air fryer to 400 o F and grease an Air fryer basket.

2. Place the steak onto a smooth surface and spread evenly with pesto.

3. Top with the cheese slices, red peppers and spinach.

4. Roll up the steak tightly around the filling and secure with the toothpicks.

5. Arrange the roll in the Air fryer basket and cook for about 14 minutes, flipping once in between.

6. Dish out in a platter and serve warm.

**Nutrition:**
Calories: 447, Fats: 23.4g, Carbohydrates: 1.8g, Sugar: 0.6g, Proteins: 53.2g, Sodium: 472mg

## 347. Tomato Stuffed Pork Roll

Preparation Time: 20 minutes
Cooking Time: 15 minutes
Servings: 4

**Ingredients:**
- 1 scallion, chopped
- ¼ cup sun-dried tomatoes, chopped finely
- 2 tablespoons fresh parsley, chopped
- 4: 6-ouncepork cutlets, pounded slightly
- Salt and freshly ground black pepper, to taste
- 2 teaspoons paprika
- ½ tablespoon olive oil

**Directions:**
1. Preheat the Air fryer to 390 o F and grease an Air fryer basket.

2. Mix scallion, tomatoes, parsley, salt and black pepper in a bowl.

3. Coat each cutlet with tomato mixture and roll up the cutlet, securing with cocktail sticks.

4. Coat the rolls with oil and rub with paprika, salt and black pepper.

5. Arrange the rolls in the Air fryer basket and cook for about 15 minutes, flipping once in between.

6. Dish out in a platter and serve warm.

**Nutrition:**
Calories: 244, Fat: 14.5g, Carbohydrates: 20.1g, Sugar: 1.7g, Protein: 8.2g, Sodium: 670mg

## 348. Ham Rolls

Preparation Time: 15 minutes
Cooking Time: 15 minutes
Servings: 4

**Ingredients:**

- 12-ounce refrigerated pizza crust, rolled into ¼ inch thickness
- 1/3 pound cooked ham, sliced
- ¾ cup Mozzarella cheese, shredded
- 3 cups Colby cheese, shredded
- 3-ounce roasted red bell peppers
- 1 tablespoon olive oil

**Directions:**

1. Preheat the Air fryer to 360 o F and grease an Air fryer basket.
2. Arrange the ham, cheeses and roasted peppers over one side of dough and fold to seal.
3. Brush the dough evenly with olive oil and cook for about 15 minutes, flipping twice in between.
4. Dish out in a platter and serve warm.

**Nutrition:**
Calories: 594, Fat: 35.8g, Carbohydrates: 35.4g, Sugar: 2.8g, Protein: 33g, Sodium: 1545mg

## 349. Ham Pinwheels

Preparation Time: 15 minutes
Cooking Time: 11 minutes
Servings: 4

**Ingredients:**

- 1 puff pastry sheet
- 10 ham slices
- 1 cup Gruyere cheese, shredded plus more for sprinkling
- 4 teaspoons Dijon mustard

**Directions:**

1. Preheat the Air fryer to 375 o F and grease an Air fryer basket.
2. Place the puff pastry onto a smooth surface and spread evenly with the mustard.
3. Top with the ham and ¾ cup cheese and roll the puff pastry.
4. Wrap the roll in plastic wrap and freeze

for about 30 minutes.

5. Remove from the freezer and slice into ½-inch rounds.
6. Arrange the pinwheels in the Air fryer basket and cook for about 8 minutes.
7. Top with remaining cheese and cook for 3 more minutes.
8. Dish out in a platter and serve warm.

**Nutrition:**
Calories: 294, Fat: 19.4g, Carbohydrates: 8.4g, Sugar: 0.2g, Protein: 20.8g, Sodium: 1090mg

## 350. Flank Steak Beef

Preparation Time: 10 minutes
Cooking Time: 20 minutes
Servings: 4

**Ingredients:**

- 1 pound flank steaks, sliced
- ¼ cup xanthum gum
- 2 teaspoon vegetable oil
- ½ teaspoon ginger
- ½ cup soy sauce
- 1 tablespoon garlic, minced
- ½ cup water
- ¾ cup swerve, packed

**Directions:**

1. Preheat the Air fryer to 390 o F and grease an Air fryer basket.
2. Coat the steaks with xanthum gum on both the sides and transfer into the Air fryer basket.
3. Cook for about 10 minutes and dish out in a platter.
4. Meanwhile, cook rest of the ingredients for the sauce in a saucepan.
5. Bring to a boil and pour over the steak slices to serve.

**Nutrition:**
Calories: 372, Fat: 11.8g, Carbohydrates: 1.8g, Sugar: 27.3g, Protein: 34g, Sodium: 871mg

## 351. Pepper Pork Chops

Preparation Time: 15 minutes
Cooking Time: 6 minutes
Servings: 2

**Ingredients:**

- 2 pork chops
- 1 egg white
- ¾ cup xanthum gum
- ½ teaspoon sea salt
- ¼ teaspoon freshly ground black pepper
- 1 oil mister

**Directions:**

1. Preheat the Air fryer to 400 o F and grease an Air fryer basket.
2. Whisk egg white with salt and black pepper in a bowl and dip the pork chops in it.
3. Cover the bowl and marinate for about 20 minutes.
4. Pour the xanthum gum over both sides of the chops and spray with oil mister.
5. Arrange the chops in the Air fryer basket and cook for about 6 minutes.
6. Dish out in a bowl and serve warm.

**Nutrition:**
Calories: 541, Fat: 34g, Carbohydrates: 3.4g, Sugar: 1g, Protein: 20.3g, Sodium: 547mg

## 352. Garlic Butter Pork Chops

Preparation Time: 10 minutes
Cooking Time: 8 minutes
Servings: 4

**Ingredients:**

- 4 pork chops
- 1 tablespoon coconut butter
- 2 teaspoons parsley
- 1 tablespoon coconut oil
- 2 teaspoons garlic, grated
- Salt and black pepper, to taste

**Directions:**

1. Preheat the Air fryer to 350 o F and grease an Air fryer basket.
2. Mix all the seasonings, coconut oil, garlic, butter, and parsley in a bowl and coat the pork chops with it.
3. Cover the chops with foil and refrigerate to marinate for about 1 hour.
4. Remove the foil and arrange the chops in the Air fryer basket.
5. Cook for about 8 minutes and dish out in a bowl to serve warm.

**Nutrition:**
Calories: 311, Fat: 25.5g, Carbohydrates: 1.4g, Sugar: 0.3g, Protein: 18.4g, Sodium: 58mg

## 353. Five Spice Pork

Preparation Time: 15 minutes
Cooking Time: 20 minutes
Servings: 4

**Ingredients:**

- 1-pound pork belly
- 2 tablespoons swerve
- 2 tablespoons dark soy sauce
- 1 tablespoon Shaoxing: cooking wine
- 2 teaspoons garlic, minced
- 2 teaspoons ginger, minced
- 1 tablespoon hoisin sauce
- 1 teaspoon Chinese Five Spice

**Directions:**

1. Preheat the Air fryer to 390 o F and grease an Air fryer basket.
2. Mix all the ingredients in a bowl and place in the Ziplock bag.
3. Seal the bag, shake it well and refrigerate to marinate for about 1 hour.
4. Remove the pork from the bag and arrange it in the Air fryer basket.
5. Cook for about 15 minutes and dish out in a bowl to serve warm.

**Nutrition:**

Calories: 604, Fat: 30.6g, Carbohydrates: 1.4g, Sugar: 20.3g, Protein: 19.8g, Sodium: 834mg

## 354. Roasted Lamb

Preparation Time: 15 minutes
Cooking Time: 1 hour 30 minutes
Servings: 4

**Ingredients:**

- 2½ pounds half lamb leg roast, slits carved
- 2 garlic cloves, sliced into smaller slithers
- 1 tablespoon dried rosemary
- 1 tablespoon olive oil
- Cracked Himalayan rock salt and cracked peppercorns, to taste

**Directions:**

1. Preheat the Air fryer to 400 o F and grease an Air fryer basket.
2. Insert the garlic slithers in the slits and brush with rosemary, oil, salt, and black pepper.
3. Arrange the lamb in the Air fryer basket and cook for about 15 minutes.
4. Set the Air fryer to 350 o F on the Roast mode and cook for 1 hour and 15 minutes.
5. Dish out the lamb chops and serve hot.

**Nutrition:**
Calories: 246, Fat: 7.4g, Carbohydrates: 9.4g, Sugar: 6.5g, Protein: 37.2g, Sodium: 353mg

## 355. Beef Roast

Preparation Time: 65 minutes
Servings: 4

**Ingredients:**

- 2 lbs. beef roast
- 1 tbsp. smoked paprika
- 3 tbsp. garlic; minced
- 3 tbsp. olive oil
- Salt and black pepper to taste

**Directions:**

1. In a bowl, combine all the ingredients and coat the roast well.
2. Place the roast in your air fryer and cook at 390°F for 55 minutes. Slice the roast, divide it between plates and serve with a side salad

## 356. Jalapeno Beef

Preparation Time: 45 minutes
Servings: 6

**Ingredients:**

- 1½ lbs. ground beef
- 16 oz. canned white beans; drained
- 20 oz. canned tomatoes; chopped.
- 1 cup beef stock
- 3 tbsp. chili powder
- 2 tbsp. olive oil
- 1 red onion; chopped.
- 6 garlic cloves; chopped.
- 7 jalapeno peppers; diced
- Salt and black pepper to taste

**Directions:**

1. Heat up the oil in a pan that fits your air fryer over medium heat.
2. Add the beef and the onions, stir and cook for 2 minutes
3. Add all remaining ingredients and stir; cook for 3 minutes more
4. Place the pan in the air fryer and cook at 380°F for 35 minutes. Divide everything into bowls and serve.

## 357. Oregano Pork Chops

Preparation Time: 20 minutes
Servings: 4

**Ingredients:**

- 4 pork chops
- 4 garlic cloves; minced
- 2 tbsp. oregano; chopped.

- 2 tbsp. olive oil
- Salt and black pepper to taste

**Directions:**
1. Place all of the ingredients in a bowl and toss / mix well
2. Transfer the chops to your air fryer's basket and cook at 400°F for 15 minutes. Serve with a side salad and enjoy!

## 358. Lamb Chops and Dill

Preparation Time: 30 minutes
Servings: 6

**Ingredients:**
- 1 lb. lamb chops
- 2 yellow onions; chopped.
- 1 tbsp. olive oil
- 2 tbsp. sweet paprika
- 2 tbsp. dill; chopped.
- 3 cups chicken stock
- 1½ cups heavy cream
- 1 garlic clove; minced
- Salt and black pepper to taste

**Directions:**
1. Put the lamb chops in your air fryer and season with the salt, pepper, garlic and paprika; rub the chops thoroughly
2. Cook at 380°F for 10 minutes
3. Transfer the lamb to a baking dish that fits your air fryer. Then add the onions, stock, cream and dill and toss.
4. Place the pan in the fryer and cook everything for 7-8 minutes more. Divide everything between plates and serve hot

## 359. Sage Pork

Preparation Time: 60 minutes
Servings: 6

**Ingredients:**
- 2½ lbs. pork loin; boneless and cubed
- 3/4 cup beef stock

- 1 tsp. basil; dried
- 3 tsp. sage; dried
- 1 tsp. oregano; dried
- 1/2 tbsp. smoked paprika
- 1/2 tbsp. garlic powder
- 2 tbsp. olive oil
- Salt and black pepper to taste

**Directions:**
1. In a pan that fits your air fryer, heat up the oil over medium heat.
2. Add the pork, toss and brown for 5 minutes
3. Add the paprika, sage, garlic powder, basil, oregano, salt and pepper; toss and cook for 2 more minutes.
4. Next add the stock and toss
5. Place the pan in the fryer and cook at 360°F for 40 minutes. Divide everything between plates and serve.

## 360. Pork and Chives

Preparation Time: 32 minutes
Servings: 6

**Ingredients:**
- 1 lb. pork tenderloin; cubed
- 1/4 cup tarragon; chopped.
- 2 tbsp. mustard
- 2 tbsp. chives; chopped.
- 1 cup mayonnaise
- 2 garlic cloves; minced
- Salt and black pepper to taste

**Directions:**
1. Place all ingredients except the mayo into a pan that fits your air fryer; mix well.
2. Put the pan in the fryer and cook at 400°F for 15 minutes
3. Add the mayo and toss
4. Put the pan in the fryer for 7 more minutes. Divide into bowls and serve.

## 361. Pork Chops and Spinach

Preparation Time: 20 minutes
Servings: 4

**Ingredients:**

- 2 pork chops
- 1/4 cup beef stock
- 3 tbsp. spinach pesto
- 2 cups baby spinach
- Salt and black pepper to taste

**Directions:**

1. Place the pork chops, salt, pepper and spinach pesto in a bowl; toss well
2. Place the pork chops in the air fryer and cook at 400°F for 4 minutes on each side.
3. Transfer the chops to a pan that fits your air fryer and add the stock and the baby spinach
4. Put the pan in the fryer and cook at 400°F for 7 minutes more. Divide everything between plates and serve.

## 362. Pork and Sprouts

Preparation Time: 35 minutes
Servings: 4

**Ingredients:**

- 1½ lbs. Brussels sprouts; trimmed
- 1 lb. pork tenderloin; cubed
- 1/2 cup sour cream
- 1 garlic clove; minced
- 2 tbsp. rosemary; chopped.
- 2 tbsp. olive oil
- Salt and black pepper to taste
- Salt and black pepper to taste

**Directions:**

1. In a pan that fits your air fryer, mix the pork with the oil, rosemary, salt, pepper, garlic, salt and pepper; toss well.
2. Place the pan in the fryer and cook at 400°F for 17 minutes
3. Next add the sprouts and the sour cream and toss
4. Place the pan in the fryer and cook for 8

more minutes. Divide everything into bowls and serve.

## 363. Cinnamon Beef

Preparation Time: 60 minutes
Servings: 6

**Ingredients:**

- 2 lbs. beef roast
- 2 yellow onions; thinly sliced
- 2 garlic cloves; minced
- Juice of 1 lemon
- 1 tbsp. cilantro; chopped.
- 1½ tbsp. cinnamon powder
- 1 cup beef stock
- Salt and black pepper to taste

**Directions:**

1. In a baking dish that fits your air fryer, mix the roast with all other ingredients and toss well.
2. Place the dish in your fryer and cook at 390°F for 55 minutes, flipping the roast halfway
3. Carve the roast, divide between plates and serve with the cooking juices drizzled on top; enjoy!

## 364. Beef and Celery

Preparation Time: 65 minutes
Servings: 6

**Ingredients:**

- 1 lb. yellow onion; chopped.
- 1 lb. celery; chopped.
- 3 lbs. beef roast
- 3 cups beef stock
- 2 tbsp. olive oil
- 16 oz. canned tomatoes; chopped.
- Salt and black pepper to taste

**Directions:**

1. Place all the ingredients into a baking dish that fits your air fryer and mix well

2. Put the pan in the fryer and cook at 390°F for 55 minutes
3. Slice the roast and then divide it and the celery mix between plates. Serve and enjoy!

## 365. Crispy Lamb Recipe

Preparation Time: 40 Minutes
Servings: 4

**Ingredients:**

- 28-ounce rack of lamb
- 2 tbsp. macadamia nuts; toasted and crushed
- 1 tbsp. bread crumbs
- 1 tbsp. olive oil
- 1 egg;
- 1 tbsp. rosemary; chopped
- 1 garlic clove; minced
- Salt and black pepper to the taste

**Directions:**

1. In a bowl; mix oil with garlic and stir well
2. Season lamb with salt, pepper and brush with the oil.
3. In another bowl, mix nuts with breadcrumbs and rosemary
4. Put the egg in a separate bowl and whisk well.
5. Dip lamb in egg, then in macadamia mix, place them in your air fryer's basket, cook at 360°F and cook for 25 minutes; increase heat to 400°F and cook for 5 minutes more. Divide among plates and serve right away

## 366. Beef Kabobs Recipe

Preparation Time: 20 Minutes
Servings: 4

**Ingredients:**

- 2 red bell peppers; chopped
- 2-pound sirloin steak; cut into medium pieces

- 2 tbsp. chili powder
- 2 tbsp. hot sauce
- 1 red onion; chopped
- 1 zucchini; sliced
- Juice form 1 lime
- 1/2 tbsp. cumin; ground
- 1/4 cup olive oil
- 1/4 cup salsa
- Salt and black pepper to the taste

**Directions:**

1. In a bowl; mix salsa with lime juice, oil, hot sauce, chili powder, cumin, salt and black pepper and whisk well.
2. Divide meat bell peppers, zucchini and onion on skewers, brush kabobs with the salsa mix you made earlier, put them in your preheated air fryer and cook them for 10 minutes at 370°F, flipping kabobs halfway. Divide among plates and serve with a side salad

## 367. Marinated Lamb and Veggies

Preparation Time: 40 Minutes
Servings: 4

**Ingredients:**

- 1 carrot; chopped
- 1 onion; sliced
- 1/2 tbsp. olive oil
- 8-ounce lamb loin; sliced
- 3-ounce bean sprouts
- For the marinade:
- 1 garlic clove; minced
- 1/2 apple; grated
- 2 tbsp. orange juice
- 5 tbsp. soy sauce
- 1 tbsp. sugar
- 1 tbsp. ginger; grated
- 1 small yellow onion; grated
- Salt and black pepper to the taste

**Directions:**

1. In a bowl; mix 1 grated onion with the apple, garlic, 1 tablespoon ginger, soy sauce, orange juice, sugar and black pepper, whisk well, add lamb and leave aside for 10 minutes
2. Heat up a pan that fits your air fryer with the olive oil over medium high heat, add 1 sliced onion, carrot and bean sprouts; stir and cook for 3 minutes.
3. Add lamb and the marinade, transfer pan to your preheated air fryer and cook at 360°F, for 25 minutes. Divide everything into bowls and serve

## 368. Garlicky Loin Roast

Preparation Time: 60 minutes
Servings: 4

**Ingredients:**

- 1 lb. pork loin roast
- 3 garlic cloves; minced
- 2 tbsp. panko breadcrumbs
- 1 tbsp. olive oil
- 1 tbsp. rosemary; chopped.
- Salt and black pepper to taste

**Directions:**

1. Place all ingredients except the roast into a bowl; stir / mix well.
2. Spread the mixture over the roast. Place the roast in the air fryer and cook at 360°F for 55 minutes
3. Slice the roast, divide it between plates and serve with a side salad

## 369. Lamb Meatballs

Preparation Time: 22 minutes
Servings: 8

**Ingredients:**

- 4 oz. lamb meat; minced
- 1 tbsp. oregano; chopped.
- 1/2 tbsp. lemon zest
- 1 egg; whisked

- Cooking spray
- Salt and black pepper to taste

**Directions:**

1. In a bowl, combine all of the ingredients except the cooking spray and stir well.
2. Shape medium-sized meatballs out of this mix
3. Place the meatballs in your air fryer's basket, grease them with cooking spray and cook at 400°F for 12 minutes. Divide between plates and serve

## 370. Hot Pork Delight

Preparation Time: 28 minutes
Servings: 4

**Ingredients:**

- 1 lb. pork tenderloin; cubed
- 1 red onion; chopped.
- 2 tbsp. olive oil
- 3 tbsp. parsley; chopped.
- 1 garlic clove; minced
- 1/2 tsp. hot chili powder
- 1 tsp. cinnamon powder
- Salt and black pepper to taste

**Directions:**

1. In a bowl, combine the chili, cinnamon, garlic, salt, pepper and the oil. Then add the pork and rub it well with the mixture
2. Transfer the meat to your air fryer and cook at 280°F for 12 minutes. Add the onions and cook for 5 minutes more
3. Divide everything between plates and serve with the parsley sprinkled on top.

## 371. Paprika Beef

Preparation Time: 30 minutes
Servings: 4

**Ingredients:**

- 1½ lbs. beef fillet
- 1 red onion; roughly chopped.

- 1 tbsp. tomato paste
- 1 tbsp. Worcestershire sauce
- 1/2 cup beef stock
- 3 tsp. sweet paprika
- 2 tbsp. olive oil
- Salt and black pepper to taste

**Directions:**

1. In a bowl, mix the beef with all remaining ingredients; toss well.
2. Transfer the mixture to a pan that fits your air fryer and cook at 400°F for 26 minutes, shaking the air fryer halfway. Divide everything between plates and serve

## 372. Lamb Ribs

Preparation Time: 20 minutes
Servings: 4

**Ingredients:**

- 4 lamb ribs
- 1 cup veggie stock
- 1/4 tsp. smoked paprika
- 1/2 tsp. chili powder
- 2 tbsp. extra virgin olive oil
- 4 garlic cloves; minced
- Salt and black pepper to taste

**Directions:**

1. In a bowl; combine all of the ingredients except the ribs and mix well.
2. Then add the ribs and rub them thoroughly with the mixture
3. Transfer the ribs to your air fryer's basket and cook at 390°F for 7 minutes on each side. Serve with a side salad

## 373. Beef and Plums

Preparation Time: 50 minutes
Servings: 6

**Ingredients:**

- 1½ lbs. beef stew meat; cubed

- 9 oz. plums; pitted and halved
- 8 oz. beef stock
- 1 tsp. ginger powder
- 1 tsp. cinnamon powder
- 1 tsp. turmeric powder
- 2 yellow onions; chopped.
- 2 garlic cloves; minced
- 3 tbsp. honey
- 2 tbsp. olive oil
- Salt and black pepper to tastes

**Directions:**

1. In a pan that fits your air fryer, heat up the oil over medium heat.
2. Add the beef, stir and brown for 2 minutes
3. Add the honey, onions, garlic, salt, pepper, turmeric, ginger and cinnamon; toss and cook for 2-3 minutes more
4. Add the plums and the stock; toss again.
5. Place the pan in the fryer and cook at 380°F for 30 minutes. Divide everything into bowls and serve

## 374. Chinese Style Beef

Preparation Time: 25 minutes
Servings: 4

**Ingredients:**

- 1 lb. beef stew meat; cut into strips
- 1/4 cup sesame seeds; toasted
- 1 cup soy sauce
- 5 garlic cloves; minced
- 1 cup green onion; chopped
- Black pepper to taste

**Directions:**

1. In a pan that fits your air fryer, place all ingredients and mix well
2. Place the pan in the fryer and cook at 390°F for 20 minutes. Divide everything into bowls and serve

## 375. Beef and Peas

Preparation Time: 25 minutes
Servings: 2

**Ingredients:**

- 2 beef steaks; cut into strips
- 2 tbsp. soy sauce
- 1 tbsp. olive oil
- 14 oz. snow peas
- Salt and black pepper to taste

**Directions:**

1. Put all of the ingredients into a pan that fits your air fryer; toss well.
2. Place the pan in the fryer and cook at 390°F for 25 minutes. Divide everything between plates and serve

## 376. Marinated Beef

Preparation Time: 30 minutes
Servings: 4

**Ingredients:**

- 3 lbs. chuck roast; cut into thin strips
- 1/2 cup soy sauce
- 1/2 cup black soy sauce
- 3 red peppers; dried and crushed
- 1 tbsp. olive oil
- 5 garlic cloves; minced
- 2 tbsp. fish sauce

**Directions:**

1. In a bowl, combine the beef with all ingredients; toss well and place in the fridge for 10 minutes.
2. Transfer the beef to your air fryer's basket and cook at 380°F for 20 minutes. Serve with a side salad

## 377. Cumin Beef

Preparation Time: 40 minutes
Servings: 4

**Ingredients:**

- 1 lb. ground beef

- 4 oz. canned kidney beans; drained
- 2 garlic cloves; minced
- 2 tbsp. olive oil
- 2 tsp. cumin; ground
- 8 oz. canned tomatoes; chopped.
- 1 yellow onion; chopped.
- Salt and black pepper to taste

**Directions:**

1. Heat up the oil in a pan that fits your air fryer over medium heat.
2. Add the onion and the beef, stir and cook for 2-3 minutes
3. Then add the garlic, salt, pepper, beans, tomatoes and the cumin; toss and cook for another 2 minutes
4. Transfer the pan to your air fryer and cook at 380°F for 30 minutes. Divide everything into bowls and serve.

## 378. Creamy Beef

Preparation Time: 55 minutes
Servings: 4

**Ingredients:**

- 1½ lbs. cubed beef
- 4 oz. brown mushrooms; sliced
- 2 garlic cloves; minced
- 2½ tbsp. vegetable oil
- 1½ tbsp. white flour
- 1 tbsp. cilantro; chopped.
- 8 oz. sour cream
- 1 red onion; chopped.
- Salt and black pepper to taste

**Directions:**

1. In a bowl, mix the beef with the salt, pepper and flour; toss.
2. Heat up the oil in a pan that fits your air fryer over medium-high heat.
3. Add the beef, onions and garlic; stir and cook for 5 minutes
4. Add the mushrooms and toss
5. Place the pan in the fryer and cook at

380°F for 35 minutes

6. Add the sour cream and cilantro and toss; cook for 5 minutes more. Divide everything between plates and serve.

## 379. Lamb and Beans

Preparation Time: 35 minutes
Servings: 4

**Ingredients:**

- 3 oz. canned kidney beans; drained
- 8 oz. lamb loin; cubed
- 1/2 tbsp. olive oil
- 1 tbsp. ginger; grated
- 3 tbsp. soy sauce
- 1 garlic clove; minced
- 1 yellow onion; sliced
- 1 carrot; chopped.
- Salt and black pepper to taste

**Directions:**

1. In baking dish that fits your air fryer, place all of the ingredients and mix well.
2. Place the dish in the fryer and cook at 390°F for 30 minutes. Divide everything into bowls and serve

## 380. Delicious Sausage

Preparation Time: 25 minutes
Servings: 4

**Ingredients:**

- 6 pork sausage links; halved
- 1 red onion; sliced
- 1 tbsp. olive oil
- 1 tbsp. rosemary; chopped.
- 2 garlic cloves; minced
- 1 tbsp. sweet paprika
- Salt and black pepper to taste

**Directions:**

1. In a pan that fits your air fryer, mix all of the ingredients and toss.

2. Place the pan in the fryer and cook at 360°F for 20 minutes. Divide between plates and serve

## 381. Beef, Arugula and Leeks

Preparation Time: 22 minutes
Servings: 4

**Ingredients:**

- 1 lb. ground beef
- 5 oz. baby arugula
- 1 tbsp. olive oil
- 2 tbsp. tomato paste
- 3 leeks; roughly chopped.
- Salt and black pepper to taste

**Directions:**

1. In a pan that fits your air fryer, mix the beef with the leeks, salt, pepper, oil and the tomato paste; toss well
2. Place the pan in the fryer and cook at 380°F for 12 minutes
3. Add the arugula and toss. Divide into bowls and serve.

## 382. Basil Beef Roast

Preparation Time: 60 minutes
Servings: 6

**Ingredients:**

- 1½ lbs. beef roast
- 2 garlic cloves; minced
- 1 cup beef stock
- 2 carrots; sliced
- 1 tbsp. basil; dried
- Salt and black pepper to taste

**Directions:**

1. In a pan that fits your air fryer, combine all ingredients well.
2. Place the pan in the fryer and cook at 390°F for 55 minutes
3. Slice the roast, divide it and the carrots between plates and serve with cooking

juices drizzled on top.

## 383. Pork Chops with Peanut Sauce

Servings: 4
Preparation Time: 20 minutes
Cooking Time: 12 minutes

### Ingredients
*For Chops:*
- 1 teaspoon fresh ginger, minced
- 1 garlic clove, minced
- 2 tablespoons soy sauce
- 1 tablespoon olive oil
- 1 teaspoon hot pepper sauce
- 1-pound boneless pork chop, cubed into 1-inch size

*For Peanut Sauce:*
- 1 tablespoon olive oil
- 1 shallot, finely chopped
- 1 garlic clove, minced
- 1 teaspoon ground coriander
- ¾ cup ground peanuts
- 1 teaspoon hot pepper sauce
- ¾ cup coconut milk

### Directions:
1. For pork: in a bowl, mix together the ginger, garlic, soy sauce, oil, and hot pepper sauce.
2. Add the pork chops and generously coat with mixture.
3. Place at the room temperature for about 15 minutes.
4. Set the temperature of air fryer to 390 degrees F. Grease an air fryer basket.
5. Arrange chops into the prepared air fryer basket in a single layer.
6. Air fry for about 12 minutes.
7. Meanwhile, for the sauce: in a pan, heat oil over medium heat and sauté the shallot and garlic for about 2-3 minutes.
8. Add the coriander and sauté for about 1 minute.
9. Stir in the remaining ingredients and cook

for about 5 minutes, stirring continuously.
10. Remove the pan of sauce from heat and let it cool slightly.
11. Remove the chops from air fryer and transfer onto serving plates.
12. Serve immediately with the topping of peanut sauce.

### Nutrition:
Calories: 725
Carbohydrate: 9.5g
Protein: 34.4g
Fat: 62.9g
Sugar: 2.8g
Sodium: 543mg

## 384. Pork Spare Ribs

Servings: 6
Preparation Time: 15 minutes
Cooking Time: 20 minutes

### Ingredients
- 5-6 garlic cloves, minced
- ½ cup rice vinegar
- 2 tablespoons soy sauce
- Salt and ground black pepper, as required
- 12: 1-inchpork spare ribs
- ½ cup cornstarch
- 2 tablespoons olive oil

### Directions:
1. In a large bowl, mix together the garlic, vinegar, soy sauce, salt, and black pepper.
2. Add the ribs and generously coat with mixture.
3. Refrigerate to marinate overnight.
4. In a shallow bowl, place the cornstarch.
5. Coat the ribs evenly with cornstarch and then, drizzle with oil.
6. Set the temperature of air fryer to 390 degrees F. Grease an air fryer basket.
7. Arrange ribs into the prepared air fryer basket in a single layer.
8. Air fry for about 10 minutes per side.
9. Remove from air fryer and transfer the

ribs onto serving plates.

10. Serve immediately.

## Nutrition:

Calories: 557

Carbohydrate: 11g

Protein: 35g

Fat: 51.3g

Sugar: 0.1g

Sodium: 997mg

## 385. BBQ Pork Ribs

Servings: 4

Preparation Time: 15 minutes

Cooking Time: 26 minutes

## Ingredients

- ¼ cup honey, divided
- ¾ cup BBQ sauce
- 2 tablespoons tomato ketchup
- 1 tablespoon Worcestershire sauce*
- 1 tablespoon soy sauce
- ½ teaspoon garlic powder
- Freshly ground white pepper, to taste
- 1¾ pounds pork ribs

## Directions:

1. In a bowl, mix together 3 tablespoons of honey and the remaining ingredients except pork ribs.
2. Add the pork ribs and generously coat with the mixture.
3. Refrigerate to marinate for about 20 minutes.
4. Set the temperature of air fryer to 355 degrees F. Grease an air fryer basket
5. Arrange ribs into the prepared air fryer basket in a single layer.
6. Air fry for about 13 minutes per side.
7. Remove from air fryer and transfer the ribs onto plates.
8. Drizzle with the remaining honey and serve immediately.

## Nutrition:

Calories: 691

Carbohydrate: 37.7g

Protein: 53.1g

Fat: 31.3g

Sugar: 32.2g

Sodium: 991mg

(Note - Worcestershire sauce* - The other ingredients that make up this savory sauce usually include onions, molasses, high fructose corn syrup: depending on the country of production), salt, garlic, tamarind, cloves, chili pepper extract, water and natural flavorings.

## 386. Glazed Pork Shoulder

Servings: 5

Preparation Time: 15 minutes

Cooking Time: 18 minutes

## Ingredients

- 1/3 cup soy sauce
- 2 tablespoons sugar
- 1 tablespoon honey
- 2 pounds pork shoulder, cut into 1½-inch thick slices

## Directions:

1. In a bowl, mix together all the soy sauce, sugar, and honey.
2. Add the pork and generously coat with marinade.
3. Cover and refrigerate to marinate for about 4-6 hours.
4. Set the temperature of air fryer to 335 degrees F. Grease an air fryer basket.
5. Place pork shoulder into the prepared air fryer basket.
6. Air fry for about 10 minutes and then, another 6-8 minutes at 390 degrees F.
7. Remove from air fryer and transfer the pork shoulder onto a platter.
8. With a piece of foil, cover the pork for about 10 minutes before serving.
9. Enjoy!

## Nutrition:

Calories: 475

Carbohydrate: 8g

Protein: 36.1g

Fat: 32.4g

Sugar: 7.1g

Sodium: 165mg

## 387. Pork Shoulder with Pineapple Sauce

Servings: 3

Preparation Time: 20 minutes

Cooking Time: 24 minutes

### Ingredients

*For Pork:*

- 10½ ounces pork shoulder, cut into bite-sized pieces
- 2 pinches of Maggi seasoning
- 1 teaspoon light soy sauce
- Dash of sesame oil
- 1 egg
- ¼ cup plain flour

*For Sauce:*

- 1 teaspoon olive oil
- 1 medium onion, sliced
- 1 tablespoon garlic, minced
- 1 large pineapple slice, cubed
- 1 medium tomato, chopped
- 2 tablespoons tomato sauce
- 2 tablespoons oyster sauce
- 1 tablespoon Worcestershire sauce
- 1 teaspoon sugar
- 1 tablespoon water
- ½ tablespoon corn flour

### Directions:

1. For pork: in a large bowl, mix together the Maggi seasoning, soy sauce, and sesame oil.
2. Add the pork cubes and generously mix with the mixture.
3. Refrigerate to marinate for about 4-6 hours.
4. In a shallow dish, beat the egg.
5. In another dish, place the plain flour.
6. Dip the cubed pork in beaten egg and then, coat evenly with the flour.
7. Set the temperature of air fryer to 248 degrees F. Grease an air fryer basket.
8. Arrange pork cubes into the prepared air fryer basket in a single layer.
9. Air fry for about 20 minutes.
10. Meanwhile, for the sauce: in a skillet, heat oil over medium heat and sauté the onion and garlic for about 1 minute.
11. Add the pineapple, and tomato and cook for about 1 minute.
12. Add the tomato sauce, oyster sauce, Worcestershire sauce, and sugar and stir to combine.
13. Meanwhile, in a bowl, mix together the water and corn flour.
14. Add the corn flour mixture into the sauce, stirring continuously.
15. Cook until the sauce is thicken enough, stirring continuously.
16. Remove pork cubes from air fryer and add into the sauce.
17. Cook for about 1-2 minutes or until coated completely.
18. Remove from the heat and serve hot.

**Nutrition:**

Calories: 557

Carbohydrate: 57.5g

Protein: 28.8g

Fat: 25.1g

Sugar: 35.1g

Sodium: 544mg

(Note: If you don't have fresh pineapple in hands, then you can use canned pineapple. But remember to skip sugar from the sauce).

## 388. Bacon Wrapped Pork tenderloin

Servings: 4

Preparation Time: 15 minutes

Cooking Time: 30 minutes

### Ingredients

- 1: 1½ poundpork tenderloins
- 4 bacon strips

- 2 tablespoons Dijon mustard

**Directions:**

1. Coat the tenderloin evenly with mustard.
2. Wrap the tenderloin with bacon strips.
3. Set the temperature of air fryer to 360 degrees F. Grease an air fryer basket.
4. Arrange pork tenderloin into the prepared air fryer basket.
5. Air fry for about 15 minutes.
6. Flip and air fry for another 10-15 minutes.
7. Remove from air fryer and transfer the pork tenderloin onto a platter, wait for about 5 minutes before slicing.
8. Cut the tenderloin into desired size slices and serve.

**Nutrition:**

Calories: 504
Carbohydrate: 0.8g
Protein:61.9
Fat: 26.2g
Sugar: 9.1g
Sodium: 867mg

## 389. Pork Tenderloin with Bell Peppers

Servings: 3
Preparation Time: 20 minutes
Cooking Time: 15 minutes

**Ingredients**

- 1 large red bell pepper, seeded and cut into thin strips
- 1 red onion, thinly sliced
- 2 teaspoons Herbs de Provence
- Salt and ground black pepper, as required
- 1 tablespoon olive oil
- 10½-ounces pork tenderloin, cut into 4 pieces
- ½ tablespoon Dijon mustard

**Directions:**

1. In a bowl, add the bell pepper, onion, Herbs de Provence, salt, black pepper, and ½ tablespoon of oil and toss to coat

well.

2. Rub the pork pieces with mustard, salt, and black pepper.
3. Drizzle with the remaining oil.
4. Set the temperature of air fryer to 390 degrees F. Grease an air fryer pan.
5. Place bell pepper mixture into the prepared Air Fryer pan and top with the pork pieces.
6. Air fry for about 15 minutes, flipping once halfway through.
7. Remove from air fryer and transfer the pork mixture onto serving plates.
8. Serve hot.

**Nutrition:**

Calories: 218
Carbohydrate: 7.1g
Protein: 27.7g
Fat: 8.8g
Sugar: 3.7g
Sodium: 110mg

## 390. Pork Tenderloin with Bacon & Veggies

Servings: 3
Preparation Time: 20 minutes
Cooking Time: 28 minutes

**Ingredients**

- 3 potatoes
- ¾ pound frozen green beans
- 6 bacon slices
- 3: 6-ouncespork tenderloins
- 2 tablespoons olive oil

**Directions:**

1. Set the temperature of air fryer to 390 degrees F. Grease an air fryer basket.
2. With a fork, pierce the potatoes.
3. Place potatoes into the prepared air fryer basket and air fry for about 15 minutes.
4. Wrap one bacon slice around 4-6 green beans.
5. Coat the pork tenderloins with oil

6. After 15 minutes, add the pork tenderloins into air fryer basket with potatoes and air fry for about 5-6 minutes.
7. Remove the pork tenderloins from basket.
8. Place bean rolls into the basket and top with the pork tenderloins.
9. Air fry for another 7 minutes.
10. Remove from air fryer and transfer the pork tenderloins onto a platter.
11. Cut each tenderloin into desired size slices.
12. Serve alongside the potatoes and green beans rolls.

**Nutrition:**

Calories: 918
Carbohydrate: 42.4g
Protein: 77.9g
Fat: 47.7g
Sugar: 4g
Sodium: 1400mg

## 391. Pork Loin with Potatoes

Servings: 5
Preparation Time: 15 minutes
Cooking Time: 25 minutes

**Ingredients**

- 2 pounds pork loin
- 3 tablespoons olive oil, divided
- 1 teaspoon fresh parsley, chopped
- Salt and ground black pepper, as required
- 3 large red potatoes, chopped
- ½ teaspoon garlic powder
- ½ teaspoon red pepper flakes, crushed

**Directions:**

1. Coat the pork loin with oil and then, season evenly with parsley, salt, and black pepper.
2. In a large bowl, add the potatoes, remaining oil, garlic powder, red pepper flakes, salt, and black pepper and toss to

coat well.
3. Set the temperature of air fryer to 325 degrees F. Grease an air fryer basket.
4. Place loin into the prepared air fryer basket.
5. Arrange potato pieces around the pork loin.
6. Air fry for about 25 minutes.
7. Remove from air fryer and transfer the pork loin onto a platter, wait for about 5 minutes before slicing.
8. Cut the pork loin into desired size slices and serve alongside the potatoes.

**Nutrition:**

Calories: 556
Carbohydrate: 29.6g
Protein: 44.9g
Fat: 28.3g
Sugar: 1.9g
Sodium: 132mg

## 392. Pork Rolls

Servings: 4
Preparation Time: 20 minutes
Cooking Time: 15 minutes

**Ingredients**

- 1 scallion, chopped
- ¼ cup sun-dried tomatoes, finely chopped
- 2 tablespoons fresh parsley, chopped
- Salt and ground black pepper, as required
- 4: 6-ouncespork cutlets, pounded slightly
- 2 teaspoons paprika
- ½ tablespoon olive oil

**Directions:**

1. In a bowl, mix well scallion, tomatoes, parsley, salt, and black pepper.
2. Spread the tomato mixture over each pork cutlet.
3. Roll each cutlet and secure with cocktail sticks.
4. Rub the outer part of rolls with paprika,

salt and black pepper.

5. Coat the rolls evenly with oil.
6. Set the temperature of air fryer to 390 degrees F. Grease an air fryer basket.
7. Arrange pork rolls into the prepared air fryer basket in a single layer.
8. Air fry for about 15 minutes.
9. Remove from air fryer and transfer the pork rolls onto serving plates.
10. Serve hot.

**Nutrition:**

Calories: 244
Carbohydrate: 14.5g
Protein: 20.1g
Fat: 8.2g
Sugar: 1.7g
Sodium: 708mg

## 393. Pork Sausage Casserole

Servings: 4
Preparation Time: 15 minutes
Cooking Time: 30 minutes

### Ingredients

- 6 ounces flour, sifted
- 2 eggs
- 1 red onion, thinly sliced
- 1 garlic clove, minced
- Salt and ground black pepper, as required
- ¾ cup milk
- 2/3 cup cold water
- 8 small sausages
- 8 fresh rosemary sprigs

### Directions:

1. In a bowl, mix together the flour, and eggs.
2. Add the onion, garlic, salt, and black pepper. Mix them well.
3. Gently, add in the milk, and water and mix until well combined.
4. In each sausage, pierce 1 rosemary sprig.
5. Set the temperature of air fryer to 320

degrees F. Grease a baking dish.

6. Arrange sausages into the prepared baking dish and top evenly with the flour mixture.
7. Air fry for about 30 minutes.
8. Remove from the air fryer and serve warm.

**Nutrition:**

Calories: 334
Carbohydrate: 37.7g
Protein: 14g
Fat: 14g
Sugar: 3.5g
Sodium: 250mg

## 394. Pork Neck Salad

Servings: 2
Preparation Time: 20 minutes
Cooking Time: 12 minutes

### Ingredients

*For Pork:*

- 1 tablespoon soy sauce
- 1 tablespoon fish sauce
- ½ tablespoon oyster sauce
- ½ pound pork neck

*For Salad:*

- 1 ripe tomato, thickly sliced
- 1 red onion, sliced
- 1 scallion, chopped
- 1 bunch fresh basil leaves
- 1 bunch fresh cilantro leaves

*For Dressing:*

- 3 tablespoons fish sauce
- 2 tablespoons olive oil
- 1 teaspoon apple cider vinegar
- 1 tablespoon palm sugar
- 1 bird eye chili
- 1 tablespoon garlic, minced

### Directions:

1. For pork: in a bowl, mix together all the

sauces.

2. Add the pork neck and generously coat with marinade.
3. Refrigerate for about 2-3 hours.
4. Set the temperature of air fryer to 340 degrees F. Grease an air fryer basket.
5. Place pork neck into the prepared basket.
6. Air fry for about 12 minutes.
7. Meanwhile, for the salad: in a serving bowl, mix together all the ingredients.
8. For dressing: in another bowl, add all the ingredients and beat until well combined.
9. Remove pork neck from air fryer and cut into desired size slices.
10. Place the pork slices over salad.
11. Add the dressing and toss to coat well.
12. Serve.

**Nutrition:**

Calories: 448
Carbohydrate: 15.2g
Protein: 20.5g
Fat: 39.7g
Sugar: 8.5g
Sodium: 2000mg

## 395. Glazed Ham

Servings: 4
Preparation Time: 15 minutes
Cooking Time: 40 minutes

**Ingredients**

- 1 pound 10½ ounces ham
- 1 cup whiskey
- 2 tablespoons French mustard
- 2 tablespoons honey

**Directions:**

1. Place the ham at room temperature for about 30 minutes before cooking.
2. In a bowl, mix together the whiskey, mustard, and honey.
3. Place the ham in a baking dish that fits in the air fryer.

4. Top with half of the honey mixture and coat well.
5. Set the temperature of air fryer to 320 degrees F. Place the baking dish into the air fryer.
6. Air fry for about 15 minutes.
7. Flip the side of ham and top with the remaining honey mixture.
8. Air fry for about 25 more minutes.
9. Remove from air fryer and place the ham onto a platter for about 10 minutes before slicing.
10. Cut the ham into desired size slices and serve.

**Nutrition:**

Calories: 558
Carbohydrate: 18.6g
Protein: 43g
Fat: 22.2g
Sugar: 8.7g
Sodium: 3000mg

## 396. Simple Lamb Chops

Servings: 2
Preparation Time: 10 minutes
Cooking Time: 6 minutes

**Ingredients**

- 1 tablespoon olive oil
- Salt and ground black pepper, as required
- 4: 4-ounceslamb chops

**Directions:**

1. In a large bowl, mix together the oil, salt, and black pepper.
2. Add the chops and coat evenly with the mixture.
3. Set the temperature of air fryer to 390 degrees F. Grease an air fryer basket.
4. Arrange chops into the prepared air fryer basket in a single layer.
5. Air fry for about 5-6 minutes.
6. Remove from air fryer and transfer the chops onto plates.

7. Serve hot.

**Nutrition:**
Calories: 486
Carbohydrate: 0.8g
Protein: 63.8g
Fat: 31.7g
Sugar: 0g
Sodium: 250mg

## 397. Lamb Loin Chops with Lemon

Servings: 4
Preparation Time: 15 minutes
Cooking Time: 30 minutes

**Ingredients**

- 2 tablespoons Dijon mustard
- 1 tablespoon fresh lemon juice
- ½ teaspoon olive oil
- 1 teaspoon dried tarragon
- Salt and ground black pepper, as required
- 8: 4-ounceslamb loin chops

**Directions:**

1. In a large bowl, mix together the mustard, lemon juice, oil, tarragon, salt, and black pepper.
2. Add chops and generously coat with the mixture.
3. Set the temperature of air fryer to 390 degrees F. Grease an air fryer basket.
4. Arrange chops into the prepared air fryer basket in a single layer in 2 batches.
5. Air fry for about 15 minutes, flipping once halfway through.
6. Remove the chops from air fryer and transfer onto serving plates.
7. Serve hot.

**Nutrition:**
Calories: 433
Carbohydrate: 0.6g
Protein: 64.1g
Fat: 17.6g
Sugar: 0.2g

Sodium: 201mg

## 398. Herbed Lamb Chops

Servings: 2
Preparation Time: 10 minutes
Cooking Time: 7 minutes

**Ingredients**

- 1 tablespoon fresh lemon juice
- 1 tablespoon olive oil
- 1 teaspoon dried rosemary
- 1 teaspoon dried thyme
- 1 teaspoon dried oregano
- ½ teaspoon ground cumin
- ½ teaspoon ground coriander
- Salt and ground black pepper, as required
- 4: 4-ounceslamb chops

**Directions:**

1. In a large bowl, mix together the lemon juice, oil, herbs, and spices.
2. Add the chops and coat evenly with the herb mixture.
3. Refrigerate to marinate for about 1 hour
4. Set the temperature of air fryer to 390 degrees F. Grease an air fryer basket.
5. Arrange chops into the prepared air fryer basket in a single layer.
6. Air fry for about 7 minutes, flipping once halfway through.
7. Remove from air fryer and transfer the chops onto plates.
8. Serve hot.

**Nutrition:**
Calories: 491
Carbohydrate: 1.6g
Protein: 64g
Fat: 24g
Sugar: 0.2g
Sodium: 253mg

## 399. Lamb Loin Chops with Garlic

Servings: 4

Preparation Time: 10 minutes

Cooking Time: 30 minutes

## Ingredients

- 3 garlic cloves, crushed
- 1 tablespoon fresh lemon juice
- 1 teaspoon olive oil
- 1 tablespoon Za'atar*
- Kosher salt and ground black pepper, as required
- 8: 3½-ouncesbone-in lamb loin chops, trimmed

## Directions:

1. In a large bowl, mix together the garlic, lemon juice, oil, Za'atar, salt, and black pepper.
2. Add chops and generously coat with the mixture.
3. Set the temperature of air fryer to 400 degrees F. Grease an air fryer basket.
4. Arrange chops into the prepared air fryer basket in a single layer in 2 batches.
5. Air Fry for about 15 minutes, flipping once after 4-5 minutes per side.
6. Remove from air fryer and transfer the chops onto plates.
7. Serve hot.

## Nutrition:

Calories: 433

Carbohydrate: 0.6g

Protein: 64.1g

Fat: 17.6g

Sugar: 0.2g

Sodium: 201mg

(Note: Za'atar* - Za'atar is generally made with ground dried thyme, oregano, marjoram, or some combination thereof, mixed with toasted sesame seeds, and salt, though other spices such as sumac might also be added. Some commercial varieties also include roasted flour.

## 400. Lamb Chops with Veggies

Servings: 4

Preparation Time: 20 minutes

Cooking Time: 8 minutes

## Ingredients

- 2 tablespoons fresh rosemary, minced
- 2 tablespoons fresh mint leaves, minced
- 1 garlic clove, minced
- 3 tablespoons olive oil
- Salt and ground black pepper, as required
- 4: 6-ounceslamb chops
- 1 purple carrot, peeled and cubed
- 1 yellow carrot, peeled and cubed
- 1 parsnip, peeled and cubed
- 1 fennel bulb, cubed

## Directions:

1. In a large bowl, mix together the herbs, garlic, oil, salt, and black pepper.
2. Add the chops and generously coat with mixture.
3. Refrigerate to marinate for about 3 hours.
4. In a large pan of water, soak the vegetables for about 15 minutes.
5. Drain the vegetables completely.
6. Set the temperature of air fryer to 390 degrees F. Grease an air fryer basket.
7. Arrange chops into the prepared air fryer basket in a single layer.
8. Air Fry for about 2 minutes.
9. Remove chops from the air fryer.
10. Place vegetables into the air fryer basket and top with the chops in a single layer.
11. Air Fry for about 6 minutes.
12. Remove from air fryer and transfer the chops and vegetables onto serving plates.
13. Serve hot.

## Nutrition:

Calories: 470

Carbohydrate: 14.8g

Protein: 49.4g

Fat: 23.5g

Sugar: 3.1g

Sodium: 186mg

## 401. Nut Crusted Rack of Lamb

Servings: 5
Preparation Time: 15 minutes
Cooking Time: 35 minutes

**Ingredients**

- 1 tablespoon olive oil
- 1 garlic clove, minced
- Salt and ground black pepper, as required
- 1¾ pounds rack of lamb
- 1 egg
- 1 tablespoon breadcrumbs
- 3 ounces almonds, finely chopped

**Directions:**

1. In a bowl, mix together the oil, garlic, salt, and black pepper.
2. Coat the rack of lamb evenly with oil mixture.
3. Crack the egg in a shallow bowl and beat well.
4. In another bowl, mix together the breadcrumbs and almonds.
5. Dip the rack of lamb in beaten egg and then, coat with almond mixture.
6. Set the temperature of air fryer to 220 degrees F. Grease an air fryer basket.
7. Place rack of lamb into the prepared air fryer basket.
8. Air fry for about 30 minutes and then 5 more minutes at 390 degrees F.
9. Remove from air fryer and place the rack of lamb onto a cutting board for about 5 minutes
10. With a sharp knife, cut the rack of lamb into individual chops and serve.

**Nutrition:**
Calories: 340
Carbohydrate: 4.1g
Protein: 31g
Fat: 21.9g
Sugar: 0.7g
Sodium: 140mg

## 402. Herbs Crumbed Rack of Lamb

Servings: 5
Preparation Time: 20 minutes
Cooking Time: 30 minutes

**Ingredients**

- 1 tablespoon butter, melted
- 1 garlic clove, finely chopped
- 1¾ pounds rack of lamb
- Salt and ground black pepper, as required
- 1 egg
- ½ cup panko breadcrumbs
- 1 tablespoon fresh thyme, minced
- 1 tablespoon fresh rosemary, minced

**Directions:**

1. In a bowl, mix together the butter, garlic, salt, and black pepper.
2. Coat the rack of lamb evenly with garlic mixture.
3. In a shallow dish, beat the egg.
4. In another dish, mix together the breadcrumbs and herbs.
5. Dip the rack of lamb in beaten egg and then, coat with breadcrumbs mixture.
6. Set the temperature of air fryer to 212 degrees F. Grease an air fryer basket.
7. Place rack of lamb into the prepared air fryer basket.
8. Air Fry for about 25 minutes and then 5 more minutes at 390 degrees F.
9. Remove from air fryer and place the rack of lamb onto a cutting board for about 5 minutes
10. With a sharp knife, cut the rack of lamb into individual chops and serve.

**Nutrition:**
Calories: 277
Carbohydrate: 5.9g
Protein: 28.6g
Fat: 14.6g
Sugar: 0.2g
Sodium: 191mg

## 403. Pesto Coated Rack of Lamb

Servings: 4
Preparation Time: 15 minutes
Cooking Time: 15 minutes

### Ingredients

- ½ bunch fresh mint
- 1 garlic clove
- ¼ cup extra-virgin olive oil
- ½ tablespoon honey
- Salt and ground black pepper, as required
- 1: 1½-poundsrack of lamb

### Directions:

1. For pesto: in a blender, add the mint, garlic, oil, honey, salt, and black pepper and pulse until smooth.
2. Coat the rack of lamb evenly with some pesto.
3. Set the temperature of air fryer to 200 degrees F. Grease an air fryer basket.
4. Place rack of lamb into the prepared air fryer basket.
5. Air fry for about 15 minutes, coating with the remaining pesto after every 5 minutes.
6. Remove from air fryer and place the rack of lamb onto a cutting board for about 5 minutes
7. Cut the rack into individual chops and serve.

### Nutrition:

Calories: 406
Carbohydrate: 2.9g
Protein: 34.9g
Fat: 27.7g
Sugar: 2.2g
Sodium: 161mg

## 404. Spiced Lamb Steaks

Servings: 3
Preparation Time: 15 minutes
Cooking Time: 15 minutes

### Ingredients

- ½ onion, roughly chopped
- 5 garlic cloves, peeled
- 1 tablespoon fresh ginger, peeled
- 1 teaspoon garam masala
- 1 teaspoon ground fennel
- ½ teaspoon ground cumin
- ½ teaspoon ground cinnamon
- ½ teaspoon cayenne pepper
- Salt and ground black pepper, as required
- 1½ pounds boneless lamb sirloin steaks

### Directions:

1. In a blender, add the onion, garlic, ginger, and spices and pulse until smooth.
2. Transfer the mixture into a large bowl.
3. Add the lamb steaks and generously coat with the mixture.
4. Refrigerate to marinate for about 24 hours.
5. Set the temperature of air fryer to 330 degrees F. Grease an air fryer basket.
6. Arrange steaks into the prepared air fryer basket in a single layer.
7. Air fry for about 15 minutes, flipping once halfway through.
8. Once done, remove the steaks from air fryer and serve.

### Nutrition:

Calories: 252406
Carbohydrate: 4.2g
Protein: 21.7g
Fat: 16.7g
Sugar: 0.7g
Sodium: 42mg

## 405. Herbed Leg of Lamb

Servings: 5
Preparation Time: 10 minutes
Cooking Time: 75 minutes

### Ingredients

- 2 pounds bone-in leg of lamb
- 2 tablespoons olive oil

- Salt and ground black pepper, as required
- 2 fresh rosemary sprigs
- 2 fresh thyme sprigs

**Directions:**
1. Coat the leg of lamb with oil and sprinkle with salt and black pepper.
2. Wrap the leg of lamb with herb sprigs.
3. Set the temperature of air fryer to 300 degrees F. Grease an air fryer basket.
4. Place leg of lamb into the prepared air fryer basket.
5. Air fry for about 75 minutes.
6. Remove from air fryer and transfer the leg of lamb onto a platter.
7. With a piece of foil, cover the leg of lamb for about 10 minutes before slicing.
8. Cut the leg of lamb into desired size pieces and serve.

**Nutrition:**
Calories: 534
Carbohydrate: 2.4g
Protein: 69.8g
Fat: 25.8g
Sugar: 0g
Sodium: 190mg

## 406. Leg of Lamb with Brussels Sprout

Servings: 6
Preparation Time: 20 minutes
Cooking Time: 90 minutes

**Ingredients**
- 2¼ pounds leg of lamb
- 3 tablespoons olive oil, divided
- 1 tablespoon fresh rosemary, minced
- 1 tablespoon fresh lemon thyme
- 1 garlic clove, minced
- Salt and ground black pepper, as required
- 1½ pounds Brussels sprouts, trimmed
- 2 tablespoons honey

**Directions:**

1. With a sharp knife, score the leg of lamb at several places.
2. In a bowl, mix together 2 tablespoons of oil, herbs, garlic, salt, and black pepper.
3. Generously coat the leg of lamb with oil mixture.
4. Set the temperature of air fryer to 300 degrees F. Grease an air fryer basket.
5. Place leg of lamb into the prepared air fryer basket.
6. Air fry for about 75 minutes.
7. Meanwhile, coat the Brussels sprout evenly with the remaining oil and honey.
8. Now, set the temperature of air fryer to 392 degrees F.
9. Arrange Brussels sprout into the air fryer basket with leg of lamb.
10. Air Fry for about 15 minutes.
11. Remove from air Fryer and transfer the leg of lamb onto a platter.
12. With a piece of foil, cover the leg of lamb for about 10 minutes before slicing.
13. Cut the leg of lamb into desired size pieces and serve alongside the Brussels sprout.

**Nutrition:**
Calories: 449
Carbohydrate: 16.6g
Protein: 51.7g
Fat: 19.9g
Sugar: 8.2g
Sodium: 185mg

## 407. Garlic Lamb Roast

Servings: 6
Preparation Time: 20 minutes
Cooking Time: 1½ hours

**Ingredients**
- 2¾ pounds half lamb leg roast
- 3 garlic cloves, cut into thin slices
- 2 tablespoons extra-virgin olive oil
- 1 tablespoon dried rosemary, crushed
- Salt and ground black pepper, as required

**Directions:**

1. In a small bowl, mix together the oil, rosemary, salt, and black pepper.
2. With the tip of a sharp knife, make deep slits on the top of lamb roast fat.
3. Insert the garlic slices into the slits.
4. Coat the lamb roast evenly with oil mixture.
5. Set the temperature of air fryer to 390 degrees F. Grease an air fryer basket.
6. Arrange lamb into the prepared air fryer basket in a single layer.
7. Air Fry for about 15 minutes and then another 1¼ hours at 320 degrees F.
8. Remove from air fryer and transfer the roast onto a platter.
9. With a piece of foil, cover the roast for about 10 minutes before slicing.
10. Cut the roast into desired size slices and serve.

**Nutrition:**

Calories: 418

Carbohydrate: 0.9g

Protein: 57.4g

Fat: 14.9g

Sugar: 0g

Sodium: 165mg

## 408. Artichoke Spinach Casserole

Preparation Time: 30 minutes
Servings: 4

**Ingredients:**
- ⅓ cup full-fat mayonnaise
- 8 oz. full-fat cream cheese; softened.
- ¼ cup diced yellow onion
- ⅓ cup full-fat sour cream.
- ¼ cup chopped pickled jalapeños.
- 2 cups fresh spinach; chopped
- 2 cups cauliflower florets; chopped
- 1 cup artichoke hearts; chopped
- 1 tbsp. salted butter; melted.

**Directions:**
1. Take a large bowl, mix butter, onion, cream cheese, mayonnaise and sour cream. Fold in jalapeños, spinach, cauliflower and artichokes.
2. Pour the mixture into a 4-cup round baking dish. Cover with foil and place into the air fryer basket
3. Adjust the temperature to 370 Degrees F and set the timer for 15 minutes. In the last 2 minutes of cooking, remove the foil to brown the top. Serve warm.
4. Nutrition: Calories: 423; Protein: 6.7g; Fiber: 5.3g; Fat: 36.3g; Carbs: 12.1g

## 409. Cheese Zucchini Boats

Preparation Time: 35 minutes
Servings: 2

**Ingredients:**
- 2 medium zucchini
- ¼ cup full-fat ricotta cheese
- ¼ cup shredded mozzarella cheese
- ¼ cup low-carb, no-sugar-added pasta sauce.
- 2 tbsp. grated vegetarian Parmesan cheese
- 1 tbsp. avocado oil
- ¼ tsp. garlic powder.
- ½ tsp. dried parsley.
- ¼ tsp. dried oregano.

**Directions:**
1. Cut off 1-inch from the top and bottom of each zucchini.
2. Slice zucchini in half lengthwise and use a spoon to scoop out a bit of the inside, making room for filling. Brush with oil and spoon 2 tbsp. pasta sauce into each shell
3. Take a medium bowl, mix ricotta, mozzarella, oregano, garlic powder and parsley
4. Spoon the mixture into each zucchini shell. Place stuffed zucchini shells into the air fryer basket.
5. Adjust the temperature to 350 Degrees F and set the timer for 20 minutes
6. To remove from the fryer basket, use tongs or a spatula and carefully lift out. Top with Parmesan. Serve immediately.

**Nutrition: Calories: 215; Protein: 10.5g; Fiber: 2.7g; Fat: 14.9g; Carbs: 9.3g**

## 410. Chocolate Chip Pan Cookie

Preparation Time: 17 minutes
Servings: 4

**Ingredients:**
- ½ cup blanched finely ground almond flour.
- 1 large egg.
- ¼ cup powdered erythritol
- 2 tbsp. unsalted butter; softened.
- 2 tbsp. low-carb, sugar-free chocolate

chips

- ½ tsp. unflavored gelatin
- ½ tsp. baking powder.
- ½ tsp. vanilla extract.

**Directions:**

1. Take a large bowl, mix almond flour and erythritol. Stir in butter, egg and gelatin until combined.
2. Stir in baking powder and vanilla and then fold in chocolate chips
3. Pour batter into 6-inch round baking pan. Place pan into the air fryer basket.
4. Adjust the temperature to 300 Degrees F and set the timer for 7 minutes
5. When fully cooked, the top will be golden brown and a toothpick inserted in center will come out clean. Let cool at least 10 minutes.

**Nutrition: Calories: 188; Protein: 5.6g; Fiber: 2.0g; Fat: 15.7g; Carbs: 16.8g**

## 411. Monkey Bread

Preparation Time: 27 minutes
Servings: 6

**Ingredients:**

- ½ cup blanched finely ground almond flour.
- 1 oz. full-fat cream cheese; softened.
- 1 large egg.
- ¼ cup heavy whipping cream.
- ½ cup low-carb vanilla protein powder
- ¾ cup granular erythritol, divided
- 8 tbsp. salted butter; melted and divided
- ½ tsp. vanilla extract.
- ½ tsp. baking powder

**Directions:**

1. Take a large bowl, combine almond flour, protein powder, ½ cup erythritol, baking powder, 5 tbsp. butter, cream cheese and egg. A soft, sticky dough will form.
2. Place the dough in the freezer for 20

minutes. It will be firm enough to roll into balls. Wet your hands with warm water and roll into twelve balls. Place the balls into a 6-inch round baking dish

3. In a medium skillet over medium heat, melt remaining butter with remaining erythritol. Lower the heat and continue stirring until mixture turns golden, then add cream and vanilla. Remove from heat and allow it to thicken for a few minutes while you continue to stir
4. While the mixture cools, place baking dish into the air fryer basket. Adjust the temperature to 320 Degrees F and set the timer for 6 minutes
5. When the timer beeps, flip the monkey bread over onto a plate and slide it back into the baking pan. Cook an additional 4 minutes until all the tops are brown.
6. Pour the caramel sauce over the monkey bread and cook an additional 2 minutes.
7. Let cool completely before serving.

**Nutrition: Calories: 322; Protein: 20.4g; Fiber: 1.7g; Fat: 24.5g; Carbs: 33.7g**

## 412. Spaghetti Squash Alfredo.

Preparation Time: 25 minutes
Servings: 2

**Ingredients:**

- ½ large cooked spaghetti squash
- ¼ cup grated vegetarian Parmesan cheese.
- ½ cup shredded Italian blend cheese
- ½ cup low-carb Alfredo sauce
- 2 tbsp. salted butter; melted.
- ¼ tsp. ground peppercorn
- ½ tsp. garlic powder.
- 1 tsp. dried parsley.

**Directions:**

1. Using a fork, remove the strands of spaghetti squash from the shell. Place into a large bowl with butter and Alfredo sauce. Sprinkle with Parmesan, garlic powder, parsley and peppercorn

2. Pour into a 4-cup round baking dish and top with shredded cheese. Place dish into the air fryer basket. Adjust the temperature to 320 Degrees F and set the timer for 15 minutes.
3. When finished, cheese will be golden and bubbling. Serve immediately

**Nutrition: Calories: 375; Protein: 13.5g; Fiber: 4.0g; Fat: 24.2g; Carbs: 24.1g**

## 413. BBQ Pulled Mushrooms

Preparation Time: 17 minutes
Servings: 2

**Ingredients:**

- 4 large portobello mushrooms
- ½ cup low-carb, sugar-free barbecue sauce
- 1 tbsp. salted butter; melted.
- 1 tsp. paprika
- ¼ tsp. onion powder.
- ¼ tsp. ground black pepper
- 1 tsp. chili powder

**Directions:**

1. Remove stem and scoop out the underside of each mushroom. Brush the caps with butter and sprinkle with pepper, chili powder, paprika and onion powder.
2. Place mushrooms into the air fryer basket. Adjust the temperature to 400 Degrees F and set the timer for 8 minutes.
3. When the timer beeps, remove mushrooms from the basket and place on a cutting board or work surface. Using two forks, gently pull the mushrooms apart, creating strands.
4. Place mushroom strands into a 4-cup round baking dish with barbecue sauce. Place dish into the air fryer basket.
5. Adjust the temperature to 350 Degrees F and set the timer for 4 minutes. Stir halfway through the cooking time. Serve warm.

**Nutrition: Calories: 108; Protein: 3.3g; Fiber:**

2.7g; Fat: 5.9g; Carbs: 10.9g

## 414. Cream Puffs

Preparation Time: 21 minutes
Servings: 8 puffs

**Ingredients:**

- 2 oz. full-fat cream cheese.
- 1 large egg.
- ¼ cup powdered erythritol
- ½ cup blanched finely ground almond flour.
- ½ cup low-carb vanilla protein powder
- ½ cup granular erythritol.
- 2 tbsp. heavy whipping cream.
- 5 tbsp. unsalted butter; melted.
- ½ tsp. baking powder.
- ¼ tsp. ground cinnamon.
- ½ tsp. vanilla extract.

**Directions:**

1. Mix almond flour, protein powder, granular erythritol, baking powder, egg and butter in a large bowl until a soft dough forms.
2. Place the dough in the freezer for 20 minutes. Wet your hands with water and roll the dough into eight balls.
3. Cut a piece of parchment to fit your air fryer basket. Working in batches as necessary, place the dough balls into the air fryer basket on top of parchment.
4. Adjust the temperature to 380 Degrees F and set the timer for 6 minutes. Flip cream puffs halfway through the cooking time.
5. When the timer beeps, remove the puffs and allow to cool.
6. Take a medium bowl, beat the cream cheese, powdered erythritol, cinnamon, cream and vanilla until fluffy.
7. Place the mixture into a pastry bag or a storage bag with the end snipped. Cut a small hole in the bottom of each puff and fill with some of the cream mixture. Store

in an airtight container up to 2 days in the refrigerator.

**Nutrition: Calories: 178; Protein: 14.9g; Fiber: 1.3g; Fat: 12.1g; Carbs: 22.1g**

## 415. Vanilla Pound Cake.

Preparation Time: 35 minutes
Servings: 6

**Ingredients:**

- ½ cup full-fat sour cream.
- 1 oz. full-fat cream cheese; softened.
- 2 large eggs.
- ½ cup granular erythritol.
- 1 cup blanched finely ground almond flour.
- ¼ cup salted butter; melted.
- 1 tsp. baking powder.
- 1 tsp. vanilla extract.

**Directions:**

1. Take a large bowl, mix almond flour, butter and erythritol.
2. Add in vanilla, baking powder, sour cream and cream cheese and mix until well combined. Add eggs and mix.
3. Pour batter into a 6-inch round baking pan. Place pan into the air fryer basket. Adjust the temperature to 300 Degrees F and set the timer for 25 minutes.
4. When the cake is done, a toothpick inserted in center will come out clean. The center should not feel wet. Allow it to cool completely, or the cake will crumble when moved.

**Nutrition: Calories: 253; Protein: 6.9g; Fiber: 2.0g; Fat: 22.6g; Carbs: 25.2g**

## 416. Toasted Coco Flakes

Preparation Time: 8 minutes
Servings: 4

**Ingredients:**

- 1 cup unsweetened coconut flakes

- ¼ cup granular erythritol.
- 2 tsp. coconut oil
- ⅛ tsp. salt

**Directions:**

1. Toss coconut flakes and oil in a large bowl until coated. Sprinkle with erythritol and salt. Place coconut flakes into the air fryer basket.
2. Adjust the temperature to 300 Degrees F and set the timer for 3 minutes.
3. Toss the flakes when 1 minute remains. Add an extra minute if you would like a more golden coconut flake. Store in an airtight container up to 3 days.

**Nutrition: Calories: 165; Protein: 1.3g; Fiber: 2.7g; Fat: 15.5g; Carbs: 20.3g**

## 417. Eggplant Stacks

Preparation Time: 17 minutes
Servings: 4

**Ingredients:**

- 2 large tomatoes; cut into ¼-inch slices
- ¼ cup fresh basil, sliced
- 4 oz. fresh mozzarella; cut into ½-oz. slices
- 1 medium eggplant; cut into ¼-inch slices
- 2 tbsp. olive oil

**Directions:**

1. In a 6-inch round baking dish, place four slices of eggplant on the bottom. Place a slice of tomato on top of each eggplant round, then mozzarella, then eggplant. Repeat as necessary.
2. Drizzle with olive oil. Cover dish with foil and place dish into the air fryer basket. Adjust the temperature to 350 Degrees F and set the timer for 12 minutes.
3. When done, eggplant will be tender. Garnish with fresh basil to serve.

**Nutrition: Calories: 195; Protein: 8.5g; Fiber: 5.2g; Fat: 12.7g; Carbs: 12.7g**

## 418. Green Beans and Lime Sauce

Preparation Time: 13 minutes
Servings: 4

**Ingredients:**

- 1 lb. green beans, trimmed
- 2 tbsp. ghee; melted
- 1 tbsp. lime juice
- 1 tsp. chili powder
- A pinch of salt and black pepper

**Directions:**

1. Take a bowl and mix the ghee with the rest of the ingredients except the green beans and whisk really well.
2. Mix the green beans with the lime sauce, toss
3. Put them in your air fryer's basket and cook at 400°F for 8 minutes. Serve right away.

**Nutrition: Calories: 151; Fat: 4g; Fiber: 2g; Carbs: 4g; Protein: 6g**

## 419. Roasted Veggie Bowl

Preparation Time: 25 minutes
Servings: 2

**Ingredients:**

- ¼ medium white onion; peeled.and sliced ¼-inch thick
- ½ medium green bell pepper; seeded and sliced ¼-inch thick
- 1 cup broccoli florets
- 1 cup quartered Brussels sprouts
- ½ cup cauliflower florets
- 1 tbsp. coconut oil
- ½ tsp. garlic powder.
- ½ tsp. cumin
- 2 tsp. chili powder

**Directions:**

1. Toss all ingredients together in a large bowl until vegetables are fully coated with

oil and seasoning. Pour vegetables into the air fryer basket.
2. Adjust the temperature to 360 Degrees F and set the timer for 15 minutes. Shake two or three times during cooking. Serve warm.

**Nutrition: Calories: 121; Protein: 4.3g; Fiber: 5.2g; Fat: 7.1g; Carbs: 13.1g**

## 420. Blackberry Crisp

Preparation Time: 20 minutes
Servings: 4

**Ingredients:**

- 1 cup Crunchy Granola
- 2 cups blackberries
- ⅓ cup powdered erythritol
- 2 tbsp. lemon juice
- ¼ tsp. xanthan gum

**Directions:**

1. Take a large bowl, toss blackberries, erythritol, lemon juice and xanthan gum.
2. Pour into 6-inch round baking dish and cover with foil. Place into the air fryer basket.
3. Adjust the temperature to 350 Degrees F and set the timer for 12 minutes.
4. When the timer beeps, remove the foil and stir.
5. Sprinkle granola over mixture and return to the air fryer basket. Adjust the temperature to 320 Degrees F and set the timer for 3 minutes or until top is golden. Serve warm.

**Nutrition: Calories: 496; Protein: 9.2g; Fiber: 12.5g; Fat: 42.1g; Carbs: 44.0g**

## 421. Peanut Butter Cookies

Preparation Time: 13 minutes
Servings: 8

**Ingredients:**

- 1 large egg.

- ⅓ cup granular erythritol.
- 1 cup no-sugar-added smooth peanut butter.
- 1 tsp. vanilla extract.

**Directions:**

1. Take a large bowl, mix all ingredients until smooth. Continue stirring for 2 additional minutes and the mixture will begin to thicken.
2. Roll the mixture into eight balls and press gently down to flatten into 2-inch round disks.
3. Cut a piece of parchment to fit your air fryer and place it into the basket. Place the cookies onto the parchment, working in batches as necessary.
4. Adjust the temperature to 320 Degrees F and set the timer for 8 minutes.
5. Flip the cookies at the 6-minute mark. Serve completely cooled.

**Nutrition: Calories: 210; Protein: 8.8g; Fiber: 2.0g; Fat: 17.5g; Carbs: 14.1g**

## 422. Cinnamon Pork Rinds

Preparation Time: 10 minutes
Servings: 2

**Ingredients:**

- 2 oz. pork rinds
- ¼ cup powdered erythritol
- 2 tbsp. unsalted butter; melted.
- ½ tsp. ground cinnamon.

**Directions:**

1. Take a large bowl, toss pork rinds and butter. Sprinkle with cinnamon and erythritol, then toss to evenly coat.
2. Place pork rinds into the air fryer basket. Adjust the temperature to 400 Degrees F and set the timer for 5 minutes. Serve immediately.

**Nutrition: Calories: 264; Protein: 16.3g; Fiber: 0.4g; Fat: 20.8g; Carbs: 18.5g**

## 423. Espresso Mini Cheesecake

Preparation Time: 20 minutes
Servings: 2

**Ingredients:**

- ½ cup walnuts
- 4 oz. full-fat cream cheese; softened.
- 1 large egg.
- 2 tbsp. salted butter
- 2 tbsp. granular erythritol.
- 2 tbsp. powdered erythritol
- 1 tsp. espresso powder
- ½ tsp. vanilla extract.
- 2 tsp. unsweetened cocoa powder

**Directions:**

1. Place walnuts, butter and granular erythritol in a food processor. Pulse until ingredients stick together and a dough forms.
2. Press dough into 4-inch springform pan and place into the air fryer basket.
3. Adjust the temperature to 400 Degrees F and set the timer for 5 minutes. When timer beeps, remove crust and let cool.
4. Take a medium bowl, mix cream cheese with egg, vanilla extract, powdered erythritol, cocoa powder and espresso powder until smooth.
5. Spoon mixture on top of baked walnut crust and place into the air fryer basket. Adjust the temperature for 300 Degrees F and set the timer for 10 minutes. Once done, chill for 2 hours before serving.

**Nutrition: Calories: 535; Protein: 11.6g; Fiber: 7.2g; Fat: 48.4g; Carbs: 37.1g**

## 424. Baked Egg and Veggies

Preparation Time: 20 minutes
Servings: 2

**Ingredients:**

- 1 cup fresh spinach; chopped
- 1 small zucchini, sliced lengthwise and

quartered

- 1 medium Roma tomato; diced
- ½ medium green bell pepper; seeded and diced
- 2 large eggs.
- 2 tbsp. salted butter
- ¼ tsp. garlic powder.
- ¼ tsp. onion powder.
- ½ tsp. dried basil
- ¼ tsp. dried oregano.

**Directions:**

1. Grease two: 4-inchramekins with 1 tbsp. butter each.
2. Take a large bowl, toss zucchini, bell pepper, spinach and tomatoes. Divide the mixture in two and place half in each ramekin.
3. Crack an egg on top of each ramekin and sprinkle with onion powder, garlic powder, basil and oregano. Place into the air fryer basket. Adjust the temperature to 330 Degrees F and set the timer for 10 minutes. Serve immediately.

**Nutrition: Calories: 150; Protein: 8.3g; Fiber: 2.2g; Fat: 10.0g; Carbs: 6.6g**

## 425. Raspberry Bites

Preparation Time: 37 minutes
Servings: 10

**Ingredients:**

- 2 oz. full-fat cream cheese; softened.
- 1 large egg.
- 1 cup blanched finely ground almond flour.
- 3 tbsp. granular Swerve.
- 1 tsp. baking powder.
- 10 tsp. sugar-free raspberry preserves.

**Directions:**

1. Mix all ingredients except preserves in a large bowl until a wet dough forms.
2. Place the bowl in the freezer for 20

minutes until dough is cool and able to roll into a ball.

3. Roll dough into ten balls and press gently in the center of each ball. Place 1 tsp. preserves in the center of each ball.
4. Cut a piece of parchment to fit your air fryer basket. Place each Danish bite on the parchment, pressing down gently to flatten the bottom.
5. Adjust the temperature to 400 Degrees F and set the timer for 7 minutes. Allow to cool completely before moving, or they will crumble.

**Nutrition: Calories: 96; Protein: 3.4g; Fiber: 1.3g; Fat: 7.7g; Carbs: 9.8g**

## 426. Coco Mug Cake

Preparation Time: 30 minutes
Servings: 1

**Ingredients:**

- 1 large egg.
- 2 tbsp. granular erythritol.
- 2 tbsp. coconut flour.
- 2 tbsp. heavy whipping cream.
- ¼ tsp. baking powder.
- ¼ tsp. vanilla extract.

**Directions:**

1. In a 4-inch ramekin, whisk egg, then add remaining ingredients. Stir until smooth. Place into the air fryer basket.
2. Adjust the temperature to 300 Degrees F and set the timer for 25 minutes.
3. When done a toothpick should come out clean. Enjoy right out of the ramekin with a spoon. Serve warm.

**Nutrition: Calories: 237; Protein: 9.9g; Fiber: 5.0g; Fat: 16.4g; Carbs: 40.7g**

## 427. Pecan Brownies

Preparation Time: 30 minutes
Servings: 6

**Ingredients:**

- ¼ cup chopped pecans
- ¼ cup low-carb, sugar-free chocolate chips.
- ¼ cup unsalted butter; softened.
- 1 large egg.
- ½ cup blanched finely ground almond flour.
- ½ cup powdered erythritol
- 2 tbsp. unsweetened cocoa powder
- ½ tsp. baking powder.

**Directions:**

1. Take a large bowl, mix almond flour, erythritol, cocoa powder and baking powder. Stir in butter and egg.
2. Fold in pecans and chocolate chips. Scoop mixture into 6-inch round baking pan. Place pan into the air fryer basket.
3. Adjust the temperature to 300 Degrees F and set the timer for 20 minutes. When fully cooked a toothpick inserted in center will come out clean. Allow 20 minutes to fully cool and firm up.

**Nutrition: Calories: 215; Protein: 4.2g; Fiber: 2.8g; Fat: 18.9g; Carbs: 21.8g**

## 428. Broccoli Crust Pizza

Preparation Time: 27 minutes
Servings: 4

**Ingredients:**

- 3 cups riced broccoli, steamed and drained well
- ½ cup shredded mozzarella cheese
- ½ cup grated vegetarian Parmesan cheese.
- 1 large egg.
- 3 tbsp. low-carb Alfredo sauce

**Directions:**

1. Take a large bowl, mix broccoli, egg and Parmesan.
2. Cut a piece of parchment to fit your air fryer basket. Press out the pizza mixture

to fit on the parchment, working in two batches if necessary. Place into the air fryer basket. Adjust the temperature to 370 Degrees F and set the timer for 5 minutes.

3. When the timer beeps, the crust should be firm enough to flip. If not, add 2 additional minutes. Flip crust.
4. Top with Alfredo sauce and mozzarella. Return to the air fryer basket and cook an additional 7 minutes or until cheese is golden and bubbling. Serve warm.

**Nutrition: Calories: 136; Protein: 9.9g; Fiber: 2.3g; Fat: 7.6g; Carbs:5.7g**

## 429. Spices Stuffed Eggplants

Preparation Time: 15 minutes
Cooking Time: 12 minutes
Servings: 4

**Ingredients:**

- 8 baby eggplants
- 4 teaspoons olive oil, divided
- ¾ tablespoon dry mango powder
- ¾ tablespoon ground coriander
- ½ teaspoon ground cumin
- ½ teaspoon ground turmeric
- ½ teaspoon garlic powder
- Salt, to taste

**Directions:**

1. Preheat the Air fryer to 370 o F and grease an Air fryer basket.
2. Make 2 slits from the bottom of each eggplant leaving the stems intact.
3. Mix one teaspoon of oil and spices in a bowl and fill each slit of eggplants with this mixture.
4. Brush the outer side of each eggplant with remaining oil and arrange in the Air fryer basket.
5. Cook for about 12 minutes and dish out in a serving plate to serve hot.

**Nutrition:**

Calories: 317, Fats: 6.7g, Carbohydrates: 65g, Sugar: 33g, Proteins: 10.9g, Sodium: 61mg

## 430. Stuffed Pumpkin

Preparation Time: 20 minutes
Cooking Time: 35 minutes
Servings: 4

**Ingredients:**

- 2 tomatoes, chopped
- 1 bell pepper, chopped
- 1 beetroot, chopped
- ½ cup green beans, shelled
- ½ of butternut pumpkin, seeded
- 2 garlic cloves, minced
- 2 teaspoons mixed dried herbs
- Salt and black pepper, to taste

**Directions:**

1. Preheat the Air fryer to 360 o F and grease an Air fryer basket.
2. Mix all the ingredients in a bowl except pumpkin and toss to coat well.
3. Stuff the vegetable mixture into the pumpkin and place into the Air fryer basket.
4. Cook for about 35 minutes and keep aside to slightly cool.
5. Dish out and serve warm.

**Nutrimmmmtion:**
Calories: 48, Fats: 0.4g, Carbohydrates: 11.1g, Sugar: 5.7g, Proteins: 1.8g, Sodium: 25mg

## 431. Glazed Veggies

Preparation Time: 20 minutes
Cooking Time: 20 minutes
Servings: 4

**Ingredients:**

- 2 ounces cherry tomatoes
- 1 large parsnip, peeled and chopped
- 1 large carrot, peeled and chopped
- 1 large zucchini, chopped

- 1 green bell pepper, seeded and chopped
- 6 tablespoons olive oil, divided
- 3 tablespoons honey
- 1 teaspoon Dijon mustard
- 1 teaspoon mixed dried herbs
- 1 teaspoon garlic paste
- Salt and black pepper, to taste

**Directions:**

1. Preheat the Air fryer to 350 o F and grease an Air fryer pan.
2. Arrange cherry tomatoes, parsnip, carrot, zucchini and bell pepper in the Air fryer pan and drizzle with 3 tablespoons of olive oil.
3. Cook for about 15 minutes and remove from the Air fryer.
4. Mix remaining olive oil, honey, mustard, herbs, garlic, salt, and black pepper in a bowl.
5. Pour this mixture over the vegetables in the Air fryer pan and set the Air fryer to 390 o F.
6. Cook for about 5 minutes and dish out to serve hot.

**Nutrition:**
Calories: 288, Fat: 21.4g, Carbohydrates: 26.7g, Sugar: 18.7g, Protein: 2.1g, Sodium: 79mg

## 432. Tofu with Capers Sauce

Preparation Time: 10 minutes
Cooking Time: 27 minutes
Servings: 4

**Ingredients:**

- 4 tablespoons fresh parsley, divided
- 1: 14-ouncesblock extra-firm tofu, pressed and cut into 8 rectangular cutlets
- 1 cup panko breadcrumbs
- 2 teaspoons cornstarch
- 2 tablespoons capers
- 1 cup vegetable broth
- ½ cup lemon juice

- 2 garlic cloves, peeled
- ½ cup mayonnaise
- Salt and black pepper, to taste

**Directions:**

1. Preheat the Air fryer to 375 o F and grease an Air fryer basket.
2. Put half of lemon juice, 2 tablespoons parsley, 2 garlic cloves, salt and black pepper in a food processor and pulse until smooth.
3. Transfer the mixture into a bowl and marinate tofu in it.
4. Place the mayonnaise in a shallow bowl and put the panko breadcrumbs in another bowl.
5. Coat the tofu pieces with mayonnaise and then, roll into the breadcrumbs.
6. Arrange the tofu pieces in the Air fryer pan and cook for about 20 minutes.
7. Mix broth, remaining lemon juice, remaining garlic, remaining parsley, cornstarch, salt and black pepper in a food processor and pulse until smooth.
8. Transfer the sauce into a small pan and stir in the capers.
9. Boil the sauce over medium heat and allow to simmer for about 7 minutes.
10. Dish out the tofu onto serving plates and drizzle with the caper sauce to serve.

**Nutrition:**
Calories: 307, Fat: 15.6g, Carbohydrates: 15.6g, Sugar: 3.4g, Protein: 10.8g, Sodium: 586mg

## 433. Tofu with Orange Sauce

Preparation Time: 20 minutes
Cooking Time: 20 minutes
Servings: 4

**Ingredients:**

- 1 pound extra-firm tofu, pressed and cubed
- ½ cup water
- 4 teaspoons cornstarch, divided
- 2 scallions: green part), chopped

- 1 tablespoon tamari
- 1/3 cup fresh orange juice
- 1 tablespoon honey
- 1 teaspoon orange zest, grated
- 1 teaspoon garlic, minced
- 1 teaspoon fresh ginger, minced
- ¼ teaspoon red pepper flakes, crushed

**Directions:**

1. Preheat the Air fryer to 390 o F and grease an Air fryer basket.
2. Mix the tofu, cornstarch, and tamari in a bowl and toss to coat well.
3. Arrange half of the tofu pieces in the Air fryer pan and cook for about 10 minutes.
4. Repeat with the remaining tofu and dish out in a bowl.
5. Put all the ingredients except scallions in a small pan over medium-high heat and bring to a boil.
6. Pour this sauce over the tofu and garnish with scallions to serve.

**Nutrition:**
Calories: 148, Fat: 6.7g, Carbohydrates: 13g, Sugar: 6.9g, Protein: 12.1g, Sodium: 263mg

## 434. Broccoli with Cauliflower

Preparation Time: 15 minutes
Cooking Time: 20 minutes
Servings: 4

**Ingredients:**

- 1½ cups broccoli, cut into 1-inch pieces
- 1½ cups cauliflower, cut into 1-inch pieces
- 1 tablespoon olive oil
- Salt, as required

**Directions:**

1. Preheat the Air fryer to 375 o F and grease an Air fryer basket.
2. Mix the vegetables, olive oil, and salt in a bowl and toss to coat well.
3. Arrange the veggie mixture in the Air

fryer basket and cook for about 20 minutes, tossing once in between.

4. Dish out in a bowl and serve hot.

**Nutrition:**
Calories: 51, Fat: 3.7g, Carbohydrates: 4.3g, Sugar: 1.5g, Protein: 1.7g, Sodium: 61mg

## 435. Herbed Veggies Combo

Preparation Time: 15 minutes
Cooking Time: 35 minutes
Servings: 4

- Ingredients:
- ½ pound carrots, peeled and sliced
- 1 pound yellow squash, sliced
- 1 pound zucchini, sliced
- ½ tablespoon fresh basil, chopped
- ½ tablespoon tarragon leaves, chopped
- 6 teaspoons olive oil, divided
- Salt and ground white pepper, to taste

**Directions:**
1. Preheat the Air fryer to 400 o F and grease an Air fryer basket.
2. Mix two teaspoons of oil and carrot slices in a bowl.
3. Arrange the carrot slices in the Air fryer basket and cook for about 5 minutes.
4. Mix the remaining oil, yellow squash, zucchini, salt, and white pepper in a large bowl and toss to coat well.
5. Transfer the zucchini mixture into air fryer basket with carrots and cook for about 30 minutes, tossing twice in between.
6. Dish out in a bowl and sprinkle with the herbs to serve.

**Nutrition:**
Calories: 120, Fat: 7.4g, Carbohydrates: 13.3g, Sugar: 6.7g, Protein: 3.3g, Sodium: 101mg

## 436. Spicy Tofu

Preparation Time: 10 minutes

Cooking Time: 13 minutes
Servings: 3

**Ingredients:**
- 1: 14-ouncesblock extra-firm tofu, pressed and cut into ¾-inch cubes
- 3 teaspoons cornstarch
- 1½ tablespoons avocado oil
- 1½ teaspoons paprika
- 1 teaspoon onion powder
- 1 teaspoon garlic powder
- Salt and black pepper, to taste

**Directions:**
1. Preheat the Air fryer to 390 o F and grease an Air fryer basket.
2. Mix the tofu, oil, cornstarch, and spices in a bowl and toss to coat well.
3. Arrange the tofu pieces in the Air fryer basket and cook for about 13 minutes, tossing twice in between.
4. Dish out the tofu onto serving plates and serve hot.

**Nutrition:**
Calories: 121, Fat: 6.6g, Carbohydrates: 7g, Sugar: 1.4g, Protein: 11.3g, Sodium: 68mg

## 437. Sweet and Spicy Parsnips

Preparation Time: 15 minutes
Cooking Time: 44 minutes
Servings: 6

**Ingredients:**
- 2 pounds parsnip, peeled and cut into 1-inch chunks
- 1 tablespoon butter, melted
- 2 tablespoons honey
- 1 tablespoon dried parsley flakes, crushed
- ¼ teaspoon red pepper flakes, crushed
- Salt and ground black pepper, to taste

**Directions:**
1. Preheat the Air fryer to 355 o F and grease an Air fryer basket.

2.  Mix the parsnips and butter in a bowl and toss to coat well.
3.  Arrange the parsnip chunks in the Air fryer basket and cook for about 40 minutes.
4.  Mix the remaining ingredients in another large bowl and stir in the parsnip chunks.
5.  Transfer the parsnip chunks in the Air fryer basket and cook for about 4 minutes.
6.  Dish out the parsnip chunks onto serving plates and serve hot.

**Nutrition:**
Calories: 155, Fat: 2.4g, Carbohydrates: 33.1g, Sugar: 13g, Protein: 1.9g, Sodium: 57mg

## 438. Herbed Carrots

Preparation Time: 15 minutes
Cooking Time: 14 minutes
Servings: 8

**Ingredients:**

*   6 large carrots, peeled and sliced lengthwise
*   2 tablespoons olive oil
*   ½ tablespoon fresh oregano, chopped
*   ½ tablespoon fresh parsley, chopped
*   Salt and black pepper, to taste
*   2 tablespoons olive oil, divided
*   ½ cup fat-free Italian dressing
*   Salt, to taste

**Directions:**

1.  Preheat the Air fryer to 360 o F and grease an Air fryer basket.
2.  Mix the carrot slices and olive oil in a bowl and toss to coat well.
3.  Arrange the carrot slices in the Air fryer basket and cook for about 12 minutes.
4.  Dish out the carrot slices onto serving plates and sprinkle with herbs, salt and black pepper.
5.  Transfer into the Air fryer basket and cook for 2 more minutes.

6.  Dish out and serve hot.

**Nutrition:**
Calories: 93, Fat: 7.2g, Carbohydrates: 7.3g, Sugar: 3.8g, Protein: 0.7g, Sodium: 252mg

## 439. Curried Eggplant

Preparation Time: 15 minutes
Cooking Time: 10 minutes
Servings: 2

**Ingredients:**

*   1 large eggplant, cut into ½-inch thick slices
*   1 garlic clove, minced
*   ½ fresh red chili, chopped
*   1 tablespoon vegetable oil
*   ¼ teaspoon curry powder
*   Salt, to taste

**Directions:**

1.  Preheat the Air fryer to 300 o F and grease an Air fryer basket.
2.  Mix all the ingredients in a bowl and toss to coat well.
3.  Arrange the eggplant slices in the Air fryer basket and cook for about 10 minutes, tossing once in between.
4.  Dish out onto serving plates and serve hot.

**Nutrition:**
Calories: 121, Fat: 7.3g, Carbohydrates: 14.2g, Sugar: 7g, Protein: 2.4g, Sodium: 83mg

## 440. Herbed Eggplant

Preparation Time: 15 minutes
Cooking Time: 15 minutes
Servings: 2

**Ingredients:**

*   1 large eggplant, cubed
*   ½ teaspoon dried marjoram, crushed
*   ½ teaspoon dried oregano, crushed
*   ½ teaspoon dried thyme, crushed

- ½ teaspoon garlic powder
- Salt and black pepper, to taste
- Olive oil cooking spray

**Directions:**
1. Preheat the Air fryer to 390 o F and grease an Air fryer basket.
2. Mix herbs, garlic powder, salt, and black pepper in a bowl.
3. Spray the eggplant cubes with cooking spray and rub with the herb mixture.
4. Arrange the eggplant cubes in the Air fryer basket and cook for about 15 minutes, flipping twice in between.
5. Dish out onto serving plates and serve hot.

**Nutrition:**
Calories: 62, Fat: 0.5g, Carbohydrates: 14.5g, Sugar: 7.1g, Protein: 2.4g, Sodium: 83mg

## 441. Salsa Stuffed Eggplants

Preparation Time: 15 minutes
Cooking Time: 25 minutes
Servings: 2

**Ingredients:**
- 1 large eggplant
- 8 cherry tomatoes, quartered
- ½ tablespoon fresh parsley
- 2 teaspoons olive oil, divided
- 2 teaspoons fresh lemon juice, divided
- 2 tablespoons tomato salsa
- Salt and black pepper, as required

**Directions:**
1. Preheat the Air fryer to 390 o F and grease an Air fryer basket.
2. Arrange the eggplant into the Air fryer basket and cook for about 15 minutes.
3. Cut the eggplant in half lengthwise and drizzle evenly with one teaspoon of oil.
4. Set the Air fryer to 355 o F and arrange the eggplant into the Air fryer basket, cut-side up.

5. Cook for another 10 minutes and dish out in a bowl.
6. Scoop out the flesh from the eggplant and transfer into a bowl.
7. Stir in the tomatoes, salsa, parsley, salt, black pepper, remaining oil, and lemon juice.
8. Squeeze lemon juice on the eggplant halves and stuff with the salsa mixture to serve.

**Nutrition:**
Calories: 192, Fat: 6.1g, Carbohydrates: 33.8g, Sugar: 20.4g, Protein: 6.9g, Sodium: 204mg

## 442. Sesame Seeds Bok Choy

Preparation Time: 10 minutes
Cooking Time: 6 minutes
Servings: 4

**Ingredients:**
- 4 bunches baby bok choy, bottoms removed and leaves separated
- 1 teaspoon sesame seeds
- Olive oil cooking spray
- 1 teaspoon garlic powder

**Directions:**
1. Preheat the Air fryer to 325 o F and grease an Air fryer basket.
2. Arrange the bok choy leaves into the Air fryer basket and spray with the cooking spray.
3. Sprinkle with garlic powder and cook for about 6 minutes, shaking twice in between.
4. Dish out in the bok choy onto serving plates and serve garnished with sesame seeds.

**Nutrition:**
Calories: 26, Fat: 0.7g, Carbohydrates: 4g, Sugar: 1.9g, Protein: 2.5g, Sodium: 98mg

## 443. Basil Tomatoes

Preparation Time: 10 minutes

Cooking Time: 10 minutes

Servings: 2

**Ingredients:**

- 2 tomatoes, halved
- 1 tablespoon fresh basil, chopped
- Olive oil cooking spray
- Salt and black pepper, as required

**Directions:**

1. Preheat the Air fryer to 320 o F and grease an Air fryer basket.
2. Spray the tomato halves evenly with olive oil cooking spray and season with salt, black pepper and basil.
3. Arrange the tomato halves into the Air fryer basket, cut sides up.
4. Cook for about 10 minutes and dish out onto serving plates.

**Nutrition:**

Calories: 22, Fat: 4.8g, Carbohydrates: 4.8g, Sugar: 3.2g, Protein: 1.1g, Sodium: 84mg

## 444. Couscous Stuffed Tomatoes

Preparation Time: 10 minutes

Cooking Time: 25 minutes

Servings: 4

**Ingredients:**

- 4 tomatoes, tops and seeds removed
- 1 parsnip, peeled and finely chopped
- 1 cup mushrooms, chopped
- 1½ cups couscous
- 1 teaspoon olive oil
- 1 garlic clove, minced
- 1 tablespoon mirin sauce

**Directions:**

1. Preheat the Air fryer to 355 o F and grease an Air fryer basket.
2. Heat olive oil in a skillet on low heat and add parsnips, mushrooms and garlic.
3. Cook for about 5 minutes and stir in the mirin sauce and couscous.

4. Stuff the couscous mixture into the tomatoes and arrange into the Air fryer basket.
5. Cook for about 20 minutes and dish out to serve warm.

**Nutrition:**

Calories: 361, Fat: 2g, Carbohydrates: 75.5g, Sugar: 5.1g, Protein: 10.4g, Sodium: 37mg

## 445. Sweet and Spicy Cauliflower

Preparation Time: 15 minutes

Cooking Time: 25 minutes

Servings: 4

**Ingredients:**

- 1 head cauliflower, cut into florets
- ¾ cup onion, thinly sliced
- 2 scallions, chopped
- 5 garlic cloves, finely sliced
- 1½ tablespoons soy sauce
- 1 tablespoon hot sauce
- 1 tablespoon rice vinegar
- 1 teaspoon coconut sugar
- Pinch of red pepper flakes
- Ground black pepper, as required

**Directions:**

1. Preheat the Air fryer to 350 o F and grease an Air fryer basket.
2. Arrange the cauliflower florets into the Air fryer basket and cook for about 10 minutes.
3. Add the onions and garlic and cook for 10 more minutes.
4. Meanwhile, mix soy sauce, hot sauce, vinegar, coconut sugar, red pepper flakes, and black pepper in a bowl.
5. Pour the soy sauce mixture into the cauliflower mixture.
6. Cook for about 5 minutes and dish out onto serving plates.
7. Garnish with scallions and serve warm.

**Nutrition:**

Calories: 72, Fat: 0.2g, Carbohydrates: 13.8g, Sugar: 3.1g, Protein: 3.6g, Sodium: 1300mg

## 446. Spiced Butternut Squash

Preparation Time: 15 minutes
Cooking Time: 20 minutes
Servings: 4

**Ingredients:**

- 1 medium butternut squash, peeled, seeded and cut into chunk
- 2 teaspoons cumin seeds
- 2 tablespoons pine nuts
- 2 tablespoons fresh cilantro, chopped
- 1/8 teaspoon garlic powder
- 1/8 teaspoon chili flakes, crushed
- Salt and ground black pepper, as required
- 1 tablespoon olive oil

**Directions:**

1. Preheat the Air fryer to 375 o F and grease an Air fryer basket.
2. Mix the squash, spices and olive oil in a bowl.
3. Arrange the butternut squash chunks into the Air fryer basket and cook for about 20 minutes.
4. Dish out the butternut squash chunks onto serving plates and serve garnished with pine nuts and cilantro.

**Nutrition:**
Calories: 165, Fat: 6.9g, Carbohydrates: 27.6g, Sugar: 5.2g, Protein: 3.1g, Sodium: 50mg

## 447. Herbed Potatoes

Preparation Time: 20 minutes
Cooking Time: 15 minutes
Servings: 4

**Ingredients:**

- 6 small potatoes, chopped
- 2 tablespoons fresh parsley, chopped
- 3 tablespoons olive oil
- 2 teaspoons mixed dried herbs
- Salt and black pepper, to taste

**Directions:**

1. Preheat the Air fryer to 360 o F and grease an Air fryer basket.
2. Mix the potatoes, oil, herbs, salt and black pepper in a bowl.
3. Arrange the chopped potatoes into the Air fryer basket and cook for about 15 minutes, tossing once in between.
4. Dish out the potatoes onto serving plates and serve garnished with parsley.

**Nutrition:**
Calories: 268, Fat: 10.8g, Carbohydrates: 40.4g, Sugar: 3g, Protein: 4.4g, Sodium: 55mg

## 448. Spicy Potatoes

Preparation Time: 10 minutes
Cooking Time: 20 minutes
Servings: 6

**Ingredients:**

- 1¾ pounds waxy potatoes, peeled and cubed
- 1 tablespoon olive oil
- ½ teaspoon ground cumin
- ½ teaspoon ground coriander
- ½ teaspoon paprika
- Salt and black pepper, to taste

**Directions:**

1. Preheat the Air fryer to 355 o F and grease an Air fryer basket.
2. Mix the potatoes, olive oil, and spices in a bowl and toss to coat well.
3. Transfer into the Air fryer basket and cook for about 20 minutes.
4. Dish out the potato cubes onto serving plates and serve hot.

**Nutrition:**
Calories: 113, Fat: 2.5g, Carbohydrates: 21g, Sugar: 1.5g, Protein: 2.3g, Sodium: 35mg

## 449. Tofu with Peanut Butter Sauce

Preparation Time: 20 minutes
Cooking Time: 15 minutes
Servings: 3

**Ingredients:**
*For Tofu*

- 1: 14-ouncesblock tofu, pressed and cut into strips
- 6 bamboo skewers, presoaked and halved

*For Tofu*

- 2 tablespoons fresh lime juice
- 2 tablespoons soy sauce
- 1 tablespoon maple syrup
- 1 teaspoon Sriracha sauce
- 2 teaspoons fresh ginger, peeled
- 2 garlic cloves, peeled

*For Sauce*

- 1: 2-inchespiece fresh ginger, peeled
- 2 garlic cloves, peeled
- ½ cup creamy peanut butter
- 1 tablespoon soy sauce
- 1 tablespoon fresh lime juice
- 1-2 teaspoons Sriracha sauce
- 6 tablespoons of water

**Directions:**

1. Preheat the Air fryer to 370 o F and grease an Air fryer basket.
2. Put all the ingredients except tofu in a food processor and pulse until smooth.
3. Transfer the mixture into a bowl and marinate tofu in it.
4. Thread one tofu strip onto each little bamboo stick and arrange them in the Air fryer basket.
5. Cook for about 15 minutes and dish out onto serving plates.
6. Mix all the ingredients for the sauce in a food processor and pulse until smooth.
7. Drizzle the sauce over tofu and serve warm.

**Nutrition:**

Calories: 385, Fats: 27.3g, Carbohydrates: 9.3g, Sugar: 9.1g, Proteins: 23g, Sodium: 1141mg

## 450. Veggie Rice

Preparation Time: 20 minutes
Cooking Time: 18 minutes
Servings: 2

**Ingredients:**

- 2 cups cooked white rice
- 1 large egg, lightly beaten
- ½ cup frozen peas, thawed
- ½ cup frozen carrots, thawed
- ½ teaspoon sesame seeds, toasted
- 1 tablespoon vegetable oil
- 2 teaspoons sesame oil, toasted and divided
- 1 tablespoon water
- Salt and ground white pepper, as required
- 1 teaspoon soy sauce
- 1 teaspoon Sriracha sauce

**Directions:**

1. Preheat the Air fryer to 380 o F and grease an Air fryer pan.
2. Mix the rice, vegetable oil, 1 teaspoon of sesame oil, water, salt, and white pepper in a bowl.
3. Transfer the rice mixture into the Air fryer basket and cook for about 12 minutes.
4. Pour the beaten egg over rice and cook for about 4 minutes.
5. Stir in the peas and carrots and cook for 2 more minutes.
6. Meanwhile, mix soy sauce, Sriracha sauce, sesame seeds and the remaining sesame oil in a bowl.
7. Dish out the potato cubes onto serving plates and drizzle with sauce to serve.

**Nutrition:**
Calories: 163, Fat: 8.4g, Carbohydrates: 15.5g, Sugar: 11.2g, Protein: 6.4g, Sodium: 324mg

## 451. Tofu with Veggies

Preparation Time: 25 minutes
Cooking Time: 22 minutes
Servings: 3

**Ingredients:**

- ½: 14-ouncesblock firm tofu, pressed and crumbled
- 1 cup carrot, peeled and chopped
- 3 cups cauliflower rice
- ½ cup broccoli, finely chopped
- ½ cup frozen peas
- 4 tablespoons low-sodium soy sauce, divided
- 1 teaspoon ground turmeric
- 1 tablespoon fresh ginger, minced
- 2 garlic cloves, minced
- 1 tablespoon rice vinegar
- 1½ teaspoons sesame oil, toasted

**Directions:**

1. Preheat the Air fryer to 370 o F and grease an Air fryer pan.
2. Mix the tofu, carrot, onion, 2 tablespoons of soy sauce, and turmeric in a bowl.
3. Transfer the tofu mixture into the Air fryer basket and cook for about 10 minutes.
4. Meanwhile, mix the cauliflower rice, broccoli, peas, ginger, garlic, vinegar, sesame oil, and remaining soy sauce in a bowl.
5. Stir in the cauliflower rice into the Air fryer pan and cook for about 12 minutes.
6. Dish out the tofu mixture onto serving plates and serve hot.

**Nutrition:**
Calories: 162, Fat: 5.5g, Carbohydrates: 20.4g, Sugar: 8.3g, Protein: 11.4g, Sodium: 1263mg

## 452. Delightful Mushrooms

Preparation Time: 20 minutes
Cooking Time: 22 minutes

Servings: 4

**Ingredients:**

- 2 cups mushrooms, sliced
- 2 tablespoons cheddar cheese, shredded
- 1 tablespoon fresh chives, chopped
- 2 tablespoons olive oil

**Directions:**

1. Preheat the Air fryer to 355 o F and grease an Air fryer basket.
2. Coat the mushrooms with olive oil and arrange into the Air fryer basket.
3. Cook for about 20 minutes and dish out in a platter.
4. Top with chives and cheddar cheese and cook for 2 more minutes.
5. Dish out and serve warm.

**Nutrition:**
Calories: 218, Fat: 7.9g, Carbohydrates: 33.6g, Sugar: 2.5g, Protein: 4.6g, Sodium: 55mg

## 453. Sesame Seeds Bok Choy

Preparation Time: 10 minutes
Cooking Time: 6 minutes
Servings: 4

**Ingredients:**

- 4 bunches spinach leaves
- 2 teaspoons sesame seeds
- 1 teaspoon garlic powder
- 1 teaspoon ginger powder
- Salt, to taste

**Directions:**

1. Preheat the Air fryer to 325 o F and grease an Air fryer basket.
2. Arrange the spinach leaves into the Air fryer basket and season with salt, garlic powder and ginger powder.
3. Cook for about 6 minutes, shaking once in between and dish out onto serving plates.
4. Top with sesame seeds and serve hot.

**Nutrition:**
Calories: 26, Fat: 0.7g, Carbohydrates: 4g, Sugar: 1.9g, Protein: 2.5g, Sodium: 98mg

## 454. Veggie Rice

Preparation Time: 38 minutes
Servings: 2

**Ingredients:**

- 1 large egg, lightly beaten
- 2 cups cooked white rice
- 1/2 cup frozen peas, thawed
- 1/2 cup frozen carrots, thawed
- 1 tbsp. water
- 1 tbsp. vegetable oil
- 1 tsp. soy sauce
- 1 tsp. Sriracha sauce
- 2 tsp. sesame oil; toasted and divided
- 1/2 tsp. sesame seeds; toasted
- Salt and ground white pepper; as your liking

**Directions:**

1. In a large bowl; mix well rice, vegetable oil, one tsp. of sesame oil, water, salt and white pepper. Set the temperature of air fryer to 380°F. Lightly, grease an air fryer pan
2. Transfer rice mixture into the prepared air fryer pan. Air fryer for about 12 minutes, stirring once halfway through. Remove the pan from air fryer and place the beaten egg over rice
3. Air fry for another 4 minutes. Again, remove the pan from air fryer and stir in the peas and carrots. Air fry for 2 more minutes.
4. Meanwhile; in a bowl; mix together soy sauce, Sriracha sauce, sesame seeds and the remaining sesame oil. Remove from air fryer and transfer the rice mixture into a serving bowl.
5. Drizzle with the sauce and serve

## 455. Croissant Rolls

Preparation Time: 16 minutes
Servings: 8

**Ingredients:**

- 4 tbsp. butter; melted
- 1: 8-ozcan croissant rolls

**Directions:**

1. Set the temperature of air fryer to 320°F. Grease an air fryer basket.
2. Arrange croissant rolls into the prepared air fryer basket. Air fry for about 4 minutes.
3. Flip the side and air fry for 1 to 2 more minutes.
4. Remove from the air fryer and transfer onto a platter.
5. Drizzle with the melted butter and serve hot.

## 456. Rice and Beans Stuffed Bell Peppers

Preparation Time: 30 minutes
Servings: 5

**Ingredients:**

- 5 large bell peppers, tops removed and seeded
- 1/2 cup mozzarella cheese, shredded
- 1/2 small bell pepper, seeded and chopped
- 1: 15-ozcan red kidney beans, rinsed and drained
- 1: 15-ozcan diced tomatoes with juice
- 1 cup cooked rice
- 1 tbsp. Parmesan cheese; grated
- 1 ½ tsp. Italian seasoning

**Directions:**

1. In a bowl; mix well chopped bell pepper, tomatoes with juice, beans, rice and Italian seasoning. Stuff each bell pepper evenly with the rice mixture.
2. Set the temperature of air fryer to 360°F. Grease an air fryer basket.
3. Arrange bell peppers into the air fryer basket in a single layer.

4. Air fry for about 12 minutes. Meanwhile; in a bowl; mix together the mozzarella and Parmesan cheese.
5. Remove the air fryer basket and top each bell pepper with cheese mixture. Air fry for 3 more minutes.
6. Remove from air fryer and transfer the bell peppers onto a serving platter. Set aside to cool slightly. Serve warm.

## 457. Ratatouille

Preparation Time: 30 minutes
Servings: 4

**Ingredients:**

- 1 zucchini; chopped
- 1 yellow bell pepper, seeded and chopped
- 1 eggplant; chopped
- 3 tomatoes; chopped
- 2 small onions; chopped
- 2 garlic cloves, minced
- 1 green bell pepper, seeded and chopped
- 1 tbsp. balsamic vinegar
- 2 tbsp. Herbs de Provence
- 1 tbsp. olive oil
- Salt and ground black pepper; as your liking

**Directions:**

1. Set the temperature of air fryer to 355°F. Grease a baking dish.
2. In a large bowl; add the vegetables, garlic, Herbs de Provence, oil, vinegar, salt and black pepper and toss to coat well.
3. Transfer vegetable mixture into the prepared baking dish. Arrange the baking dish into air fryer and air fry for about 15 minutes.
4. Remove from air fryer and transfer the vegetable mixture into a serving bowl. Serve immediately.

## 458. Breadcrumbs Stuffed Mushrooms

Preparation Time: 25 minutes
Servings: 4

**Ingredients:**

- 16 small button mushrooms, stemmed and gills removed
- 1 garlic clove; crushed
- 1 ½ spelt bread slices
- 1 tbsp. flat-leaf parsley, finely chopped
- 1 ½ tbsp. olive oil
- Salt and ground black pepper; as your liking

**Directions:**

1. In a food processor, add the bread slices and pulse until fine crumbs form. Transfer the crumbs into a bowl. Add the garlic, parsley, salt and black pepper and stir to combine.
2. Stir in the olive oil. Set the temperature of air fryer to 390°F. Grease an air fryer basket.
3. Stuff each mushroom cap with the breadcrumbs mixture.
4. Arrange mushroom caps into the prepared air fryer basket. Air fry for about 9 to 10 minutes.
5. Remove from air fryer and transfer the mushrooms onto a serving platter.
6. Set aside to cool slightly. Serve warm.

## 459. Glazed Veggies

Preparation Time: 40 minutes
Servings: 4

**Ingredients:**

- 2-oz cherry tomatoes
- 1 large zucchini; chopped
- 1 large carrot; peeled and chopped
- 1 green bell pepper, seeded and chopped
- 1 large parsnip; peeled and chopped
- 6 tbsp. olive oil, divided
- 3 tbsp. honey
- 1 tsp. garlic paste
- 1 tsp. Dijon mustard
- 1 tsp. mixed dried herbs
- Salt and ground black pepper; as your

liking

**Directions:**

1. Set the temperature of air fryer to 350°F. Grease an air fryer pan.
2. Arrange vegetables into the prepared air fryer pan and drizzle with 3 tbsp. of oil. Air fry for about 15 minutes.
3. Meanwhile; in a baking dish, mix well remaining oil, honey, mustard, herbs, garlic, salt and black pepper.
4. Remove the vegetables from air fryer. Transfer the vegetables into baking dish with honey mixture and mix until well combined.
5. set the temperature of air fryer to 392°F. Arrange the baking dish into air fryer and air fry for about 5 minutes. Remove from air fryer and transfer the vegetable mixture into a serving bowl. Serve immediately.

## 460. Jacket Potatoes

Preparation Time: 30 minutes
Servings: 2

**Ingredients:**

- 2 potatoes
- 3 tbsp. sour cream
- 1 tbsp. butter; softened
- 1 tbsp. mozzarella cheese, shredded
- 1 tsp. chives, minced
- Salt and ground black pepper; as your liking

**Directions:**

1. Set the temperature of air fryer to 355°F. Grease an air fryer basket.
2. With a fork, prick the potatoes. Arrange potatoes into the prepared air fryer basket.
3. Air fry for about 15 minutes. In a bowl; add the remaining Ingredients and mix until well combined.
4. Remove from air fryer and transfer the potatoes onto a platter.

5. Open potatoes from the center and stuff them with cheese mixture. Serve immediately

## 461. Salsa Stuffed Eggplants

Preparation Time: 40 minutes
Servings: 2

**Ingredients:**

- 1 large eggplant
- 8 cherry tomatoes, quartered
- 2 tbsp. tomato salsa
- 1/2 tbsp. fresh parsley
- 2 tsp. fresh lemon juice, divided
- 2 tsp. olive oil, divided
- Salt and ground black pepper; as your liking

**Directions:**

1. Set the temperature of air fryer to 390°F.
2. Grease an air fryer basket. Place eggplant into the prepared air fryer basket.
3. Air fry for about 15 minutes. Remove from air fryer and cut the eggplant in half lengthwise.
4. Drizzle the eggplant halves evenly with one tsp. of oil. Now; set the temperature of air fryer to 355°F. Grease the air fryer basket.
5. Arrange eggplant into the prepared air fryer basket, cut-side up. Air fry for another 10 minutes.
6. Remove eggplant from the air fryer and set aside for about 5 minutes.
7. Carefully; scoop out the flesh, leaving about ¼-inch away from edges.
8. Drizzle the eggplant halves with one tsp. of lemon juice. Transfer the eggplant flesh into a bowl.
9. Add the tomatoes, salsa, parsley, salt, black pepper, remaining oil and lemon juice and mix well.
10. Stuff the eggplant haves with salsa mixture and serve.

## 462. Herbed Potatoes

Preparation Time: 26 minutes
Servings: 4

**Ingredients:**

- 6 small potatoes; chopped
- 2 tbsp. fresh parsley; chopped
- 3 tbsp. olive oil
- 2 tsp. mixed dried herbs
- Salt and ground black pepper; as your liking

**Directions:**

1. Set the temperature of air fryer to 356°F. Grease an air fryer basket. In a large bowl; add the potatoes, oil, herbs, salt and black pepper and toss to coat well.
2. Arrange the chopped potatoes into the prepared air fryer basket in a single layer.
3. Air fry for about 16 minutes, tossing once halfway through.
4. Remove from air fryer and transfer the potatoes onto serving plates. Garnish with parsley and serve.

## 463. Sautéed Green Beans

Preparation Time: 20 minutes
Servings: 2

**Ingredients:**

- 8-oz fresh green beans, trimmed and cut in half
- 1 tsp. sesame oil
- 1 tbsp. soy sauce

**Directions:**

1. In a bowl; mix well green beans, soy sauce and sesame oil.
2. Set the temperature of air fryer to 390°F. Lightly, grease an air fryer basket.
3. Arrange green beans into the prepared air fryer basket. Air fry for about 10 minutes, tossing once halfway through.
4. Remove from air fryer and transfer the green beans onto serving plates. Serve

hot.

## 464. Sesame Seeds Bok Choy

Preparation Time: 16 minutes
Servings: 4

**Ingredients:**

- 4 bunches baby bok choy, bottoms removed and leaves separated
- 1 tsp. garlic powder
- Olive oil cooking spray
- 1 tsp. sesame seeds

**Directions:**

1. Set the temperature of air fryer to 325°F. Arrange bok choy leaves into the air fryer basket in a single layer.
2. Spray with the cooking spray and sprinkle with garlic powder.
3. Air fry for about 5 to 6 minutes, shaking after every 2 minutes.
4. Remove from air fryer and transfer the bok choy onto serving plates. Garnish with sesame seeds and serve hot.

## 465. Stuffed Okra

Preparation Time: 27 minutes
Servings: 2

**Ingredients:**

- 8-oz large okra
- 1/4 of onion; chopped
- 1/4 cup chickpea flour
- 2 tbsp. coconut; grated freshly
- 1 tsp. garam masala powder
- 1/2 tsp. ground turmeric
- 1/2 tsp. red chili powder
- 1/2 tsp. ground cumin
- Salt, to taste

**Directions:**

1. With a knife, make a slit in each okra vertically without cutting in 2 halves. In a bowl; mix together the flour, onion;

grated coconut and spices.

2. Stuff each okra with the mixture. Set the temperature of air fryer to 390°F. Grease an air fryer basket.

3. Arrange stuffed okra into the prepared air fryer basket. Air fry for about 12 minutes.

4. Remove from air fryer and transfer the okra onto serving plates. Serve hot.

## 466. Almond Asparagus

Preparation Time: 21 minutes
Servings: 3

**Ingredients:**

- 1 lb. asparagus
- 1/3 cup almonds, sliced
- 2 tbsp. balsamic vinegar
- 2 tbsp. olive oil
- Salt and ground black pepper; as your liking

**Directions:**

1. In a bowl; mix together the asparagus, oil, vinegar, salt and black pepper. Set the temperature of air fryer to 400°F. Grease an air fryer basket.

2. Arrange asparagus into the prepared air fryer basket in a single layer and top with the almond slices.

3. Air fry for about 5 to 6 minutes.

4. Remove from air fryer and transfer the asparagus onto serving plates. Serve hot.

## 467. Stuffed Tomatoes

Preparation Time: 37 minutes
Servings: 4

**Ingredients:**

- 4 tomatoes
- 1 carrot; peeled and finely chopped
- 1 onion; chopped
- 1 cup frozen peas, thawed
- 1 garlic clove, minced
- 2 cups cold cooked rice

- 1 tbsp. soy sauce
- 1 tsp. olive oil

**Directions:**

1. Cut the top of each tomato and scoop out pulp and seeds. In a skillet, heat oil over low heat and sauté the carrot, onion, garlic and peas for about 2 minutes.

2. Stir in the soy sauce and rice and remove from heat. Set the temperature of air fryer to 355°F. Grease an air fryer basket.

3. Stuff each tomato with the rice mixture.

4. Arrange tomatoes into the prepared air fryer basket. Air fry for about 20 minutes.

5. Remove from air fryer and transfer the tomatoes onto a serving platter. Set aside to cool slightly. Serve warm.

## 468. Spicy Tofu

Preparation Time: 20 minutes
Servings: 2

**Ingredients:**

- 1: 14-ozblock extra-firm tofu, pressed and cut into ¾-inch cubes
- 1 ½ tbsp. avocado oil
- 1 tsp. onion powder
- 1 tsp. garlic powder
- 3 tsp. cornstarch
- 1 ½ tsp. paprika
- Salt and ground black pepper; as your liking

**Directions:**

1. In a bowl; mix well tofu, oil, cornstarch and spices. Set the temperature of air fryer to 390°F.

2. Grease an air fryer basket.

3. Arrange tofu pieces into the prepared air fryer basket in a single layer. Air fry for about 13 minutes, shaking twice halfway through.

4. Remove from air fryer and transfer the tofu onto serving plates. Serve hot.

## 469. Sweet and Spicy Cauliflower

Preparation Time: 45 minutes
Servings: 4

**Ingredients:**

- 1 head cauliflower; cut into florets
- 3/4 cup onion, thinly sliced
- 2 scallions; chopped
- 5 garlic cloves, finely sliced
- 1 tbsp. hot sauce
- 1 tbsp. rice vinegar
- 1 ½ tbsp. soy sauce
- 1 tsp. coconut sugar
- Pinch of red pepper flakes
- Ground black pepper; as your liking

**Directions:**

1. Set the temperature of air fryer to 350°F. Grease an air fryer pan. Arrange cauliflower florets into the prepared air fryer pan in a single layer.
2. Air fry for about 10 minutes. Remove from air fryer and stir in the onions.
3. Air fry for another 10 minutes. Remove from air fryer and stir in the garlic.
4. Air fry for 5 more minutes. Meanwhile; in a bowl; mix well soy sauce, hot sauce, vinegar, coconut sugar, red pepper flakes and black pepper.
5. Remove from the air fryer and stir in the sauce mixture. Air fry for about 5 minutes.
6. Remove from air fryer and transfer the cauliflower mixture onto serving plates. Garnish with scallions and serve.

## 470. Tofu with Capers Sauce

Preparation Time: 40 minutes
Servings: 4

**Ingredients:**

*For Marinade:*

- 1/4 cup fresh lemon juice
- 1 garlic clove; peeled
- 2 tbsp. fresh parsley
- Salt and ground black pepper; as your liking

*For Tofu:*

- 1/2 cup mayonnaise
- 1: 14-ozblock extra-firm tofu, pressed and cut into 8 rectangular cutlets
- 1 cup panko breadcrumbs

*For Sauce:*

- 1 garlic clove; peeled
- 1 cup vegetable broth
- 1/4 cup lemon juice
- 2 tbsp. fresh parsley
- 2 tbsp. capers
- 2 tsp. cornstarch
- Salt and ground black pepper; as your liking

**Directions:**

1. For marinade: in a food processor, add all the Ingredients and pulse until smooth. In a bowl; mix together the marinade and tofu.
2. Set aside for about 15 to 30 minutes. In two shallow bowls, place the mayonnaise and panko breadcrumbs respectively.
3. Coat the tofu pieces with mayonnaise and then, roll into the panko. Set the temperature of air fryer to 375°F. Grease an air fryer basket.
4. Arrange tofu pieces into the prepared air fryer basket in a single layer.
5. Air fry for about 20 minutes, shaking once halfway through.
6. Meanwhile; for the sauce: add broth, lemon juice, garlic, parsley, cornstarch, salt and black pepper in a food processor and pulse until smooth.
7. Transfer the sauce into a small pan and stir in the capers. Place the sauce over medium heat and bring to a boil.
8. Reduce the heat to low and simmer for about 5 to 7 minutes, stirring continuously.
9. Remove the tofu from air fryer and

transfer onto serving plates. Top with the sauce and serve.

## 471. Spiced Butternut Squash

Preparation Time: 35 minutes
Servings: 4

**Ingredients:**

- 1 medium butternut squash, peeled, seeded and cut into chunk
- 2 tbsp. pine nuts
- 2 tbsp. fresh cilantro; chopped
- 1 tbsp. olive oil
- 1/8 tsp. chili flakes; crushed
- 1/8 tsp. garlic powder
- 2 tsp. cumin seeds
- Salt and ground black pepper; as your liking

**Directions:**

1. Set the temperature of air fryer to 375°F. Grease an air fryer basket. In a bowl; mix together the squash, spices and oil.
2. Arrange butternut squash chunks into the prepared fryer basket. Air fry for about 20 minutes, flipping occasionally.
3. Remove from air fryer and transfer the squash chunks onto serving plates.
4. Garnish with pine nuts and cilantro. Serve.

## 472. Herbed Veggies Combo

Preparation Time: 50 minutes
Servings: 4

**Ingredients:**

- 1 lb. yellow squash, sliced
- 1/2 lb. carrots; peeled and sliced
- 1 lb. zucchini, sliced
- 1/2 tbsp. tarragon leaves; chopped
- 1/2 tbsp. fresh basil; chopped
- 6 tsp. olive oil, divided
- Salt and ground white pepper; as your

liking

**Directions:**

1. Set the temperature of air fryer to 400°F. In a bowl; mix together 2 tsp. of oil and carrot slices.
2. Place carrot slices into the air fryer basket Air fry for about 5 minutes.
3. Meanwhile; in a large bowl; add the remaining oil, yellow squash, zucchini, salt and white pepper and toss to coat well. Transfer the zucchini mixture into air fryer basket with carrots.
4. Air fry for about 30 minutes, tossing 2 to 3 times. Remove from air fryer and transfer the vegetable mixture into a serving bowl.
5. Add the herbs and mix until well combined. Serve.

## 473. Broccoli with Cauliflower

Preparation Time: 35 minutes
Servings: 4

**Ingredients:**

- 1 ½ cups cauliflower; cut into 1-inch pieces
- 1 ½ cups broccoli; cut into 1-inch pieces
- 1 tbsp. olive oil
- Salt; as your liking

**Directions:**

1. In a bowl; add the vegetables, oil and salt and toss to coat well.
2. Set the temperature of air fryer to 375°F. Grease an air fryer basket.
3. Arrange veggie mixture into the prepared air fryer basket. Air fry for about 15 to 20 minutes, tossing once halfway through.
4. Remove from air fryer and transfer the veggie mixture onto serving plates. Serve hot.

## 474. Sautéed Spinach

Preparation Time: 24 minutes
Servings: 2

**Ingredients:**

- 1 garlic clove, minced
- 6-oz fresh spinach
- 1 small onion; chopped
- 2 tbsp. olive oil
- Salt and ground black pepper; as your liking

**Directions:**

1. Set the temperature of air fryer to 340°F. In an air fryer pan, heat the oil for about 2 minutes.
2. Add the onion and garlic and air fry for about 3 minutes.
3. Add the spinach, salt and black pepper and air fry for about 4 more minutes.
4. Remove from air fryer and transfer the spinach mixture onto serving plates. Serve hot.

## 475. Crispy Marinated Tofu

Preparation Time: 35 minutes
Servings: 3

**Ingredients:**

- 1: 14-ozblock firm tofu, pressed and cut into 1-inch cubes
- 1 tbsp. cornstarch
- 2 tbsp. low sodium soy sauce
- 1 tsp. seasoned rice vinegar
- 2 tsp. sesame oil; toasted

**Directions:**

1. In a bowl; mix well tofu, soy sauce, sesame oil and vinegar. Set aside to marinate for about 25 to 30 minutes. Coat the tofu cubes evenly with cornstarch.
2. Set the temperature of air fryer to 370°F. Grease an air fryer basket. Arrange tofu pieces into the prepared air fryer basket in a single layer.
3. Air fry for about 20 minutes, shaking once halfway through.
4. Remove from air fryer and transfer the tofu onto serving plates. Serve warm.

## 476. Spices Stuffed Eggplants

Preparation Time: 27 minutes
Servings: 4

**Ingredients:**

- 8 baby eggplants
- 3/4 tbsp. ground coriander
- 3/4 tbsp. dry mango powder
- 1/2 tsp. ground cumin
- 1/2 tsp. ground turmeric
- 1/2 tsp. garlic powder
- 4 tsp. olive oil, divided
- Salt, to taste

**Directions:**

1. In a small bowl; mix together one tsp. of oil and spices. From the bottom of each eggplant, make 2 slits, leaving the stems intact.
2. With a small spoon, fill each slit of eggplants with spice mixture. Now; brush the outer side of each eggplant with remaining oil.
3. Set the temperature of air fryer to 369°F. Grease an air fryer basket.
4. Arrange eggplants into the prepared air fryer basket in a single layer.
5. Air fry for about 8 to 12 minutes. Remove from air fryer and transfer the eggplants onto serving plates. Serve hot.

## 477. Tofu in Sweet and Spicy Sauce

Preparation Time: 43 minutes
Servings: 3

**Ingredients:**
*For Tofu:*

- 1/2 cup arrowroot flour
- 1: 14-ozblock firm tofu, pressed and cubed
- 1/2 tsp. sesame oil

*For Sauce:*

- 2 large garlic cloves, minced
- 2 scallions: green part); chopped

- 1 ½ tbsp. chili sauce
- 1 tbsp. agave nectar
- 4 tbsp. low-sodium soy sauce
- 1 ½ tbsp. rice vinegar
- 1 tsp. fresh ginger; peeled and grated

**Directions:**

1. In a bowl; mix together the tofu, arrowroot flour and sesame oil. Set the temperature of air fryer to 360°F. Generously, grease an air fryer basket
2. Arrange tofu pieces into the prepared air fryer basket in a single layer
3. Air fry for about 20 minutes, shaking once halfway through.
4. Meanwhile; for the sauce: in a bowl; add all the Ingredients except scallions and beat until well combined.
5. Remove from air fryer and transfer the tofu into a skillet with sauce over medium heat and cook for about 3 minutes, stirring occasionally. Garnish with scallions and serve hot

## 478. Rice Flour Crusted Tofu

Preparation Time: 43 minutes
Servings: 3

**Ingredients:**

- 1: 14-ozblock firm tofu, pressed and cubed into ½-inch size
- 1/4 cup rice flour
- 2 tbsp. olive oil
- 2 tbsp. cornstarch
- Salt and ground black pepper; as your liking

**Directions:**

1. In a bowl; mix together cornstarch, rice flour, salt and black pepper.
2. Coat the tofu evenly with flour mixture. Drizzle the tofu with oil.
3. Set the temperature of air fryer to 360°F. Grease an air fryer basket.
4. Arrange tofu cubes into the prepared air

fryer basket in a single layer.
5. Air fry for about 14 minutes per side. Remove from air fryer and transfer the tofu onto serving plates. Serve warm.

## 479. Mushrooms with Peas

Preparation Time: 30 minutes
Servings: 4

**Ingredients:**

- 16-oz cremini mushrooms, halved
- 4 garlic cloves, finely chopped
- 1/2 cup soy sauce
- 1/2 cup frozen peas
- 4 tbsp. maple syrup
- 4 tbsp. rice vinegar
- 1/2 tsp. ground ginger
- 2 tsp. Chinese five spice powder

**Directions:**

1. In a bowl; mix well soy sauce, maple syrup, vinegar, garlic, five spice powder and ground ginger. Set the temperature of air fryer to 350°F. Grease an air fryer pan.
2. Arrange mushroom into the prepared air fryer pan in a single layer. Air fry for about 10 minutes.
3. Remove from air fryer and stir the mushrooms.
4. Add the peas and vinegar mixture and stir to combine. Air fry for about 5 more minutes.
5. Remove from air fryer and transfer the mushroom mixture onto serving plates. Serve hot.

## 480. Wine Infused Mushrooms

Servings: 6
Preparation Time: 15 minutes
Cooking Time: 32 minutes

**Ingredients**

- 1 tablespoon butter
- 2 teaspoons Herbs de Provence

- ½ teaspoon garlic powder
- 2 pounds fresh mushrooms, quartered
- 2 tablespoons white vermouth*

**Directions:**

1. Set the temperature of air fryer to 320 degrees F.
2. In an air fryer pan, mix together the butter, Herbs de Provence, and garlic powder and air fry for about 2 minutes.
3. Stir in the mushrooms and air fry for about 25 minutes.
4. Stir in the vermouth and air fry for 5 more minutes.
5. Remove from air fryer and transfer the mushrooms onto serving plates.
6. Serve hot.

**Nutrition:**

Calories: 54
Carbohydrate: 5.3g
Protein: 4.8g
Fat: 2.4g
Sugar: 2.7g
Sodium: 23mg

(Note: White vermouth* - Vermouth is an aromatized, fortified white wine flavored with various botanicals and sometimes colored. The modern versions of the beverage were first produced in the mid to late 18th century in Turin, Italy.

## 481. Cheese Stuffed Mushrooms

Servings: 4
Preparation Time: 15 minutes
Cooking Time: 8 minutes

**Ingredients**

- 4 fresh large mushrooms, stemmed and gills removed
- 4 ounces cream cheese, softened
- ¼ cup Parmesan cheese, shredded
- 2 tablespoons white cheddar cheese, shredded
- 2 tablespoons sharp cheddar cheese, shredded
- 1 teaspoon Worcestershire sauce
- 2 garlic cloves, chopped
- Salt and ground black pepper, as required

**Directions:**

1. In a bowl, mix well cream cheese, Parmesan, cheddar cheeses, Worcestershire sauce, garlic, salt, and black pepper.
2. Set the temperature of air fryer to 370 degrees F. Grease an air fryer basket.
3. Stuff each mushroom with the cheese mixture.
4. Arrange stuffed mushrooms into the prepared air fryer basket.
5. Air fry for about 8 minutes.
6. Remove from air fryer and transfer the mushrooms onto a serving platter.
7. Set aside to cool slightly.
8. Serve warm.

**Nutrition:**

Calories: 156
Carbohydrate: 2.6g
Protein: 6.5g
Fat: 13.6g
Sugar: 0.7g
Sodium: 267mg

## 482. Cheesy Mushroom Pizza

Servings: 2
Preparation Time: 15 minutes
Cooking Time: 6 minutes

**Ingredients**

- 2 Portobello mushroom caps, stemmed
- 2 tablespoons olive oil
- 1/8 teaspoon dried Italian seasonings
- Salt, to taste
- 2 tablespoons canned tomatoes, chopped
- 2 tablespoons mozzarella cheese, shredded
- 2 Kalamata olives, pitted and sliced

- 2 tablespoons Parmesan cheese, grated freshly
- 1 teaspoon red pepper flakes, crushed

**Directions:**

1. Set the temperature of air fryer to 320 degrees F. Grease an air fryer basket.
2. With a spoon, scoop out the center of each mushroom cap.
3. Coat each mushroom cap with oil from both sides.
4. Sprinkle the inside of caps with Italian seasoning and salt.
5. Place the canned tomato evenly over both caps, followed by the olives and mozzarella cheese.
6. Arrange mushroom caps into the prepared air fryer basket.
7. Air fry for about 5-6 minutes.
8. Remove from air fryer and immediately sprinkle with the Parmesan cheese and red pepper flakes.
9. Serve.

**Nutrition:**

Calories: 251
Carbohydrate: 5.7g
Protein: 13.4g
Fat: 21g
Sugar: 0.7g
Sodium: 330mg

## 483. Cheesy Spinach

Servings: 3
Preparation Time: 15 minutes
Cooking Time: 15 minutes

**Ingredients**

- 1: 10-ouncespackage frozen spinach, thawed
- ½ cup onion, chopped
- 2 teaspoons garlic, minced
- 4 ounces cream cheese, chopped
- ½ teaspoon ground nutmeg
- Salt and ground black pepper, as required

- ¼ cup Parmesan cheese, shredded

**Directions:**

1. In a bowl, mix well spinach, onion, garlic, cream cheese, nutmeg, salt, and black pepper.
2. Set the temperature of air fryer to 350 degrees F. Grease an air fryer pan.
3. Place spinach mixture into the prepared air fryer pan.
4. Air fry for about 10 minutes.
5. Remove from air fryer and stir the mixture well.
6. Sprinkle the spinach mixture evenly with Parmesan cheese.
7. Now, set the temperature of air fryer to 400 degrees F and air fry for 5 more minutes.
8. Remove from air fryer and transfer the spinach mixture onto serving plates.
9. Serve hot.

**Nutrition:**

Calories: 194
Carbohydrate: 7.3g
Protein: 8.4g
Fat: 15.5g
Sugar: 1.4g
Sodium: 351mg

## 484. Parmesan Asparagus

Servings: 3
Preparation Time: 15 minutes
Cooking Time: 10 minutes

**Ingredients**

- 1 pound fresh asparagus, trimmed
- 1 tablespoon Parmesan cheese, grated
- 1 tablespoon butter, melted
- 1 teaspoon garlic powder
- Salt and ground black pepper, as required

**Directions:**

1. In a bowl, mix together the asparagus, cheese, butter, garlic powder, salt, and black pepper.

2. Set the temperature of air fryer to 400 degrees F. Grease an air fryer basket.
3. Arrange asparagus into the prepared air fryer basket.
4. Air fry for about 10 minutes.
5. Remove from air fryer and transfer the asparagus onto serving plates.
6. Serve hot.

**Nutrition:**

Calories: 73
Carbohydrate: 6.6g
Protein: 4.2g
Fat: 2.7g
Sugar: 3.1g
Sodium: 95mg

# 485. Lemony Green Beans

Servings: 3
Preparation Time: 15 minutes
Cooking Time: 12 minutes

**Ingredients**

- 1 pound green beans, trimmed and halved
- 1 teaspoon butter, melted
- 1 tablespoon fresh lemon juice
- ¼ teaspoon garlic powder
- Salt and ground black pepper, as required

**Directions:**

1. In a large bowl, add all the ingredients and toss to coat well.
2. Set the temperature of air fryer to 400 degrees F. Grease an air fryer basket.
3. Arrange green beans into the prepared air fryer basket.
4. Air fry for about 10-12 minutes.
5. Remove from air fryer and transfer the green beans onto serving plates.
6. Serve hot.

**Nutrition:**

Calories: 60
Carbohydrate: 11.1g
Protein: 2.8g

Fat: 1.5g
Sugar: 2.3g
Sodium: 70mg

# 486.Veggie Stuffed Bell Peppers

Servings: 6
Preparation Time: 20 minutes
Cooking Time: 25 minutes

**Ingredients**

- 6 large bell peppers
- 1 bread roll, finely chopped
- 1 carrot, peeled and finely chopped
- 1 onion, finely chopped
- 1 potato, peeled and finely chopped
- ½ cup fresh peas, shelled
- 2 garlic cloves, minced
- 2 teaspoons fresh parsley, chopped
- Salt and ground black pepper, as required
- 1/3 cup cheddar cheese, grated

**Directions:**

1. Remove the tops of each bell pepper and discard the seeds.
2. Finely chop the bell pepper tops.
3. In a bowl, mix well chopped bell pepper tops, loaf, vegetables, garlic, parsley, salt and black pepper.
4. Stuff each bell pepper with the vegetable mixture.
5. Set the temperature of air fryer to 350 degrees F. Grease an air fryer basket.
6. Arrange peppers into the prepared air fryer basket.
7. Air fry for about 20 minutes.
8. Remove the air fryer basket and top each bell pepper with cheese.
9. Air fry for 5 more minutes.
10. Remove from air fryer and transfer the bell peppers onto a serving platter.
11. Set aside to cool slightly.
12. Serve warm.

**Nutrition:**
Calories: 123
Carbohydrate: 21.7g
Protein: 4.8g
Fat: 2.7g
Sugar: 8.7g
Sodium: 105mg

## 487. Rice & Beans Stuffed Bell Peppers

Servings: 5
Preparation Time: 15 minutes
Cooking Time: 15 minutes

**Ingredients**

- ½ small bell pepper, seeded and chopped
- 1: 15-ouncescan diced tomatoes with juice
- 1: 15-ouncescan red kidney beans, rinsed and drained
- 1 cup cooked rice
- 1½ teaspoons Italian seasoning
- 5 large bell peppers, tops removed and seeded
- ½ cup mozzarella cheese, shredded
- 1 tablespoon Parmesan cheese, grated

**Directions:**

1. In a bowl, mix well chopped bell pepper, tomatoes with juice, beans, rice, and Italian seasoning.
2. Stuff each bell pepper evenly with the rice mixture.
3. Set the temperature of air fryer to 360 degrees F. Grease an air fryer basket.
4. Arrange bell peppers into the air fryer basket in a single layer.
5. Air fry for about 12 minutes.
6. Meanwhile, in a bowl, mix together the mozzarella and Parmesan cheese.
7. Remove the air fryer basket and top each bell pepper with cheese mixture.
8. Air fry for 3 more minutes.
9. Remove from air fryer and transfer the bell peppers onto a serving platter.
10. Set aside to cool slightly.

11. Serve warm.

**Nutrition:**
Calories: 288
Carbohydrate: 55g
Protein: 11.3g
Fat: 3.1g
Sugar: 9.7g
Sodium: 286mg

## 488. Stuffed Pumpkin

Servings: 5
Preparation Time: 20 minutes
Cooking Time: 30 minutes

**Ingredients**

- 1 sweet potato, peeled and chopped
- 1 parsnip, peeled and chopped
- 1 carrot, peeled and chopped
- ½ cup fresh peas, shelled
- 1 onion, chopped
- 2 garlic cloves, minced
- 1 egg, beaten
- 2 teaspoons mixed dried herbs
- Salt and ground black pepper, as required
- ½ of butternut pumpkin, seeded

**Directions:**

1. In a large bowl, mix well vegetables, garlic, egg, herbs, salt, and black pepper.
2. Stuff the pumpkin half with vegetable mixture.
3. Set the temperature of air fryer to 355 degrees F. Grease an air fryer basket.
4. Arrange pumpkin half into the prepared air fryer basket.
5. Air fry for about 30 minutes.
6. Remove from air fryer and transfer the pumpkin onto a serving platter.
7. Set aside to cool slightly.
8. Serve warm.

**Nutrition:**
Calories: 157

Carbohydrate: 35.9g

Protein: 4.6g

Fat: 1.1g

Sugar: 4.6g

Sodium: 64mg

## 489. Glazed Veggies

Servings: 4

Preparation Time: 20 minutes

Cooking Time: 20 minutes

**Ingredients**

- 2 ounces cherry tomatoes
- 1 large parsnip, peeled and chopped
- 1 large carrot, peeled and chopped
- 1 large zucchini, chopped
- 1 green bell pepper, seeded and chopped
- 6 tablespoons olive oil, divided
- 3 tablespoons honey
- 1 teaspoon Dijon mustard
- 1 teaspoon mixed dried herbs
- 1 teaspoon garlic paste
- Salt and ground black pepper, as required

**Directions:**

1. Set the temperature of air fryer to 350 degrees F. Grease an air fryer pan.
2. Arrange vegetables into the prepared air fryer pan and drizzle with 3 tablespoons of oil.
3. Air fry for about 15 minutes.
4. Meanwhile, in a baking dish, mix well remaining oil, honey, mustard, herbs, garlic, salt, and black pepper.
5. Remove the vegetables from air fryer.
6. Transfer the vegetables into baking dish with honey mixture and mix until well combined.
7. Now, set the temperature of air fryer to 392 degrees F.
8. Arrange the baking dish into air fryer and air fry for about 5 minutes.
9. Remove from air fryer and transfer the vegetable mixture into a serving bowl.

10. Serve immediately.

**Nutrition:**

Calories: 288

Carbohydrate: 26.7g

Protein: 2.1g

Fat: 21.4g

Sugar: 18.7g

Sodium: 79mg

## 490. Tofu with Capers Sauce

Servings: 4

Preparation Time: 20 minutes

Cooking Time: 20 minutes

**Ingredients**

*For Marinade:*

- ¼ cup fresh lemon juice
- 2 tablespoons fresh parsley
- 1 garlic clove, peeled
- Salt and ground black pepper, as required

*For Tofu:*

- 1: 14-ouncesblock extra-firm tofu, pressed and cut into 8 rectangular cutlets
- ½ cup mayonnaise
- 1 cup panko breadcrumbs

*For Sauce:*

- 1 cup vegetable broth
- ¼ cup lemon juice
- 1 garlic clove, peeled
- 2 tablespoons fresh parsley
- 2 teaspoons cornstarch
- Salt and ground black pepper, as required
- 2 tablespoons capers

**Directions:**

1. For marinade: in a food processor, add all the ingredients and pulse until smooth.
2. In a bowl, mix together the marinade and tofu.
3. Set aside for about 15-30 minutes.
4. In two shallow bowls, place the

mayonnaise and panko breadcrumbs respectively.

5. Coat the tofu pieces with mayonnaise and then, roll into the panko.

6. Set the temperature of air fryer to 375 degrees F. Grease an air fryer basket.

7. Arrange tofu pieces into the prepared air fryer basket in a single layer.

8. Air fry for about 20 minutes, shaking once halfway through.

9. Meanwhile, for the sauce: add broth, lemon juice, garlic, parsley, cornstarch, salt and black pepper in a food processor and pulse until smooth.

10. Transfer the sauce into a small pan and stir in the capers.

11. Place the sauce over medium heat and bring to a boil.

12. Reduce the heat to low and simmer for about 5-7 minutes, stirring continuously.

13. Remove the tofu from air fryer and transfer onto serving plates.

14. Top with the sauce and serve.

**Nutrition:**

Calories: 307
Carbohydrate: 15.6g
Protein: 10.8g
Fat: 16.5g
Sugar: 3.4g
Sodium: 586mg

## 491. Tofu with Orange Sauce

Servings: 4
Preparation Time: 20 minutes
Cooking Time: 20 minutes

**Ingredients**

*For Tofu:*

- 1 pound extra-firm tofu, pressed and cubed

- 1 tablespoon cornstarch

- 1 tablespoon tamari*

*For Sauce:*

- ½ cup water

- 1/3 cup fresh orange juice

- 1 tablespoon honey

- 1 teaspoon orange zest, grated

- 1 teaspoon garlic, minced

- 1 teaspoon fresh ginger, minced

- 2 teaspoons cornstarch

- ¼ teaspoon red pepper flakes, crushed

*For Garnishing:*

- 2 scallions: green part), chopped

**Directions:**

1. In a bowl, add the tofu, cornstarch, and tamari and toss to coat well.

2. Set the tofu aside to marinate for at least 15 minutes.

3. Set the temperature of air fryer to 390 degrees F. Grease an air fryer basket.

4. Arrange tofu pieces into the prepared air fryer basket in 2 batches in a single layer.

5. Air fry for about 10 minutes, shaking once halfway through.

6. Meanwhile, for the sauce: in a small pan, add all the ingredients over medium-high heat and bring to a boil, stirring continuously.

7. Remove from air fryer and transfer the tofu into a serving bowl.

8. Top with the sauce and gently stir to combine.

9. Garnish with scallions and serve.

**Nutrition:**

Calories: 148
Carbohydrate: 13g
Protein: 12.1g
Fat: 6.7g
Sugar: 6.9g
Sodium: 263mg
(Note: Tamari* - Tamari is soy sauce without the normally added wheat.

## 492. Buttered Dinner Rolls

Servings: 12

Preparation Time: 15 minutes
Cooking Time: 30 minutes

## Ingredients

- 1 cup milk
- 1 tablespoon coconut oil
- 1 tablespoon olive oil
- 3 cups plain flour
- 7½ tablespoons unsalted butter
- 1 teaspoon yeast
- Salt and ground black pepper, as required

## Directions:

1. In a pan, add the milk, coconut oil, and olive oil and cook until lukewarm.
2. Remove from the heat and stir well.
3. In a large bowl, add the flour, butter, yeast, salt, black pepper, and milk mixture and mix until a dough forms.
4. With your hands, knead for about 4-5 minutes
5. With a damp cloth, cover the dough and set aside in a warm place for about 5 minutes.
6. Again, with your hands, knead the dough for about 4-5 minutes
7. With a damp cloth, cover the dough and set aside in a warm place for about 30 minutes.
8. Place the dough onto a lightly floured surface.
9. Divide the dough into 12 equal pieces and form each into a ball.
10. Set the temperature of air fryer to 360 degrees F. Grease an air fryer basket.
11. Arrange rolls into the prepared air fryer basket in 2 batches in a single layer.
12. Air fry for about 15 minutes.
13. Remove from the air fryer and serve warm.

## Nutrition:

Calories: 208
Carbohydrate: 25g
Protein: 4.1g
Fat: 10.3g

Sugar: 1g
Sodium: 73mg

## 493. Cheesy Dinner Rolls

Servings: 2
Preparation Time: 10 minutes
Cooking Time: 5 minutes

## Ingredients

- 2 dinner rolls
- ½ cup Parmesan cheese, grated
- 2 tablespoons unsalted butter, melted
- ½ teaspoon garlic bread seasoning mix

## Directions:

1. Cut the dinner rolls into cross style, but not the all way through.
2. Stuff the slits evenly with cheese.
3. Coat the tops of each roll with butter and then, sprinkle with the seasoning mix.
4. Set the temperature of air fryer to 355 degrees F. Grease an air fryer basket.
5. Arrange dinner rolls into the prepared air fryer basket.
6. Air fry for about 5 minutes or until cheese melts completely.
7. Remove from the air fryer and serve hot.

## Nutrition:

Calories: 608
Carbohydrate: 48.8g
Protein: 33.5g
Fat: 33.1g
Sugar: 4.8g
Sodium: 2000mg

## 494. Croissant Rolls

Servings: 8
Preparation Time: 10 minutes
Cooking Time: 6 minutes

## Ingredients

- 1: 8-ouncescan croissant rolls

- 4 tablespoons butter, melted

**Directions:**

1. Set the temperature of air fryer to 320 degrees F. Grease an air fryer basket.
2. Arrange croissant rolls into the prepared air fryer basket.
3. Air fry for about 4 minutes.
4. Flip the side and air fry for 1-2 more minutes.
5. Remove from the air fryer and transfer onto a platter.
6. Drizzle with the melted butter and serve hot.

**Nutrition:**

Calories: 152
Carbohydrate: 11.1g
Protein: 2.1g
Fat: 10.8g
Sugar: 3g
Sodium: 223mg

## 495. Sweet & Spicy Parsnips

Servings: 6
Preparation Time: 15 minutes
Cooking Time: 44 minutes

**Ingredients**

- 2 pounds parsnip, peeled and cut into 1-inch chunks

- 1 tablespoon butter, melted

- 2 tablespoons honey

- 1 tablespoon dried parsley flakes, crushed

- ¼ teaspoon red pepper flakes, crushed

- Salt and ground black pepper, as required

**Directions:**

1. Set the temperature of air fryer to 355 degrees F. Grease an air fryer basket.
2. In a large bowl, mix together the parsnips and butter.
3. Arrange parsnip chunks into the prepared air fryer basket in a single layer.
4. Air fry for about 40 minutes.
5. Meanwhile, in another large bowl, mix well remaining ingredients.
6. After 40 minutes, transfer parsnips into the bowl of honey mixture and toss to coat well.
7. Again, arrange the parsnip chunks into air fryer basket in a single layer.
8. Air fry for 3-4 more minutes.
9. Remove from air fryer and transfer the parsnip chunks onto serving plates.
10. Serve hot.

**Nutrition:**

Calories: 155
Carbohydrate: 33.1g
Protein: 1.9g
Fat: 2.4g
Sugar: 13g
Sodium: 57mg

# Vegan

## 496. Herbed Carrots

Servings: 8
Preparation Time: 15 minutes
Cooking Time: 14 minutes

**Ingredients**

- 6 large carrots, peeled and sliced lengthwise
- 2 tablespoons olive oil
- ½ tablespoon fresh oregano, chopped
- ½ tablespoon fresh parsley, chopped
- Salt and ground black pepper, as required

**Directions:**

1. Set the temperature of air fryer to 360 degrees F. Grease an air fryer basket.
2. In a bowl, mix together the carrot slices, and oil.
3. Arrange carrot slices into the prepared air fryer basket in a single layer.
4. Air fry for about 12 minutes.
5. Remove from air fryer and sprinkle the carrots evenly with herbs, salt and black pepper.
6. Air fry for 2 more minutes.
7. Remove from air fryer and transfer the carrot slices onto serving plates.
8. Serve hot.

**Nutrition:**
Calories: 53
Carbohydrate: 5.5g
Protein: 0.5g
Fat: 3.5g
Sugar: 2.7g
Sodium: 57mg

## 497. Curried Eggplant

Servings: 2
Preparation Time: 15 minutes
Cooking Time: 10 minutes

**Ingredients**

- 1 large eggplant, cut into ½-inch thick slices
- 1 garlic clove, minced
- ½ fresh red chili, chopped
- 1 tablespoon vegetable oil
- ¼ teaspoon curry powder
- Salt, as required

**Directions:**

1. Set the temperature of air fryer to 300 degrees F. Grease an air fryer basket.
2. In a bowl, add all the ingredients and toss to coat well.
3. Arrange eggplant slices into the prepared air fryer basket in a single layer.
4. Air fry for about 10 minutes, shaking once halfway through.
5. Remove from air fryer and transfer the eggplant slices onto serving plates.
6. Serve hot.

**Nutrition:**
Calories: 121
Carbohydrate: 14.2g
Protein: 2.4g
Fat: 7.3g
Sugar: 7g
Sodium: 83mg

## 498. Herbed Eggplant

Servings: 2
Preparation Time: 15 minutes
Cooking Time: 15 minutes

**Ingredients**

- ½ teaspoon dried marjoram, crushed
- ½ teaspoon dried oregano, crushed
- ½ teaspoon dried thyme, crushed

- ½ teaspoon garlic powder
- Salt and ground black pepper, as required
- 1 large eggplant, cubed
- Olive oil cooking spray

**Directions:**

1. Set the temperature of air fryer to 390 degrees F. Grease an air fryer basket.
2. In a small bowl, mix well herbs, garlic powder, salt, and black pepper.
3. Spray the eggplant cubes evenly with cooking spray and then, rub with the herbs mixture.
4. Arrange eggplant cubes into the prepared air fryer basket in a single layer.
5. Air fry for about 6 minutes.
6. Flip and spray the eggplant cubes with cooking spray.
7. Air fry for another 6 minutes.
8. Flip and again, spray the eggplant cubes with cooking spray.
9. Air fry for 2-3 more minutes.
10. Remove from air fryer and transfer the eggplant cubes onto serving plates.
11. Serve hot.

**Nutrition:**

Calories: 62
Carbohydrate: 14.5g
Protein: 2.4g
Fat: 0.5g
Sugar: 7.1g
Sodium: 83mg

## 499. Spices Stuffed Eggplants

Servings: 4
Preparation Time: 15 minutes
Cooking Time: 12 minutes

**Ingredients**

- 4 teaspoons olive oil, divided
- ¾ tablespoon dry mango powder
- ¾ tablespoon ground coriander
- ½ teaspoon ground cumin

- ½ teaspoon ground turmeric
- ½ teaspoon garlic powder
- Salt, to taste
- 8 baby eggplants

**Directions:**

1. In a small bowl, mix together one teaspoon of oil, and spices.
2. From the bottom of each eggplant, make 2 slits, leaving the stems intact.
3. With a small spoon, fill each slit of eggplants with spice mixture.
4. Now, brush the outer side of each eggplant with remaining oil.
5. Set the temperature of air fryer to 369 degrees F. Grease an air fryer basket.
6. Arrange eggplants into the prepared air fryer basket in a single layer.
7. Air fry for about 8-12 minutes.
8. Remove from air fryer and transfer the eggplants onto serving plates.
9. Serve hot.

**Nutrition:**

Calories: 317
Carbohydrate: 65g
Protein: 10.9g
Fat: 6.7g
Sugar: 33g
Sodium: 61mg

## 500. Salsa Stuffed Eggplants

Servings: 2
Preparation Time: 15 minutes
Cooking Time: 25 minutes

**Ingredients**

- 1 large eggplant
- 2 teaspoons olive oil, divided
- 2 teaspoons fresh lemon juice, divided
- 8 cherry tomatoes, quartered
- 2 tablespoons tomato salsa
- ½ tablespoon fresh parsley
- Salt and ground black pepper, as required

**Directions:**

1. Set the temperature of air fryer to 390 degrees F. Grease an air fryer basket.
2. Place eggplant into the prepared air fryer basket.
3. Air fry for about 15 minutes.
4. Remove from air fryer and cut the eggplant in half lengthwise.
5. Drizzle the eggplant halves evenly with one teaspoon of oil.
6. Now, set the temperature of air fryer to 355 degrees F. Grease the air fryer basket.
7. Arrange eggplant into the prepared air fryer basket, cut-side up.
8. Air fry for another 10 minutes.
9. Remove eggplant from the air fryer and set aside for about 5 minutes.
10. Carefully, scoop out the flesh, leaving about ¼-inch away from edges.
11. Drizzle the eggplant halves with one teaspoon of lemon juice.
12. Transfer the eggplant flesh into a bowl.
13. Add the tomatoes, salsa, parsley, salt, black pepper, remaining oil, and lemon juice and mix well.
14. Stuff the eggplant haves with salsa mixture and serve.

**Nutrition:**

Calories: 192
Carbohydrate: 33.8g
Protein: 6.9g
Fat: 6.1g
Sugar: 20.4g
Sodium: 204mg

## 501. Sesame Seeds Bok Choy

Servings: 4
Preparation Time: 10 minutes
Cooking Time: 6 minutes

**Ingredients**

- 4 bunches baby bok choy, bottoms removed and leaves separated
- Olive oil cooking spray
- 1 teaspoon garlic powder
- 1 teaspoon sesame seeds

**Directions:**

1. Set the temperature of air fryer to 325 degrees F.
2. Arrange bok choy leaves into the air fryer basket in a single layer.
3. Spray with the cooking spray and sprinkle with garlic powder.
4. Air fry for about 5-6 minutes, shaking after every 2 minutes.
5. Remove from air fryer and transfer the bok choy onto serving plates.
6. Garnish with sesame seeds and serve hot.

**Nutrition:**

Calories: 26
Carbohydrate: 4g
Protein: 2.5g
Fat: 0.7g
Sugar: 1.9g
Sodium: 98mg

## 502. Basil Tomatoes

Servings: 2
Preparation Time: 10 minutes
Cooking Time: 10 minutes

**Ingredients**

- 2 tomatoes, halved
- Olive oil cooking spray
- Salt and ground black pepper, as required
- 1 tablespoon fresh basil, chopped

**Directions:**

1. Set the temperature of air fryer to 320 degrees F. Grease an air fryer basket.
2. Spray the tomato halves evenly with cooking spray and sprinkle with salt, black pepper and basil.
3. Arrange tomato halves into the prepared air fryer basket, cut sides up.
4. Air fry for about 10 minutes or until desired doneness.

5. Remove from air fryer and transfer the tomatoes onto serving plates.
6. Serve warm.

**Nutrition:**
Calories: 22
Carbohydrate: 4.8g
Protein: 1.1g
Fat: 4.8g
Sugar: 3.2g
Sodium: 84mg

## 503. Stuffed Tomatoes

Servings: 4
Preparation Time: 15 minutes
Cooking Time: 22 minutes

**Ingredients**

- 4 tomatoes
- 1 teaspoon olive oil
- 1 carrot, peeled and finely chopped
- 1 onion, chopped
- 1 cup frozen peas, thawed
- 1 garlic clove, minced
- 2 cups cold cooked rice
- 1 tablespoon soy sauce

**Directions:**
1. Cut the top of each tomato and scoop out pulp and seeds.
2. In a skillet, heat oil over low heat and sauté the carrot, onion, garlic, and peas for about 2 minutes.
3. Stir in the soy sauce and rice and remove from heat.
4. Set the temperature of air fryer to 355 degrees F. Grease an air fryer basket.
5. Stuff each tomato with the rice mixture.
6. Arrange tomatoes into the prepared air fryer basket.
7. Air fry for about 20 minutes.
8. Remove from air fryer and transfer the tomatoes onto a serving platter.
9. Set aside to cool slightly.

10. Serve warm.

**Nutrition:**
Calories: 421
Carbohydrate: 89.1g
Protein: 10.5g
Fat: 2.2g
Sugar: 7.2g
Sodium: 277mg

## 504. Sweet & Spicy Cauliflower

Servings: 4
Preparation Time: 15 minutes
Cooking Time: 30 minutes

**Ingredients**

- 1 head cauliflower, cut into florets
- ¾ cup onion, thinly sliced
- 5 garlic cloves, finely sliced
- 1½ tablespoons soy sauce
- 1 tablespoon hot sauce
- 1 tablespoon rice vinegar
- 1 teaspoon coconut sugar
- Pinch of red pepper flakes
- Ground black pepper, as required
- 2 scallions, chopped

**Directions:**
1. Set the temperature of air fryer to 350 degrees F. Grease an air fryer pan.
2. Arrange cauliflower florets into the prepared air fryer pan in a single layer.
3. Air fry for about 10 minutes.
4. Remove from air fryer and stir in the onions.
5. Air fry for another 10 minutes.
6. Remove from air fryer and stir in the garlic.
7. Air fry for 5 more minutes.
8. Meanwhile, in a bowl, mix well soy sauce, hot sauce, vinegar, coconut sugar, red pepper flakes, and black pepper.
9. Remove from the air fryer and stir in the sauce mixture.

10. Air fry for about 5 minutes.
11. Remove from air fryer and transfer the cauliflower mixture onto serving plates.
12. Garnish with scallions and serve.

**Nutrition:**

Calories: 72
Carbohydrate: 13.8g
Protein: 3.6g
Fat: 0.2g
Sugar: 3.1g
Sodium: 1300mg

## 505. Spiced Butternut Squash

Servings: 4
Preparation Time: 15 minutes
Cooking Time: 20 minutes

### Ingredients

- 1 medium butternut squash, peeled, seeded and cut into chunk
- 2 teaspoons cumin seeds
- 1/8 teaspoon garlic powder
- 1/8 teaspoon chili flakes, crushed
- Salt and ground black pepper, as required
- 1 tablespoon olive oil
- 2 tablespoons pine nuts
- 2 tablespoons fresh cilantro, chopped

### Directions:

Set the temperature of air fryer to 375 degrees F. Grease an air fryer basket.

In a bowl, mix together the squash, spices, and oil.

Arrange butternut squash chunks into the prepared fryer basket.

Air fry for about 20 minutes, flipping occasionally.

Remove from air fryer and transfer the squash chunks onto serving plates.

Garnish with pine nuts and cilantro.

Serve.

**Nutrition:**

Calories: 165

Carbohydrate: 27.6g
Protein: 3.1g
Fat: 6.9g
Sugar: 5.2g
Sodium: 50mg

## 506. Herbed Potatoes

Servings: 4
Preparation Time: 10 minutes
Cooking Time: 16 minutes

### Ingredients

- 6 small potatoes, chopped
- 3 tablespoons olive oil
- 2 teaspoons mixed dried herbs
- Salt and ground black pepper, as required
- 2 tablespoons fresh parsley, chopped

### Directions:

1. Set the temperature of air fryer to 356 degrees F. Grease an air fryer basket.
2. In a large bowl, add the potatoes, oil, herbs, salt and black pepper and toss to coat well.
3. Arrange the chopped potatoes into the prepared air fryer basket in a single layer.
4. Air fry for about 16 minutes, tossing once halfway through.
5. Remove from air fryer and transfer the potatoes onto serving plates.
6. Garnish with parsley and serve.

**Nutrition:**

Calories: 268
Carbohydrate: 40.4g
Protein: 4.4g
Fat: 10.8g
Sugar: 3g
Sodium: 55mg

## 507. Spicy Potatoes

Servings: 6
Preparation Time: 10 minutes
Cooking Time: 20 minutes

## Ingredients

- 1¾ pounds waxy potatoes, peeled and cubed
- 1 tablespoon olive oil
- ½ teaspoon ground cumin
- ½ teaspoon ground coriander
- ½ teaspoon paprika
- Salt and freshly ground black pepper, as required

## Directions:

1. In a large bowl of water, add the potatoes and set aside for about 30 minutes.
2. Drain the potatoes completely and dry with paper towels.
3. In a bowl, add the potatoes, oil, and spices and toss to coat well.
4. Set the temperature of air fryer to 355 degrees F. Grease an air fryer basket.
5. Arrange potato pieces into the prepared air fryer basket in a single layer.
6. Air fry for about 20 minutes.
7. Remove from air fryer and transfer the potato pieces onto serving plates.
8. Serve hot.

## Nutrition:

Calories: 113
Carbohydrate: 21g
Protein: 2.3g
Fat: 2.5g
Sugar: 1.5g
Sodium: 35mg

## 508. Crispy Kale Chips

Servings: 3
Cooking Time: 7 minutes

## Ingredients:

- 3 cups kale leaves, stems removed
- 1 tablespoon olive oil
- Salt and pepper, to taste

## Directions

1. In a bowl, combine all of the ingredients.

Toss to coat the kale leaves with oil, salt, and pepper.

2. Arrange the kale leaves on the double layer rack and insert inside the air fryer.
3. Close the air fryer and cook for 7 minutes at 3700F.
4. Allow to cool before serving.

## Nutrition

Calories: 48; Carbs: 1.4g; Protein: 0.7g; Fat: 4.8g

## 509. Grilled Buffalo Cauliflower

Servings: 1
Cooking Time: 5 minutes

## Ingredients:

- 1 cup cauliflower florets
- Cooking oil spray
- Salt and pepper, to taste
- ½ cup buffalo sauce

## Directions

1. Place the cauliflower florets in a bowl and spray with cooking oil. Season with salt and pepper.
2. Toss to coat.
3. Place the grill pan in the air fryer and add the cauliflower florets.
4. Close the lid and cook for 5 minutes at 3900F.
5. Once cooked, place in a bowl and pour the buffalo sauce over the top. Toss to coat.

## Nutrition

Calories: 25; Carbs: 5.3g; Protein: 2g; Fat: 0.1g

## 510. Faux Fried Pickles

Servings: 1
Cooking Time: 5 minutes

## Ingredients:

- 1 cup pickle slices
- 1 egg, beaten
- ½ cup grated Parmesan cheese

- ½ cup almond flour
- ¼ cup pork rinds, crushed
- Salt and pepper, to taste

**Directions**

1. Place the pickles in a bowl and pour the beaten egg over the top. Allow to soak.
2. In another dish or bowl, combine the Parmesan cheese, almond flour, pork rinds, salt, and pepper.
3. Dredge the pickles in the Parmesan cheese mixture and place on the double layer rack.
4. Place the rack with the pickles inside of the air fryer.
5. Close the lid and cook for 5 minutes at 3900F.

**Nutrition**

Calories: 664; Carbs: 17.9g; Protein: 42g; Fat: 49.9g

## 511. Greatest Green Beans

Servings: 1
Cooking Time: 5 minutes

**Ingredients:**

- 1 cup green beans, trimmed
- ½ teaspoon oil
- Salt and pepper, to taste

**Directions**

1. Place the green beans in a bowl and add in oil, salt, and pepper.
2. Toss to coat the beans.
3. Place the grill pan in the air fryer and add the green beans in a single layer.
4. Close the lid and cook for 5 minutes at 3900F.

**Nutrition**

Calories: 54; Carbs: 7.7g; Protein: 2g; Fat: 2.5g

## 512. Summer Grilled Corn

Servings: 2

Cooking Time: 6 minutes

**Ingredients:**

- 2 corn on the cob, cut into halves widthwise
- ½ teaspoon oil
- Salt and pepper, to taste

**Directions**

1. Brush the corn cobs with oil and season with salt and pepper.
2. Place the grill pan accessory into the air fryer.
3. Place the corn cobs on the grill pan.
4. Close the lid and cook for 3 minutes at 3900F.
5. Open the air fryer and turn the corn cobs.
6. Cook for another 3 minutes at the same temperature.

**Nutrition**

Calories: 173; Carbs: 29g; Protein: 4.5 g; Fat: 4.5g

# Chicken

## 513. Teriyaki Grilled Chicken

Servings: 3
Cooking Time: 40 minutes

**Ingredients:**

- ½ cup soy sauce
- ½ cup water
- 3 tablespoons brown sugar
- 3 tablespoon honey
- 3 cloves of garlic, minced
- 1 tablespoon minced ginger
- 1 tablespoons rice vinegar
- 3 tablespoons olive oil
- 1 ½ pounds boneless skinless chicken breasts

**Directions**

1. Place all ingredients in a Ziploc bag and give a good shake. Allow to marinate in the fridge for at least 2 hours.
2. Preheat the air fryer at 3750F.
3. Place the grill pan accessory in the air fryer.
4. Grill the chicken for 40 minutes making sure to flip the chicken every 10 minutes.
5. Meanwhile, prepare the teriyaki glaze by pouring the marinade on a saucepan and allow to simmer over medium flame until the sauce thickens.
6. Before serving, brush the chicken with the teriyaki glaze.

**Nutrition**
Calories: 603; Carbs: 33.7g; Protein: 54.4g; Fat: 27.3g

## 514. Sweet and Spicy Grilled Chicken

Servings: 4
Cooking Time: 35 minutes

**Ingredients:**

- ½ cup brown sugar
- 2 tablespoons chili powder
- 1 teaspoon salt
- ½ teaspoon garlic powder
- 1 teaspoon liquid smoke seasoning
- 4 boneless chicken breasts

**Directions**

1. Place all ingredients in a Ziploc bag and give a good shake. Allow to marinate in the fridge for at least 2 hours.
2. Preheat the air fryer at 3750F.
3. Place the grill pan accessory in the air fryer.
4. Grill the chicken for 35 minutes.
5. Make sure to flip the chicken every 10 minute to grill evenly.

**Nutrition**
Calories: 446; Carbs: 29.6g; Protein: 61.8g; Fat: 7.7g

## 515. Honey Lime Grilled Chicken

Servings: 4
Cooking Time: 40 minutes

**Ingredients:**

- 2 pounds boneless chicken breasts
- ¼ cup lime juice, freshly squeezed
- ½ cup honey
- 2 tablespoons soy sauce
- 1 tablespoon olive oil
- 2 cloves of garlic, minced
- ½ cup cilantro, chopped finely
- Salt and pepper to taste

**Directions**

1. Place all ingredients in a Ziploc bag and give a good shake. Allow to marinate in the fridge for at least 2 hours.
2. Preheat the air fryer at 3750F.
3. Place the grill pan accessory in the air fryer.
4. Grill the chicken for 40 minutes making sure to flip the chicken every 10 minutes

to grill evenly on all sides.

**Nutrition**

Calories:467; Carbs: 38.9g; Protein:52.5 g; Fat: 10.2g

## 516. Grilled Jerk Chicken

Servings: 8
Cooking Time: 60 minutes

**Ingredients:**

- 4 habanero chilies
- 5 cloves of garlic, minced
- ¾ malt vinegar
- ¾ soy sauce
- 2 tablespoons rum
- 2tablespoon salt
- 2 ½ teaspoons ground allspice
- 1 ½ teaspoons ground nutmeg
- ¾ ground cloves
- 8 pieces chicken legs

**Directions**

1. Place all ingredients in a Ziploc bag and give a good shake. Allow to marinate in the fridge for at least 2 hours.
2. Preheat the air fryer at 3750F.
3. Place the grill pan accessory in the air fryer.
4. Grill the chicken for 60 minutes and flip the chicken every 10 minutes for even grilling.

**Nutrition**

Calories: 204; Carbs: 1.2g; Protein:28.7 g; Fat: 8.1g

## 517. Butterflied Chicken with Herbs

Servings: 4
Cooking Time: 1 hour

**Ingredients:**

- 2 pounds whole chicken, backbones removed and butterflied
- Salt and pepper to taste
- 6 cloves of garlic, minced
- ¼ cup Aleppo-style pepper
- 1 and 1/4 cup chopped rosemary
- ¼ cup fresh lemon juice
- ¼ cup oregano
- 1 cup green olives, pitted and cracked

**Directions**

1. Place the chicken breast side up and slice through the breasts. Using your palms, press against the breastbone to flatten the breasts or you may remove the bones altogether.
2. Once the bones have been removed, season the chicken with salt, pepper, garlic, pepper, rosemary, lemon juice, and oregano.
3. Allow to marinate in the fridge for at least 12 hours.
4. Preheat the air fryer at 3750F.
5. Place the grill pan accessory in the air fryer.
6. Place the chicken on the grill pan and place the olives around the chicken.
7. Grill for 1 hour and make sure to flip the chicken every 10 minutes for even grilling.

**Nutrition**

Calories: 492; Carbs:50.4 g; Protein:37.6 g; Fat: 16.6g

## 518. 4-Ingredient Garlic Herb Chicken Wings

Servings: 4
Cooking Time: 35 minutes

**Ingredients:**

- 2 pounds chicken wings
- 6 medium garlic cloves, grated
- ¼ cup chopped rosemary
- Salt and pepper to taste

**Directions**

1. Season the chicken with garlic, rosemary,

salt, and pepper.
2. Preheat the air fryer at 3750F.
3. Place the grill pan accessory in the air fryer.
4. Grill for 35 minutes and make sure to flip the chicken every 10 minutes.

**Nutrition**

Calories:299; Carbs: 2.9g; Protein: 50.4g; Fat: 8.2g

## 520. Pesto Grilled Chicken

Servings: 8
Cooking Time: 30 minutes

**Ingredients:**

- 1 ¾ cup of your favorite pesto
- 8 chicken thighs
- Salt and pepper to taste

**Directions**

1. Place all ingredients in the Ziploc bag and allow to marinate in the fridge for at least 2 hours.
2. Preheat the air fryer at 3750F.
3. Place the grill pan accessory in the air fryer.
4. Grill the chicken for at least 30 minutes.
5. Make sure to flip the chicken every 10 minutes for even grilling.

**Nutrition**

Calories: 481; Carbs: 3.8g; Protein: 32.6g; Fat: 36.8g

## 520. Chili and Yogurt Marinated Chicken

Servings: 3
Cooking Time: 40 minutes

**Ingredients:**

- 7 dried chilies, seeds removed and broken into pieces
- 1-inch ginger, peeled and chopped
- 4 cloves of garlic, minced
- ½ cup whole milk yogurt
- 3 tablespoons fresh lime juice

- 2 tablespoons prepared mustard
- 1 tablespoon ground coriander
- 1 tablespoon smoked paprika
- 1 ½ teaspoon garam masala
- ½ teaspoon ground cumin
- 1 ½ pounds skinless chicken thighs
- Salt and pepper to taste

**Directions**

1. Place all ingredients in a Ziploc bag and give a good shake to combine everything.
2. Allow to marinate for at least 2 hours in the fridge.
3. Preheat the air fryer at 3750F.
4. Place the grill pan accessory in the air fryer.
5. Grill for at least 40 minutes.
6. Make sure to flip the chicken every 10 minutes.

**Nutrition**

Calories: 583; Carbs: 25.5g; Protein:54.6 g; Fat: 29.8g

## 521. Grilled Chicken with Bold Dressing

Servings: 8
Cooking Time: 40 minutes

**Ingredients:**

- 1 dried Mexican chili, shredded
- ½ teaspoon crushed red pepper flakes
- ¾ cup fresh cilantro
- ¼ cup chopped oregano
- 1 teaspoon lime zest
- Salt and pepper to taste
- 4 pounds chicken breasts

**Directions**

1. Place all ingredients in a Ziploc bag and give a good shake.
2. Allow to marinate in the fridge for at least 2 hours.
3. Preheat the air fryer at 3750F.
4. Place the grill pan accessory in the air

5. Grill for at least 40 minutes making sure to flip the chicken every 10 minutes for even grilling.

**Nutrition**

522. Calories: 394; Carbs:0.9 g; Protein: 47.4g; Fat: 21g

## 522. Indian Spiced Chicken, Eggplant, and Tomato Skewers

Servings: 4
Cooking Time: 25 minutes

**Ingredients:**

- 4 cloves of garlic, minced
- 1-inch ginger, grated
- 1 can coconut milk
- 3 teaspoons lime zest
- 2 tablespoons fresh lime juice
- 2 tablespoons tomato paste
- Salt and pepper to taste
- 1 ½ teaspoon ground turmeric
- ¼ teaspoon cayenne pepper
- ¼ teaspoon ground cardamom
- 2 pounds boneless chicken breasts, cut into cubes
- 1 medium eggplant, cut into cubes
- 1 onion, cut into wedges
- 1 cup cherry tomatoes

**Directions**

1. In a bowl, place the garlic, ginger, coconut milk, lime zest, lime juice, tomato paste, salt, pepper, turmeric, cayenne pepper, cardamom, and chicken breasts. Allow to marinate in the fridge for at least for 2 hours.
2. Preheat the air fryer at 3750F.
3. Place the grill pan accessory in the air fryer.
4. Skewer the chicken cubes with eggplant, onion, and cherry tomatoes on bamboo skewers.

5. Place on the grill pan and cook for 25 minutes making sure to flip the skewers every 5 minutes for even cooking.

**Nutrition**

Calories: 479; Carbs:19.7 g; Protein: 55.2g; Fat: 20.6g

## 523. Easy Curry Grilled Chicken Wings

Servings: 4
Cooking Time: 35 minutes

**Ingredients:**

- 2 pounds chicken wings
- ½ cup plain yogurt
- 1 tablespoons curry powder
- Salt and pepper to taste

**Directions**

1. Season the chicken wings with yogurt, curry powder, salt, and pepper. Toss to combine everything.
2. Allow to marinate in the fridge for at least 2 hours.
3. Preheat the air fryer at 3750F.
4. Place the grill pan accessory in the air fryer.
5. Grill the chicken for 35 minutes and make sure to flip the chicken halfway through the cooking time.

**Nutrition**

Calories:314; Carbs: 3.3g; Protein: 51.3g; Fat: 9.2g

## 524. Spicy Chicken with Lemon and Parsley in A Packet

Servings: 4
Cooking Time: 45 minutes

**Ingredients:**

- 2 pounds chicken thighs
- ¼ cup smoked paprika
- ½ teaspoon liquid smoke seasoning
- Salt and pepper to taste
- 1 ½ tablespoon cayenne pepper

- 4 lemons, halved
- ½ cup parsley leaves

**Directions**

1. Preheat the air fryer at 3750F.
2. Place the grill pan accessory in the air fryer.
3. In a large piece of foil, place the chicken and season with paprika, liquid smoke seasoning, salt, pepper, and cayenne pepper.
4. Top with lemon and parsley.
5. Place on the grill and cook for 45 minutes.

**Nutrition**

Calories: 546; Carbs: 10.4g; Protein: 39.2g; Fat: 39.1g

## 525. Korean Grilled Chicken

Servings: 4
Cooking Time: 30 minutes

**Ingredients:**

- 2 pounds chicken wings
- 1 teaspoon salt
- ½ teaspoon fresh ground black pepper
- ½ cup gochujang
- 1 scallion, sliced thinly

**Directions**

1. Place in a Ziploc bag the chicken wings, salt, pepper, and gochujang sauce.
2. Allow to marinate in the fridge for at least 2 hours.
3. Preheat the air fryer at 3750F.
4. Place the grill pan accessory in the air fryer.
5. Grill the chicken wings for 30 minutes making sure to flip the chicken every 10 minutes.
6. Top with scallions and serve with more gochujang.

**Nutrition**

Calories: 289; Carbs: 0.8g; Protein: 50.1g; Fat: 8.2g

## 526. Grilled Chicken with Shishito Peppers

Servings: 6
Cooking Time: 30 minutes

**Ingredients:**

- 3 pounds chicken wings
- Salt and pepper to taste
- 2 tablespoons sesame oil
- 1 ½ cups shishito peppers, pureed

**Directions**

1. Place all ingredients in a Ziploc bag and allow to marinate for at least 2 hours in the fridge.
2. Preheat the air fryer at 3750F.
3. Place the grill pan accessory in the air fryer.
4. Grill for at least 30 minutes flipping the chicken every 5 minutes and basting with the remaining sauce.

**Nutrition**

Calories: 333; Carbs: 1.7g; Protein: 50.2g; Fat: 12.6g

## 527. Grilled Chicken with Scallions

Servings: 4
Cooking Time: 1 hour

**Ingredients:**

- 2 pounds whole chicken
- Salt and pepper to taste
- 4 sprigs rosemary
- 2 cloves of garlic, peeled and crushed
- 2 bunches scallions

**Directions**

1. Season the whole chicken with salt and pepper.
2. Place inside the chicken cavity the rosemary, garlic, and scallions.
3. Preheat the air fryer at 3750F.

4.  Place the grill pan accessory in the air fryer.
5.  Grill the chicken for 1 hour.

**Nutrition**

Calories: 470; Carbs: 46.2g; Protein: 37.2g; Fat: 15.9g

## 528. PiriPiri Chicken

Servings: 6
Cooking Time: 45 minutes

**Ingredients:**

- 3 pounds chicken breasts
- ½ cup piripiri sauce
- ¼ cup fresh lemon juice
- Salt and pepper to taste
- 1-inch fresh ginger, peeled, and sliced thinly
- 1 large shallot, quartered
- 3 cloves of garlic, minced

**Directions**

1.  Preheat the air fryer at 3750F.
2.  Place the grill pan accessory in the air fryer.
3.  On a large piece of foil, place the chicken and top with the rest of the ingredients.
4.  Fold the foil and crimp the edges.
5.  Grill for 45 minutes.

**Nutrition**

Calories:404; Carbs: 3.4g; Protein: 47.9g; Fat: 21.1g

## 529. Grilled Turmeric and Lemongrass Chicken

Servings: 6
Cooking Time: 40 minutes

**Ingredients:**

- 3 shallots, chopped
- 3 cloves of garlic, minced
- 2 lemongrass stalks

- 1 teaspoon turmeric
- Salt and pepper to taste
- 2 tablespoons fish sauce
- 3 pounds whole chicken

**Directions**

1.  Place all ingredients in a Ziploc bag and allow to marinate for at least 2 hours in the fridge.
2.  Preheat the air fryer at 3750F.
3.  Place the grill pan accessory in the air fryer.
4.  Grill the chicken for 40 minutes making sure to flip every 10 minutes for even grilling.

**Nutrition**

Calories: 486; Carbs: 49.1g; Protein: 38.5g; Fat: 16.1g

## 530. Peruvian Grilled Chicken

Servings: 4
Cooking Time: 40 minutes

**Ingredients:**

- 1/3 cup soy sauce
- 2 tablespoons fresh lime juice
- 5 cloves of garlic, minced
- 2 teaspoons ground cumin
- 1 teaspoon paprika
- ½ teaspoon dried oregano
- 2 ½ pounds chicken, quartered

**Directions**

1.  Place all ingredients in a Ziploc bag and shake to mix everything.
2.  Allow to marinate for at least 2 hours in the fridge.
3.  Preheat the air fryer at 3750F.
4.  Place the grill pan accessory in the air fryer.
5.  Grill the chicken for 40 minutes making sure to flip the chicken every 10 minutes for even grilling.

**Nutrition**

Calories:389; Carbs: 7.9g; Protein: 59.7g; Fat: 11.8g

## 531. Broccoli Dip

Preparation Time: 25 minutes
Servings: 4

**Ingredients:**

- 1 ½ cups veggie stock
- 1/3 cup coconut milk
- 3 cups broccoli florets
- 2 garlic cloves; minced
- 1 tbsp. olive oil
- 1 tbsp. balsamic vinegar
- Salt and black pepper to taste.

**Directions:**

1. In a pan that fits your air fryer, mix all the ingredients, toss.
2. Introduce in the fryer and cook at 390°F for 15 minutes. Divide into bowls and serve

**Nutrition: Calories: 163; Fat: 4g; Fiber: 2g; Carbs: 4g; Protein: 5g**

## 532. Crab and Artichoke Dip

Preparation Time: 25 minutes
Servings: 4

**Ingredients:**

- 8 oz. cream cheese, soft
- 12 oz. jumbo crab meat
- 1 bunch green onions; minced
- 14 oz. canned artichoke hearts, drained and chopped.
- 1 cup coconut cream
- 1 ½ cups mozzarella; shredded
- 1 tbsp. lemon juice
- 1 tbsp. lemon juice
- A pinch of salt and black pepper

**Directions:**

1. In a bowl, combine all the ingredients except half of the cheese and whisk them really well.
2. Transfer this to a pan that fits your air fryer, introduce in the machine and cook at 400°F for 15 minutes
3. Sprinkle the rest of the mozzarella on top and cook for 5 minutes more. Divide the mix into bowls and serve as a party dip

**Nutrition: Calories: 240; Fat: 8g; Fiber: 2g; Carbs: 4g; Protein: 14g**

## 533. Mozzarella and Tomato Salad

Preparation Time: 17 minutes
Servings: 6

**Ingredients:**

- 1 lb. tomatoes; sliced
- 1 cup mozzarella; shredded
- 1 tbsp. ginger; grated
- 1 tbsp. balsamic vinegar
- 1 tsp. sweet paprika
- 1 tsp. chili powder
- ½ tsp. coriander, ground

**Directions:**

1. In a pan that fits your air fryer, mix all the ingredients except the mozzarella, toss, introduce the pan in the air fryer and cook at 360°F for 12 minutes
2. Divide into bowls and serve cold as an appetizer with the mozzarella sprinkled all over.

**Nutrition: Calories: 185; Fat: 8g; Fiber: 2g; Carbs: 4g; Protein: 8g**

## 534. Cheese Bread.

Preparation Time: 20 minutes

Servings: 2

**Ingredients:**

- ¼ cup grated Parmesan cheese.
- 1 cup shredded mozzarella cheese
- 1 large egg.
- ½ tsp. garlic powder.

**Directions:**

1. Mix all ingredients in a large bowl. Cut a piece of parchment to fit your air fryer basket. Press the mixture into a circle on the parchment and place into the air fryer basket
2. Adjust the temperature to 350 Degrees F and set the timer for 10 minutes.

**Nutrition: Calories: 258; Protein: 19.2g; Fiber: 0.1g; Fat: 16.6g; Carbs: 3.7g**

## 535. Bacon Wrapped Onion Rings.

Preparation Time: 15 minutes
Servings: 4

**Ingredients:**

- 1 large onion; peeled.
- 8 slices sugar-free bacon.
- 1 tbsp. sriracha

**Directions:**

1. Slice onion into ¼-inch-thick slices. Brush sriracha over the onion slices. Take two slices of onion and wrap bacon around the rings. Repeat with remaining onion and bacon
2. Place into the air fryer basket. Adjust the temperature to 350 Degrees F and set the timer for 10 minutes.
3. Use tongs to flip the onion rings halfway through the cooking time. When fully cooked, bacon will be crispy. Serve warm

**Nutrition: Calories: 105; Protein: 7.5g; Fiber: 0.6g; Fat: 5.9g; Carbs: 4.3g**

## 536. Cheesy Meatballs

Preparation Time: 30 minutes
Servings: 16 meatballs

**Ingredients:**

- 1 lb. 80/20 ground beef.
- 3 oz. low-moisture, whole-milk mozzarella, cubed
- 1 large egg.
- ½ cup low-carb, no-sugar-added pasta sauce.
- ¼ cup grated Parmesan cheese.
- ¼ cup blanched finely ground almond flour.
- ¼ tsp. onion powder.
- 1 tsp. dried parsley.
- ½ tsp. garlic powder.

**Directions:**

1. Take a large bowl, add ground beef, almond flour, parsley, garlic powder, onion powder and egg. Fold ingredients together until fully combined
2. Form the mixture into 2-inch balls and use your thumb or a spoon to create an indent in the center of each meatball. Place a cube of cheese in the center and form the ball around it.
3. Place the meatballs into the air fryer, working in batches if necessary. Adjust the temperature to 350 Degrees F and set the timer for 15 minutes
4. Meatballs will be slightly crispy on the outside and fully cooked when at least 180 Degrees F internally.
5. When they are finished cooking, toss the meatballs in the sauce and sprinkle with grated Parmesan for serving.

**Nutrition: Calories: 447; Protein: 29.6g; Fiber: 1.8g; Fat: 29.7g; Carbs: 5.4g**

## 537. Jalapeño Bacon Cheese Bread

Preparation Time: 25 minutes
Servings: 8 sticks

**Ingredients:**

- 4 slices sugar-free bacon; cooked and chopped
- 2 large eggs.
- ¼ cup chopped pickled jalapeños.
- ¼ cup grated Parmesan cheese.
- 2 cups shredded mozzarella cheese

**Directions:**
1. Mix all ingredients in a large bowl. Cut a piece of parchment to fit your air fryer basket.
2. Dampen your hands with a bit of water and press out the mixture into a circle. You may need to separate this into two smaller cheese breads, depending on the size of your fryer
3. Place the parchment and cheese bread into the air fryer basket
4. Adjust the temperature to 320 Degrees F and set the timer for 15 minutes. Carefully flip the bread when 5 minutes remain
5. When fully cooked, the top will be golden brown. Serve warm.

**Nutrition: Calories: 273; Protein: 20.1g; Fiber: 0.1g; Fat: 18.1g; Carbs: 2.3g**

## 538. Peppers and Cheese Dip

Preparation Time: 25 minutes
Servings: 6

**Ingredients:**
- 2 bacon slices, cooked and crumbled
- 4 oz. parmesan; grated
- 4 oz. mozzarella; grated
- 8 oz. cream cheese, soft
- 2 roasted red peppers; chopped.
- A pinch of salt and black pepper

**Directions:**
1. In a pan that fits your air fryer, mix all the ingredients and whisk really well.
2. Introduce the pan in the fryer and cook at 400°F for 20 minutes. Divide into bowls and serve cold

**Nutrition: Calories: 173; Fat: 8g; Fiber: 2g; Carbs: 4g; Protein: 11g**

## 539. Avocado Bites

Preparation Time: 13 minutes
Servings: 4

**Ingredients:**
- 4 avocados, peeled, pitted and cut into wedges
- 1 ½ cups almond meal
- 1 egg; whisked
- A pinch of salt and black pepper
- Cooking spray

**Directions:**
1. Put the egg in a bowl and the almond meal in another.
2. Season avocado wedges with salt and pepper, coat them in egg and then in meal almond
3. Arrange the avocado bites in your air fryer's basket, grease them with cooking spray and cook at 400°F for 8 minutes. Serve as a snack right away

**Nutrition: Calories: 200; Fat: 12g; Fiber: 3g; Carbs: 5g; Protein: 16g**

## 540. Zucchini Salsa

Preparation Time: 20 minutes
Servings: 6

**Ingredients:**
- 1 ½ lb. zucchinis, roughly cubed
- 2 tomatoes; cubed
- 2 spring onions; chopped.
- 1 tbsp. balsamic vinegar
- Salt and black pepper to taste.

**Directions:**
1. In a pan that fits your air fryer, mix all the ingredients, toss, introduce the pan in the fryer and cook at 360°F for 15 minutes
2. Divide the salsa into cups and serve cold.

**Nutrition: Calories: 164; Fat: 6g; Fiber: 2g; Carbs: 3g; Protein: 8g**

## 541. Crab Balls

Preparation Time: 25 minutes
Servings: 8

**Ingredients:**

- 16 oz. lump crabmeat; chopped.
- 2/3 cup almond meal
- ½ cup coconut cream
- 1 egg; whisked
- 2 tbsp. chives, mined
- 1 tsp. lemon juice
- 1 tsp. mustard
- A pinch of salt and black pepper
- Cooking spray

**Directions:**

1. Take a bowl and mix all the ingredients except the cooking spray and stir well.
2. Shape medium balls out of this mix, place them in the fryer and cook at 390°F for 20 minutes

**Nutrition: Calories: 141; Fat: 7g; Fiber: 2g; Carbs: 4g; Protein: 9g**

## 542. Fennel Spread

Preparation Time: 25 minutes
Servings: 8

**Ingredients:**

- 3 fennel bulbs; trimmed and cut into wedges
- 4 garlic cloves; minced
- ¼ cup parmesan; grated
- 3 tbsp. olive oil
- A pinch of salt and black pepper

**Directions:**

1. Put the fennel in the air fryer's basket and bake at 380°F for 20 minutes.
2. In a blender, combine the roasted fennel with the rest of the ingredients and pulse well
3. Put the spread in a ramekin, introduce it in the fryer and cook at 380°F for 5 minutes more
4. Divide into bowls and serve as a dip.

**Nutrition: Calories: 240; Fat: 11g; Fiber: 3g; Carbs: 4g; Protein: 12g**

## 543. Sweet Pepper Poppers

Preparation Time: 23 minutes
Servings: 16 halves

**Ingredients:**

- 8 mini sweet peppers
- 4 slices sugar-free bacon; cooked and crumbled
- ¼ cup shredded pepper jack cheese
- 4 oz. full-fat cream cheese; softened.

**Directions:**

1. Remove the tops from the peppers and slice each one in half lengthwise. Use a small knife to remove seeds and membranes
2. In a small bowl, mix cream cheese, bacon and pepper jack
3. Place 3 tsp. of the mixture into each sweet pepper and press down smooth. Place into the fryer basket. Adjust the temperature to 400 Degrees F and set the timer for 8 minutes. Serve warm.

**Nutrition: Calories: 176; Protein: 7.4g; Fiber: 0.9g; Fat: 13.4g; Carbs: 3.6g**

## 544. Parmesan Chicken Wings

Preparation Time: 30 minutes
Servings: 4

**Ingredients:**

- 2 lb. raw chicken wings
- ⅓ cup grated Parmesan cheese.
- 1 tbsp. baking powder
- 4 tbsp. unsalted butter; melted.

- ¼ tsp. dried parsley.
- ½ tsp. garlic powder.
- 1 tsp. pink Himalayan salt

**Directions:**

1. Take a large bowl, place chicken wings, salt, ½ tsp. garlic powder. and baking powder, then toss. Place wings into the air fryer basket
2. Adjust the temperature to 400 Degrees F and set the timer for 25 minutes. Toss the basket two or three times during the cooking time
3. In a small bowl, combine butter, Parmesan and parsley.
4. Remove wings from the fryer and place into a clean large bowl. Pour the butter mixture over the wings and toss until coated. Serve warm.

**Nutrition: Calories: 565; Protein: 41.8g; Fiber: 0.1g; Fat: 42.1g; Carbs: 2.2g**

## 545. Bacon Wrapped Brie

Preparation Time: 15 minutes
Servings: 8

**Ingredients:**

- 1: 8-oz.round Brie
- 4 slices sugar-free bacon.

**Directions:**

1. Place two slices of bacon to form an X. Place the third slice of bacon horizontally across the center of the X. Place the fourth slice of bacon vertically across the X. It should look like a plus sign: +on top of an X. Place the Brie in the center of the bacon
2. Wrap the bacon around the Brie, securing with a few toothpicks. Cut a piece of parchment to fit your air fryer basket and place the bacon-wrapped Brie on top. Place inside the air fryer basket.
3. Adjust the temperature to 400 Degrees F and set the timer for 10 minutes. When 3 minutes remain on the timer, carefully flip

Brie

4. When cooked, bacon will be crispy and cheese will be soft and melty. To serve; cut into eight slices.

**Nutrition: Calories: 116; Protein: 7.7g; Fiber: 0.0g; Fat: 8.9g; Carbs: 0.2g**

## 546. Buffalo Chicken Dip

Preparation Time: 20 minutes
Servings: 4

**Ingredients:**

- 1 ½ cups shredded medium Cheddar cheese, divided.
- 2 scallions, sliced on the bias
- 8 oz. full-fat cream cheese; softened.
- 1 cup cooked; diced chicken breast
- ½ cup buffalo sauce
- ⅓ cup chopped pickled jalapeños.
- ⅓ cup full-fat ranch dressing

**Directions:**

1. Place chicken into a large bowl. Add cream cheese, buffalo sauce and ranch dressing. Stir until the sauces are well mixed and mostly smooth. Fold in jalapeños and 1 cup Cheddar.
2. Pour the mixture into a 4-cup round baking dish and place remaining Cheddar on top. Place dish into the air fryer basket.
3. Adjust the temperature to 350 Degrees F and set the timer for 10 minutes. When done, the top will be brown and the dip bubbling. Top with sliced scallions. Serve warm.

**Nutrition: Calories: 472; Protein: 25.6g; Fiber: 0.6g; Fat: 32.0g; Carbs: 9.1g**

## 547. Feta Cheese Dip

Preparation Time: 10 minutes
Servings: 6

**Ingredients:**

- 2 avocados, peeled, pitted and mashed
- ¼ cup spring onion; chopped.
- 1 garlic clove; minced
- ¼ cup parsley; chopped.
- ½ cup feta cheese, crumbled
- 1 tbsp. jalapeno; minced
- Juice of 1 lime

**Directions:**

1. In a ramekin, mix all the ingredients and whisk them well.
2. Introduce in the fryer and cook at 380°F for 5 minutes. Serve as a party dip right away

**Nutrition: Calories: 200; Fat: 12g; Fiber: 2g; Carbs: 4g; Protein: 9g**

## 548. Cheese and Leeks Dip

Preparation Time: 17 minutes
Servings: 6

**Ingredients:**

- 2 spring onions; minced
- 4 leeks; sliced
- ¼ cup coconut cream
- 3 tbsp. coconut milk
- 2 tbsp. butter; melted
- Salt and white pepper to the taste

**Directions:**

1. In a pan that fits your air fryer, mix all the ingredients and whisk them well.
2. Introduce the pan in the fryer and cook at 390°F for 12 minutes. Divide into bowls and serve

**Nutrition: Calories: 204; Fat: 12g; Fiber: 2g; Carbs: 4g; Protein: 14g**

## 549. Mozzarella Sticks

Preparation Time: 1 hour 10 minutes
Servings: 12 sticks

**Ingredients:**

- 6: 1-oz.mozzarella string cheese sticks
- ½ oz. pork rinds, finely ground
- 2 large eggs.
- ½ cup grated Parmesan cheese.
- 1 tsp. dried parsley.

**Directions:**

1. Place mozzarella sticks on a cutting board and cut in half. Freeze 45 minutes or until firm. If freezing overnight, remove frozen sticks after 1 hour and place into airtight zip-top storage bag and place back in freezer for future use.
2. Take a large bowl, mix Parmesan, ground pork rinds and parsley
3. Take a medium bowl, whisk eggs
4. Dip a frozen mozzarella stick into beaten eggs and then into Parmesan mixture to coat.
5. Repeat with remaining sticks. Place mozzarella sticks into the air fryer basket.
6. Adjust the temperature to 400 Degrees F and set the timer for 10 minutes or until golden. Serve warm.

**Nutrition: Calories: 236; Protein: 19.2g; Fiber: 0.0g; Fat: 13.8g; Carbs: 4.7g**

## 550. Garlic Cheese Dip

Preparation Time: 15 minutes
Servings: 10

**Ingredients:**

- 1 lb. mozzarella; shredded
- 6 garlic cloves; minced
- 3 tbsp. olive oil
- 1 tbsp. thyme; chopped.
- 1 tsp. rosemary; chopped.
- A pinch of salt and black pepper

**Directions:**

1. In a pan that fits your air fryer, mix all the ingredients, whisk really well, introduce in the air fryer and cook at 370°F for 10 minutes.
2. Divide into bowls and serve right away.

**Nutrition: Calories: 184; Fat: 11g; Fiber: 3g; Carbs: 5g; Protein: 7g**

## 551. Crustless Pizza

Preparation Time: 10 minutes
Servings: 1

**Ingredients:**

- 2 slices sugar-free bacon; cooked and crumbled
- 7 slices pepperoni
- ½ cup shredded mozzarella cheese
- ¼ cup cooked ground sausage
- 2 tbsp. low-carb, sugar-free pizza sauce, for dipping
- 1 tbsp. grated Parmesan cheese

**Directions:**

1. Cover the bottom of a 6-inch cake pan with mozzarella. Place pepperoni, sausage and bacon on top of cheese and sprinkle with Parmesan
2. Place pan into the air fryer basket. Adjust the temperature to 400 Degrees F and set the timer for 5 minutes.
3. Remove when cheese is bubbling and golden. Serve warm with pizza sauce for dipping.

**Nutrition: Calories: 466; Protein: 28.1g; Fiber: 0.5g; Fat: 34.0g; Carbs: 5.2g**

## 552. Bow Tie Pasta Chips

Preparation Time: 10 minutes
Cooking Time: 10 minutes
Servings: 6

**Ingredients:**

- 2 cups white bow tie pasta
- 1 tablespoon olive oil
- 1 tablespoon nutritional yeast
- 1½ teaspoons Italian seasoning blend
- ½ teaspoon salt

**Directions:**

1. Cook the pasta for 1/2 the time called for on the package. Toss the drained pasta
2. with the olive oil or aquafaba, nutritional yeast, Italian seasoning, and salt.
3. Place about half of the mixture in your air fryer basket if yours is small; larger ones may be able to do cook in one batch.
4. Cook on 390°F: 200°C for 5 minutes. Shake the basket and cook 3 to 5 minutes more or until crunchy.

**Nutrition:**
Calories: 408, Fat: 23.1g, Carbohydrates: 52.6g, Sugar: 0g, Protein: 14.6g, Sodium: 688mg

## 553. Stuffed Mushrooms with Sour Cream

Preparation Time: 15 minutes
Cooking Time: 8 minutes
Servings: 12

**Ingredients:**

- ¼ orange bell pepper, diced
- ¾ cup Cheddar cheese, shredded
- 12 mushrooms caps, stems diced
- ½ onion, diced
- ½ small carrot, diced
- ¼ cup sour cream

**Directions:**

1. Preheat the Air fryer to 350 o F and grease a baking tray.
2. Place mushroom stems, onion, orange bell pepper and carrot over medium heat in a skillet.
3. Cook for about 5 minutes until softened and stir in ½ cup Cheddar cheese and sour cream.
4. Stuff this mixture in the mushroom caps and arrange them on the baking tray.
5. Top with rest of the cheese and place the baking tray in the Air fryer basket.
6. Cook for about 8 minutes until cheese is melted and serve warm.

**Nutrition:**

Calories: 43, Fat: 3.1g, Carbohydrates: 1.7g, Sugar: 1g, Protein: 2.4g, Sodium: 55mg

## 554. Crispy Shrimps

Preparation Time: 15 minutes
Cooking Time: 8 minutes
Servings: 2

**Ingredients:**

- 1 egg
- ¼ pound nacho chips, crushed
- 10 shrimps, peeled and deveined
- 1 tablespoon olive oil
- Salt and black pepper, to taste

**Directions:**

1. Preheat the Air fryer to 365 o F and grease an Air fryer basket.
2. Crack egg in a shallow dish and beat well.
3. Place the nacho chips in another shallow dish.
4. Season the shrimps with salt and black pepper, coat into egg and then roll into nacho chips.
5. Place the coated shrimps into the Air fryer basket and cook for about 8 minutes.
6. Dish out and serve warm.

**Nutrition:**
Calories: 514, Fat: 25.8g, Carbohydrates: 36.9g, Sugar: 2.3g, Protein: 32.5g, Sodium: 648mg

## 555. Sunflower Seeds Bread

Preparation Time: 15 minutes
Cooking Time: 18 minutes
Servings: 4

**Ingredients:**

- 2/3 cup whole wheat flour
- 2/3 cup plain flour
- 1/3 cup sunflower seeds
- 1 cup lukewarm water
- ½ sachet instant yeast
- 1 teaspoon salt

**Directions:**

1. Preheat the Air fryer to 390 o F and grease a cake pan.
2. Mix together flours, sunflower seeds, yeast and salt in a bowl.
3. Add water slowly and knead for about 5 minutes until a dough is formed.
4. Cover the dough with a plastic wrap and keep in warm place for about half an hour.
5. Arrange the dough into a cake pan and transfer into an Air fryer basket.
6. Cook for about 18 minutes and dish out to serve warm.

**Nutrition:**
Calories: 156, Fat: 2.4g, Carbohydrates: 28.5g, Sugar: 0.5g, Protein: 4.6g, Sodium: 582mg

## 556. Air Fried Chicken Tenders

Preparation Time: 15 minutes
Cooking Time: 10 minutes
Servings: 4

**Ingredients:**

- 12 oz chicken breasts, cut into tenders
- 1 egg white
- 1/8 cup flour
- ½ cup panko bread crumbs
- Salt and black pepper, to taste

**Directions:**

1. Preheat the Air fryer to 350 o F and grease an Air fryer basket.
2. Season the chicken tenders with salt and black pepper.
3. Coat the chicken tenders with flour, then dip in egg whites and then dredge in the panko bread crumbs.
4. Arrange in the Air fryer basket and cook for about 10 minutes.
5. Dish out in a platter and serve warm.

**Nutrition:**

Calories: 220, Fat: 17.1g, Carbohydrates: 6g, Sugar: 3.5g, Protein: 12.8g, Sodium: 332mg

## 557. Air Fryer Plantains

Preparation Time: 10 minutes
Cooking Time: 10 minutes
Servings: 4

**Ingredients:**

- 2 ripe plantains
- 2 teaspoons avocado oil
- 1/8 teaspoon salt

**Directions:**

1. Preheat the Air fryer to 400 o F and grease an Air fryer basket.
2. Mix the plantains with avocado oil and salt in a bowl.
3. Arrange the coated plantains in the Air fryer basket and cook for about 10 minutes.
4. Dish out in a bowl and serve immediately.

**Nutrition:**

Calories: 112, Fat: 0.6g, Carbohydrates: 28.7g, Sugar: 13.4g, Protein: 1.2g, Sodium: 77mg

## 558. Pita Bread Cheese Pizza

Preparation Time: 10 minutes
Cooking Time: 6 minutes
Servings: 4

**Ingredients:**

- 1 pita bread
- ¼ cup Mozzarella cheese
- 7 slices pepperoni
- ¼ cup sausage
- 1 tablespoon yellow onion, sliced thinly
- 1 tablespoon pizza sauce
- 1 drizzle extra-virgin olive oil
- ½ teaspoon fresh garlic, minced

**Directions:**

1. Preheat the Air fryer to 350 o F and grease an Air fryer basket.
2. Spread pizza sauce on the pita bread and add sausages, pepperoni, onions, garlic and cheese.
3. Drizzle with olive oil and place it in the Air fryer basket.
4. Cook for about 6 minutes and dish out to serve warm.
5. **Nutrition:**

Calories: 56, Fat: 3.6g, Carbohydrates: 6.7g, Sugar: 3.6g, Protein: 0.3g, Sodium: 0mg

## 559. Buttered Dinner Rolls

Preparation Time: 15 minutes
Cooking Time: 30 minutes
Servings: 12

**Ingredients:**

- 1 cup milk
- 3 cups plain flour
- 7½ tablespoons unsalted butter
- 1 tablespoon coconut oil
- 1 tablespoon olive oil
- 1 teaspoon yeast
- Salt and black pepper, to taste

**Directions:**

1. Preheat the Air fryer to 360 o F and grease an Air fryer basket.
2. Put olive oil, milk and coconut oil in a pan and cook for about 3 minutes.
3. Remove from the heat and mix well.
4. Mix together plain flour, yeast, butter, salt and black pepper in a large bowl.
5. Knead well for about 5 minutes until a dough is formed.
6. Cover the dough with a damp cloth and keep aside for about 5 minutes in a warm place.
7. Knead the dough for about 5 minutes again with your hands.
8. Cover the dough with a damp cloth and keep aside for about 30 minutes in a warm place.

9. Divide the dough into 12 equal pieces and roll each into a ball.
10. Arrange 6 balls into the Air fryer basket in a single layer and cook for about 15 minutes.
11. Repeat with the remaining balls and serve warm.

**Nutrition:**
Calories: 208, Fat: 10.3g, Carbohydrates: 25g, Sugar: 1g, Protein: 4.1g, Sodium: 73mg

## 560. Cheesy Dinner Rolls

Preparation Time: 10 minutes
Cooking Time: 5 minutes
Servings: 2

**Ingredients:**

- 2 dinner rolls
- ½ cup Parmesan cheese, grated
- 2 tablespoons unsalted butter, melted
- ½ teaspoon garlic bread seasoning mix

**Directions:**

1. Preheat the Air fryer to 355 o F and grease an Air fryer basket.
2. Cut the dinner rolls in slits and stuff cheese in the slits.
3. Top with butter and garlic bread seasoning mix.
4. Arrange the dinner rolls into the Air fryer basket and cook for about 5 minutes.
5. Dish out in a platter and serve hot.

**Nutrition:**
Calories: 608, Fat: 33.1g, Carbohydrates: 48.8g, Sugar: 4.8g, Protein: 33.5g, Sodium: 2000mg

## 561. Croissant Rolls

Preparation Time: 10 minutes
Cooking Time: 6 minutes
Servings: 8

**Ingredients:**

- 1: 8-ouncescan croissant rolls

- 4 tablespoons butter, melted
- 1 tablespoon olive oil

**Directions:**

1. Preheat the Air fryer to 320 o F and grease an Air fryer basket with olive oil.
2. Coat the croissant rolls with butter and arrange into the Air fryer basket.
3. Cook for about 6 minutes, flipping once in between.
4. Dish out in a platter and serve hot.

**Nutrition:**
Calories: 167, Fat: 12.6g, Carbohydrates: 11.1g, Sugar: 3g, Protein: 2.1g, Sodium: 223mg

## 562. Healthy Veggie Lasagna

Preparation Time: 15 minutes
Cooking Time: 1 hour; Serves 4

**Ingredients:**

- 1½ pounds pumpkin, peeled and chopped finely
- ¾ pound tomatoes, cubed
- 1 pound cooked beets, sliced thinly
- ½ pound fresh lasagna sheets
- ¼ cup Parmesan cheese, grated
- 2 tablespoons sunflower oil

**Directions:**

1. Preheat the Air fryer to 300 o F and lightly grease a baking dish.
2. Put pumpkin and 1 tablespoon sunflower oil in a skillet and cook for about 10 minutes.
3. Put the pumpkin mixture and tomatoes in a blender and pulse until smooth.
4. Return to the skillet and cook on low heat for about 5 minutes.
5. Transfer the pumpkin puree into the baking dish and layer with lasagna sheets.
6. Top with the beet slices and cheese and place in the Air fryer.
7. Cook for about 45 minutes and dish out to serve warm.

**Nutrition:**
Calories: 368, Fats: 10.3g, Carbohydrates: 59.8g,
Sugar: 16.9g, Proteins: 13.4g, Sodium: 165mg

## 563. Portabella Pizza Treat

Preparation Time: 10 minutes
Cooking Time: 6 minutes
Servings: 2

**Ingredients:**

- 2 Portabella caps, stemmed
- 2 tablespoons canned tomatoes with basil
- 2 tablespoons mozzarella cheese, shredded
- 4 pepperoni slices
- 2 tablespoons Parmesan cheese, grated freshly
- 2 tablespoon olive oil
- 1/8 teaspoon dried Italian seasonings
- Salt, to taste
- 1 teaspoon red pepper flakes, crushed

**Directions:**

1. Preheat the Air fryer to 320 o F and grease an Air fryer basket.
2. Drizzle olive oil on both sides of portabella cap and season salt, red pepper flakes and Italian seasonings.
3. Top canned tomatoes on the mushrooms, followed by mozzarella cheese.
4. Place portabella caps in the Air fryer basket and cook for about 2 minutes.
5. Top with pepperoni slices and cook for about 4 minutes.
6. Sprinkle with Parmesan cheese and dish out to serve warm.

**Nutrition:**
Calories: 242, Fat: 21.8g, Carbohydrates: 5.8g,
Sugar: 2g, Protein: 8.8g, Sodium: 350mg

## 564. Heirloom Tomato Sandwiches with Pesto

Preparation Time: 20 minutes

Cooking Time: 16 minutes
Servings: 4

**Ingredients:**

- 3 tablespoons pine nuts
- ½ cup fresh basil, chopped
- ½ cup fresh parsley, chopped
- 2 heirloom tomatoes, cut into ½ inch thick slices
- 8-ounce feta cheese, cut into ½ inch thick slices
- ½ cup plus 2 tablespoons olive oil, divided
- Salt, to taste
- 1 garlic clove, chopped

**Directions:**

1. Preheat the Air fryer to 390 o F and grease an Air fryer basket.
2. Mix together 1 tablespoon of olive oil, pine nuts and pinch of salt in a bowl.
3. Place pine nuts in the Air fryer and cook for about 2 minutes.
4. Put the pine nuts, remaining oil, fresh basil, fresh parsley, garlic and salt and pulse until combined.
5. Dish out the pesto in a bowl, cover and refrigerate.
6. Spread 1 tablespoon of pesto on each tomato slice and top with a feta slice and onion.
7. Drizzle with olive oil and arrange the prepared tomato slices in the Air fryer basket.
8. Cook for about 14 minutes and serve with remaining pesto.

**Nutrition:**
Calories: 559, Fat: 55.7g, Carbohydrates: 8g,
Sugar: 2.6g, Protein: 11.8g, Sodium: 787mg

## 565. Cheese Stuffed Tomatoes

Preparation Time: 15 minutes
Cooking Time: 15 minutes
Servings: 2

**Ingredients:**

- 2 large tomatoes, sliced in half and pulp scooped out
- ½ cup broccoli, finely chopped
- ½ cup cheddar cheese, shredded
- 1 tablespoon unsalted butter, melted
- ½ teaspoon dried thyme, crushed

**Directions:**

1. Preheat the Air fryer to 355 o F and grease an Air fryer basket.
2. Mix together broccoli and cheese in a bowl.
3. Stuff the broccoli mixture in each tomato.
4. Arrange the stuffed tomatoes into the Air fryer basket and drizzle evenly with butter.
5. Cook for about 15 minutes and dish out in a serving platter.
6. Garnish with thyme and serve warm.

**Nutrition:**
Calories: 206, Fat: 15.6g, Carbohydrates: 9.1g, Sugar: 5.3g, Protein: 9.4g, Sodium: 233mg

## 566. Hummus Mushroom Pizza

Preparation Time: 20 minutes
Cooking Time: 6 minutes
Servings: 4

**Ingredients:**

- 4 Portobello mushroom caps, stemmed and gills removed
- 3 ounces zucchini, shredded
- 2 tablespoons sweet red pepper, seeded and chopped
- 4 Kalamata olives, sliced
- ½ cup hummus
- 1 tablespoon balsamic vinegar
- Salt and black pepper, to taste
- 4 tablespoons pasta sauce
- 1 garlic clove, minced
- 1 teaspoon dried basil

**Directions:**

1. Preheat the Air fryer to 330 o F and grease an Air fryer basket.
2. Coat both sides of all Portobello mushroom cap with vinegar.
3. Season the inside of each mushroom cap with salt and black pepper.
4. Divide pasta sauce and garlic inside each mushroom.
5. Arrange mushroom caps into the Air fryer basket and cook for about 3 minutes.
6. Remove from the Air fryer and top zucchini, red peppers and olives on each mushroom cap.
7. Season with basil, salt, and black pepper and transfer into the Air fryer basket.
8. Cook for about 3 more minutes and dish out in a serving platter.
9. Spread hummus on each mushroom pizza and serve.

**Nutrition:**
Calories: 115, Fat: 4.1g, Carbohydrates: 15.4g, Sugar: 4.8g, Protein: 6.7g, Sodium: 264mg

## 567. Jacket Potatoes

Preparation Time: 15 minutes
Cooking Time: 15 minutes
Servings: 2

**Ingredients:**

- 2 potatoes
- 1 tablespoon parmesan cheese, shredded
- 1 tablespoon butter, softened
- 1 teaspoon parsley, minced
- ¼ cup tomatoes, chopped
- 3 tablespoons sour cream
- Salt and black pepper, to taste

**Directions:**

1. Preheat the Air fryer to 355 o F and grease an Air fryer basket.
2. Make holes in the potatoes and transfer into the Air fryer basket.
3. Cook for about 15 minutes and dish out

in a bowl.

4. Mix together rest of the ingredients in a bowl and combine well.

5. Cut the potatoes from the center and stuff in the cheese mixture to serve.

**Nutrition:**

Calories: 277, Fats: 12.2g, Carbohydrates: 34.8g, Sugar: 2.5g, Proteins: 8.2g, Sodium: 226mg

## 568. Cheese Stuffed Mushrooms

Preparation Time: 15 minutes
Cooking Time: 8 minutes
Servings: 4

**Ingredients:**

- 4 fresh large mushrooms, stemmed and gills removed
- ¼ cup Parmesan cheese, shredded
- 2 tablespoons white cheddar cheese, shredded
- 2 tablespoons sharp cheddar cheese, shredded
- Salt and black pepper, to taste
- 1/3 cup vegetable oil4 ounces cream cheese, softened
- 1 teaspoon Worcestershire sauce
- 2 garlic cloves, chopped
- Salt and ground black pepper, as required

**Directions:**

1. Preheat the Air fryer to 375 o F and grease an Air fryer basket.

2. Mix together Parmesan cheese, cheddar cheese, Worcestershire sauce, cream cheese, garlic, salt and black pepper in a bowl,

3. Stuff the cheese mixture in each mushroom and arrange in the Air fryer basket.

4. Cook for about 8 minutes and dish out in a serving platter.

**Nutrition:**

Calories: 156, Fat: 13.6g, Carbohydrates: 2.6g, Sugar: 0.7g, Protein: 6.5g, Sodium: 267mg

## 569. Cheesy Mushroom Pizza

Preparation Time: 15 minutes
Cooking Time: 6 minutes
Servings: 2

**Ingredients:**

- 2 Portobello mushroom caps, stemmed
- 2 tablespoons canned tomatoes, chopped
- 2 tablespoons Monterey Jack cheese, shredded
- 2 jalapeno peppers, pitted and sliced
- 2 tablespoons onions, chopped
- 2 tablespoons olive oil
- 1 teaspoon dried oregano
- Salt and white pepper, to taste

**Directions:**

1. Preheat the Air fryer to 320 o F and grease an Air fryer basket.

2. Coat both sides of all Portobello mushroom cap with olive oil.

3. Season the inside of each mushroom cap with salt and white pepper.

4. Divide pasta sauce and garlic inside each mushroom.

5. Arrange mushroom caps into the Air fryer basket and top with canned tomatoes, jalapeno peppers, onions and cheese.

6. Sprinkle with dried oregano and cook for about 6 minutes.

7. Remove from the Air fryer and serve warm.

**Nutrition:**

Calories: 251, Fat: 21g, Carbohydrates: 5.7g, Sugar: 0.7g, Protein: 13.4g, Sodium: 330mg

## 570. Rice Flour Crusted Tofu

Preparation Time: 15 minutes
Cooking Time: 28 minutes
Servings: 3

**Ingredients:**

- 1: 14-ouncesblock firm tofu, pressed and cubed into ½-inch size

- 2 tablespoons cornstarch
- ¼ cup rice flour
- Salt and ground black pepper, as required
- 2 tablespoons olive oil

**Directions:**
1. Preheat the Air fryer to 360 o F and grease an Air fryer basket.
2. Mix together cornstarch, rice flour, salt, and black pepper in a bowl.
3. Coat the tofu with flour mixture evenly and drizzle with olive oil.
4. Arrange the tofu cubes into the Air fryer basket and cook for about 28 minutes.
5. Dish out the tofu in a serving platter and serve warm.

**Nutrition:**
Calories: 241, Fat: 15g, Carbohydrates: 17.7g, Sugar: 0.8g, Protein: 11.6g, Sodium: 67mg

## 571. Beans and Veggie Burgers

Preparation Time: 20 minutes
Cooking Time: 23 minutes
Servings: 4

**Ingredients:**
- 1 cup cooked black beans
- 2 cups boiled potatoes, peeled and mashed
- 1 cup fresh spinach, chopped
- 1 cup fresh mushrooms, chopped
- 6 cups fresh baby greens
- 2 teaspoons Chile lime seasoning
- Olive oil cooking spray

**Directions:**
1. Preheat the Air fryer to 375 o F and grease an Air fryer basket.
2. Mix together potatoes, spinach, beans, mushrooms and Chile lime seasoning in a large bowl.
3. Make 4 equal-sized patties from this mixture and place the patties into the prepared Air fryer basket.

4. Spray with olive oil cooking spray and cook for about 20 minutes, flipping once in between.
5. Set the Air fryer to 90 o F and cook for about 3 more minutes.
6. Dish out in a platter and serve alongside the baby greens.

**Nutrition:**
Calories: 249, Fat: 1.1g, Carbohydrates: 48.8g, Sugar: 2.9g, Protein: 13.7g, Sodium: 47mg

## 572. Spiced Soy Curls

Preparation Time: 15 minutes
Cooking Time: 10 minutes
Servings: 2

**Ingredients:**
- 3 cups boiling water
- 4 ounces soy curls, soaked in boiling water for about 10 minutes and drained
- ¼ cup fine ground cornmeal
- ¼ cup nutritional yeast
- 2 teaspoons Cajun seasoning
- 1 teaspoon poultry seasoning
- Salt and ground white pepper, to taste

**Directions:**
1. Preheat the Air fryer to 385 o F and grease an Air fryer basket.
2. Mix together cornmeal, nutritional yeast, Cajun seasoning, poultry seasoning, salt and white pepper in a bowl.
3. Coat the soy curls generously with this mixture and arrange in the Air fryer basket.
4. Cook for about 10 minutes, flipping in between and dis out in a serving platter.

**Nutrition:**
Calories: 317, Fat: 10.2g, Carbohydrates: 30.8g, Sugar: 2g, Protein: 29.4g, Sodium: 145mg

## 573. Tofu in Sweet and Spicy Sauce

Preparation Time: 15 minutes

Cooking Time: 6 minutes

Servings: 2

**Ingredients:**

- 1: 14-ouncesblock firm tofu, pressed and cubed
- ½ cup arrowroot flour
- 2 scallions: green part), chopped
- ½ teaspoon sesame oil
- 4 tablespoons low-sodium soy sauce
- 1½ tablespoons rice vinegar
- 1½ tablespoons chili sauce
- 1 tablespoon agave nectar
- 2 large garlic cloves, minced
- 1 teaspoon fresh ginger, peeled and grated

**Directions:**

1. Preheat the Air fryer to 360 o F and grease an Air fryer basket.
2. Mix together tofu, arrowroot flour, and sesame oil in a bowl.
3. Arrange the tofu into the Air fryer basket and cook for about 20 minutes.
4. Meanwhile, mix together remaining ingredients except scallions in a bowl to make a sauce.
5. Place the tofu and sauce in a skillet and cook for about 3 minutes, stirring occasionally.
6. Garnish with green parts of scallions and serve hot.

**Nutrition:**

Calories: 153, Fat: 6.4g, Carbohydrates: 13.5g, Sugar: 13.4g, Protein: 13.4g, Sodium: 1300mg

## 574. Ranch Dipped Fillets

Preparation Time: 5 minutes

Cooking Time: 13 minutes

Servings: 2

**Ingredients:**

- ¼ cup panko breadcrumbs
- 1 egg beaten
- 2 tilapia fillets
- Garnish: Herbs and chilies
- ½ packet ranch dressing mix powder
- 1¼ tablespoons vegetable oil

**Directions:**

1. Preheat the Air fryer to 350 o F and grease an Air fryer basket.
2. Mix ranch dressing with panko breadcrumbs in a bowl.
3. Whisk eggs in a shallow bowl and dip the fish fillet in the eggs.
4. Dredge in the breadcrumbs and transfer into the Air fryer basket.
5. Cook for about 13 minutes and garnish with chilies and herbs to serve.

**Nutrition:**

Calories: 301, Fat: 12.2g, Carbohydrates: 1.5g, Sugar: 1.4g, Protein: 28.8g, Sodium: 276mg

## 575. Bacon Filled Poppers

Preparation Time: 5 minutes

Cooking Time: 15 minutes

Servings: 4

**Ingredients:**

- 4 strips crispy cooked bacon
- 3 tablespoons butter
- ½ cup jalapeno peppers, diced
- 2/3 cup almond flour
- 2 oz. Cheddar cheese, white, shredded
- 1 pinch cayenne pepper
- 1 tablespoon bacon fat
- 1 teaspoon kosher salt
- Black pepper, ground, to taste

**Directions:**

1. Preheat the Air fryer to 390 o F and grease an Air fryer basket.
2. Mix together butter with salt and water on medium heat in a skillet.
3. Whisk in the flour and sauté for about 3 minutes.
4. Dish out in a bowl and mix with the remaining ingredients to form a dough.

5. Wrap plastic wrap around the dough and refrigerate for about half an hour.

6. Make small popper balls out of this dough and arrange in the Air fryer basket.

7. Cook for about 15 minutes and dish out to serve warm.

**Nutrition:**

Calories: 385, Fat: 32.8g, Carbohydrates: 5.2g, Sugar: 0.4g, Protein: 17g, Sodium: 1532mg

## 576. Baked Egg Plant with Bacon

Preparation Time: 15 minutes
Cooking Time: 35 minutes
Servings: 2

**Ingredients:**

- 2 egg plants, cut in half lengthwise
- ½ cup cheddar cheese, shredded
- ½ can: 7.5 oz.chili without beans
- 2 tablespoons cooked bacon bits
- Fresh scallions, thinly sliced
- 2 teaspoons kosher salt
- 2 tablespoons sour cream

**Directions:**

1. Preheat the Air fryer to 390 o F and grease an Air fryer basket.

2. Place the egg plants with their skin side down in the Air fryer basket.

3. Cook for about 35 minutes and remove the egg plants from the Air fryer basket.

4. Top each half with salt, chili and cheddar cheese and transfer them back in the Air fryer basket.

5. Cook for 3 more minutes and dish out in a bowl.

6. Garnish with sour cream, bacon bits and scallions to serve.

**Nutrition:**

Calories: 548, Fat: 22.9g, Carbohydrates: 7.5g, Sugar: 10.9g, Protein: 40.1g, Sodium: 350mg

## 577. Zucchini Air Fried Gratin

Preparation Time: 10 minutes
Cooking Time: 15 minutes
Servings: 4

**Ingredients:**

- 2 zucchinis, cut into 8 equal sized pieces
- 1 tablespoon fresh parsley, chopped
- 2 tablespoons bread crumbs
- 4 tablespoons Parmesan cheese, grated
- 1 tablespoon vegetable oil
- Salt and black pepper, to taste

**Directions:**

1. Preheat the Air fryer to 360 o F and grease an Air fryer basket.

2. Arrange the zucchini pieces in the Air fryer basket with their skin side down.

3. Top with the remaining ingredients and cook for about 15 minutes.

4. Dish out and serve warm.

**Nutrition:**

Calories: 481, Fat: 11.1g, Carbohydrates: 9.1g, Sugar: 3g, Protein: 7g, Sodium: 203mg

## 578. Chicken Stuffed Mushrooms

Preparation Time: 10 minutes
Cooking Time: 15 minutes
Servings: 12

**Ingredients:**

- 12 large fresh mushrooms, stems removed
- 1 cup chicken meat, cubed
- ½ lb. imitation crabmeat, flaked
- 2 cups butter
- Garlic powder, to taste
- 2 cloves garlic, peeled and minced
- Salt and black pepper, to taste
- 1: 8 oz.package cream cheese, softened
- Crushed red pepper, to taste

**Directions:**

1. Preheat the Air fryer to 375 o F and

grease an Air fryer basket.

2. Heat butter on medium heat in a nonstick skillet and add chicken.

3. Sauté for about 5 minutes and stir in the remaining ingredients except mushrooms.

4. Stuff this filling mixture in the mushroom caps and arrange in the Air fryer basket.

5. Cook for about 10 minutes and dish out to serve warm.

**Nutrition:**

Calories: 383, Fat: 36.3g, Carbohydrates: 4.3g, Sugar: 1.7g, Protein: 7.3g, Sodium: 444mg

## 579. Cocoa and Nuts Bombs

Preparation Time: 13 minutes
Servings: 12

**Ingredients:**

- 2 cups macadamia nuts; chopped.
- ¼ cup cocoa powder
- 1/3 cup swerve
- 4 tbsp. coconut oil; melted
- 1 tsp. vanilla extract

**Directions:**

1. Take a bowl and mix all the ingredients and whisk well.
2. Shape medium balls out of this mix, place them in your air fryer and cook at 300°F for 8 minutes. Serve cold

**Nutrition: Calories: 120; Fat: 12g; Fiber: 1g; Carbs: 2g; Protein: 1g**

## 580. Sponge Ricotta Cake

Preparation Time: 35 minutes
Servings: 8

**Ingredients:**

- 3 eggs, whisked
- 1 cup almond flour
- 1 cup ricotta, soft
- 1/3 swerve
- 7 tbsp. ghee; melted
- 1 tsp. baking powder
- Cooking spray

**Directions:**

1. In a bowl, combine all the ingredients except the cooking spray and stir them very well.
2. Grease a cake pan that fits the air fryer with the cooking spray and pour the cake mix inside.
3. Put the pan in the fryer and cook at 350°F for 30 minutes
4. Cool the cake down, slice and serve.

**Nutrition: Calories: 210; Fat: 12g; Fiber: 3g; Carbs: 6g; Protein: 9g**

## 581. Cream and Coconut Cups

Preparation Time: 15 minutes
Servings: 6

**Ingredients:**

- 8 oz. cream cheese, soft
- 3 eggs
- 2 tbsp. butter; melted
- 3 tbsp. coconut, shredded and unsweetened
- 4 tbsp. swerve

**Directions:**

1. Take a bowl and mix all the ingredients and whisk really well.
2. Divide into small ramekins, put them in the fryer and cook at 320°F and bake for 10 minutes. Serve cold

**Nutrition: Calories: 164; Fat: 4g; Fiber: 2g; Carbs: 5g; Protein: 5g**

## 582. Plum Cake

Preparation Time: 40 minutes
Servings: 8

**Ingredients:**

- 4 plums, pitted and chopped.
- 1 ½ cups almond flour
- ½ cup coconut flour
- ¾ cup almond milk
- ½ cup butter, soft
- 3 eggs

- ½ cup swerve
- 1 tbsp. vanilla extract
- 2 tsp. baking powder
- ¼ tsp. almond extract

**Directions:**

1. Take a bowl and mix all the ingredients and whisk well.
2. Pour this into a cake pan that fits the air fryer after you've lined it with parchment paper, put the pan in the machine and cook at 370°F for 30 minutes.
3. Cool the cake down, slice and serve

**Nutrition: Calories: 183; Fat: 4g; Fiber: 3g; Carbs: 4g; Protein: 7g**

## 583. Currant Cream

Preparation Time: 35 minutes
Servings: 4

**Ingredients:**

- 7 cups red currants
- 6 sage leaves
- 1 cup water
- 1 cup swerve

**Directions:**

1. In a pan that fits your air fryer, mix all the ingredients, toss, put the pan in the fryer and cook at 330°F for 30 minutes
2. Discard sage leaves, divide into cups and serve cold.

**Nutrition: Calories: 171; Fat: 4g; Fiber: 2g; Carbs: 3g; Protein: 6g**

## 584. Almond Cupcakes

Preparation Time: 30 minutes
Servings: 4

**Ingredients:**

- 1/3 cup coconut flour
- 4 eggs, whisked
- ¼ cup almond milk

- ½ cup cocoa powder
- 3 tbsp. stevia
- 4 tbsp. coconut oil; melted
- 1 tsp. vanilla extract
- ½ tsp. baking soda
- 1 tsp. baking powder
- Cooking spray

**Directions:**

1. Take a bowl and mix all the ingredients except the cooking spray and whisk well.
2. Grease a cupcake tin that fits the air fryer with the cooking spray, pour the cupcake mix, put the pan in your air fryer, cook at 350°F for 25 minutes, cool down and serve

**Nutrition: Calories: 103; Fat: 4g; Fiber: 2g; Carbs: 6g; Protein: 3g**

## 585. Baked Plums

Preparation Time: 25 minutes
Servings: 6

**Ingredients:**

- 6 plums; cut into wedges
- 10 drops stevia
- Zest of 1 lemon, grated
- 2 tbsp. water
- 1 tsp. ginger, ground
- ½ tsp. cinnamon powder

**Directions:**

1. In a pan that fits the air fryer, combine the plums with the rest of the ingredients, toss gently.
2. Put the pan in the air fryer and cook at 360°F for 20 minutes. Serve cold

**Nutrition: Calories: 170; Fat: 5g; Fiber: 1g; Carbs: 3g; Protein: 5g**

## 586. Cauliflower Rice and Plum Pudding

Preparation Time: 30 minutes
Servings: 4

**Ingredients:**

- 4 plums, pitted and roughly chopped.
- 1 ½ cups cauliflower rice
- 2 cups coconut milk
- 2 tbsp. ghee; melted
- 3 tbsp. stevia

**Directions:**

1. Take a bowl and mix all the ingredients, toss, divide into ramekins, put them in the air fryer and cook at 340°F for 25 minutes. Cool down and serve

**Nutrition: Calories: 221; Fat: 4g; Fiber: 1g; Carbs: 3g; Protein: 3g**

## 587. Avocado and Raspberries Cake

Preparation Time: 40 minutes
Servings: 4

**Ingredients:**

- 2 avocados, peeled, pitted and mashed
- 4 oz. raspberries
- 1 cup swerve
- 1 cup almonds flour
- 4 eggs, whisked
- 4 tbsp. butter; melted
- 3 tsp. baking powder

**Directions:**

1. Take a bowl and mix all the ingredients, toss, pour this into a cake pan that fits the air fryer after you've lined it with parchment paper.
2. Put the pan in the fryer and cook at 340°F for 30 minutes
3. Leave the cake to cool down, slice and serve.

**Nutrition: Calories: 193; Fat: 4g; Fiber: 2g; Carbs: 5g; Protein: 5g**

## 588. Walnut and Vanilla Bars

Preparation Time: 21 minutes
Servings: 4

**Ingredients:**

- 1 egg
- ¼ cup almond flour
- ¼ cup walnuts; chopped.
- 1/3 cup cocoa powder
- 7 tbsp. ghee; melted
- 3 tbsp. swerve
- ½ tsp. baking soda
- 1 tsp. vanilla extract

**Directions:**

1. Take a bowl and mix all the ingredients and stir well.
2. Spread this on a baking sheet that fits your air fryer lined with parchment paper.
3. Put it in the fryer and cook at 330°F and bake for 16 minutes
4. Leave the bars to cool down, cut and serve

**Nutrition: Calories: 182; Fat: 12g; Fiber: 1g; Carbs: 3g; Protein: 6g**

## 589. Plum Cream

Preparation Time: 25 minutes
Servings: 4

**Ingredients:**

- 1 lb. plums, pitted and chopped.
- 1 ½ cups heavy cream
- ¼ cup swerve
- 1 tbsp. lemon juice

**Directions:**

1. Take a bowl and mix all the ingredients and whisk really well.
2. Divide this into 4 ramekins, put them in the air fryer and cook at 340°F for 20 minutes. Serve cold

**Nutrition: Calories: 171; Fat: 4g; Fiber: 2g; Carbs: 4g; Protein: 4g**

## 590. Mini Lava Cakes

Preparation Time: 30 minutes

Servings: 4

**Ingredients:**

- 3 oz. dark chocolate; melted
- 2 eggs, whisked
- ¼ cup coconut oil; melted
- 1 tbsp. almond flour
- 2 tbsp. swerve
- ¼ tsp. vanilla extract
- Cooking spray

**Directions:**

1. In bowl, combine all the ingredients except the cooking spray and whisk really well.
2. Divide this into 4 ramekins greased with cooking spray, put them in the fryer and cook at 360°F for 20 minutes

**Nutrition: Calories: 161; Fat: 12g; Fiber: 1g; Carbs: 4g; Protein: 7g**

## 591. Currant Pudding

Preparation Time: 25 minutes
Servings: 6

**Ingredients:**

- 1 cup red currants, blended
- 1 cup coconut cream
- 1 cup black currants, blended
- 3 tbsp. stevia

**Directions:**

1. In a bowl, combine all the ingredients and stir well.
2. Divide into ramekins, put them in the fryer and cook at 340°F for 20 minutes
3. Serve the pudding cold.

**Nutrition: Calories: 200; Fat: 4g; Fiber: 2g; Carbs: 4g; Protein: 6g**

## 592. Lemon Blackberries Cake

Preparation Time: 35 minutes
Servings: 4

**Ingredients:**

- 2 eggs, whisked
- ¼ cup almond milk
- 1 ½ cups almond flour
- 1 cup blackberries; chopped.
- 2 tbsp. ghee; melted
- 4 tbsp. swerve
- 1 tsp. lemon zest, grated
- 1 tsp. lemon juice
- ½ tsp. baking powder

**Directions:**

1. Take a bowl and mix all the ingredients and whisk well.
2. Pour this into a cake pan that fits the air fryer lined with parchment paper, put the pan in your air fryer and cook at 340°F for 25 minutes. Cool the cake down, slice and serve

**Nutrition: Calories: 193; Fat: 5g; Fiber: 1g; Carbs: 4g; Protein: 4g**

## 593. Yogurt Cake

Preparation Time: 35 minutes
Servings: 12

**Ingredients:**

- 6 eggs, whisked
- 8 oz. Greek yogurt
- 9 oz. coconut flour
- 4 tbsp. stevia
- 1 tsp. vanilla extract
- 1 tsp. baking powder

**Directions:**

1. Take a bowl and mix all the ingredients and whisk well.
2. Pour this into a cake pan that fits the air fryer lined with parchment paper.
3. Put the pan in the air fryer and cook at 330°F for 30 minutes

**Nutrition: Calories: 181; Fat: 13g; Fiber: 2g; Carbs: 4g; Protein: 5g**

## 594. Currant Cookies

Preparation Time: 35 minutes
Servings: 6

**Ingredients:**

- ½ cup currants
- ½ cup swerve
- 2 cups almond flour
- ½ cup ghee; melted
- 1 tsp. vanilla extract
- 2 tsp. baking soda

**Directions:**

1. Take a bowl and mix all the ingredients and whisk well.
2. Spread this on a baking sheet lined with parchment paper, put the pan in the air fryer and cook at 350°F for 30 minutes
3. Cool down; cut into rectangles and serve.

**Nutrition: Calories: 172; Fat: 5g; Fiber: 2g; Carbs: 3g; Protein: 5g**

## 595. Spiced Avocado Pudding

Preparation Time: 30 minutes
Servings: 6

**Ingredients:**

- 4 small avocados, peeled, pitted and mashed
- 2 eggs, whisked
- ¾ cup swerve
- 1 cup coconut milk
- 1 tsp. cinnamon powder
- ½ tsp. ginger powder

**Directions:**

1. Take a bowl and mix all the ingredients and whisk well.
2. Pour into a pudding mould, put it in the air fryer and cook at 350°F for 25 minutes. Serve warm

**Nutrition: Calories: 192; Fat: 8g; Fiber: 2g; Carbs: 5g; Protein: 4g**

## 596. Lemon Cookies

Preparation Time: 30 minutes
Servings: 12

**Ingredients:**

- ¼ cup cashew butter, soft
- 1 egg, whisked
- ¾ cup swerve
- 1 cup coconut cream
- Juice of 1 lemon
- 1 tsp. baking powder
- 1 tsp. lemon peel, grated

**Directions:**

1. In a bowl, combine all the ingredients gradually and stir well.
2. Spoon balls this on a cookie sheet lined with parchment paper and flatten them.
3. Put the cookie sheet in the fryer and cook at 350°F for 20 minutes. Serve the cookies cold

**Nutrition: Calories: 121; Fat: 5g; Fiber: 1g; Carbs: 4g; Protein: 2g**

## 597. Chocolate Strawberry Cups

Preparation Time: 15 minutes
Servings: 8

**Ingredients:**

- 16 strawberries; halved
- 2 cups chocolate chips; melted
- 2 tbsp. coconut oil

**Directions:**

1. In a pan that fits your air fryer, mix the strawberries with the oil and the melted chocolate chips, toss gently, put the pan in the air fryer and cook at 340°F for 10 minutes.
2. Divide into cups and serve cold

**Nutrition: Calories: 162; Fat: 5g; Fiber: 3g; Carbs: 5g; Protein: 6g**

## 598. Fruity Oreo Muffins

Preparation Time: 15 minutes
Cooking Time: 10 minutes
Servings: 6

**Ingredients:**

- 1 cup milk
- 1 pack Oreo biscuits, crushed
- ¾ teaspoon baking powder
- 1 banana, peeled and chopped
- 1 apple, peeled, cored and chopped
- 1 teaspoon cocoa powder
- 1 teaspoon honey
- 1 teaspoon fresh lemon juice
- A pinch of ground cinnamon

**Directions:**

1. Preheat the Air fryer to 320 o F and grease 6 muffin cups lightly.
2. Mix milk, biscuits, cocoa powder, baking soda, and baking powder in a bowl until well combined.
3. Transfer the mixture into the muffin cups and cook for about 10 minutes.
4. Remove from the Air fryer and invert the muffin cups onto a wire rack to cool.
5. Meanwhile, mix the banana, apple, honey, lemon juice, and cinnamon in another bowl.
6. Scoop some portion of muffins from the center and fill with fruit mixture to serve.

**Nutrition:**
Calories: 182, Fat: 3.1g, Carbohydrates: 31.4g, Sugar: 19.5g, Protein: 3.1g, Sodium: 196mg

## 599. Chocolate Mug Cake

Preparation Time: 15 minutes
Cooking Time: 13 minutes
Servings: 1

**Ingredients:**

- ¼ cup self-rising flour
- 1 tablespoon cocoa powder
- 3 tablespoons whole milk
- 5 tablespoons caster sugar
- 3 tablespoons coconut oil

**Directions:**

1. Preheat the Air fryer to 390 o F and grease a large mug lightly.
2. Mix all the ingredients in a shallow mug until well combined.
3. Arrange the mug into the Air fryer basket and cook for about 13 minutes.
4. Dish out and serve warm.

**Nutrition:**
Calories: 729, Fat: 43.3g, Carbohydrates: 88.8g, Sugar: 62.2g, Protein: 5.7g, Sodium: 20mg

## 600. Dark Chocolate Cheesecake

Preparation Time: 20 minutes
Cooking Time: 34 minutes
Servings: 6

**Ingredients:**

- 3 eggs, whites and yolks separated
- 1 cup dark chocolate, chopped
- ½ cup cream cheese, softened
- 2 tablespoons cocoa powder
- ¼ cup dates jam
- 2 tablespoons powdered sugar

**Directions:**

1. Preheat the Air fryer to 285 o F and grease a cake pan lightly.
2. Refrigerate egg whites in a bowl to chill before using.
3. Microwave chocolate and cream cheese on high for about 3 minutes.
4. Remove from microwave and whisk in the egg yolks.
5. Whisk together egg whites until firm peaks form and combine with the chocolate mixture.
6. Transfer the mixture into a cake pan and arrange in the Air fryer basket.
7. Cook for about 30 minutes and dish out.

8. Dust with powdered sugar and spread dates jam on top to serve.

**Nutrition:**
Calories: 298, Fat: 18.3g, Carbohydrates: 29.7g, Sugar: 24.5g, Protein: 6.3g, Sodium: 119mg

## 601. Cream Doughnuts

Preparation Time: 15 minutes
Cooking Time: 16 minutes
Servings: 8

**Ingredients:**
- 4 tablespoons butter, softened and divided
- 2 egg yolks
- 2¼ cups plain flour
- 1½ teaspoons baking powder
- ½ cup sugar
- 1 teaspoon salt
- ½ cup sour cream
- ½ cup heavy cream

**Directions:**
1. Preheat the Air fryer to 355 o F and grease an Air fryer basket lightly.
2. Sift together flour, baking powder and salt in a large bowl.
3. Add sugar and cold butter and mix until a coarse crumb is formed.
4. Stir in the egg yolks, ½ of the sour cream and 1/3 of the flour mixture and mix until a dough is formed.
5. Add remaining sour cream and 1/3 of the flour mixture and mix until well combined.
6. Stir in the remaining flour mixture and combine well.
7. Roll the dough into ½ inch thickness onto a floured surface and cut into donuts with a donut cutter.
8. Coat butter on both sides of the donuts and arrange in the Air fryer basket.
9. Cook for about 8 minutes until golden and top with heavy cream to serve.

**Nutrition:**
Calories: 297, Fats: 13g, Carbohydrates: 40.7g, Sugar: 12.6g, Proteins: 5g, Sodium: 346mg

## 602. Apple Doughnuts

Preparation Time: 20 minutes
Cooking Time: 5 minutes
Servings: 6

**Ingredients:**
- 2½ cups plus 2 tablespoons all-purpose flour
- 1½ teaspoons baking powder
- 2 tablespoons unsalted butter, softened
- 1 egg
- ½ pink lady apple, peeled, cored and grated
- 1 cup apple cider
- ½ teaspoon ground cinnamon
- ½ teaspoon salt
- ½ cup brown sugar

**Directions:**
1. Preheat the Air fryer to 360 o F and grease an Air fryer basket lightly.
2. Boil apple cider in a medium pan over medium-high heat and reduce the heat.
3. Let it simmer for about 15 minutes and dish out in a bowl.
4. Sift together flour, baking powder, baking soda, cinnamon, and salt in a large bowl.
5. Mix the brown sugar, egg, cooled apple cider and butter in another bowl.
6. Stir in the flour mixture and grated apple and mix to form a dough.
7. Wrap the dough with a plastic wrap and refrigerate for about 30 minutes.
8. Roll the dough into 1-inch thickness and cut the doughnuts with a doughnut cutter.
9. Arrange the doughnuts into the Air fryer basket and cook for about 5 minutes, flipping once in between.
10. Dish out and serve warm.

**Nutrition:**

Calories: 433, Fat: 11g, Carbohydrates: 78.3g, Sugar: 35g, Protein: 6.8g, Sodium: 383mg

## 603. Doughnuts Pudding

Preparation Time: 15 minutes
Cooking Time: 1 hour; Serves 4

**Ingredients:**

- 6 glazed doughnuts, cut into small pieces
- ¾ cup frozen sweet cherries
- ½ cup raisins
- ½ cup semi-sweet chocolate baking chips
- 4 egg yolks
- ¼ cup sugar
- 1 teaspoon ground cinnamon
- 1½ cups whipping cream

**Directions:**

1. Preheat the Air fryer to 310 o F and grease a baking dish lightly.
2. Mix doughnut pieces, cherries, raisins, chocolate chips, sugar, and cinnamon in a large bowl.
3. Whisk the egg yolks with whipping cream in another bowl until well combined.
4. Combine the egg yolk mixture into the doughnut mixture and mix well.
5. Arrange the doughnuts mixture evenly into the baking dish and transfer into the Air fryer basket.
6. Cook for about 60 minutes and dish out to serve warm.

**Nutrition:**
Calories: 786, Fat: 43.2g, Carbohydrates: 9.3g, Sugar: 60.7g, Protein: 11g, Sodium: 419mg

## 604. Chocolate Soufflé

Preparation Time: 15 minutes
Cooking Time: 16 minutes
Servings: 2

**Ingredients:**

- 3 ounces semi-sweet chocolate, chopped

- ¼ cup butter
- 2 eggs, egg yolks and whites separated
- 2 tablespoons all-purpose flour
- 3 tablespoons sugar
- ½ teaspoon pure vanilla extract
- 1 teaspoon powdered sugar plus extra for dusting

**Directions:**

1. Preheat the Air fryer to 330 o F and grease 2 ramekins lightly.
2. Microwave butter and chocolate on high heat for about 2 minutes until smooth.
3. Whisk the egg yolks, sugar, and vanilla extract in a bowl.
4. Add the chocolate mixture and flour and mix until well combined.
5. Whisk the egg whites in another bowl until soft peaks form and fold into the chocolate mixture.
6. Sprinkle each with a pinch of sugar and transfer the mixture into the ramekins.
7. Arrange the ramekins into the Air fryer basket and cook for about 14 minutes.
8. Dish out and serve sprinkled with the powdered sugar to serve.

**Nutrition:**
Calories: 569, Fat: 38.8g, Carbohydrates: 54.1g, Sugar: 42.2g, Protein: 6.9g, Sodium: 225mg

## 605. Fried Banana Slices

Preparation Time: 15 minutes
Cooking Time: 15 minutes
Servings: 8

**Ingredients:**

- 4 medium ripe bananas, peeled and cut in 4 pieces lengthwise
- 1/3 cup rice flour, divided
- 4 tablespoons corn flour
- 2 tablespoons desiccated coconut
- ½ teaspoon baking powder
- ½ teaspoon ground cardamom

- A pinch of salt

**Directions:**

1. Preheat the Air fryer to 390 o F and grease an Air fryer basket.
2. Mix coconut, 2 tablespoons of rice flour, corn flour, baking powder, cardamom, and salt in a shallow bowl.
3. Stir in the water gradually and mix until a smooth mixture is formed.
4. Place the remaining rice flour in a second bowl and dip in the coconut mixture.
5. Dredge in the rice flour and arrange the banana slices into the Air fryer basket in a single layer.
6. Cook for about 15 minutes, flipping once in between and dish out onto plates to serve.

**Nutrition:**
Calories: 260, Fat: 6g, Carbohydrates: 51.2g, Sugar: 17.6g, Protein: 4.6g, Sodium: 49mg

## 606. Chocolaty Squares

Preparation Time: 15 minutes
Cooking Time: 20 minutes
Servings: 4

**Ingredients:**

- 2-ounce cold butter
- 3-ounce self-rising flour
- ½ tablespoon milk
- 2-ounce chocolate, chopped
- 1¼-ounce brown sugar
- 1/8 cup honey

**Directions:**

1. Preheat the Air fryer to 320 o F and grease a tin lightly.
2. Mix butter, brown sugar, flour and honey and beat till smooth.
3. Stir in the chocolate and milk and pour the mixture into a tin.
4. Transfer into the Air fryer basket and cook for about 20 minutes.
5. Dish out and cut into desired squares to

serve.

**Nutrition:**
Calories: 322, Fat: 15.9g, Carbohydrates: 42.2g, Sugar: 24.8g, Protein: 3.5g, Sodium: 97mg

## 607. Cherry Pie

Preparation Time: 20 minutes
Cooking Time: 15 minutes
Servings: 4

**Ingredients:**

- ½: 21-ouncecan cherry pie filling
- 1 refrigerated pre-made pie crust
- ½ tablespoon milk
- 1 egg yolk
- 1 tablespoon vegetable oil

**Directions:**

1. Preheat the Air fryer to 320 o F and press pie crust into a pie pan.
2. Poke the holes with a fork all over dough and transfer the pie pan into the Air fryer basket.
3. Cook for about 5 minutes and remove from the Air fryer.
4. Pour the cherry pie filling into pie crust.
5. Cut the remaining pie crust into ¾-inch strips and place the strips in a crisscross manner.
6. Whisk egg and milk in a small bowl and brush the egg wash on the top of pie.
7. Transfer the pie pan into the Air fryer basket and cook for about 15 minutes to serve.

**Nutrition:**
Calories: 307, Fat: 1.4g, Carbohydrates: 70g, Sugar: 57.9g, Protein: 1g, Sodium: 130mg

## 608. Marshmallow Pastries

Preparation Time: 20 minutes
Cooking Time: 5 minutes
Servings: 8

**Ingredients:**

- 4-ounce butter, melted
- 8 phyllo pastry sheets, thawed
- ½ cup chunky peanut butter
- 8 teaspoons marshmallow fluff
- Pinch of salt

**Directions:**
1. Preheat the Air fryer to 360 o F and grease an Air fryer basket.
2. Brush butter over 1 filo pastry sheet and top with a second filo sheet.
3. Brush butter over second filo pastry sheet and repeat with all the remaining sheets.
4. Cut the phyllo layers in 8 strips and put 1 tablespoon of peanut butter and 1 teaspoon of marshmallow fluff on the underside of a filo strip.
5. Fold the tip of the sheet over the filling to form a triangle and fold repeatedly in a zigzag manner.
6. Arrange the pastries into the Air fryer basket and cook for about 5 minutes.
7. Season with a pinch of salt and serve warm.

**Nutrition:**
Calories: 283, Fat: 20.6g, Carbohydrates: 20.2g, Sugar: 3.4g, Protein: 6g, Sodium: 320mg

## 609. Avocado Walnut Bread

Preparation Time: 5 minutes
Cooking Time: 35 minutes
Servings: 6

**Ingredients:**
- ¾ cup: 3 oz. almond flour, white
- ¼ teaspoon baking soda
- 2 ripe avocados, cored, peeled and mashed
- 2 large eggs, beaten
- 2 tablespoons: 3/4 oz. Toasted walnuts, chopped roughly
- 1 teaspoon cinnamon ground
- ½ teaspoon kosher salt
- 2 tablespoons vegetable oil

- ½ cup granulated swerve
- 1 teaspoon vanilla extract

**Directions:**
1. Preheat the Air fryer to 310 o F and line a 6-inch baking pan with parchment paper.
2. Mix almond flour, salt, baking soda, and cinnamon in a bowl.
3. Whisk eggs with avocado mash, yogurt, swerve, oil, and vanilla in a bowl.
4. Stir in the almond flour mixture and mix until well combined.
5. Pour the batter evenly into the pan and top with the walnuts.
6. Place the baking pan into the Air fryer basket and cook for about 35 minutes.
7. Dish out in a platter and cut into slices to serve.

**Nutrition:**
Calories: 248, Fat: 15.7g, Carbohydrates: 8.4g, Sugar: 1.1g, Protein: 14.1g, Sodium: 94mg

## 610. Pumpkin Bars

Preparation Time: 10 minutes
Cooking Time: 25 minutes
Servings: 6

**Ingredients:**
- ¼ cup almond butter
- 1 tablespoon unsweetened almond milk
- ½ cup coconut flour
- ¾ teaspoon baking soda
- ½ cup dark sugar free chocolate chips, divided
- 1 cup canned sugar free pumpkin puree
- ¼ cup swerve
- 1 teaspoon cinnamon
- 1 teaspoon vanilla extract
- ¼ teaspoon nutmeg
- ½ teaspoon ginger
- 1/8 teaspoon salt
- 1/8 teaspoon ground cloves

**Directions:**

1. Preheat the Air fryer to 360 o F and layer a baking pan with wax paper.
2. Mix pumpkin puree, swerve, vanilla extract, milk, and butter in a bowl.
3. Combine coconut flour, spices, salt, and baking soda in another bowl.
4. Combine the two mixtures and mix well until smooth.
5. Add about 1/3 cup of the sugar free chocolate chips and transfer this mixture into the baking pan.
6. Transfer into the Air fryer basket and cook for about 25 minutes.
7. Microwave sugar free chocolate bits on low heat and dish out the baked cake from the pan.
8. Top with melted chocolate and slice to serve.

**Nutrition:**

Calories: 249, Fat: 11.9g, Carbohydrates: 1.8g, Sugar: 0.3g, Protein: 5g, Sodium: 79mg

## 611. Double Layer Lemon Bars

Preparation Time: 10 minutes
Cooking Time: 25 minutes
Servings: 6

**Ingredients:**

*For the crust:*

- 1 cup coconut flour, sifted
- 1 tablespoon butter, melted

*For the lemon topping:*

- 3 eggs
- 2 teaspoons coconut flour, sifted

*For the crust:*

- ½ cup coconut oil, melted
- A pinch of salt
- Swerve, to taste

*For the lemon topping:*

- Swerve, to taste
- 2 teaspoons lemon zest
- ½ cup fresh lemon juice

**Directions:**

1. Preheat the Air fryer to 350 o F and grease a 6-inch baking pan lightly.
2. Mix butter, swerve, salt, and oil in a bowl until foamy.
3. Stir in the coconut flour and mix until a smooth dough is formed.
4. Place the dough into the baking pan and press it thoroughly.
5. Transfer into the Air fryer and cook for about 8 minutes.
6. Meanwhile, whisk eggs with swerve, lemon zest, coconut flour and lemon juice in a bowl and mix well until smooth.
7. Pour this filling into the air fried crust and place into the Air fryer.
8. Set the Air fryer to 370 o F and cook for about 23 minutes.
9. Cut into slices and serve.

**Nutrition:**

Calories: 301, Fat: 12.2g, Carbohydrates: 2.5g, Sugar: 1.4g, Protein: 8.8g, Sodium: 276mg

## 612. Air Fryer Chocolate Cake

Preparation Time: 10 minutes
Cooking Time: 25 minutes
Servings: 6

**Ingredients:**

- 3 eggs
- 1 cup almond flour
- 1 stick butter, room temperature
- 1/3 cup cocoa powder
- 1½ teaspoons baking powder
- ½ cup sour cream
- 2/3 cup swerve
- 2 teaspoons vanilla

**Directions:**

1. Preheat the Air fryer to 360 o F and grease a cake pan lightly.
2. Mix all the ingredients in a bowl and beat well.
3. Pour the batter in the cake pan and

transfer into the Air fryer basket.

4. Cook for about 25 minutes and cut into slices to serve.

**Nutrition:**

Calories: 313, Fats: 134g, Carbohydrates: 5.3g, Sugar: 19g, Proteins: 4.6g, Sodium: 62mg

## 613. Cinnamon Doughnuts

Preparation Time: 10 minutes
Cooking Time: 12 minutes
Servings: 6

**Ingredients:**

- 1 cup white almond flour
- 1 teaspoon baking powder
- 2 tablespoons water
- ¼ cup almond milk
- ¼ cup swerve
- ½ teaspoon salt
- 1 tablespoon coconut oil, melted
- 2 teaspoons cinnamon

**Directions:**

1. Preheat the Air fryer to 360 o F and grease an Air fryer basket.
2. Mix flour, swerve, salt, cinnamon and baking powder in a bowl.
3. Stir in the coconut oil, water, and soy milk until a smooth dough is formed.
4. Cover this dough and refrigerate for about 1 hour.
5. Mix ground cinnamon with 2 tablespoons swerve in another bowl and keep aside.
6. Divide the dough into 12 equal balls and roll each ball in the cinnamon swerve mixture.
7. Transfer 6 balls in the Air fryer basket and cook for about 6 minutes.
8. Repeat with the remaining balls and dish out to serve.

**Nutrition:**

Calories: 166, Fat: 4.9g, Carbohydrates: 9.3g, Sugar: 2.7g, Protein: 2.4g, Sodium: 3mg

## 614. Dark Chocolate Cake

Preparation Time: 10 minutes
Cooking Time: 10 minutes
Servings: 4

**Ingredients:**

- 1½ tablespoons almond flour
- 3½ oz. unsalted butter
- 3½ oz. sugar free dark chocolate, chopped
- 2 eggs
- 3½ tablespoons swerve

**Directions:**

1. Preheat the Air fryer to 375 o F and grease 4 regular sized ramekins.
2. Microwave all chocolate bits with butter in a bowl for about 3 minutes.
3. Remove from the microwave and whisk in the eggs and swerve.
4. Stir in the flour and mix well until smooth.
5. Transfer the mixture into the ramekins and arrange in the Air fryer basket.
6. Cook for about 10 minutes and dish out to serve.

**Nutrition:**

Calories: 379, Fat: 29.7g, Carbohydrates: 3.7g, Sugar: 1.3g, Protein: 5.2g, Sodium: 193mg

## 615. Ninja Pop-Tarts

Preparation Time: 10 minutes
Cooking Time: 1 hour; Serves 6

**Ingredients:**

*Pop-tarts:*

- 1 cup coconut flour
- 1 cup almond flour
- ½ cup of ice-cold water

*Pop-tarts:*

- ¼ teaspoon salt
- 2 tablespoons swerve
- 2/3 cup very cold coconut oil

- ½ teaspoon vanilla extract

*Lemon Glaze:*

- 1¼ cups powdered swerve
- 2 tablespoons lemon juice
- zest of 1 lemon
- 1 teaspoon coconut oil, melted
- ¼ teaspoon vanilla extract

## Directions:

*Pop-tarts:*

1. Preheat the Air fryer to 375 o F and grease an Air fryer basket.
2. Mix all the flours, swerve, and salt in a bowl and stir in the coconut oil.
3. Mix well with a fork until an almond meal mixture is formed.
4. Stir in vanilla and 1 tablespoon of cold water and mix until a firm dough is formed.
5. Cut the dough into two equal pieces and spread in a thin sheet.
6. Cut each sheet into 12 equal sized rectangles and transfer 4 rectangles in the Air fryer basket.
7. Cook for about 10 minutes and repeat with the remaining rectangles.

*Lemon Glaze:*

1. Meanwhile, mix all the ingredients for the lemon glaze and pour over the cooked tarts.
2. Top with sprinkles and serve.

## Nutrition:

Calories: 368, Fat: 6g, Carbohydrates: 2.8g, Sugar: 2.9g, Protein: 7.2g, Sodium: 103mg

## 616. Blueberry Cake

Preparation Time: 10 minutes
Cooking Time: 25 minutes
Servings: 6

## Ingredients:

- 3 eggs
- 1 cup almond flour
- 1 stick butter, room temperature

- 1/3 cup blueberries
- 1½ teaspoons baking powder
- ½ cup sour cream
- 2/3 cup swerve
- 2 teaspoons vanilla

## Directions:

1. Preheat the Air fryer to 370 o F and grease a baking pan lightly.
2. Mix all the ingredients in a bowl except blueberries.
3. Pour the batter in the baking pan and fold in the blueberries.
4. Mix well and transfer the pan in the Air fryer basket.
5. Cook for about 25 minutes and cut into slices to serve.

## Nutrition:

Calories: 323, Fat: 14g, Carbohydrates: 5.3g, Sugar: 1.4g, Protein: 4.6g, Sodium: 92mg

## 617. Crème Brûlée

Preparation Time: 10 minutes
Cooking Time: 13 minutes
Servings: 8

## Ingredients:

- 10 egg yolks
- 4 cups heavy cream
- 2 tablespoons sugar
- 2 tablespoons vanilla extract

## Directions:

1. Preheat the Air fryer to 370 o F and grease 8: 6-ounceramekins lightly.
2. Mix all the ingredients in a bowl except stevia until well combined.
3. Divide the mixture evenly in the ramekins and transfer into the Air fryer.
4. Cook for about 13 minutes and remove from the Air fryer.
5. Let it cool slightly and refrigerate for about 3 hours to serve.

## Nutrition:

Calories: 295, Fat: 27.8g, Carbohydrates: 5.8g, Sugar: 3.6g, Protein: 4.6g, Sodium: 33mg

## 618. Tea Cookies

Preparation Time: 15 minutes
Cooking Time: 25 minutes
Servings: 15

**Ingredients:**

- ½ cup salted butter, softened
- 2 cups almond meal
- 1 organic egg
- 1 teaspoon ground cinnamon
- 2 teaspoons sugar
- 1 teaspoon organic vanilla extract

**Directions:**

1. Preheat the Air fryer to 370 o F and grease an Air fryer basket.
2. Mix all the ingredients in a bowl until well combined.
3. Make equal sized balls from the mixture and transfer in the Air fryer basket.
4. Cook for about 5 minutes and press down each ball with fork.
5. Cook for about 20 minutes and allow the cookies cool to serve with tea.

**Nutrition:**

Calories: 291, Fat: 14g, Carbohydrates: 30.3g, Sugar: 2.3g, Protein: 11.9g, Sodium: 266mg

## 619. Zucchini Brownies

Preparation Time: 5 minutes
Cooking Time: 35 minutes
Servings: 12

**Ingredients:**

- 1 cup butter
- 1 cup dark chocolate chips
- 1½ cups zucchini, shredded
- ¼ teaspoon baking soda
- 1 egg
- 1 teaspoon vanilla extract

- 1/3 cup applesauce, unsweetened
- 1 teaspoon ground cinnamon
- ½ teaspoon ground nutmeg

**Directions:**

1. Preheat the Air fryer to 345 o F and grease 3 large ramekins.
2. Mix all the ingredients in a large bowl until well combined.
3. Pour evenly into the prepared ramekins and smooth the top surface with the back of spatula.
4. Transfer the ramekin in the Air fryer basket and cook for about 35 minutes.
5. Dish out and cut into slices to serve.

**Nutrition:**

Calories: 195, Fat: 18.4g, Carbohydrates: 8.2g, Sugar: 6.4g, Protein: 1.5g, Sodium: 143mg

## 620. Lemon Mousse

Preparation Time: 15 minutes
Cooking Time: 10 minutes
Servings: 6

**Ingredients:**

- 12-ounces cream cheese, softened
- ¼ teaspoon salt
- 1 teaspoon lemon liquid stevia
- 1/3 cup fresh lemon juice
- 1½ cups heavy cream

**Directions:**

1. Preheat the Air fryer to 345 degrees F and grease a large ramekin lightly.
2. Mix all the ingredients in a large bowl until well combined.
3. Pour into the ramekin and transfer into the Air fryer.
4. Cook for about 10 minutes and pour into the serving glasses.
5. Refrigerate to cool for about 3 hours and serve chilled.

**Nutrition:**

Calories: 305, Fat: 31g, Carbohydrates: 2.6g,

Sugar: 0.4g, Protein: 5g, Sodium: 279mg

## 621. Strawberry Cobbler Recipe

Preparation Time: 35 Minutes
Servings: 6

### Ingredients:

- 3/4 cup sugar
- 6 cups strawberries; halved
- 1/2 cup flour
- 1/8 tsp. baking powder
- 1/2 cup water
- 3 ½ tbsp. olive oil
- 1 tbsp. lemon juice
- A pinch of baking soda
- Cooking spray

### Directions:

1. In a bowl; mix strawberries with half of sugar, sprinkle some flour, add lemon juice, whisk and pour into the baking dish that fits your air fryer and greased with cooking spray.
2. In another bowl, mix flour with the rest of the sugar, baking powder and soda and stir well
3. Add the olive oil and mix until the whole thing with your hands
4. Add 1/2 cup water and spread over strawberries
5. Introduce in the fryer at 355°F and bake for 25 minutes. Leave cobbler aside to cool down, slice and serve.

## 622. Lemon Cake

Preparation Time: 22 minutes
Servings: 6

### Ingredients:

- 3 oz. brown sugar
- 3 oz. flour
- 1 tsp. dark chocolate; grated
- 3½ oz. butter; melted

- 3 eggs
- 1/2 tsp. lemon juice

### Directions:

1. Mix all of the ingredients in a bowl.
2. Pour the mixture into a greased cake pan and place in the fryer
3. Cook at 360°F for 17 minutes. Let cake cool before serving

## 623. Pear Delight

Preparation Time: 25 minutes
Servings: 4

### Ingredients:

- 4 pears; peeled and roughly cut into cubes
- 1/4 cup brown sugar
- 4 tbsp. butter; melted
- 1 tbsp. maple syrup
- 2 tsp. cinnamon powder

### Directions:

1. In a pan that fits your air fryer, place all the ingredients and toss.
2. Place the pan in the air fryer and cook at 300°F for 20 minutes. Divide into cups, refrigerate and serve cold

## 624. Butter Donuts

Preparation Time: 25 minutes
Servings: 4

### Ingredients:

- 8 oz. flour
- 4 oz. whole milk
- 1 egg
- 2½ tbsp. butter
- 1 tbsp. brown sugar
- 1 tbsp. white sugar
- 1 tsp. baking powder

### Directions:

1. Place all of the ingredients in a bowl and mix well.

2. Shape donuts from this mix and place them in your air fryer's basket

3. Cook at 360°F for 15 minutes. Arrange the donuts on a platter and serve them warm

## 625. Apple Bread Pudding

Preparation Time: 59 minutes
Servings: 8

**Ingredients:**
*For Bread Pudding:*
- 10½-oz bread, cubed
- 1 ½ cups milk
- 1/2 cup raisins
- 1/4 cup walnuts; chopped
- 3/4 cup water
- 1/2 cup apple, peeled, cored and chopped
- 5 tbsp. honey
- 2 tsp. ground cinnamon
- 2 tsp. cornstarch
- 1 tsp. vanilla extract

*For Topping:*
- 3/5 cup brown sugar
- 1 ⅓ cups plain flour
- 7 tbsp. butter

**Directions:**
1. In a large bowl; mix well bread, apple, raisins and walnuts. In another bowl; add the remaining pudding Ingredients and mix until well combined. Add the milk mixture into bread mixture and mix until well combined. Refrigerate for about 15 minutes, tossing occasionally

2. For topping: in a bowl; mix together the flour and sugar. With a pastry cutter, cut in the butter until a crumbly mixture forms. Set the temperature of air fryer to 355°F

3. Place the mixture evenly into 2 baking pans and spread the topping mixture on top of each. Place 1 pan into an air fryer basket. Air fry for about 22 minutes. Repeat with the remaining pan. Remove

from the air fryer and serve warm.

## 626. Creamy Blackberry

Preparation Time: 18 minutes
Servings: 4

**Ingredients:**
- 1 cup blackberries
- 1/2 cup heavy cream
- 5 tbsp. sugar
- 2 tsp. vanilla extract
- 2 tsp. baking powder
- 1/2 cup butter; melted
- 2 eggs

**Directions:**
1. Place all of the ingredients in a bowl and whisk well.
2. Divide the mixture between 4 ramekins and place the ramekins in the fryer
3. Cook at 320°F for 12 minutes. Refrigerate and serve cold

## 627. Cranberry Jam

Preparation Time: 25 minutes
Servings: 8

**Ingredients:**
- 2 lbs. cranberries
- 4 oz. black currant
- 3 tbsp. water
- 2 lbs. sugar
- Zest of 1 lime

**Directions:**
1. In a pan that fits your air fryer, add all the ingredients and stir.
2. Place the pan in the fryer and cook at 360°F for 20 minutes. Stir the jam well, divide into cups, refrigerate and serve cold

## 628. Yummy Rice Pudding

Preparation Time: 25 minutes

Servings: 6

**Ingredients:**

- 7 oz. white rice
- 1 tbsp. butter; melted
- 1 tbsp. heavy cream
- 16 oz. milk
- 1/3 cup sugar
- 1 tsp. vanilla extract

**Directions:**

1. Place all ingredients in a pan that fits your air fryer and stir well
2. Put the pan in the fryer and cook at 360°F for 20 minutes. Stir the pudding, divide it into bowls, refrigerate and serve cold.

## 629. Chocolate Pudding

Preparation Time: 34 minutes
Servings: 4

**Ingredients:**

- 1/4 cup fresh orange juice
- 2/3 cup dark chocolate; chopped
- 1/2 cup butter
- 1/4 cup caster sugar
- 2 medium eggs
- 2 tbsp. self-rising flour
- 2 tsp. fresh orange rind, finely grated

**Directions:**

1. In a microwave-safe bowl; add the butter and chocolate. Microwave on high heat for about 2 minutes or until melted completely, stirring after every 30 seconds. Remove from microwave and stir the mixture until smooth. Add the sugar and eggs and whisk until frothy
2. Add the orange rind and juice, followed by flour and mix until well combined. Set the temperature of air fryer to 355°F. Grease 4 ramekins.
3. Divide mixture into the prepared ramekins about ¾ full. Air fry for about 12 minutes

4. Remove from the air fryer and set aside to completely cool before serving. Serve warm

## 630. Apple Doughnuts

Preparation Time: 25 minutes
Servings: 6

**Ingredients:**

*For Doughnuts:*

- 1/2 cup brown sugar
- 1 cup apple cider
- 1/2 pink lady apple, peeled, cored and grated
- 2 ½ cups plus 2 tbsp. all-purpose flour
- 1 egg
- 2 tbsp. unsalted butter; softened
- 1 tsp. baking powder
- 1/2 tsp. baking soda
- 1/2 tsp. ground cinnamon
- 1/2 tsp. salt

*For Topping:*

- 3 tbsp. butter; melted
- 1/2 cup sugar
- 1/2 tbsp. ground cinnamon

**Directions:**

1. In a medium pan, add the apple cider over medium-high heat and bring it to a boil. Lower the heat and simmer for about 15 minutes or until the cider reduces to 1/4 cup. Remove the pan from heat and transfer the apple cider into a bowl. Refrigerate to cool. In a large bowl; mix well flour, baking powder, baking soda, cinnamon and salt
2. In another bowl; add the brown sugar and butter and with an electric hand mixer, whisk until light and fluffy. Add the egg and whisk well.
3. Add the cooled apple cider and mix well. Put the flour mixture and mix until well combined. Add the grated apple and mix until a dough forms.
4. put the dough onto a lightly floured

surface and with your hands, knead until a soft dough comes together. With a plastic wrap, wrap the dough and refrigerate for about 30 minutes

5. place the dough onto a lightly floured surface and roll into 1-inch thickness. With a 3-inches doughnut cutter, cut the doughnuts.

6. Set the temperature of air fryer to 360°F for about 2 minutes. Grease an air fryer basket. Now; turn off the air fryer.

7. Arrange doughnuts into the prepared air fryer basket and let the dough rest in the turned off air fryer for about 5 minutes. Again, set the temperature of air fryer to 360°F

8. Air fry for about 5 minutes, flipping once halfway through. Meanwhile; in a shallow bowl; mix together the sugar and cinnamon. Remove from air fryer and transfer the doughnuts onto a platter. Brush both sides of doughnuts with melted butter and then, coat with the cinnamon sugar. Serve

# 631. Coffee Cheesecakes Recipe

Preparation Time: 30 Minutes
Servings: 6

**Ingredients:**
*For the cheesecakes:*
- 2 tbsp. butter
- 3 tbsp. coffee
- 3 eggs
- 8-ounce cream cheese
- 1/3 cup sugar
- 1 tbsp. caramel syrup

*For the frosting:*
- 3 tbsp. caramel syrup
- 2 tbsp. sugar
- 3 tbsp. butter
- 8-ounce mascarpone cheese; soft

**Directions:**
1. In your blender, mix cream cheese with

eggs, 2 tablespoon butter, coffee, 1 tablespoon caramel syrup and ⅓ cup sugar and pulse very well, spoon into a cupcakes pan that fits your air fryer, introduce in the fryer and cook at 320°F and bake for 20 minutes.

2. Leave aside to cool down and then keep in the freezer for 3 hours. Meanwhile; in a bowl, mix 3 tablespoon butter with 3 tablespoon caramel syrup, 2 tablespoon sugar and mascarpone, blend well, spoon this over cheesecakes and serve them

# 632. Grape Stew

Preparation Time: 20 minutes
Servings: 4

**Ingredients:**
- 1 lb. red grapes
- 26 oz. grape juice
- Juice and zest of 1 lemon

**Directions:**
1. In a pan that fits your air fryer, add all ingredients and toss
2. Place the pan in the fryer and cook at 320°F for 14 minutes. Divide into cups, refrigerate and serve cold

# 633. Chocolate Banana Pastries

Preparation Time: 27 minutes
Servings: 4

**Ingredients:**
- 2 bananas; peeled and sliced
- 1 puff pastry sheet
- 1/2 cup Nutella

**Directions:**
1. Cut the pastry sheet into 4 equal-sized squares. Spread Nutella evenly on each square of pastry. Divide the banana slices over Nutella. Fold each square into a triangle and with wet fingers, slightly press the edges. Then with a fork, press the edges firmly

2. Set the temperature of air fryer to 375°F. Lightly, grease an air fryer basket. Arrange pastries into the prepared air fryer basket in a single layer. Air fry for about 10 to 12 minutes. Remove from air fryer and transfer the pastries onto a platter. Serve warm

## 634. Raisin Bread Pudding

Preparation Time: 27 minutes
Servings: 3

**Ingredients:**

- 2 bread slices; cut into small cubes
- 1 cup milk
- 1 egg
- 1 tbsp. brown sugar
- 2 tbsp. raisins, soaked in hot water for about 15 minutes
- 1 tbsp. chocolate chips
- 1 tbsp. sugar
- 1/2 tsp. ground cinnamon
- 1/4 tsp. vanilla extract

**Directions:**

1. In a bowl; mix well milk, egg, brown sugar, cinnamon and vanilla extract. Stir in the raisins
2. In a baking dish, spread the bread cubes and top evenly with the milk mixture. Refrigerate for about 15 to 20 minutes. Set the temperature of air fryer to 375°F. Remove from refrigerator and sprinkle with chocolate chips and sugar on top
3. Arrange the baking dish into an air fryer basket. Air fry for about 12 minutes. Remove from the air fryer and serve warm.

## 635. Apple and Cinnamon Sauce

Preparation Time: 40 minutes
Servings: 6

**Ingredients:**

- 6 apples; peeled, cored and cut into wedges
- 1 cup red wine
- 1 cup sugar
- 1 tbsp. cinnamon powder

**Directions:**

1. In a pan that fits your air fryer, place all of the ingredients and toss
2. Place the pan in the fryer and cook at 320°F for 30 minutes. Divide into cups and serve right away

## 636. Raspberry Wontons

Preparation Time: 36 minutes
Servings: 12

**Ingredients:**

*For Wonton Wrappers:*

- 18-oz cream cheese; softened
- 1/2 cup powdered sugar
- 1 package of wonton wrappers
- 1 tsp. vanilla extract

*For Raspberry Syrup:*

- 1: 12-ozpackage frozen raspberries
- 1/4 cup water
- 1/4 cup sugar
- 1 tsp. vanilla extract

**Directions:**

1. For wrappers: in a bowl; add the sugar, cream cheese and vanilla extract and whisk until smooth. Place a wonton wrapper onto a smooth surface. Place one tbsp. of cream cheese mixture in the center of each wrapper. With wet fingers, fold wrappers around the filling and then, pinch the edges to seal
2. Set the temperature of air fryer to 350°F. Lightly, grease an air fryer basket. Arrange wonton wrappers into the prepared air fryer basket in 2 batches
3. Air fry for about 8 minutes. Meanwhile; for the syrup: in a medium skillet, add water, sugar, raspberries and vanilla extract over medium heat and cook for

about 5 minutes, stirring continuously

4. Remove from the heat and set aside to cool slightly. Transfer the mixture into food processor and blend until smooth. Remove the wontons from air fryer and transfer onto a platter. Serve the wontons with topping of raspberry syrup.

## 637. Doughnuts Pudding

Preparation Time: 75 minutes
Servings: 4

**Ingredients:**

- 6 glazed doughnuts; cut into small pieces
- 4 egg yolks
- 1/2 cup semi-sweet chocolate baking chips
- 1/4 cup sugar
- 1 ½ cups whipping cream
- 3/4 cup frozen sweet cherries
- 1/2 cup raisins
- 1 tsp. ground cinnamon

**Directions:**

1. In a large bowl; mix together doughnut pieces, cherries, raisins, chocolate chips, sugar and cinnamon. In another bowl; add the egg yolks and whipping cream and whisk until well combined. Add the egg yolk mixture into doughnut mixture and mix well. Set the temperature of air fryer to 310°F. Line a baking dish with a piece of foil
2. Place doughnuts mixture evenly into the prepared baking dish. Arrange the baking dish into an air fryer basket. Air fry for about 60 minutes. Remove from the air fryer and serve warm

## 638. Cinnamon Rolls

Preparation Time: 12 minutes
Servings: 8

**Ingredients:**

- 1 lb. bread dough

- 3/4 cup brown sugar
- 1/4 cup butter; melted
- 1½ tbsp. cinnamon; ground

**Directions:**

1. Roll the dough on a floured working surface, shape a rectangle and brush with the butter.
2. In a bowl, combine the cinnamon and sugar and then sprinkle this over the dough
3. Roll the dough into a log, seal, cut into 8 pieces and leave the rolls to rise for 2 hours
4. Place the rolls in your air fryer's basket and cook at 350°F for 5 minutes on each side. Serve warm and enjoy!

## 639. Brioche Pudding

Preparation Time: 35 minutes
Servings: 4

**Ingredients:**

- 3 cups brioche; cubed
- 2 cups half and half
- 2 cups milk
- 1/2 tsp. vanilla extract
- 1/2 cup raisins
- 1 cup sugar
- 4 egg yolks; whisked
- 2 tbsp. butter; melted
- Zest of 1/2 lemon

**Directions:**

1. In a bowl, add all of the ingredients and whisk well
2. Pour the mixture into a pudding mould and place it in the air fryer
3. Cook at 330°F for 30 minutes. Cool down and serve.

## 640. Pineapple and Carrot Cake

Preparation Time: 55 minutes
Servings: 6

**Ingredients:**

- 5 oz. flour
- 1/4 cup pineapple juice
- 1/3 cup carrots; grated
- 1/3 cup coconut flakes; shredded
- 1/2 cup sugar
- 3/4 tsp. baking powder
- 1/2 tsp. baking soda
- 1/2 tsp. cinnamon powder
- 1 egg; whisked
- 3 tbsp. yogurt
- 4 tbsp. vegetable oil
- Cooking spray

**Directions:**

1. Place all of the ingredients: except the cooking spray in a bowl and mix well.
2. Pour the mixture into a spring form pan, greased with cooking spray, that fits your air fryer
3. Place the pan in your air fryer and cook at 320°F for 45 minutes. Allow the cake to cool before cutting and serving

## 641. Rum Cheesecake

Preparation Time: 30 minutes
Servings: 6

**Ingredients:**

- 16 oz. cream cheese; softened
- 2 eggs
- 1/2 tsp. vanilla extract
- 1/2 cup sugar
- 1/2 cup graham cookies; crumbled
- 2 tsp. butter; melted
- 1 tsp. rum

**Directions:**

1. Grease a pan with the butter and spread the cookie crumbs on the bottom.
2. In a bowl, mix all the remaining ingredients and whisk well; then spread this mixture over the cookie crumbs

3. Place the pan in your air fryer and cook at 340°F for 20 minutes. Let the cheesecake cool down, refrigerate and serve cold

## 642. Amaretto Cream

Preparation Time: 18 minutes
Servings: 8

**Ingredients:**

- 12 oz. chocolate chips
- 1 cup heavy cream
- 1 cup sugar
- 1/2 cup butter; melted
- 2 tbsp. amaretto liqueur

**Directions:**

1. Place all of the ingredients in a bowl and stir
2. Pour the mixture into small ramekins and place in the air fryer
3. Cook at 320°F for 12 minutes. Refrigerate / freeze for a while… best when served really cold.

## 643. Oreo Cheesecake

Preparation Time: 30 minutes
Servings: 8

**Ingredients:**

- 1 lb. cream cheese; softened
- 1/2 tsp. vanilla extract
- 4 tbsp. sugar
- 1 cup Oreo cookies; crumbled
- 2 eggs; whisked
- 2 tbsp. butter; melted

**Directions:**

1. In a bowl, mix the cookies with the butter and then press this mixture onto the bottom of a cake pan lined with parchment paper.
2. Place the pan in your air fryer and cook at 350°F for 4 minutes
3. In a bowl, mix the sugar with the cream

cheese, eggs and vanilla; whisk until combined and smooth and spread this over the crust

4. Cook the cheesecake in your air fryer at 310°F for 15 minutes. Place the cheesecake in the fridge for a couple of hours before serving.

## 644. Cream of Tartar Bread

Preparation Time: 50 minutes
Servings: 6

**Ingredients:**

- 3/4 cup sugar
- 1½ cups flour
- 1/3 cup milk
- 1/3 cup butter
- 2 zucchinis; grated
- 1 tsp. vanilla extract
- 1 egg
- 1 tsp. baking powder
- 1/2 tsp. baking soda
- 1½ tsp. cream of tartar

**Directions:**

1. Place all ingredients in a bowl and mix well.
2. Pour the mixture into a lined loaf pan and place the pan in the air fryer
3. Cook at 320°F for 40 minutes Cool down, slice and serve.

## 645. Pumpkin Cake

Preparation Time: 35 minutes
Servings: 8

**Ingredients:**

- 8 oz. canned pumpkin puree
- 1/2 cup Greek yogurt
- 1 egg; whisked
- 3/4 cup sugar
- 3/4 tsp. pumpkin pie spice
- 1 tsp. baking powder

- 1 cup white flour
- Cooking spray

**Directions:**

1. Place all ingredients: other than the cooking sprayin a bowl and mix well.
2. Grease a cake pan with cooking spray, pour the cake batter inside and spread
3. Place the pan in the air fryer and cook at 330°F for 25 minutes. Let the cake cool down, slice and serve.

## 646. Raspberry-Coconut Cupcake

Servings: 6
Cooking Time: 30 minutes

**Ingredients**

- ½ cup butter
- ½ teaspoon salt
- ¾ cup erythritol
- 1 cup almond milk, unsweetened
- 1 cup coconut flour
- 1 tablespoon baking powder
- 3 teaspoons vanilla extract
- 7 large eggs, beaten

**Directions:**

1. Preheat the air fryer for 5 minutes.
2. Mix all ingredients using a hand mixer.
3. Pour into hard cupcake molds.
4. Place in the air fryer basket.
5. Bake for 30 minutes at 3500F or until a toothpick inserted in the middle comes out clean.
6. Bake by batches if possible.
7. Allow to chill before serving.

**Nutrition:**
Calories: 235; Carbohydrates: 7.4g; Protein: 3.8g; Fat: 21.1g

## 647. Easy Baked Chocolate Mug Cake

Servings: 3
Cooking Time: 15 minutes

## Ingredients

- ½ cup cocoa powder
- ½ cup stevia powder
- 1 cup coconut cream
- 1 package cream cheese, room temperature
- 1 tablespoon vanilla extract
- 4 tablespoons butter

## Directions:

1. Preheat the air fryer for 5 minutes.
2. In a mixing bowl, combine all ingredients.
3. Use a hand mixer to mix everything until fluffy.
4. Pour into greased mugs.
5. Place the mugs in the fryer basket.
6. Bake for 15 minutes at 3500F.
7. Place in the fridge to chill before serving.

## Nutrition:

Calories: 744; Carbohydrates:15.3 g; Protein: 13.9g; Fat: 69.7g

## 648. Keto-Friendly Doughnut Recipe

Servings: 4
Cooking Time: 20 minutes

## Ingredients

- ¼ cup coconut milk
- ¼ cup erythritol
- ¼ cup flaxseed meal
- ¾ cup almond flour
- 1 tablespoon cocoa powder
- 1 teaspoon vanilla extract
- 2 large eggs, beaten
- 3 tablespoons coconut oil

## Directions:

1. Place all ingredients in a mixing bowl.
2. Mix until well-combined.
3. Scoop the dough into individual doughnut molds.
4. Preheat the air fryer for 5 minutes.
5. Cook for 20 minutes at 3500F.

6. Bake in batches if possible.

## Nutrition:

Calories: 222; Carbohydrates: 5.1g; Protein: 3.9g; Fat: 20.7g

## 649. Zucchini-Choco Bread

Servings: 12
Cooking Time: 20 minutes

## Ingredients

- ¼ teaspoon salt
- ½ cup almond milk
- ½ cup maple syrup
- ½ cup sunflower oil
- ½ cup unsweetened cocoa powder
- 1 cup oat flour
- 1 cup zucchini, shredded and squeezed
- 1 tablespoon flax egg: 1 tablespoon flax meal + 3 tablespoons water
- 1 teaspoon apple cider vinegar
- 1 teaspoon baking soda
- 1 teaspoon vanilla extract
- 1/3 cup chocolate chips

## Directions:

1. Preheat the air fryer to 3500F.
2. Line a baking dish that will fit the air fryer with parchment paper.
3. In a bowl, combine the flax meal, zucchini, sunflower oil, maple, vanilla, apple cider vinegar and milk.
4. Stir in the oat flour, baking soda, cocoa powder, and salt. Mix until well combined.
5. Add the chocolate chips.
6. Pour over the baking dish and cook for 15 minutes or until a toothpick inserted in the middle comes out clean.

## Nutrition:

Calories: 213; Carbohydrates:24.2 g; Protein: 4.6g; Fat: 10.9g

## 650. Apple-Toffee Upside-Down Cake

Servings: 9
Cooking Time: 30 minutes

## Ingredients

- ¼ cup almond butter
- ¼ cup sunflower oil
- ½ cup walnuts, chopped
- ¾ cup + 3 tablespoon coconut sugar
- ¾ cup water
- 1 ½ teaspoon mixed spice
- 1 cup plain flour
- 1 lemon, zest
- 1 teaspoon baking soda
- 1 teaspoon vinegar
- 3 baking apples, cored and sliced

## Directions:

1. Preheat the air fryer to 3900F.
2. In a skillet, melt the almond butter and 3 tablespoons sugar. Pour the mixture over a baking dish that will fit in the air fryer. Arrange the slices of apples on top. Set aside.
3. In a mixing bowl, combine flour, ¾ cup sugar, and baking soda. Add the mixed spice.
4. In another bowl, mix the oil, water, vinegar, and lemon zest. Stir in the chopped walnuts.
5. Combine the wet ingredients to the dry ingredients until well combined.
6. Pour over the tin with apple slices.
7. Bake for 30 minutes or until a toothpick inserted comes out clean.

## Nutrition:

Calories: 335; Carbohydrates: 39.6g; Protein: 3.8g; Fat: 17.9g

## 651. Cherry-Choco Bars

Servings: 8
Cooking Time: 15 minutes

## Ingredients

- ¼ teaspoon salt

- ½ cup almonds, sliced
- ½ cup chia seeds
- ½ cup dark chocolate, chopped
- ½ cup dried cherries, chopped
- ½ cup prunes, pureed
- ½ cup quinoa, cooked
- ¾ cup almond butter
- 1/3 cup honey
- 2 cups old-fashioned oats
- 2 tablespoon coconut oil

## Directions:

1. Preheat the air fryer to 3750F.
2. In a mixing bowl, combine the oats, quinoa, chia seeds, almond, cherries, and chocolate.
3. In a saucepan, heat the almond butter, honey, and coconut oil.
4. Pour the butter mixture over the dry mixture. Add salt and prunes.
5. Mix until well combined.
6. Pour over a baking dish that can fit inside the air fryer.
7. Cook for 15 minutes.
8. Let it cool for an hour before slicing into bars.

**Nutrition: Calories: 321; Carbohydrates: 35g; Protein: 7g; Fat: 17g**

## 652. Maple Cinnamon Buns

Servings: 9
Cooking Time: 30 minutes

## Ingredients

- ¼ cup icing sugar
- ½ cup pecan nuts, toasted
- ¾ cup tablespoon unsweetened almond milk
- 1 ½ cup plain white flour, sifted
- 1 ½ tablespoon active yeast
- 1 cup wholegrain flour, sifted
- 1 tablespoon coconut oil, melted

- 1 tablespoon ground flaxseed
- 2 ripe bananas, sliced
- 2 teaspoons cinnamon powder
- 4 Medjool dates, pitted
- 4 tablespoons maple syrup

**Directions:**

1. Heat the ¾ cup almond milk to lukewarm and add the maple syrup and yeast. Allow the yeast to activate for 5 to 10 minutes.
2. Meanwhile, mix together flaxseed and 3 tablespoons of water to make the egg replacement. Allow flaxseed to soak for 2 minutes. Add the coconut oil.
3. Pour the flaxseed mixture to the yeast mixture.
4. In another bowl, combine the two types of flour and the 1 tablespoon cinnamon powder. Pour the yeast-flaxseed mixture and combine until dough forms.
5. Knead the dough on a floured surface for at least 10 minutes.
6. Place the kneaded dough in a greased bowl and cover with a kitchen towel. Leave in a warm and dark area for the bread to rise for 1 hour.
7. While the dough is rising, make the filling by mixing together the pecans, banana slices, and dates. Add 1 tablespoon of cinnamon powder.
8. Preheat the air fryer to 3900F.
9. Roll the risen dough on a floured surface until it is thin. Spread the pecan mixture on to the dough.
10. 10Roll the dough and cut into nine slices.
11. Place inside a dish that will fit in the air fryer and cook for 30 minutes.
12. 12Once cooked, sprinkle with icing sugar.

**Nutrition:**
Calories: 293; Carbohydrates: 44.9g; Protein: 5.6g; Fat:10.1 g

## 653. Yummy Banana Cookies

Servings: 6
Cooking Time: 10 minutes

**Ingredients**

- 1 cup dates, pitted and chopped
- 1 teaspoon vanilla
- 1/3 cup vegetable oil
- cups rolled oats
- ripe bananas

**Directions:**

1. Preheat the air fryer to 3500F.
2. In a bowl, mash the bananas and add in the rest of the ingredients.
3. Let it rest inside the fridge for 10 minutes.
4. Drop a teaspoonful on cut parchment paper.
5. Place the cookies on parchment paper inside the air fryer basket. Make sure that the cookies do not overlap.
6. Cook for 20 minutes or until the edges are crispy.
7. Serve with almond milk.

**Nutrition:**
Calories: 382; Carbohydrates: 50.14g; Protein: 6.54g; Fat: 17.2g

## 654. Coffee Flavored Doughnuts

Servings: 6
Cooking Time: 6 minutes

**Ingredients**

- ¼ cup coconut sugar
- ¼ cup coffee
- ½ teaspoon salt
- 1 cup white all-purpose flour
- 1 tablespoon sunflower oil
- 1 teaspoon baking powder
- 2 tablespoon aquafaba

**Directions:**

1. In a mixing bowl mix together the dry Ingredients flour, sugar, salt, and baking powder.
2. In another bowl, combine the aquafaba, sunflower oil, and coffee.
3. Mix to form a dough.

4. Let the dough rest inside the fridge.
5. Preheat the air fryer to 4000F.
6. Knead the dough and create doughnuts.
7. Arrange inside the air fryer in single layer and cook for 6 minutes.
8. Do not shake so that the donut maintains its shape.

**Nutrition:**
Calories: 113; Carbohydrates: 20.45g; Protein: 2.16g; Fat:2.54g

## 655. Crisped 'n Chewy Chonut Holes

Servings:  6
Cooking Time: 10 minutes

**Ingredients**
- ¼ cup almond milk
- ¼ cup coconut sugar
- ¼ teaspoon cinnamon
- ½ teaspoon salt
- 1 cup white all-purpose flour
- 1 tablespoon coconut oil, melted
- 1 teaspoon baking powder
- 2 tablespoon aquafaba or liquid from canned chickpeas

**Directions:**
1. In a mixing bowl, mix the flour, sugar, and baking powder. Add the salt and cinnamon and mix well.
2. In another bowl, mix together the coconut oil, aquafaba, and almond milk.
3. Gently pour the dry ingredients to the wet ingredients. Mix together until well combined or until you form a sticky dough.
4. Place the dough in the refrigerator to rest for at least an hour.
5. Preheat the air fryer to 370oF.
6. Create small balls of the dough and place inside the air fryer and cook for 10 minutes. Do not shake the air fryer.
7. Once cooked, sprinkle with sugar and cinnamon.

8. Serve with your breakfast coffee.

**Nutrition:**
Calories: 120; Carbohydrates: 21.62g; Protein: 2.31g; Fat:2.76g

## 656. Oriental Coconut Cake

Servings: 8
Cooking Time: 40 minutes

**Ingredients**
- 1 cup gluten-free flour
- 2 eggs
- 1/2 cup flaked coconut
- 1-1/2 teaspoons baking powder
- 1/2 teaspoon baking soda
- 1/2 teaspoon xanthan gum
- 1/2 teaspoon salt
- 1/2 cup coconut milk
- 1/2 cup vegetable oil
- 1/2 teaspoon vanilla extract
- 1/4 cup chopped walnuts
- 3/4 cup white sugar

**Directions:**
1. In blender blend all wet Ingredients. Add dry ingredients and blend thoroughly.
2. Lightly grease baking pan of air fryer with cooking spray.
3. Pour in batter. Cover pan with foil.
4. For 30 minutes, cook on 330oF.
5. Let it rest for 10 minutes
6. Serve and enjoy.

**Nutrition:**
Calories: 359; Carbs: 35.2g; Protein: 4.3g; Fat: 22.3g

## 657. Coffee 'n Blueberry Cake

Servings: 6
Cooking Time: 35 minutes

**Ingredients**
- 1 cup white sugar

- 1 egg
- 1/2 cup butter, softened
- 1/2 cup fresh or frozen blueberries
- 1/2 cup sour cream
- 1/2 teaspoon baking powder
- 1/2 teaspoon ground cinnamon
- 1/2 teaspoon vanilla extract
- 1/4 cup brown sugar
- 1/4 cup chopped pecans
- 1/8 teaspoon salt
- 1-1/2 teaspoons confectioners' sugar for dusting
- 3/4 cup and 1 tablespoon all-purpose flour

**Directions:**

1. In a small bowl, whisk well pecans, cinnamon, and brown sugar.
2. In a blender, blend well all wet Ingredients. Add dry Ingredients except for confectioner's sugar and blueberries. Blend well until smooth and creamy.
3. Lightly grease baking pan of air fryer with cooking spray.
4. Pour half of batter in pan. Sprinkle half of pecan mixture on top. Pour the remaining batter. And then topped with remaining pecan mixture.
5. Cover pan with foil.
6. For 35 minutes, cook on 330oF.
7. Serve and enjoy with a dusting of confectioner's sugar.

**Nutrition:**

Calories: 471; Carbs: 59.5g; Protein: 4.1g; Fat: 24.0g

## 658. Mouth-Watering Strawberry Cobbler

Servings: 4
Cooking Time: 25 minutes

**Ingredients**

- 1 tablespoon butter, diced

- 1 tablespoon and 2 teaspoons butter
- 1-1/2 teaspoons cornstarch
- 1/2 cup water
- 1-1/2 cups strawberries, hulled
- 1/2 cup all-purpose flour
- 1-1/2 teaspoons white sugar
- 1/4 cup white sugar
- 1/4 teaspoon salt
- 1/4 cup heavy whipping cream
- 3/4 teaspoon baking powder

**Directions:**

1. Lightly grease baking pan of air fryer with cooking spray. Add water, cornstarch, and sugar. Cook for 10 minutes 390oF or until hot and thick. Add strawberries and mix well. Dot tops with 1 tbsp butter.
2. In a bowl, mix well salt, baking powder, sugar, and flour. Cut in 1 tbsp and 2 tsp butter. Mix in cream. Spoon on top of berries.
3. Cook for 15 minutes at 390oF, until tops are lightly browned.
4. Serve and enjoy.

**Nutrition:**

Calories: 255; Carbs: 32.0g; Protein: 2.4g; Fat: 13.0g

## 659. Lusciously Easy Brownies

Servings: 8
Cooking Time: 20 minutes

**Ingredients**

- 1 egg
- 2 tablespoons and 2 teaspoons unsweetened cocoa powder
- 1/2 cup white sugar
- 1/2 teaspoon vanilla extract
- 1/4 cup butter
- 1/4 cup all-purpose flour
- 1/8 teaspoon salt
- 1/8 teaspoon baking powder

*Frosting Ingredients*

- 1 tablespoon and 1-1/2 teaspoons butter, softened
- 1 tablespoon and 1-1/2 teaspoons unsweetened cocoa powder
- 1-1/2 teaspoons honey
- 1/2 teaspoon vanilla extract
- 1/2 cup confectioners' sugar

**Directions:**

1. Lightly grease baking pan of air fryer with cooking spray. Melt ¼ cup butter for 3 minutes. Stir in vanilla, eggs, and sugar. Mix well.
2. Stir in baking powder, salt, flour, and cocoa mix well. Evenly spread.
3. For 20 minutes, cook on 300oF.
4. In a small bowl, make the frosting by mixing well all Ingredients. Frost brownies while still warm.
5. Serve and enjoy.

**Nutrition:**

Calories: 191; Carbs: 25.7g; Protein: 1.8g; Fat: 9.0g

## 660. Bread Pudding with Cranberry

Servings: 4
Cooking Time: 45 minutes

**Ingredients**

- 1-1/2 cups milk
- 2-1/2 eggs
- 1/2 cup cranberries1 teaspoon butter
- 1/4 cup and 2 tablespoons white sugar
- 1/4 cup golden raisins
- 1/8 teaspoon ground cinnamon
- 3/4 cup heavy whipping cream
- 3/4 teaspoon lemon zest
- 3/4 teaspoon kosher salt
- 3/4 French baguettes, cut into 2-inch slices
- 3/8 vanilla bean, split and seeds scraped away

**Directions:**

1. Lightly grease baking pan of air fryer with cooking spray. Spread baguette slices, cranberries, and raisins.
2. In blender, blend well vanilla bean, cinnamon, salt, lemon zest, eggs, sugar, and cream. Pour over baguette slices. Let it soak for an hour.
3. Cover pan with foil.
4. For 35 minutes, cook on 330oF.
5. Let it rest for 10 minutes.
6. Serve and enjoy.

**Nutrition:**

Calories: 581; Carbs: 76.1g; Protein: 15.8g; Fat: 23.7g

## 661. Pound Cake with Fresh Apples

Servings: 6
Cooking Time: 60 minutes

**Ingredients**

- 1 cup white sugar
- 1 teaspoon vanilla extract
- 1 medium Granny Smith apples - peeled, cored and chopped
- 1-1/2 eggs
- 1-1/2 cups all-purpose flour
- 1/2 teaspoon baking soda
- 1/2 teaspoon salt
- 1/4 teaspoon ground cinnamon
- 2/3 cup and 1 tablespoon chopped walnuts
- 3/4 cup vegetable oil

**Directions:**

1. In blender, blend all Ingredients except for apples and walnuts. Blend thoroughly. Fold in apples and walnuts.
2. Lightly grease baking pan of air fryer with cooking spray. Pour batter.
3. Cover pan with foil.
4. For 30 minutes, cook on preheated 330oF air fryer.
5. Remove foil and cook for another 20

minutes.

6. Let it stand for 10 minutes.

7. Serve and enjoy.

**Nutrition:**

Calories: 696; Carbs: 71.1g; Protein: 6.5g; Fat: 42.8g

## 662. Quick 'n Easy Pumpkin Pie

Servings: 8

Cooking Time: 35 minutes

**Ingredients**

- 1: 14 ouncecan sweetened condensed milk
- 1: 15 ouncecan pumpkin puree
- 1 9-inch unbaked pie crust
- 1 large egg
- 1 teaspoon ground cinnamon
- 1/2 teaspoon fine salt
- 1/2 teaspoon ground ginger
- 1/4 teaspoon freshly grated nutmeg
- 1/8 teaspoon Chinese 5-spice powder
- egg yolks

**Directions:**

1. Lightly grease baking pan of air fryer with cooking spray. Press pie crust on bottom of pan, stretching all the way up to the sides of the pan. Pierce all over with fork.

2. In blender, blend well egg, egg yolks, and pumpkin puree. Add Chinese 5-spice powder, nutmeg, salt, ginger, cinnamon, and condensed milk. Pour on top of pie crust.

3. Cover pan with foil.

4. For 15 minutes, cook on preheated 390oF air fryer.

5. Remove foil and continue cooking for 20 minutes at 330oF until middle is set.

6. Allow to cool in air fryer completely.

7. Serve and enjoy.

**Nutrition:**

Calories: 326; Carbs: 41.9g; Protein: 7.6g; Fat: 14.2g

## 663. Melts in Your Mouth Caramel Cheesecake

Servings: 8

Cooking Time: 40 minutes

**Ingredients**

- 1 Can Dulce de Leche
- 1 Tbsp Melted Chocolate
- 1 Tbsp Vanilla Essence
- 250 g Caster Sugar
- Large Eggs
- 50 g Melted Butter
- 500 g Soft Cheese
- Digestives, crumbled

**Directions:**

1. Lightly grease baking pan of air fryer with cooking spray. Mix and press crumbled digestives and melted butter on pan bottom. Spread dulce de leche.

2. In bowl, beat well soft cheese and sugar until fluffy. Stir in vanilla and egg. Pour over dulce de leche.

3. Cover pan with foil. For 15 minutes, cook on 390oF.

4. Cook for 10 minutes at 330oF. And then 15 minutes at 300oF.

5. Let it cool completely in air fryer. Refrigerate for at least 4 hours before slicing.

6. Serve and enjoy.

**Nutrition:**

Calories: 463; Carbs: 44.1g; Protein: 17.9g; Fat: 23.8g

## 664. Crispy Good Peaches

Servings: 4

Cooking Time: 30 minutes

**Ingredients**

- teaspoon  cinnamon
- teaspoon  sugar, white
- 1/cup  oats, dry rolled

- 1/4 cup Flour, white
- tablespoon Flour, white
- tablespoon butter, unsalted
- tablespoon sugar
- tablespoon pecans, chopped
- cup sliced peaches, frozen

**Directions:**
1. Lightly grease baking pan of air fryer with cooking spray. Mix in a tsp cinnamon, 2 tbsp flour, 3 tbsp sugar, and peaches.
2. For 20 minutes, cook on 300oF.
3. Mix the rest of the Ingredients in a bowl. Pour over peaches.
4. Cook for 10 minutes at 330oF.
5. Serve and enjoy.

**Nutrition:**
Calories: 435; Carbs: 74.1g; Protein: 4.3g; Fat: 13.4g

## 665. Apple Pie in Air Fryer

Servings: 4
Cooking Time: 35 minutes

**Ingredients**
- ½ teaspoon vanilla extract
- 1 beaten egg
- 1 large apple, chopped
- 1 Pillsbury Refrigerator pie crust
- 1 tablespoon butter
- 1 tablespoon ground cinnamon
- 1 tablespoon raw sugar
- 2 tablespoon sugar
- 2 teaspoons lemon juice
- Baking spray

**Directions:**
1. Lightly grease baking pan of air fryer with cooking spray. Spread pie crust on bottom of pan up to the sides.
2. In a bowl, mix vanilla, sugar, cinnamon, lemon juice, and apples. Pour on top of pie crust. Top apples with butter slices.
3. Cover apples with the other pie crust. Pierce with knife the tops of pie.
4. Spread beaten egg on top of crust and sprinkle sugar.
5. Cover with foil.
6. For 25 minutes, cook on 390oF.
7. Remove foil cook for 10 minutes at 330oF until tops are browned.
8. Serve and enjoy.

**Nutrition:**
Calories: 372; Carbs: 44.7g; Protein: 4.2g; Fat: 19.6g

## 666. Leche Flan Filipino Style

Servings: 4
Cooking Time: 30 minutes

**Ingredients**
- 1 cup heavy cream
- 1 teaspoon vanilla extract
- 1/2: 14 ouncecan sweetened condensed milk
- 1/2 cup milk
- 2-1/2 eggs
- 1/3 cup white sugar

**Directions:**
1. In blender, blend well vanilla, eggs, milk, cream, and condensed milk.
2. Lightly grease baking pan of air fryer with cooking spray. Add sugar and heat for 10 minutes at 370oF until melted and caramelized. Lower heat to 300oF and continue melting and swirling.
3. Pour milk mixture into caramelized sugar. Cover pan with foil.
4. Cook for 20 minutes at 330oF.
5. Let it cool completely in the fridge.
6. Place a plate on top of pan and invert pan to easily remove flan.
7. Serve and enjoy.

**Nutrition:**
Calories: 498; Carbs: 46.8g; Protein: 10.0g; Fat: 30.0g

## 667. Blueberry & Lemon Cake

Servings: 4
Cooking Time: 17 minutes

**Ingredients**

- 2 eggs
- 1 cup blueberries
- zest from 1 lemon
- juice from 1 lemon
- 1 tsp. vanilla
- brown sugar for topping: a little sprinkling on top of each muffin-less than a teaspoon
- 2 1/2 cups self-rising flour
- 1/2 cup Monk Fruit: or use your preferred sugar
- 1/2 cup cream
- 1/4 cup avocado oil: any light cooking oil

**Directions:**

1. In mixing bowl, beat well wet Ingredients. Stir in dry ingredients and mix thoroughly.
2. Lightly grease baking pan of air fryer with cooking spray. Pour in batter.
3. For 12 minutes, cook on 330oF.
4. Let it stand in air fryer for 5 minutes.
5. Serve and enjoy.

**Nutrition:**
Calories: 589; Carbs: 76.7g; Protein: 13.5g; Fat: 25.3g

## 668. Strawberry Pop Tarts

Servings: 6
Cooking Time: 25 minutes

**Ingredients**

- 1 oz reduced-fat Philadelphia cream cheese
- 1 tsp cornstarch
- 1 tsp stevia
- 1 tsp sugar sprinkles

- 1/2 cup plain, non-fat vanilla Greek yogurt
- 1/3 cup low-sugar strawberry preserves
- 2 refrigerated pie crusts
- olive oil or coconut oil spray

**Directions:**

1. Cut pie crusts into 6 equal rectangles.
2. In a bowl, mix cornstarch and preserves. Add preserves in middle of crust. Fold over crust. Crimp edges with fork to seal. Repeat process for remaining crusts.
3. Lightly grease baking pan of air fryer with cooking spray. Add pop tarts in single layer. Cook in batches for 8 minutes at 370oF.
4. Meanwhile, make the frosting by mixing stevia, cream cheese, and yogurt in a bowl. Spread on top of cooked pop tart and add sugar sprinkles.
5. Serve and enjoy.

**Nutrition:**
Calories: 317; Carbs: 34.8g; Protein: 4.7g; Fat: 17.6g

## 669. Apple Pie

Servings: 6
Preparation Time: 15 minutes
Cooking Time: 30 minutes

**Ingredients**

- 1 frozen pie crust, thawed
- 1 large apple, peeled, cored and chopped
- 3 tablespoons sugar, divided
- 1 tablespoon ground cinnamon
- 2 teaspoons fresh lemon juice
- ½ teaspoon vanilla extract
- 1 tablespoon butter, chopped
- 1 egg, beaten

**Directions:**

1. Grease a pie pan.
2. With a smaller baking tin, cut 1 crust from thawed pie crust about 1/8-inch larger

than pie pan.

3. Now, cut the second crust from the pie crust a little smaller than first one.
4. Arrange the large crust in the bottom of prepared pie pan.
5. In a bowl, mix together the apple, 2 tablespoons of sugar, cinnamon, lemon juice, and vanilla extract.
6. Place apple mixture evenly over the bottom crust.
7. Add the chopped butter over apple mixture.
8. Arrange the second crust on top and pinch the edges to seal.
9. Carefully, cut 3-4 slits in the top crust.
10. Spread the beaten egg evenly over top crust and sprinkle with the remaining sugar.
11. Set the temperature of air fryer to 320 degrees F.
12. Arrange the pie pan into an air fryer basket.
13. Air fry for about 30 minutes.
14. Remove from air fryer and place the pie pan onto a wire rack to cool for about 10-15 minutes before serving.
15. Serve warm.

**Nutrition:**

Calories: 190
Carbohydrate: 25.3g
Protein: 11.3g
Fat: 3.1g
Sugar: 1.6g
Sodium: 160mg

## 670. Sweet Potato Pie

Servings: 6
Preparation Time: 25 minutes
Cooking Time: 60 minutes

**Ingredients**

- ounces sweet potato
- 1 teaspoon olive oil
- 1: 9-inchesprepared frozen pie dough,

thawed
- ¼ cup heavy cream
- 2 large eggs
- 2 tablespoons maple syrup
- 1 tablespoon butter, melted
- 1 tablespoon light brown sugar
- ½ teaspoon ground cinnamon
- 1/8 teaspoon ground nutmeg
- Salt, to taste
- ¾ teaspoon vanilla extract

**Directions:**

1. Set the temperature of air fryer to 400 degrees F.
2. Coat the sweet potato evenly with oil.
3. Arrange the sweet potato into an air fryer basket.
4. Air fry for about 30 minutes.
5. Remove from air fryer and set aside to cool completely.
6. Peel the sweet potato and mash it completely.
7. Place the pie dough onto a floured surface and cut into 8-inch pie shell.
8. Arrange the dough shell into a greased pie pan.
9. In a large bowl, add the mashed sweet potato, and remaining ingredients and mix until well combined.
10. Place sweet potato mixture evenly over the pie shell.
11. Set the temperature of air fryer to 320 degrees F.
12. Arrange the pie pan into an air fryer basket.
13. Air fry for about 30 minutes.
14. Remove from air fryer and place the pie pan onto a wire rack to cool for about 10-15 minutes before serving.
15. Serve warm.

**Nutrition:**

Calories: 233
Carbohydrate: 27.8g
Protein: 3.8g

Fat: 12.2g
Sugar: 16.6g
Sodium: 212mg

## 671. Pecan Pie

Servings: 5
Preparation Time: 15 minutes
Cooking Time: 35 minutes

### Ingredients

- ¾ cup brown sugar
- ¼ cup caster sugar
- 1/3 cup butter, melted
- 2 large eggs
- 1¾ tablespoons flour
- 1 tablespoon milk
- 1 teaspoon vanilla extract
- 1 cup pecan halves
- 1 frozen pie crust, thawed

### Directions:

1. In a large bowl, mix well sugars, and butter.
2. Add the eggs and whisk until foamy.
3. Add the flour, milk, and vanilla extract and whisk until well combined.
4. Fold in the pecan halves.
5. Set the temperature of air fryer to 300 degrees F. Grease a pie pan.
6. Arrange the crust in the bottom of prepared pie pan.
7. Transfer pecan mixture evenly over the crust.
8. Arrange the pan in an air fryer basket.
9. Air fry for about 22 minutes and then, another 13 minutes at 285 degrees F.
10. Remove from air fryer and place the pie pan onto a wire rack to cool for about 10-15 minutes before serving.
11. Serve warm.

### Nutrition:

Calories: 575
Carbohydrate: 49.9g

Protein: 6.9g
Fat: 40.5g
Sugar: 33.5g
Sodium: 286mg

## 672. Apple Tart

Servings: 3
Preparation Time: 10 minutes
Cooking Time: 25 minutes

### Ingredients

- 2½ ounces butter, chopped and divided
- 3½ ounces flour
- 1 egg yolk
- 1 ounce sugar
- 1 large granny smith apple, peeled, cored and cut into 12 wedges

### Directions:

1. In a bowl, add half of the butter, flour, and egg yolk and mix until a soft dough forms.
2. Now, put the dough onto a floured surface and roll into a 6-inch round circle.
3. Set the temperature of air fryer to 390 degrees F.
4. In a baking pan, add the remaining butter and sprinkle with sugar.
5. Top with the apple wedges in a circular pattern.
6. Place the rolled dough over apple wedges and gently press along the edges of the pan.
7. Arrange the pan into an air fryer basket.
8. Air fry for about 25 minutes.
9. Remove from the air fryer and serve warm.

### Nutrition:

Calories: 382
Carbohydrate: 45.2g
Protein: 4.7g
Fat: 21.1g
Sugar: 17.3g
Sodium: 140mg

## 673. Fudge Brownies

Servings: 8
Preparation Time: 15 minutes
Cooking Time: 20 minutes

**Ingredients**

1 cup sugar
½ cup butter, melted
½ cup flour
1/3 cup cocoa powder
1 teaspoon baking powder
2 eggs
1 teaspoon vanilla extract

**Directions:**

1. Set the temperature of Air fryer to 350 degrees F. Grease a baking pan.
2. In a large bowl, add the sugar, and butter and whisk until light and fluffy.
3. Add the remaining ingredients and mix until well combined.
4. Place mixture evenly into the prepared pan and with the back of spatula, smooth the top surface.
5. Arrange the baking pan into an air fryer basket.
6. Air fry pan for about 20 minutes.
7. Remove the baking pan from air fryer and set aside to cool completely.
8. Cut into 8 equal-sized squares and serve.

**Nutrition:**

Calories: 250
Carbohydrate: 33.4g
Protein: 13g
Fat: 13.2g
Sugar: 25.2g
Sodium: 99mg

## 674. Walnut Brownies

Servings: 4
Preparation Time: 15 minutes
Cooking Time: 22 minutes

**Ingredients**

- ½ cup chocolate, roughly chopped
- 1/3 cup butter
- 5 tablespoons sugar
- 1 egg, beaten
- 1 teaspoon vanilla extract
- A pinch of salt
- 5 tablespoons self-rising flour
- ¼ cup walnuts, chopped

**Directions:**

1. In a microwave-safe bowl, add the chocolate and butter. Microwave on high heat for about 2 minutes, stirring after every 30 seconds.
2. Remove from microwave and set aside to cool.
3. Now, in a bowl, add the sugar, egg, vanilla extract, and salt and whisk until creamy and light.
4. Add the chocolate mixture and whisk until well combined.
5. Add the flour, and walnuts and mix until well combined.
6. Set the temperature of air fryer to 355 degrees F. Line a baking pan with a greased parchment paper.
7. Place mixture evenly into the prepared pan and with the back of spatula, smooth the top surface.
8. Arrange the baking pan into an air fryer basket.
9. Air fry for about 20 minutes.
10. Remove the baking pan from air fryer and set aside to cool completely.
11. Cut into 4 equal-sized squares and serve.

**Nutrition:**

Calories: 205
Carbohydrate: 1g
Protein: 3.1g
Fat: 13.8g
Sugar: 13.1g
Sodium: 91mg

## 675. Shortbread Fingers

Servings: 10
Preparation Time: 15 minutes
Cooking Time: 12 minutes

**Ingredients**

- 1/3 cup caster sugar
- 1 2/3 cups plain flour
- ¾ cup butter

**Directions:**

1. In a large bowl, mix together the sugar and flour.
2. Add the butter and mix until a smooth dough forms.
3. Cut the dough into 10 equal-sized fingers.
4. With a fork, lightly prick the fingers.
5. Set the temperature of air fryer to 355 degrees F. Lightly, grease a baking sheet.
6. Arrange fingers into the prepared baking sheet in a single layer.
7. Arrange the baking sheet into an air fryer basket.
8. Air fry for about 12 minutes.
9. Remove the baking sheet from air fryer and place onto a wire rack to cool for about 5-10 minutes.
10. Now, invert the short bread fingers onto wire rack to completely cool before serving.
11. Serve.

**Nutrition:**

Calories: 223
Carbohydrate: 22.6g
Protein: 2.3g
Fat: 14g
Sugar: 6.7g
Sodium: 99mg

## 676. Cream Doughnuts

Servings: 8
Preparation Time: 15 minutes
Cooking Time: 16 minutes

**Ingredients**

*For Doughnuts:*

- ½ cup sugar
- 2 tablespoons butter, softened
- 2 egg yolks
- 2¼ cups plain flour
- 1½ teaspoons baking powder
- 1 teaspoon salt
- ½ cup sour cream
- 2 tablespoons butter, melted

*For Topping:*

- 1/3 cup caster sugar
- 1 teaspoon cinnamon

**Directions:**

1. In a large bowl, add the sugar and 2 tablespoons of softened butter and whisk until crumbly mixture forms.
2. Add the egg yolks and whisk until well combined.
3. In another bowl, sift together the flour, baking powder, and salt.
4. Divide the flour mixture in 3 portions.
5. Add first portion of flour mixture and ½ of sour cream in the bowl of sugar mixture and mix well.
6. Add the second portion of flour mixture, and remaining sour cream and mix well.
7. Now, add the remaining portion and mix until a dough forms.
8. Refrigerate the dough before rolling.
9. Now, put the dough onto a lightly floured surface and roll into 2-inch thickness.
10. With a floured doughnut cutter, cut the dough.
11. Set the temperature of air fryer to 355 degrees F. Grease an air fryer basket.
12. Coat both sides of the doughnut with melted butter.
13. Arrange doughnuts into the prepared air fryer basket in 2 batches.
14. Air fry for about 8 minutes or until golden brown.
15. Meanwhile, in a bowl, mix together the sugar and cinnamon.
16. Remove from air fryer and transfer the doughnuts onto a platter to cool

completely.

17. Sprinkle the doughnuts with cinnamon sugar and serve.

**Nutrition:**
Calories: 272
Carbohydrate: 40.8g
Protein: 4.8g
Fat: 10.2g
Sugar: 12.6g
Sodium: 343mg

## 677. Milky Doughnuts

Servings: 12
Preparation Time: 15 minutes
Cooking Time: 24 minutes

**Ingredients**
*For Doughnuts:*
- 1 cup all-purpose flour
- 1 cup whole wheat flour
- 2 teaspoons baking powder
- Salt, to taste
- ¾ cup sugar
- 1 egg
- 1 tablespoon butter, softened
- ½ cup milk
- 2 teaspoons vanilla extract

*For Glaze:*
- 2 tablespoons icing sugar
- 2 tablespoons condensed milk
- 1 tablespoon cocoa powder

**Directions:**
1. In a large bowl, mix well flours, baking powder, and salt.
2. In another bowl, add the sugar and egg. Whisk until fluffy and light.
3. Add the flour mixture and stir until well combined.
4. Add the butter, milk, and vanilla extract and mix until a soft dough forms.
5. Refrigerate the dough for at least 1 hour.
6. Now, put the dough onto a lightly floured surface and roll into ½-inch thickness.
7. With a small doughnut cutter, cut 24 small doughnuts from the rolled dough.
8. Set the temperature of air fryer to 390 degrees F. Grease an air fryer basket.
9. Place doughnuts into the prepared air fryer basket in 3 batches.
10. Air fry for about 6-8 minutes.
11. Remove from air fryer and transfer the doughnuts onto a platter to cool completely.
12. In a small bowl, mix together the condensed milk and cocoa powder.
13. Spread the glaze over doughnuts and sprinkle with icing sugar.
14. Serve.

**Nutrition:**
Calories: 166
Carbohydrate: 33.4g
Protein: 3.9g
Fat: 2.3g
Sugar: 16.2g
Sodium: 34mg

## 678. Apple Doughnuts

Servings: 6
Preparation Time: 20 minutes
Cooking Time: 5 minutes

**Ingredients**
*For Doughnuts:*
- 1 cup apple cider
- 2½ cups plus 2 tablespoons all-purpose flour
- 1 teaspoon baking powder
- ½ teaspoon baking soda
- ½ teaspoon ground cinnamon
- ½ teaspoon salt
- ½ cup brown sugar
- 2 tablespoons unsalted butter, softened
- 1 egg
- ½ pink lady apple, peeled, cored and grated

*For Topping:*

- ½ cup sugar
- ½ tablespoon ground cinnamon
- 3 tablespoons butter, melted

**Directions:**

1. In a medium pan, add the apple cider over medium-high heat and bring it to a boil.
2. Lower the heat and simmer for about 15 minutes or until the cider reduces to ¼ cup.
3. Remove the pan from heat and transfer the apple cider into a bowl. Refrigerate to cool.
4. In a large bowl, mix well flour, baking powder, baking soda, cinnamon, and salt.
5. In another bowl, add the brown sugar, and butter and with an electric hand mixer, whisk until light and fluffy.
6. Add the egg and whisk well.
7. Add the cooled apple cider and mix well.
8. Put the flour mixture and mix until well combined.
9. Add the grated apple and mix until a dough forms.
10. Now, put the dough onto a lightly floured surface and with your hands, knead until a soft dough comes together.
11. With a plastic wrap, wrap the dough and refrigerate for about 30 minutes.
12. Now, place the dough onto a lightly floured surface and roll into 1-inch thickness.
13. With a 3-inches doughnut cutter, cut the doughnuts.
14. Set the temperature of air fryer to 360 degrees F for about 2 minutes. Grease an air fryer basket.
15. Now, turn off the air fryer.
16. Arrange doughnuts into the prepared air fryer basket and let the dough rest in the turned off air fryer for about 5 minutes.
17. Again, set the temperature of air fryer to 360 degrees F.
18. Air fry for about 5 minutes, flipping once halfway through.
19. Meanwhile, in a shallow bowl, mix together the sugar, and cinnamon.
20. Remove from air fryer and transfer the doughnuts onto a platter.
21. Brush both sides of doughnuts with melted butter and then, coat with the cinnamon sugar.
22. Serve.

**Nutrition:**

Calories: 433
Carbohydrate: 78.3g
Protein: 6.8g
Fat: 11g
Sugar: 35g
Sodium: 383mg

## 679. Chocolate Banana Pastries

Servings: 4
Preparation Time: 15 minutes
Cooking Time: 12 minutes

**Ingredients**

- 1 puff pastry sheet
- ½ cup Nutella
- 2 bananas, peeled and sliced

**Directions:**

1. Cut the pastry sheet into 4 equal-sized squares.
2. Spread Nutella evenly on each square of pastry.
3. Divide the banana slices over Nutella.
4. Fold each square into a triangle and with wet fingers, slightly press the edges.
5. Then with a fork, press the edges firmly.
6. Set the temperature of air fryer to 375 degrees F. Lightly, grease an air fryer basket.
7. Arrange pastries into the prepared air fryer basket in a single layer.
8. Air fry for about 10-12 minutes.
9. Remove from air fryer and transfer the pastries onto a platter.
10. Serve warm.

**Nutrition:**

Calories: 205

Carbohydrate: 30.3g

Protein: 3.2g

Fat: 8.9g

Sugar: 14.4g

Sodium: 96mg

## 680. Pear Pastry Pouch

Servings: 4

Preparation Time: 15 minutes

Cooking Time: 15 minutes

**Ingredients**

- 2 small pears, peeled, cored and halved
- 2 cups vanilla custard
- 4 puff pastry sheets
- 2 tablespoons sugar
- Pinch of ground cinnamon
- 1 egg, lightly beaten
- 2 tablespoons whipped cream

**Directions:**

1. Carefully, make small cuts in each pear half.
2. In the center of each pastry sheet, place a spoonful of vanilla custard and top with a pear half.
3. In a bowl, mix together the sugar and cinnamon.
4. Sprinkle the sugar mixture evenly over pear halves.
5. Pinch the corners to shape into a pouch.
6. Now, coat each pear with egg.
7. Set the temperature of air fryer to 330 degrees F. Lightly, grease an air fryer basket.
8. Arrange pear pouches into the prepared air fryer basket in a single layer.
9. Air fry for about 15 minutes.
10. Remove from air fryer and transfer the pear pouches onto a platter.
11. Top with whipped cream and serve with the remaining custard.

**Nutrition:**

Calories: 467

Carbohydrate: 56.1g

Protein: 8g

Fat: 24.4g

Sugar: 36.5g

Sodium: 140mg

## 681. Apple Pastry Pouch

Servings: 2

Preparation Time: 15 minutes

Cooking Time: 25 minutes

**Ingredients**

- 1 tablespoon brown sugar
- 2 tablespoons raisins
- 2 small apples, peeled and cored
- 2 puff pastry sheets
- 2 tablespoons butter, melted

**Directions:**

1. In a bowl, mix together the sugar and raisins.
2. Fill the core of each apple with raisins mixture.
3. Place one apple in the center of each pastry sheet and fold dough to cover the apple completely.
4. Then, pinch the edges to seal.
5. Coat each apple evenly with butter.
6. Set the temperature of air fryer to 355 degrees F. Lightly, grease an air fryer basket.
7. Arrange apple pouches into the prepared air fryer basket in a single layer.
8. Air fry for about 25 minutes.
9. Remove from air fryer and transfer the apple pouches onto a platter.
10. Serve warm.

**Nutrition:**

Calories: 418

Carbohydrate: 55.2g

Protein: 3.1g

Fat: 22.8g

Sugar: 33.2g
Sodium: 157mg

## 682. Raspberry Wontons

Servings: 12
Preparation Time: 20 minutes
Cooking Time: 16 minutes

### Ingredients

*For Wonton Wrappers:*

- ½ cup powdered sugar
- 18 ounces cream cheese, softened
- 1 teaspoon vanilla extract
- 1 package of wonton wrappers

*For Raspberry Syrup:*

- ¼ cup water
- ¼ cup sugar
- 1: 12-ouncespackage frozen raspberries
- 1 teaspoon vanilla extract

### Directions:

1. For wrappers: in a bowl, add the sugar, cream cheese, and vanilla extract and whisk until smooth.
2. Place a wonton wrapper onto a smooth surface.
3. Place one tablespoon of cream cheese mixture in the center of each wrapper.
4. With wet fingers, fold wrappers around the filling and then, pinch the edges to seal.
5. Set the temperature of air fryer to 350 degrees F. Lightly, grease an air fryer basket.
6. Arrange wonton wrappers into the prepared air fryer basket in 2 batches.
7. Air fry for about 8 minutes.
8. Meanwhile, for the syrup: in a medium skillet, add water, sugar, raspberries, and vanilla extract over medium heat and cook for about 5 minutes, stirring continuously.
9. Remove from the heat and set aside to cool slightly.
10. Transfer the mixture into food processor and blend until smooth.
11. Remove the wontons from air fryer and transfer onto a platter.
12. Serve the wontons with topping of raspberry syrup.

### Nutrition:

Calories: 325
Carbohydrate: 39.6g
Protein: 7.1g
Fat: 15.5g
Sugar: 15.4g
Sodium: 343mg

## 683. Fruity Tacos

Servings: 2
Preparation Time: 10 minutes
Cooking Time: 5 minutes

### Ingredients

- 2 soft shell tortillas
- 4 tablespoons strawberry jelly
- ¼ cup blueberries
- ¼ cup raspberries
- 2 tablespoons powdered sugar

### Directions:

1. Set the temperature of air fryer to 300 degrees F. Lightly, grease an air fryer basket.
2. Arrange the tortillas onto a smooth surface.
3. Spread two tablespoons of strawberry jelly over each tortilla and top each with berries.
4. Sprinkle each with the powdered sugar.
5. Arrange tortillas into the prepared air fryer basket.
6. Air fry for about 5 minutes or until crispy.
7. Remove from the air fryer and transfer the tortillas onto a platter.
8. Serve warm.

### Nutrition:

Calories: 272

Carbohydrate: 63.4g

Protein: 3.5g

Fat: 1.8g

Sugar: 34.8g

Sodium: 26mg

## 684. Raisin Bread Pudding

Servings: 3

Preparation Time: 15 minutes

Cooking Time: 12 minutes

### Ingredients

- 1 cup milk
- 1 egg
- 1 tablespoon brown sugar
- ½ teaspoon ground cinnamon
- ¼ teaspoon vanilla extract
- 2 tablespoons raisins, soaked in hot water for about 15 minutes
- 2 bread slices, cut into small cubes
- 1 tablespoon chocolate chips
- 1 tablespoon sugar

### Directions:

1. In a bowl, mix well milk, egg, brown sugar, cinnamon, and vanilla extract.
2. Stir in the raisins.
3. In a baking dish, spread the bread cubes and top evenly with the milk mixture.
4. Refrigerate for about 15-20 minutes.
5. Set the temperature of air fryer to 375 degrees F.
6. Remove from refrigerator and sprinkle with chocolate chips and sugar on top.
7. Arrange the baking dish into an air fryer basket.
8. Air fry for about 12 minutes.
9. Remove from the air fryer and serve warm.

### Nutrition:

Calories: 143

Carbohydrate: 21.3g

Protein: 5.5g

Fat: 4.4g

Sugar: 16.4g

Sodium: 104mg

## 685. Apple Bread Pudding

Servings: 8

Preparation Time: 15 minutes

Cooking Time: 44 minutes

### Ingredients

*For Bread Pudding:*

- 10½ ounces bread, cubed
- ½ cup apple, peeled, cored and chopped
- ½ cup raisins
- ¼ cup walnuts, chopped
- 1½ cups milk
- ¾ cup water
- 5 tablespoons honey
- 2 teaspoons ground cinnamon
- 2 teaspoons cornstarch
- 1 teaspoon vanilla extract

*For Topping:*

- 1 1/3 cups plain flour
- 3/5 cup brown sugar
- tablespoons butter

### Directions:

1. In a large bowl, mix well bread, apple, raisins, and walnuts.
2. In another bowl, add the remaining pudding ingredients and mix until well combined.
3. Add the milk mixture into bread mixture and mix until well combined.
4. Refrigerate for about 15 minutes, tossing occasionally.
5. For topping: in a bowl, mix together the flour and sugar.
6. With a pastry cutter, cut in the butter until a crumbly mixture forms.
7. Set the temperature of air fryer to 355 degrees F.
8. Place the mixture evenly into 2 baking pans and spread the topping mixture on top of each.

9. Place 1 pan into an air fryer basket.
10. Air fry for about 22 minutes.
11. Repeat with the remaining pan.
12. Remove from the air fryer and serve warm.

**Nutrition:**

Calories: 432
Carbohydrate: 69.1g
Protein: 7.9g
Fat: 14.8g
Sugar: 32g
Sodium: 353mg

## 686. Doughnuts Pudding

Servings: 4
Preparation Time: 15 minutes
Cooking Time: 60 minutes

**Ingredients**

- 6 glazed doughnuts, cut into small pieces
- ¾ cup frozen sweet cherries
- ½ cup raisins
- ½ cup semi-sweet chocolate baking chips
- ¼ cup sugar
- 1 teaspoon ground cinnamon
- 4 egg yolks
- 1½ cups whipping cream

**Directions:**

1. In a large bowl, mix together doughnut pieces, cherries, raisins, chocolate chips, sugar, and cinnamon.
2. In another bowl, add the egg yolks, and whipping cream and whisk until well combined.
3. Add the egg yolk mixture into doughnut mixture and mix well.
4. Set the temperature of air fryer to 310 degrees F. Line a baking dish with a piece of foil.
5. Place doughnuts mixture evenly into the prepared baking dish.
6. Arrange the baking dish into an air fryer basket.
7. Air fry for about 60 minutes.

8. Remove from the air fryer and serve warm.

**Nutrition:**

Calories: 786
Carbohydrate: 9.3g
Protein: 11g
Fat: 43.2g
Sugar: 60.7g
Sodium: 419mg

## 687. Chocolate Pudding

Servings: 4
Preparation Time: 20 minutes
Cooking Time: 14 minutes

**Ingredients**

- ½ cup butter
- 2/3 cup dark chocolate, chopped
- ¼ cup caster sugar
- 2 medium eggs
- 2 teaspoons fresh orange rind, finely grated
- ¼ cup fresh orange juice
- 2 tablespoons self-rising flour

**Directions:**

1. In a microwave-safe bowl, add the butter, and chocolate. Microwave on high heat for about 2 minutes or until melted completely, stirring after every 30 seconds.
2. Remove from microwave and stir the mixture until smooth.
3. Add the sugar, and eggs and whisk until frothy.
4. Add the orange rind and juice, followed by flour and mix until well combined.
5. Set the temperature of air fryer to 355 degrees F. Grease 4 ramekins.
6. Divide mixture into the prepared ramekins about ¾ full.
7. Air fry for about 12 minutes.
8. Remove from the air fryer and set aside to completely cool before serving.
9. Serve warm.

**Nutrition:**

Calories: 454

Carbohydrate: 34.2g

Protein: 5.7g

Fat: 33.6g

Sugar: 28.4g

Sodium: 217mg

## 688. Vanilla Soufflé

Servings: 6

Preparation Time: 15 minutes

Cooking Time: 39 minutes

**Ingredients**

- ¼ cup butter, softened
- ¼ cup all-purpose flour
- ½ cup plus 2 tablespoons sugar, divided
- 1 cup milk
- 3 teaspoons vanilla extract, divided
- 4 egg yolks
- 5 egg whites
- 1 teaspoon cream of tartar
- 2 tablespoons powdered sugar plus extra for dusting

**Directions:**

1. In a bowl, add the butter, and flour and mix until a smooth paste forms.
2. In a medium pan, mix together ½ cup of sugar and milk over medium-low heat and cook for about 3 minutes or until the sugar is dissolved, stirring continuously.
3. Add the flour mixture, whisking continuously and simmer for about 3-4 minutes or until mixture becomes thick.
4. Remove from the heat and stir in 1 teaspoon of vanilla extract.
5. Set aside for about 10 minutes to cool.
6. In a bowl, mix together the egg yolks and 1 teaspoon of vanilla extract.
7. Add the egg yolk mixture into milk mixture and mix until well combined.
8. In another bowl, add the egg whites, cream of tartar, remaining sugar, and vanilla extract and whisk until stiff peaks form.

9. Fold the egg whites mixture into milk mixture.
10. Set the temperature of air fryer to 330 degrees F. Grease 6 ramekins and sprinkle each with a pinch of sugar.
11. Place mixture evenly into the prepared ramekins and with the back of a spoon, smooth the top surface.
12. Arrange the ramekins into an air fryer basket in 2 batches.
13. Air fry for about 14-16 minutes.
14. Remove from air fryer and set aside to cool slightly.
15. Sprinkle with the powdered sugar and serve warm.

**Nutrition:**

Calories: 250

Carbohydrate: 29.8g

Protein: 6.8g

Fat: 11.6g

Sugar: 25g

Sodium: 107mg

## 689. Chocolate Soufflé

Servings: 2

Preparation Time: 15 minutes

Cooking Time: 16 minutes

**Ingredients**

- 3 ounces semi-sweet chocolate, chopped
- ¼ cup butter
- 2 eggs, egg yolks and whites separated
- 3 tablespoons sugar
- ½ teaspoon pure vanilla extract
- 2 tablespoons all-purpose flour
- 1 teaspoon powdered sugar plus extra for dusting

**Directions:**

1. In a microwave-safe bowl, put the butter, and chocolate. Microwave on high heat for about 2 minutes or until melted completely, stirring after every 30 seconds.
2. Remove from microwave and stir the

mixture until smooth.

3. In another bowl, add the egg yolks and whisk well.
4. Add the sugar, and vanilla extract and whisk well.
5. Add the chocolate mixture and mix until well combined.
6. Add the flour and mix well.
7. In a clean glass bowl, add the egg whites and whisk until soft peaks form.
8. Fold the whipped egg whites in 3 portions into the chocolate mixture.
9. Set the temperature of air fryer to 330 degrees F. Grease 2 ramekins and sprinkle each with a pinch of sugar.
10. Place mixture evenly into the prepared ramekins and with the back of a spoon, smooth the top surface.
11. Arrange the ramekins into an air fryer basket.
12. Air fry for about 14 minutes.
13. Remove from air fryer and set aside to cool slightly.
14. Sprinkle with the powdered sugar and serve warm.

**Nutrition:**
Calories: 569
Carbohydrate: 54.1g
Protein: 6.9g
Fat: 38.8g
Sugar: 42.2g
Sodium: 225mg

## 690. Stuffed Apples

Servings: 4
Preparation Time: 15 minutes
Cooking Time: 13 minutes

**Ingredients**
*For Stuffed Apples:*
- 4 small firm apples, cored
- ½ cup golden raisins
- ½ cup blanched almonds
- 2 tablespoons sugar

*For Vanilla Sauce:*
- ½ cup whipped cream
- 2 tablespoons sugar
- ½ teaspoon vanilla extract

**Directions:**
1. In a food processor, add raisins, almonds, and sugar and pulse until chopped.
2. Carefully, stuff each apple with raisin mixture.
3. Set the temperature of air fryer to 355 degrees F. Line a baking dish with a parchment paper.
4. Now, place apples into the prepared baking dish.
5. Arrange the baking dish into an air fryer basket.
6. Air fry for about 10 minutes.
7. Meanwhile, for vanilla sauce: in a pan, add the cream, sugar, and vanilla extract over medium heat and cook for about 2-3 minutes or until sugar is dissolved, stirring continuously.
8. Remove the baking dish from air fryer and transfer the apples onto plates to cool slightly
9. Top with the vanilla sauce and serve.

**Nutrition:**
Calories: 329
Carbohydrate: 60.2g
Protein: 4g
Fat: 11.1g
Sugar: 46.5g
Sodium: 9mg

## 691. Crispy Banana Split

Servings: 8
Preparation Time: 15 minutes
Cooking Time: 14 minutes

**Ingredients**
- 3 tablespoons coconut oil
- 1 cup panko breadcrumbs
- ½ cup corn flour
- 2 eggs

- 4 bananas, peeled and halved lengthwise
- 3 tablespoons sugar
- ¼ teaspoon ground cinnamon
- 2 tablespoons walnuts, chopped

**Directions:**

1. In a medium skillet, heat the oil over medium heat and cook breadcrumbs for about 3-4 minutes or until golden browned and crumbled, stirring continuously.
2. Transfer the breadcrumbs into a shallow bowl and set aside to cool.
3. In a second bowl, place the corn flour.
4. In a third bowl, whisk the eggs.
5. Coat the banana slices with flour and then, dip into eggs and finally, coat evenly with the breadcrumbs.
6. In a small bowl, mix together the sugar and cinnamon
7. Set the temperature of air fryer to 280 degrees F. Grease an air fryer basket.
8. Arrange banana slices into the prepared air fryer basket in a single layer and sprinkle with cinnamon sugar
9. Air fry for about 10 minutes.
10. Remove from air fryer and transfer the banana slices onto plates to cool slightly
11. Sprinkle with chopped walnuts and serve.

**Nutrition:**

Calories: 216
Carbohydrate: 26g
Protein: 3.4g
Fat: 8.8g
Sugar: 11.9g
Sodium: 16mg

## 692. Fried Banana Slices

Servings: 8
Preparation Time: 15 minutes
Cooking Time: 15 minutes

### Ingredients

- 4 medium ripe bananas, peeled
- 1/3 cup rice flour, divided

- 2 tablespoons all-purpose flour
- 2 tablespoons corn flour
- 2 tablespoons desiccated coconut
- ½ teaspoon baking powder
- ½ teaspoon ground cardamom
- A pinch of salt
- Water, as required
- ¼ cup sesame seeds

**Directions:**

1. In a shallow bowl, mix well 2 tablespoons of rice flour, all-purpose flour, corn flour, coconut, baking powder, cardamom, and salt.
2. Gradually, add the water and mix until a thick and smooth mixture forms.
3. In a second bowl, place the remaining rice flour.
4. In a third bowl, add the sesame seeds.
5. Cut each banana into half and then, cut each half in 2 pieces lengthwise.
6. Dip the banana slices into coconut mixture and then, coat with the remaining rice flour, followed by the sesame seeds.
7. Set the temperature of air fryer to 392 degrees F. Line an air fryer basket with a greased and floured piece of foil.
8. Arrange banana slices into the prepared air fryer basket in a single layer.
9. Air fry for about 10-15 minutes, flipping once halfway through.
10. Remove from air fryer and transfer the banana slices onto plates to cool slightly.
11. Serve warm.

**Nutrition:**

Calories: 260
Carbohydrate: 51.2g
Protein: 4.6g
Fat: 6g
Sugar: 17.6g
Sodium: 49mg

## 693. Plum Cream

Preparation Time: 25 minutes
Servings: 4

**Ingredients:**

- 1 lb. plums, pitted and chopped.
- 1 ½ cups heavy cream
- ¼ cup swerve
- 1 tbsp. lemon juice

**Directions:**

1. Take a bowl and mix all the ingredients and whisk really well.
2. Divide this into 4 ramekins, put them in the air fryer and cook at 340°F for 20 minutes. Serve cold

**Nutrition:**

Calories: 171

Fat: 4g

Fiber: 2g

Carbs: 4g

Protein: 4g

## 694. Lemon Chocolate Cookies

Servings: 4

Preparation Time: 15 minutes

Cooking Time: 5 minutes

**Ingredients:**

- 1 cup almond flour
- 6 tablespoons butter
- 4 tablespoons Stevia
- 1 egg yolk
- ½ cup semi-sweet chocolate chips

**Directions**

1. Place butter and stevia in a mixing bowl then using an electric mixer beat until fluffy.
2. Add egg yolk to the bowl then continue beating until incorporated.
3. Stir almond flour into the mixture then using a wooden spatula mix until becoming dough.
4. Add chocolate chips to the dough then mix until just combined.
5. Preheat an Air Fryer to 180°F (82°C).
6. Shape the dough into small ball forms then arrange in the Air Fryer.

7. Press the cookie balls until becoming coin forms then cook in the Air Fryer for 5 minutes.
8. Once it is done, remove from the Air Fryer then place on a cooling rack. Let them cool.
9. Serve and enjoy.

**Nutrition Values:**

Net Carbs: 5.4g; Calories: 246; Total Fat: 23.9g; Saturated Fat: 12.6g

Protein: 2.9g; Carbs: 6.7g

## 695. Blueberry Muffins

Servings: 5

Preparation Time: 10 minutes

Cooking Time: 14 minutes

**Ingredients:**

- 1 egg
- 3/4 cup blueberries
- 3 tbsp grass-fed butter, melted
- 1/3 cup almond milk
- 1 tsp vanilla
- 2 tbsp erythritol
- 1 tsp baking powder
- 2/3 cup almond flour

**Directions**

1. Add all ingredients into the mixing bowl and mix until well combined.
2. Pour batter into the silicon muffin molds.
3. Place in air fryer and cook for 14 minutes at 320 F/ 160 C.
4. Serve and enjoy.

**Nutrition Values:**

Calories 212; Fat 19.1 g; Carbohydrates 12.7 g; Sugar 3.4 g; Protein 4.9 g; Cholesterol 51 mg

## 696. Strawberry Muffins

Servings: 12

Preparation Time: 10 minutes

Cooking Time: 20 minutes

**Ingredients:**

- 3 eggs
- 2/3 cup strawberries, diced
- 1/3 cup heavy cream
- 1 tsp vanilla
- 1/2 cup Swerve
- 5 tbsp butter, melted
- 1 tsp cinnamon
- 2 tsp baking powder
- 2 ½ cups almond flour
- 1/4 tsp Himalayan salt

## Directions
1. Preheat the air fryer to 176 C/ 350 F.
2. In a bowl, beat together butter and swerve. Add eggs, cream, and vanilla and beat until frothy.
3. Sift together almond flour, cinnamon, baking powder, and salt.
4. Add almond flour mixture to the wet ingredients and mix until well combined.
5. Add strawberries and stir well.
6. Pour batter into the muffin molds and place in air fryer. In batches.
7. Bake in for 20 minutes.
8. Serve and enjoy.

## Nutrition Values:
Net Carbs: 3.6g; Calories: 208; Total Fat: 18.8g; Saturated Fat: 5g
Protein: 6.6g; Carbs: 6.4g

## 697. Gluten Free Chocó Lava Cake

Preparation Time: 15 minutes
Servings: 2

## Ingredients:
- 1 egg
- 1/2 tsp baking powder
- 1 tbsp coconut oil, melted
- 1 tbsp flax meal
- 1/8 tsp stevia
- 2 tbsp erythritol
- 2 tbsp water
- 2 tbsp cocoa powder
- 1/8 tsp vanilla

- Pinch of salt

## Directions:
1. Spray two ramekins with cooking spray and set aside.
2. Add all ingredients to the bowl and whisk well.
3. Preheat the air fryer to 176 C/ 350 F for a minute.
4. Pour batter into the prepared ramekins. Place ramekins into the air fryer basket and cook for 8-9 minutes.
5. Serve warm and enjoy.

## Nutrition Values:
Calories 122 Fat 11 g Carbohydrates 17 g Sugar 0.3 g Protein 4.5 g Cholesterol 82 mg

## 698. Cinnamon Chocolate Churros

Servings: 6
Preparation Time: 10 minutes
Cooking Time: 8 minutes

## Ingredients
- ¼ cup butter
- ½ cup warm water
- ½ cup almond flour
- 2 eggs
- 2 ½ teaspoons cinnamon
- ¼ cup semi-sweet chocolate chips
- 2 tablespoons almond milk

## Directions
1. Place water and butter in a saucepan then bring to boil.
2. Once it is boiled, add almond flour to the saucepan then stir until becoming a soft dough.
3. Wait until the dough is soft then add eggs to the dough.
4. Using an electric mixer mix until fluffy.
5. Transfer the fluffy dough to a piping bag then set aside.
6. Preheat an Air Fryer to 380°F (193°C).
7. Pipe several pieces of 3-inch-long dough in the Air Fryer then cook for 10 minutes.

8. Remove the churros from the Air Fryer then repeat with the remaining dough.

9. Meanwhile, place semi-sweet chocolate chips in a microwave-safe bowl. Melt the butter in the microwave.

10. Pour almond milk into the melted chocolate then stir until incorporated.

11. Arrange the churros on a serving dish then drizzle melted chocolate over the churros.

12. Sprinkle cinnamon on top then serve.

13. Enjoy.

**Nutrition Values:**

Net Carbs: 3.4g; Calories: 194; Total Fat: 18.3g; Saturated Fat: 10.2g
Protein: 4.1g; Carbs: 5g

## 699. Delicious Grilled Pineapple

Servings: 4
Preparation Time: 5 minutes
Cooking Time: 20 minutes

### Ingredients

- 4 pineapple slices
- 1 tsp ground cinnamon
- 4 tbsp coconut sugar

### Directions

1. Add cinnamon and coconut sugar in a zip-lock bag and mix well.

2. Now add pineapple slices into the bag and shake until well coated. Place in refrigerator for half an hour.

3. Preheat the air fryer at 180 C/ 356 F for 5 minutes.

4. Place pineapple slices on the air fryer's wire rack and grill them for 10 minutes.

5. After 10 minutes flip pineapple slices to other side and grill them for 10 minutes more.

6. Serve and enjoy.

**Nutrition Values:**

Calories 141; Fat 0 g; Carbohydrates 29.5 g; Sugar 10 g; Protein 1 g; Cholesterol 0 mg

## 700. Cinnamon Mug Cake

Servings: 1
Preparation Time: 5 minutes
Cooking Time: 10 minutes

### Ingredients

- 1/4 tsp vanilla extract
- 1/4 cup almond milk, unsweetened
- 1 scoop vanilla protein powder
- 1/2 tsp cinnamon
- 1 tsp granulated sweetener
- 1 tbsp almond flour
- 1/2 tsp baking powder

### Directions

1. Add protein powder, sweetener, cinnamon, almond flour, and baking powder into the heat-safe mug and mix well.

2. Add vanilla extract and almond milk and stir well. If the batter is crumbly add more milk until formed thick batter.

3. Place mug in air fryer and cook at 200 C/ 392 F for 10 minutes.

4. Serve and enjoy.

**Nutrition Values:**

Net Carbs: 6.3g; Calories: 180; Total Fat: 6.3g; Saturated Fat: 1.3g
Protein: 23.9g; Carbs: 8.2g

## 701. Lemon Blueberry Muffin

Servings: 12
Preparation Time: 10 minutes
Cooking Time: 10 minutes

### Ingredients

- 2 eggs
- 2 1/2 cups almond flour
- 1 tsp vanilla
- 1 tbsp lemon juice
- 1 cup blueberries
- 1/4 cup olive oil

- 1/2 cup coconut cream
- 1/2 cup monk fruit

**Directions**

1. In a small bowl, mix together almond flour and monk fruit and set aside.
2. In a mixing bowl, combine together coconut cream, eggs, vanilla, and lemon juice.
3. Add almond flour mixture to the coconut cream mixture and stir until well blended.
4. Pour the batter into silicone cupcake holders.
5. Place in air fryer and cook for 10 minutes at 320 F/ 160 C.
6. Serve and enjoy.

**Nutrition Values**

: Calories 211; Fat 19 g; Carbohydrates 7.4 g; Sugar 2.5 g; Protein 6.3 g; Cholesterol 27 mg

# Conclusion

Unlike frying things in a typical pan on gas which fails to make your fries crisp and leaves your samosa uncooked due to uneven heat. The inbuilt kitchen deep fryers do it all; you can have perfectly crisp French fries like the one you get in restaurants. Your samosas will be perfectly cooked inside- out. Well, the list doesn't end here it goes on and on the potato wedges, chicken and much more. You can make many starters and dishes using fryer and relish the taste buds of your loved ones.

The new air fryers come along with a lot of features, so you don't mess up doing things enjoy your cooking experience. The free hot to set the temperature according to your convenience both mechanically and electronically. Oil filters to reuse the oil and use it for a long run. With the ventilation system to reduce and eliminate the frying odor. In a few models you also get the automatic timers and alarm set for convenient cooking, frying I mean. Also, the auto- push and raise feature to immerse or hold back the frying basket to achieve the perfect frying aim.

So, why should you wait? I am sure you don't want to mess in your kitchen when grilling, baking of frying your food, right? Get yourself an air fryer. Thank you for purchasing this cookbook I hope you will apply all the acquired knowledge productively.

Made in the USA
Middletown, DE
27 August 2020